COLOR MATTERS

In the United States, as in many parts of the world, people are discriminated against based on gradations of skin color. This type of skin tone bias, or colorism, is both related to and distinct from discrimination on the basis of race, with which it is often conflated. Preferential treatment of lighter skin tones over darker occurs within racial and ethnic groups as well as between them. While America has made progress in issues of race over the past decades, discrimination on the basis of color continues to be a constant and often unremarked part of life.

In *Color Matters*, Kimberly Jade Norwood has collected the most up-to-date research on this insidious form of discrimination, including perspectives from the disciplines of history, law, sociology, and psychology. Anchored with historical chapters that show how the influence and legacy of slavery have shaped the treatment of skin color in American society, the contributors to this volume bring to light the ways in which colorism affects us all—influencing what we wear, who we see on television, and even which child we might pick to adopt. Sure to be an eye-opening collection for anyone curious about how race and color continue to affect society, *Color Matters* provides students of race in America with a wide-ranging overview of a crucial topic.

Kimberly Jade Norwood is Professor of Law and Professor of African and African American Studies at Washington University, St. Louis.

NEW DIRECTIONS IN AMERICAN HISTORY

COLOR MATTERS

Skin Tone Bias and the Myth of a Post-Racial America

Edited by
Kimberly Jade Norwood

Routledge
Taylor & Francis Group

NEW YORK AND LONDON

First published 2014
by Routledge
711 Third Avenue, New York, NY 10017

and by Routledge
2 Park Square, Milton Park, Abingdon, Oxon OX14 4RN

Routledge is an imprint of the Taylor & Francis Group, an informa business

Library of Congress Cataloging in Publication Data
Color matters: skin tone bias and the myth of a postracial America/
    edited by Kimberly Jade Norwood.
    pages cm. — (New directions in American history)
    1. African Americans—Race identity. 2. Human skin color—Social
aspects—United States. 3. Race awareness—United States. 4. Race
discrimination—United States. 5. Racism—United States. I. Norwood,
Kimberly Jade.
    E185.625.C646 2013
    305.896′073—dc23
    2013021054

ISBN: 978-0-415-51774-4 (hbk)
ISBN: 978-0-415-51775-1 (pbk)
ISBN: 978-1-315-81933-4 (ebk)

Typeset in Bembo and Stone Sans
by Florence Production Ltd, Stoodleigh, Devon, UK

CONTENTS

ACKNOWLEDGMENTS

I first would like to thank my husband, Ronald Alan Norwood, for his patience, guidance, and support during the years that this project was in incubation. He was my go-to man for every question, concern, and challenge, and I have been blessed to have his input in this work. I owe a special thanks to Paul Finkelman. Paul was the first colleague I spoke to about the colorism epiphany I experienced while visiting China in the spring of 2010. It is because of my many communications with and support from Paul that this project came to fruition. Professor Leland Ware was the next colleague I contacted about this book. He was a tremendous supporter of this project and spent valuable time working on the book. I also thank all contributors for their dedication and enthusiasm during the life of the project. A special thank you to my research assistants, Violeta Solonova Foreman and Adrienne Johnson. Both were very gracious, patient, diligent, and hard-working during our time together. Thank you to my colleagues at Washington University School of Law, my assistant Beverly Owens, and the law school library staff. All were crucial to the success of the project. I also would like to thank Jean McDonald, lecturer of Journalism at the University of Illinois at Urbana-Champaign, who provided invaluable editing advice to me during the past few months. My oldest child, Candice Norwood, a 2013 graduate of the University of Illinois, also deserves acknowledgment. In addition to introducing me to Jean McDonald, she also brainstormed with me about the scope and depth of colorism on many occasions. Finally, I must thank my editor, Kimberly Guinta, at Routledge. Always positive, always supportive, always sure, she has been a calming, reassuring voice, and it has been a pleasure to work with someone of her stability and balance.

INTRODUCTION

Kimberly Jade Norwood

Data collected within the industry shows that 90 percent of the pistachios sold in the Chinese market have been bleached, said Fang Ming, dean of the food science and engineering department at the East China University of Science and Technology. Pistachios have become a major snack in China only within the past few years, Fang said. With no knowledge of the nuts' natural look, most consumers mistake the white-shelled pistachios as the good ones. The bleaching is to cater to the mass consumer idea of "the brighter, the better," which covers up quality flaws.[1]

Bleached nuts. This might strike you as an odd way to start a book on the continuing and increasing relevance of skin tone, but it is the springboard from which this project ascends. It was, in fact, the concept that brought a half-century of skin color unrest in my mind to fruition. For fifty years, I normalized evidence of skin tone bias in the world and in my community, and then I read a newspaper article about the bleaching of pistachio nuts. That article jarred the buried concerns I had about how skin color affected the world, American society, and black and brown communities.

While teaching in China during the spring of 2010, I came across a newspaper, written in English: the *China Daily*. I was so excited to find a paper in my language that I digested every word. Every day, I searched for the *China Daily*. On the day in question, I read a story in the *China Daily* titled "New Standards to Ban Bleaching of Pistachios." While I like pistachios, I tend to read more political and social news. Yet, being starved for the written English word, I went ahead and read the story. It turned out to be a most intriguing read. According to the article, China is the world's largest consumer of pistachio nuts. Before making them available to the consuming public, however, the nuts in China are bleached.

They are not bleached to clean them or to remove harmful chemicals or to dissolve natural impurities. Rather, they are bleached for one reason: "to cater to the mass consumer idea of 'the brighter, the better.'"

I have always known that the world I lived in valued lighter skin colors over darker. I suspect my earliest memories on this were established growing up as the brown-skinned child of a mother whose skin color was not only many shades lighter than mine, but who also had a head of long, flowing hair. Comments made to my mother in my presence to the effect of "Wow! Where did she come from?!" always revolved around my much darker skin and very short and wooly hair. Somehow I grew past the sting of the insults and made a decision to remain unaffected by skin tone bias. But, of course, no matter what I told myself, the world revealed something different. Boys lighter in complexion from me never asked me out. Interestingly, I married the one who did! (I wonder if that reflected my own unconscious color preferences.) Indeed, people have often teased me over the course of my twenty-five year marriage for marrying a "white boy" (my husband is considered light skin in black circles). A friend who met my dark chocolate-colored sister-in-law at a social gathering at my home on one occasion said aloud, "OK, now I understand." When I asked my friend what she meant by her comment, she stated that she always found it odd that my light-skinned husband chose someone of my complexion as a spouse, but after meeting his sister she understood why. Many of my own children—neither dark-skinned nor light-skinned but a blend of their parents' complexions—have grappled with these issues. I've seen in my sons a clear preference for light skin; I've seen a daughter lament over the preference for light and white skin among boys of all races and colors in her age group; and several years ago my then 7-year-old told me that she wished she had "the cool skin." As she elaborated, it was the same color skin her favorite Disney and Nickelodeon characters had and the same as that of all the cool singers she saw on television and would later hear on the Disney radio channel. The cool skin was skin much lighter than hers—"more pink," she said. So, although I had tried to stay immune to skin color discrimination, the world around me had not. Skin color preferences were alive and thriving, even in my own home. Somehow I had stopped thinking about it, pushed it to the side, tried to forget or ignore—*maybe accept?*—that lighter is more acceptable. And then I visited China.

The words of the newspaper story in the *China Daily* kept flashing in my mind: "mass perception," "brighter, better," "the good ones." From that day on, I began to experience my surroundings while traveling in China through colored lenses. I began to notice the skin colors of the professionals—usually legal professionals as I found myself, invariably, at one law firm or another—and compared their skin tone with that of the working class. I noticed television commercials and programming, magazines, billboards, advertisements of all sorts. In virtually every case, the professionals were lighter in skin tone than the laborers, and the Chinese images portrayed in the media were of very fair Chinese people. Indeed, not only were models, particularly the women, very fair in skin tone, one could just barely spot any remnants of their "Asianness." Eye shape, eyebrows, noses and mouths looked strikingly Caucasian. Residents of China make up almost 20 percent of the world population.[2] They are not Caucasian, and yet many clamor for skin as light as possible.[3] Not only is light, bright, or white preferred on skin in this land, but as the *China Daily* story revealed, even white food is better! Of course, the preference for white food is neither new nor foreign. Consider white flour, rice, bread, potatoes, and sugar.[4] Yes, there is a slow (and ironically healthy) movement back to brown—that is, the *unbleached* versions of flour, sugar, rice, and the like—but one has to wonder where the concept that removing the color, bleaching the nuts, so to speak, came from. I even found evidence in Native American communities that white animals are preferred over darker ones. Consider, for example, the rare white bison, which when born is glorified and cherished in some Native American communities as the rare jewel that not only is a sign of prosperity from a prophet but that also brings good things to all people in the world.[5] Lighter is better, the world says, in food, in animals, and in people.

On the flight back home, I opened up my *American Way* magazine. I found very few discernible people of color depicted therein. Page 15 advertised makeup to brighten one's complexion. Page 16 advertised a page full of "flesh-toned" shoes, not one of which was in the brown family.[6] I discussed these issues with a colleague once I arrived back in the States. This person is of Jewish descent and has written on race and on slavery in America. I complained to him about flesh-toned shoes and stockings. I worried about the millions of people of color around the world who want to be lighter. I nagged about music videos with light-skinned women always as the prize. My colleague seemed to sympathize with me but went on to say something like: "Black people are everywhere now: TV, movies, advertisements, corporate America. There have been tremendous strides. We still need to do more, yes, but it is not the case where blacks simply are not at the table anymore. Those days are gone."

At that moment the decision to put this anthology together was made. Now, it is true that discrimination based on race is harder to get away with today. American society has clearly advanced in that regard. But I believe that, as race is evolving, another form of discrimination is on the rise. In other words, while it is true that more people of color—and blacks in particular—are visible in the media and in corporate America, why are these people more often light in skin tone? When I raised this concern with my colleague, he questioned my observation. "Blacks are on television, in movies, professors at universities, part of corporate America. Indeed, the president of the United States is black![7] You're looking at society through race lenses, Kim! Take them off! See the light!"

I asked my colleague to do something that I would like you to do as well. Put this work down, and for a few days go watch television—news channels (national and local), dramas, children's programming, sitcoms, crime dramas, soap operas, commercials. Go to a few movies. Go to the theater. Walk on your college and university campuses and look at the professors (and students) there. Start paying attention to the advertisements in your doctors' office magazines, at the advertisements in newspapers, on the walls at the malls, on the sides of buses, trains, and storefront walls. Look at the skin color of the images on your telephone apps. Become conscious of the skin tones of the people you are viewing. How often do you come across a dark-skinned person of color versus a light-skinned person of color? To put this in context, how often was the person closer in skin color to President Obama, Newark Mayor Corey Booker, singer Alicia Keyes or actress Halle Berry? Or is their skin color closer to that of First Lady Michelle Obama, singer Jennifer Hudson, or actor Don Cheadle, Jr.?

This experiment involves doing something we say we do not like to do: Notice color. American society pretends to be colorblind, and yet the results of this experiment will clearly reveal that in no way are we blind to color; in fact, noticing color is precisely what we do. Everyday choices are made based on skin color: who you date, who your friends are, who you vote for, who you hire. After participating in my experiment for just a mere day, my colleague called me back, admitting to me what was already in plain view: There is a color hierarchy in America, and for black people in particular! Finding visible darker-skinned images anywhere—in the media, in business, in government—was both hard and rare. The results simply could not be disputed. Blacks are visible, but more often than not the visual representation of blackness is in the form of light skin.[8]

Over the years, many scholars have written on colorism throughout the world, colorism within America, and colorism within black America. This anthology continues these earlier efforts to expose the colorism that currently thrives in colorblind America. It will demonstrate to the reader that there is no such thing as colorblindness—not in theory, not in practice, not even in our minds. Using black Americans as an example of the ways in which colorism thrives in the larger society and within a group of people, this anthology further supports early works that we truly *do* see color but only certain ones.[9]

In Chapter 1 I team up with my former research assistant, J.D. candidate Violeta Solonova Foreman to provide an overview of the global reach of color-ism and drill down to its effects in the United States. Using black Americans as an example of how colorism in the United States has affected a group of people, the chapter links the unique development of colorism in the United States to current practice. Law professor Paul Finkelman builds on that unique develop-ment in Chapter 2. There the author writes on the origins of colorism in early American law with a highlight on the ways in which color came to signify race. The chapter provides the historical context for color preferences within the United States and demonstrates how (and when) the preference for white and eventually grand acceptance of skin tones a few shades less than white secured prominent places within the American psyche, fabric, and culture. In Chapter 3, law professor Kevin D. Brown continues with a look at the history of the "one-drop" rule. As he explains, there was a time in American history when one drop of blood determined whether a person was considered black (and thus presumably a slave). Today this rule is being roundly rejected as the indicator of racial identity. The offspring of that rejection portends the decreasing significance of race and corresponding increasing significance of skin color. In Chapter 4, law professor Taunya Lovell Banks continues with the modern-day effects of this trend. Picking up on comments made by Senator Majority Leader Harry Reid in 2010 about white voters' preference for Barack Obama because he, Obama, is a "light-skinned African American" "with no Negro dialect," the author discusses the significance of media profiling of black Americans in the Obama administration who have lighter to medium skin tones and elite educational credentials. The chapter asks whether blackness in the United States is being disaggregated in the minds of both African Americans and the dominant culture, and whether we are witnessing the emergence of a buffer class of people who—unlike in Latin America—identify culturally as black, and whose success is asserted as proof that we are post-racial.

Taking another direction, in Chapter 5 Dr. Kellina M. Craig-Henderson revisits some of her earlier work on how colorism affects interracial marriage and intimacy within the African American community. She explores African Americans' increased involvement in intimate interracial relationships as proof of the elimination of racial barriers and racial discrimination. The chapter will look at some of the reasons behind African American motives to establish interracial romantic relationships and any connection they have to racial progress or post-racial existences.

Chapter 6 begins a focus in the book on resolution. There Dr. Vetta Sanders Thompson explores connections between race and color in the context of a concept she calls "fragmented peoplehood." Focusing on the African American community's experience in America, the author discusses how people of color compartmentalize their identity, allowing them to resolve any anxiety about their conflicting and contradictory attitudes about race and color. Psychological reactions to experiences of racism and discrimination through the centuries have created psychological insecurities that are both rejected and perpetuated, as fragmented identity psychosis permits strategic, self-serving, and sometimes harmful decisions. These fragmented ways of identifying and surviving are explored. The chapter ends with a discussion of the lingering influence of racism and colorism among African Americans in the United States in a so-called post-racial society and the need for dialogue to begin to repair fragmented psyches.

Some of the mental stress referred to by Dr. Sanders Thompson is further explored by law professor Kimberly Jade Norwood in Chapter 7. There the author looks at two forms of differential treatment based on skin color that are practiced within black communities. First, the preference for lighter skin within black America is studied. The author then looks at another form of reliance on the color of one's skin to discriminate or preference individuals. This is a practice the author has dubbed "blackthink." Blackthink is a phenomenon that polices black identity. The author believes that both practices—preference of some blacks over others based on skin color, and the marginalization of blacks based on skin color—result in an internal war that is derisive, hypocritical, and destructive to the souls of black folks. This mindset, in the author's view, is a modern augmentation of the double consciousness phenomenon Dr. W. E. B. Du Bois identified over a century ago and poses a threat of implosion of a people unless these issues are aired and discussed.

In Chapter 8, Dr. Ronald E. Hall and Adrienne Johnson, J.D., suggest other ways in which colorism can be eradicated through jurisprudence and hiring policies to eradicate differences in treatment based on skin color. Specifically, the authors suggest that employers take a fresh look at affirmative action policies, focusing not on pilloried racial grounds but rather with a nonracial colorism approach. Colorism exists in America, and because current laws pay scant attention to color this type of differential treatment is largely ignored. Courts are beginning to recognize color-discrimination claims as actionable under the law, but the progress here has been painfully slow as courts, and indeed society alike, often appear unaware of or unclear on the distinction between race discrimination and color discrimination. Focusing on race has not only caused a backlash today but also leaves colorism intact. This issue cannot be addressed and eradicated unless it is first acknowledged. Focusing on skin color and fostering a broader framework of inclusion will move the country toward equal treatment of all people.

Finally, Chapter 9 introduces valuable resources for businesses, schools, communities, and even individuals to use to help expose and eradicate colorism. Specifically, Dr. Richard D. Harvey, assistant professor Kira Hudson Banks, and doctoral candidate Rachel E. Tennial, after reviewing the nature of colorism and prior attempts to measure colorism, discuss the development and validated two colorism scales. One scale, "the in-group colorism scale" (ICS), was developed to measure the meaning and significance of colorism for members of communities of color. The second scale, "the out-group colorism scale" (OCS), was developed to measure the meaning and significance of colorism for those outside of communities of color. The scales are proffered as research tools for those interested in finding ways to address colorism, and the chapter concludes with ideas and guidelines on how these scales can be used in various institutional and community settings.

As this book will demonstrate, millions of people of color not only hate the skin they live in but they also long to be lighter in skin color. It is time to send a different message to those people and the young children who look up to them. We hope this work will do just that. This focus is more urgent now than ever before. Black and brown people will become a majority in the United States in the next few decades. In other words, America is becoming less white. Yet, unless colorism is acknowledged, the rising black and brown majority will continue to associate power and privilege with white skin and that association will continue the color caste hierarchy currently entrenched in American society. As Carter Woodson observed long ago, hatred of your own skin is "the worst sort of lynching."[10] If we are not careful, a new form of slavery will rise and while it will not be based on race, it will surely *look* and *act* like race-based slavery censored long ago.

Notes

1 Wang Yan, "New Standards to Ban Bleaching of Pistachios," *China Daily*, May 24, 2010, 5.
2 Of the total world population of approximately 7 billion, the population of China is over 1 billion. See https://www.cia.gov/library/publications/the-world-factbook/geos/xx.html. This comes out to approximately 19.13 percent of the world population as of the end of 2012.
3 See, e.g., Joanne L. Bondilla and Paul Spickard, *Is Lighter Better? Skin-Tone Discrimination among Asian Americans* (Lanham, MD: Rowman & Littlefield Publishers, 2007).
4 There is even a color preference for chicken: White meat costs more than dark meat, allegedly because the demand for white meat is greater than that for dark. Ironically, that is the same conclusion we reach when we are talking about people.
5 Michael Melia, "Birth of White Bison Is Cause for Celebration; American Indians Consider Sacred Event Worthy of Gifts of Tobacco and Colored Flags at New England Farm," *St. Louis Post Dispatch*, July 7, 2012, A19.
6 *American Way*, May 15, 2010. Cosmetics are another interesting issue here. If you have brown skin, it is not always easy to find a foundation for your skin color. Things are much better, true, but the color spectrum remains a work in progress.
7 Biologically, President Obama is half black and half white. I have identified him here as black partly because this is the label, life, and culture he has chosen to identify with, partly because his tanned skin color has caused many others in the United States to view him and treat him as a black man, and partly because I believe that if you put a hoodie on him at night in New York he'd have just as hard of a time getting a taxicab in NYC as any other black man. Commentary, "The Blackness of Obama," available at http://www.blackcommentator.com/216/216_blackness_of_obama_norwood_guest. html. He might be accused of stealing. See "Forest Whitaker Blasts NY Deli: I Was Falsely Accused of Stealing," http://www.tmz.com/2013/02/16/forest-whitaker-deli-shoplifting-frisked/. He might even be shot. See the Trayvon Martin case, http://www.huffingtonpost.com/news/trayvon-martin/.
8 See, e.g., Ron Dicker, "Seinfeld Super Bowl Acura Ad Faces Controversy Over Casting Call for Black Actors: 'Not Too Dark,'" http://www.huffingtonpost.com/2012/04/18/acura-commercial-casting-_n_1434783.html.
9 With white America still being in positions of power and privilege, *and in charge of hiring*, we see over and over again color-based, *as opposed to colorblind*, choices being made every day. For studies on the depth of implicit in-group bias, see, e.g., Jerry Kang and Kristin Lane, "Seeing through Colorblindness: Implicit Bias and the Law," *UCLA Law Review* 58 (2010): 476; Brian A. Nosek, Frederick L. Smyth, Feffrey J. Hansen, Thierry Devos, Nicole M. Lindner, Kate A. Ranganath, Colin Tucker Smith, Kristina R. Olson, Dolly Chugh, Anthony G. Greenwald, and Mahzarin R. Banaji, "Pervasiveness and Correlates of Implicit Attitudes and Stereotypes," *European Review of Social Psychology* 18 (2007): 36–88; Jerry Kang, "Trojan Horses of Race," *Harvard Law Journal* 118 (2005):

1489; Marilynn B. Brewer, "In-Group Favoritism: The Subtle Side of Intergroup Discrimination," in *Codes of Conduct: Behavioral Research into Business Ethics*, ed. David M. Messick and Ann E. Tenbrunsel (New York: Russell Sage Foundation, 1996), 160, 164–165.

10 Carter G. Woodson, *The Mis-education of the Negro*, (Washington, DC: Associated Publishers, 1933), 3.

1

THE UBIQUITOUSNESS OF COLORISM

Then and Now

*Kimberly Jade Norwood and
Violeta Solonova Foreman*

> Black: dirty, soiled, sinister, evil, associated with the Devil, calamitous, disastrous. White: innocent, favorable, fortunate, free from moral impunity, free from spot or blemish.[1]

Black smoke represents the devil; white smoke brings us a pope. Black vs. White: These words have meaning, and they are not limited to good vs. evil or dark vs. light. They also govern how we feel about the people who wear the skin associated with these colors.[2] The term "colorism" is believed to have been first coined in 1982 by Pulitzer Prize-winner Alice Walker. It was defined by her as the "prejudicial or preferential treatment of same-race people based solely on their color."[3] It not only applies within racial communities but also between them. It is a global phenomenon,[4] and because of its tie to beauty it affects women more than men.[5]

An International Look at Color

> Cuban society was thus built with a strict code in which skin color placed human beings in certain social classes and even within varying degrees of humanity: Black, in many cases, was synonymous with beast.[6]

Historically, distinctions based on skin color have appeared independently in different societies around the globe. Centuries ago, for example, "bronze-brown Aztec women [in Central America] . . . used to smear themselves with an ointment made of yellow earth . . . [during courtship,] since golden skin was considered more attractive than brown."[7] In classical antiquity, the Greeks and

Romans used white lead as a cosmetic to lighten their skin, and the Egyptian queen Cleopatra (69–30 BCE) used mercury and "is said to have taken pains to keep her skin light . . . by bathing in asses' milk."[8] In some societies, colorism was specifically tied to class. Agrarian societies placed value on white skin to distinguish the upper class from outdoor laborers.[9] Western colonization, however, used colorism to dehumanize enslaved populations, thus making discrimination based on skin color more than a class imperative, turning it instead into a system of hatred and denigration. This chapter will look briefly at colorism around the globe, focusing particularly on colorism in the United States, and will examine colorism's unique history in America, its tie to racism, and some present-day implications.

Latin America

During the colonial period, Latin America experienced genetic and cultural mixing between the natives, Europeans, and Africans, which, as a result of mixed unions, led to a socially distinct group of people.[10] Social classifications proliferated as racially mixed individuals came to define their place in society.[11] Racial labels multiplied as the Spanish colonists pursued a system of hierarchical classes based on socioracial classifications called "*sociedad de castas* ('society of castes, or breeds')."[12] During the postcolonial period, when most Latin American countries became independent republics, those in power had to reconcile the racial mixture of their populations with the popular theories about the inferiority of colored people. To solve this dilemma, some Latin Americans invoked the notion of "progressive mixture," which acknowledged the mixed nature of Latin America but "also assumed that the region was moving toward a 'superior' state of increasing 'whiteness.'"[13] Many countries encouraged European immigration in order to hasten the process of *blanqueamiento* ("whitening").[14] The concept of "whitening" can be traced to the "1783 Cédula de Gracias al Sacar (petition to 'cleanse' persons of 'impure origins'), which allowed mulattoes[15] to buy certificates that officially declared them to be white."[16]

Today distinctions based on skin color are manifold. Brazil, for example, has at least 300 terms to define skin color.[17] Unlike racial categories in the old American South, however, where one drop of black blood rendered an individual black, the Latino/a equivalent is almost the mirror opposite: One drop of white blood is a start on the path to whiteness.[18] Moreover, appearance, gender, status, and social situation play a role in determining who is classified as black, mulatto, or white.[19] Skin color, though, remains dominant and telling. There is evidence, for example, that black families earn 10 percent less than brown families in Brazil, and both brown and black families earn 60 percent less than white families.[20] The studies also show that light-skinned Latinos are "substantially better off than their dark skinned compatriots regarding their educational attainment, occupational status and household income."[21]

This preference is depicted in Spanish social media as well. Dark-skinned Latinas tend to be overly sexualized and portrayed as morally lacking.[22] Most actors are represented as having lighter skin, unless they appear in secondary roles, such as maids, janitors, and gardeners, in which case their skin is noticeably darker.[23] This is true in print media as well.[24] Even Disney's first Latina princess, introduced in the fall of 2012, has blue eyes, light brown hair, and a Caucasian skin tone.[25]

Asia

Asia is the largest and the most populated continent.[26] While some of its countries, such as Japan and Korea, have individuals whose skin color ranges from light to medium light, many other countries, such as India and Pakistan, include people with darker skin pigmentation.[27] Despite the existence of a full spectrum of skin color in Asia, colorism is widespread in many Asian countries. This section will touch on the practice as it exists in India, China, Japan, and the Philippines.[28]

India

The relation between skin color and class in India is complex and often mistakenly attributed to the caste system. The caste system originated in the Vedic period. It was religiously sanctioned and was designed to "describe the cultural development of each class."[29] While each cast was associated with a color—serfs were affiliated with black, peasants with yellow, warriors with red, and priests with white—skin color did not determine a person's caste.[30] There is evidence that darkly pigmented persons could belong to one of the higher castes.[31] Over time, however, the caste system came to incorporate the negative associations between darker skin and outdoor activities, particularly because both warriors and peasants labored outdoors and were consequently darker-skinned than priests.[32] By the fifteenth and sixteenth centuries, and ultimately influenced by increased contacts with Europe as a result of trade, the caste line became a color line.[33] When the British colonized India, they not only used skin color to distinguish themselves physically, socially, and culturally from the Indians, but they also used skin color to distinguish the Aryan North and the high castes, from the Dravidian South and the lower castes.[34] Following the Aryan conquest of the indigenous and darker-skinned Dravidians, society became segregated into castes. The upper castes, and particularly the priests, were thought to be the descendants of the light-skinned Aryans and the lower castes as descendants of the dark-skinned Dravidians.[35] This cemented ideas of racial theory of caste and dominance of light-skinned people over dark.[36]

The preference for light skin is widely accepted in India today. India has the largest market for skin lighteners,[37] with sales rates increasing nearly 18 percent a year, and far outstripping those of Coca-Cola and tea.[38] Fueling this demand is the country's entertainment industry in which fair skin is imperative for success.[39] Even on popular social media outlets such as Facebook, Indian users are urged to appear whiter and thus more attractive.[40] Skin-whitening creams are not only advertised for the face, but even for the female genital area.[41]

China and Japan

The preference for light skin in Asian society was present long before encounters with Europeans in the modern era.[42] Indeed, white skin was associated with the upper class, while darker skin was viewed as belonging to the lower class that had to labor outdoors.[43] In ancient Japan, lighter skin was associated with color symbolism, as well as notions of purity.[44] The use of makeup to simulate appearance of white skin can be traced as far back as the eighth century in Japan,[45] where pale skin was associated with beauty and spiritual purity.[46] Similarly, in medieval China, women tried to lighten their skin by, among other things, eating ground seashell and applying skin whiteners made out of mercury or lead oxide.[47]

Although the preference for light skin existed before contact with Europeans, it is often cited that in the period following World War II, the "advancement of Westernization and the wide presence of U.S. military bases in Asia have significantly affected aesthetic ideals among Asian peoples."[48] For example, although Japan has had many contacts with white Spanish, English, Dutch, and Portuguese traders before the Tokugawa government sealed off Japan from the West in 1639, the Japanese viewed their own whiteness as superior and often depicted white foreigners as having darker skins than themselves. After Japan was forced to open its doors to trade in 1853, increased commercialism with the West began to gradually alter the country's perception of attractiveness.[49] By the 1920s, motion pictures completely changed Japanese attitudes toward beauty, with Japanese women cutting their hair into fashionable Western bob styles and curling it, despite the traditional samurai notions that valued straight long hair.[50] Anything Western came to be considered modern and superior, and therefore desirable.

Increased globalization and the proliferation of Western mass-media notions of attractiveness have combined with the Asian cultural values associated with white skin to produce a new, heavily Westernized understanding of beauty.[51] Today, European-like phenotypic traits are more desirable[52] and whiter skin pigmentation and more angular facial structures abound. Virtually all advertisements in both countries are of Asian women who are not only pale in skin color, but who possess almost no hint of their Asian lineage. Surgically corrected eyes, lips, mouths, and noses are common.[53] Cosmetic surgery is one of the most popular ways to spend one's discretionary income. The most common operation, blepharoplasty, is used to create a double eyelid that makes eyes appear larger, and the second most popular procedure heightens the bridge of the nose in order to make it more prominent.[54] Blepharoplasty was the world's third most popular plastic surgery in 2009.[55] A Chinese-born student of one of the authors shared that her "own mother would prefer [her] to marry a white man over a Chinese man because [her] children would be whiter and would have a better chance of success."[56] Interestingly, recent data reveal that "Asian women are almost twice as likely to marry a white person than are Asian men.[57]

The desire to appear more Western and less Asian can also be evidenced in Japanese comics, which depict Japanese characters as having light skin, round, and often blue eyes, and bright or even blond hair, while Korean and Chinese characters have exaggerated Asian features.[58]

The Philippines

The Philippines have a long history of colonization. After about 300 years of Spanish rule, the Philippines were colonized by the United States from 1898 to 1946.[59] During the Spanish period, interracial mixing created a substantial population of mestizos,[60] but they were not formally relegated to a separate social class.[61] Although discrimination based on color did exist in the Spanish era, particularly between the mestizos and the natives, it intensified during the U.S. colonization. In fact, it was during the U.S. colonization period that color ranking became the most pronounced, as many U.S. colonial administrators were Southern military officers who drew on American Jim Crow racial distinctions.[62] Scholars note, however, that although colonial rule did, to a great extent, exacerbate skin color prejudices, the Philippines associated light skin color with beauty before the Spanish arrival, as ancient Filipino poets valorized fair-skinned women.[63]

Today, Filipinos have a preference for lighter skin, much like the Japanese, Chinese, and Indians. Skin-whitening creams proliferate, with statistics showing four out of ten women using skin-whitening products.[64] In the entertainment industry, movie stars and famous singers are often very light skinned and have round eyes.[65] For example, the light-skinned Filipina actress Bela Padilla was recently pictured on a controversial men's magazine cover in which she was emerging from a group of dark-skinned models, some of them darkly painted Filipinas, with the caption "Stepping out of the Shadows."[66] The cover was supposed to capture Padilla jettisoning her inhibitions and revamping her image to appeal to an older demographic, but instead the image served as a glaring testament to the colorism issues in the country.[67]

Africa

There is varied information available pinpointing the exact source of the preference for light skin in Africa. Some scholars pin the contemporary African preferences for light skin on colonization.[68] Others have offered evidence that the preference for light skin had some hold prior to colonization. In some parts of precolonial Africa, light-brown, yellow, or reddish tints were the favored pigmentations for women.[69] Yet, in precolonial Congo, dark skin was preferred to such an extent that babies were put in the sun to become darker.[70] It is clear, though, that socioracial hierarchies were established in its colonized countries and this "cemented and generalized the privilege attached to light skin."[71]

Today many African countries continue to be affected by colonialist skin color ideologies. For example, 77 percent of women in parts of Nigeria, 60 percent of Zambian women ages 30–39, 59 percent of the population in Togo, 50–60 percent of adult Ghanaian women, 52 percent of the population in Dakar, Senegal, 50 percent of women in Barnako, Mali, and 35 percent of the population in Pretoria, South Africa, report using skin-whitening products on a regular basis.[72] Lighter-complexioned women in many parts of Africa are considered more beautiful.[73] Light skin is believed to be necessary to attract, and even keep, a husband.[74] Some use skin-whitening products so regularly that they are known as "the bleachers."[75] This dangerous practice risks cancer and mercury poisoning, among other ailments,[76] but it is the price these women are willing to pay for desirability, love, and economic stability.[77] Indeed, in the words of Marita Golden, "they are buying a dream of a better life."[78]

Colorism in Black and White: The United States[79]

Colonialism of the New World played a pivotal role in the centuries-old preference we see in the United States today for white and light skin.[80] In the United States, this preference was a mixture of the culture carried to the New World by the colonists and the unique institution of enslavement of dark-skinned peoples here. Of course, slavery was not invented in the New World, but it did take on a life of its own and became so connected with dark skin that it was almost impossible to separate the two. Specifically, faced with the need for a controllable and cheap labor force to harvest tobacco, which was the chief source of wealth and very labor intensive, colonists began to pass laws that increasingly restricted Africans and their offspring permanently as servants and later as slaves, as well as established and harbored differential treatment of freed servants with European ancestry.[81] In early years of American slavery, African slaves in the Virginia and Carolina colonies could be released from bondage if they converted to Christianity, but after 1667 this loophole was eliminated and the legal status of Africans became tied to skin color.[82] By the late 1600s white skin came to be synonymous with freedom, and black skin with slavery.[83]

Colonists needed labor to secure wealth both for the colonists and for England's elite. Africans, unlike the Irish who were enslaved on plantations in the Caribbean, knew how to raise food in tropical soil, were immune to Old World diseases that killed Native Americans, and, most importantly, were less likely to run away than Native Americans, who were familiar with the territory. Moreover, using white servants for the same labor assigned to Africans was problematic because the former were protected by English law and any mistreatment would be criticized abroad.[84] To justify permanent enslavement of Africans and the horrific treatment they received, the colonists began to publicize grotesque descriptions of Africans to foster fear and loathing and to associate black-skinned people with the cursed descendants of Ham.[85] As Africans were increasingly projected as alien and not quite human, skin color began to play an important role: "[G]reat meaning was attached to human blackness, because black had consistently negative connotations in Indo-European languages, and darkness—such as the darkness of night—ha[d] a long-standing association with evil."[86] Moreover, slave trade was justified because descendants of Ham were thought to be inferior, and the very fact that slavery existed was thought to support the theory behind the curse of Ham.[87] In tandem with popular beliefs about the distinctiveness of dark-skinned people, writings in the eighteenth century began to bolster such views with so-called scientific arguments. Thus,

> the European world sought to justify not only the institution of slavery but also its increasingly brutal marginalization of all non-European peoples, slave or free. Science became the vehicle through which the delineation of races was confirmed, and scientists in Europe and America provided the arguments and evidence to document the inferiority of non-Europeans.[88]

This coalescence of needs, beliefs, justifications, and practices had the effect of placing white skin at a premium and dehumanizing black skin.[89] It was during these times, as well, that colorism took root. The sexual unions between whites and blacks—and largely between enslaved African women and their white male captors—produced children, half black, half white, then commonly called mulattoes.[90] Mulattoes were often lighter than Africans in skin color. Eventually the lighter-skinned mulattoes were preferred by white society over their darker-skin brethren because the lighter-skin blacks were considered more aesthetically appealing and intellectually superior to pure Africans.[91]

These beliefs and preferences hold true today. The closer one's skin color is to white, the closer one is to being treated with an elevated status: that of an "honorary white person," a term created by Professor Eduardo Bonilla-Silva.[92] Focusing on current ways in which skin color impacts the lives of blacks in America today, for example, consider the following:

- To the extent blacks are represented in the most powerful positions in the United States, most in those leadership roles (CEOs and other corporate executives; federal and state government officials in the executive, legislative and judicial branches, and governors and mayors) are light in skin tone.
- Tenured and tenure-track professors at universities throughout America, particularly elite ones, are more likely to be light in skin tone.
- Not only are darker-skinned blacks arrested and incarcerated at higher percentages, but they receive longer prison sentences for comparable offenses

than lighter-skinned blacks and are more likely to be on death row for comparable offenses than lighter-skin blacks. Moreover, the "blacker" one's features (skin color, hair, lips), the greater the penalty.[93]

- Dark-skinned blacks are more likely to be the victims of racial discrimination than lighter-skin blacks.[94]
- In the employment context, lighter-skinned blacks are both more employable and employed. Data on interviews and callbacks even demonstrate that lighter skin is preferred over academic credentials.[95]
- Lighter-skinned blacks are more prevalent in all forms of advertising (store advertisements, magazines, and billboards) and on television: as news anchors,[96] as cast members in television shows, as dancers and love interests in music videos, and as actors in commercials.[97]
- Hollywood has long expressed its preference for light-skin women of color, and even today it is rare to find a dark-skin woman in a positive leading role or as a love interest.[98]
- Many of today's successful entertainers—actors and actresses, singers and musicians—tend to be lighter, rather than darker, in skin tone.
- Lighter-skinned blacks are often better educated, have higher occupational status (better jobs, careers, higher incomes), earn more money, have more overall wealth, tend to marry higher on the socioeconomic ladder, and are perceived as being more competent than darker-skinned blacks.[99]
- Lighter-skinned blacks, particularly females, are more likely to be married than darker-skinned blacks.[100]
- In nationwide beauty pageants, such as the Miss America Pageant, the rare black contestant and (even rarer) black winner have almost always been women with European features: light skin tone, keen features, and long, straight flowing hair.[101]
- In the adoption market, white children are preferred over nonwhite.[102] When African American children are considered, there is a preference for light skin and biracial children over dark-skinned children.[103] There is also a price hierarchy based on demand, with white children commanding top dollar, biracial children half as much, and black children being the cheapest.[104]
- Parents have been known to request light-skinned child-care providers for their children.[105]
- Even in cases where the media has taken a lead role in exposing colorism, it paradoxically continues to broadcast its own preference for light skin tones. CNN, for example, has recently run a series of shows titled *Who is Black in America* and *The State of Black America*. Ironically, while many of the issues explored in these shows involved the preference for light skin over dark skin in black America, the shows were reported to the viewers by the very fair Soledad O'Brien. And, indeed, the overwhelming majority of the newsmen and women of color visible on CNN in 2012—Soledad

O'Brien, Suzanne Malveaux, Tony Harris, T. J. Holmes, Don Lemon, and Fredricka Whitfield—are all people of color who are very fair in skin tone.[106]

• Twenty-first-century doll tests, where white and black preschool and elementary school children are asked various questions about an array of colored faces on a palette placed in front of them, reveal overwhelming preferences for light skin and associate negative connotations with dark skin.[107]

We make choices —consciously in some cases and unconsciously in others— based on skin color every day.[108] By and large, however, Americans continue to believe they are colorblind. The data clearly establishes, though, we cannot help but see color.[109] Even babies see color.[110] The refusal to acknowledge this elephant in the room comes at a high price: It results in a divisive society that continues to pit one color against another. This fosters stereotypes and tensions and negatively affects the people the practice purports not to see.[111]

Focusing on colorism in the United States today is particularly interesting given its recent progress on racial fronts. It is commonly said that, with the election of the first black president, America has entered a post-racial status. Post-racial, undoubtedly, means that the United States has cured its race problem. Many of those who admit that there is still great inequality between whites and nonwhites —especially between whites and blacks—usually advance that this is a result of economic and social conditions, not racism. Indeed, many believe that the election of Barack Obama into the nation's highest office proves that a post-racial sphere has been entered. This is supported by other notable black achievements, such as the success of Colin Powell as both chairman of the Joint Chiefs of Staff and secretary of state, followed by Condoleezza Rice as U.S. Secretary of State, and more recently the election of Deval Patrick as the governor of Massachusetts.

Despite the election of President Obama, though, race continues to matter. There remain exorbitant differences in employment rates, salaries, personal income, family income, wealth, percentages living below poverty, educational attainment, incarceration rates, health care access, and life expectancy rates between whites and blacks.[112] Moreover, negative stereotypes, bigotry, and discrimination based on race continue to thrive. Events following the election of Barack Obama in 2008 and his reelection in 2012 reveal that, far from improving, racial tensions, racist actions, and discriminatory practices have increased.[113] Indeed, some believe that racism has worsened during the Barack Obama presidency.[114] So, during a time when real racial progress is being made, there are increasingly alarming racial disparities and tensions.[115]

It is true, however, that we have entered unchartered territory: 2012 marked the first time in America's history when there were more nonwhite babies born in the United States than white babies, and by the year 2045 whites will be a minority in the United States.[116] Additionally, racial boundaries have become more blurred. There was a time in America when race had a concrete legal significance. It decided whether you were an enslaved person or not; it decided whether you were a citizen, whether you had the right to vote, and whether you had the right to an education. It decided where you could live and work, what water fountain you could drink from, and whether you could eat at a restaurant or stay at a hotel. It determined where you attended school and even where you could be buried. In the twenty-first century, however, the legal spine for these distinctions has been crushed. While *de facto* racial segregation still exists, in many cases *de jure* racial segregation is a thing of the past.

We also have evolved in our thinking about race. It is largely believed today, for example, that there is no such thing as biologically different races; that the genetic markers between two black people, for example, could be greater than the difference between a black person and a white person; and that race, rather, is more a social construction as opposed to a biological one.[117] Moreover, as the United States' biracial and multiracial population increases, it is more difficult to look at a given individual and identify the person by race.

Racial transformation in America is currently evolving, caught in a tug of war between regression and progress. In the midst of this still-morphing concept, America also finds itself in the midst of a growing preference for lighter skin. The evidence is clear on this. Blacks are getting hired, yes, but which ones? Blacks are getting married, yes, but which ones? Blacks are chosen as leaders in government positions and in social/political organizations, *including black organizations*, yes, but which ones? The existing color hierarchy in America keeps dark-skinned people at the bottom of the ladder. This practice is so normalized that even very young black girls pray, as Toni Morrison's Pecola did in *The Bluest Eye*, for something whiter.[118] It is so normal and natural that it can even go undetected by people of color. In his signature piece on colorism, law professor Leonard Baynes once made the following observation:

> [T]here was something that one of my colleagues told me that I really had not considered or noticed before. He said that when he worked at the NAACP Legal Defense Fund, all the attorneys were light-skinned. I had also worked there one summer while I was in law school, and my initial reaction was: "No!" But, upon reflection, I realized that many of the attorneys were light to medium brown in complexion. A light bulb went off in my head. I also realized that in many of the legal jobs that I have held, there have been few African Americans, and I have been one of the darker people employed. And I'm not that dark![119]

Despite America's legal evolution on race during and after the Civil War,[120] one thing did not change: the value of white skin.[121] It represented then, and represents now, power and privilege in America. And the closer one's skin tone is to white, the better one's chances of success; you may not be white but if you are light, you are good enough.[122] For black Americans, this distinction has had very damming effects, particularly on young black girls. Longing for lighter skin makes a dark chocolate-colored girl long to be the color of milk chocolate; the milk chocolate-colored girl long to be the color of a cinnamon-colored girl. The cinnamon-colored girl longs to be a little lighter: Coffee—but with a lot of cream. Incremental shades of light matter, and lighter is always better. This reality persists today even in a world where the café au lait-colored leader of the free world is married to a dark chocolate-colored beauty.

Despite the fact that the world, and America, is becoming less and less white, the preference for white and light continues to maintain a stronghold. Colorism is everywhere. It is so widely practiced and normalized in our lives that one might conclude that it is insurmountable. Yet, colorism begins *in the mind*. If we consciously recognize the dynamics of color in our lives, its power will be revealed. We can then begin and sustain dialogue on why colorism continues its power over people striving to be colorblind.

Notes

1 See http://www.merriam-webster.com/dictionary/.
2 Light skin is associated with good attributes and dark with bad attributes, and there is a universal preference for light skin over dark. See Brian A. Nosek, Frederick L. Smyth, Feffrey J. Hansen, Thierry Devos, Nicole M. Lindner, Kate A. Ranganath, Colin Tucker Smith, Kristina R. Olson, Dolly Chugh, Anthony G. Greenwald, and Mahzarin R. Banaji, "Pervasiveness and Correlates of Implicit Attitudes and Stereotypes," *European Review of Social Psychology* 18 (2007): 36–88.
3 Alice Walker, "If the Present Looks Like the Past, What Does the Future Look Like?" in *In Search of Our Mothers' Gardens* (New York: Harcourt Brace Jovanovich, 1983), 290.
4 See, e.g., Tanya Katerí Hernández, *Racial Subordination in Latin America: The Role of the State, Customary Law, and the New Civil Rights Response* (New York: Cambridge University Press, 2012); Evelyn Nakano Glenn, ed., *Shades of Difference: Why Skin Color Matters* (Stanford, CA: Stanford University Press, 2009); Ronald E. Hall, ed., *Racism in the 21st Century: An Empirical Analysis of Skin Color* (New York: Springer Science & Business Media, LLC, 2008); Joanne L. Rondilla and Paul Spickard, *Is Lighter Better* (Lanham, MD: Rowman & Littlefield, 2007); Marita Golden, *Don't Play in the Sun: One Woman's Journey through the Color Complex* (New York: Anchor Books, 2005); Edward E. Telles, *Race in Another America: The Significance of Skin Color in Brazil* (Princeton, NJ: Princeton University Press, 2004).
5 Yaba Amgborale Blay, "Struck by Lightening: The Transdiasporan Phenomenon of Skin Bleaching," *JENdA* 14 (2009): 2. See also Imani Perry, "Buying White Beauty," *Cardozo Journal of Law and Gender* 12 (2006): 579–607. Men engage in skin bleaching as well. In India, where skin bleaching among men is a huge industry, see Saritha Rai, "Indian Men Seek Whiter Shade of Pale," *Global Post*, July 29, 2010, accessed May 8, 2013, http://www.globalpost.com/dispatch/india/100727/indian-culture-skin-lightening-shahid-kapur#1.
6 See, e.g., Leonardo Padura, "Race in Cuba: The Eternal 'Black Problem,'" http://www.theroot.com/views/race-cuba-eternal-black-problem; see also PBS's *Black in Latin America*, multimedia website, http://www.pbs.org/wnet/black-in-latin-america/.

7   Kathy Russell, Midge Wilson, and Ronald E. Hall, *The Color Complex: The Politics of Skin Color among African Americans* (New York: Harcourt Brace Jovanovich, 1992), 65.
8   Nina G. Jablonski, *Living Color: The Biological and Social Meaning of Skin Color* (Berkeley: University of California Press, 2012), 170.
9   Interestingly, modern-day United States and Europe place value on tanned skin because it is associated with leisure, and thus affluence.
10 *Encyclopædia Britannica Online*, s.v. "race," accessed January 2, 2013, http://www. britannica.com.
11 Ibid. "Although *mestizo* ('mixed person') was a general label, it often referred specifically to people of indigenous and European heritage, while the term *mulato* ('mulatto') usually referred to a person of African and European descent. Labels multiplied as time went on, as with *zambo* (black–indigenous mix) and *pardo* (literally, 'brown person,' commonly used to denote a person of African and European descent)." Ibid.
12 Ibid.
13 Ibid.; Jesús María Herrera Salas, "Ethnicity and Revolution: The Political Economy of Racism in Venezuela," *Latin American Perspectives* 32(2) (2005): 72.
14 Ibid.
15 A person of mixed African heritage. Lillian Guerra, *Popular Expression and National Identity in Puerto Rico: The Struggle for Self, Community, and Nation* (Gainesville, FL: University Press of Florida, 1998), 215.
16 Ibid.
17 Berta Esperanza Hernández-Truyol and Stephen J. Powell, *Just Trade: A New Covenant Linking Trade and Human Rights* (New York: New York University Press, 2009), 161.
18 Ibid.
19 Edward Telles, "The Social Consequences of Skin Color in Brazil," in *Shades of Difference: Why Skin Color Matters*, ed. Evelyn Glenn (Palo Alto, CA: Stanford University Press, 2009), 9; Tanya Golash-Boza and William Darity, Jr., "Latino Racial Choices: The Effects of Skin Colour and Discrimination on Latinos' and Latinas' Racial Self-Identifications," *Ethnic and Racial Studies* 31(5) (2008): 904.
20 Ibid.
21 Edward Telles et al., "Skin Color, Racial Identity and Socioeconomic Outcomes in Latin America's Pigmentocracy" (paper presented at the annual meetings of Population Association of America, Washington, DC, March 31–April 2, 2011), 7. This study included the following six countries: Bolivia, Brazil, Colombia, Dominican Republic, Mexico, and Peru. Telles found "that Brazilians with darker skin color have lower earnings and occupational status than do those with lighter skin; they also have less access to education and experience various forms of discrimination." Andrés Villarreal, "Stratification by Skin Color in Contemporary Mexico," *American Sociological Review* 75(5) (2010): 653. Andrés Villarreal also "found evidence of profound social stratification by skin color in contemporary Mexico. Individuals with darker skin tone have significantly lower levels of educational attainment and occupational status, and they are more likely to live in poverty and less likely to be affluent, even after controlling for other individual characteristics." Villarreal, "Stratification by Skin Color," 671.
22 Lucila Vargas, *Latina Teens, Migration, and Popular Culture* (New York: Peter Lang Pub., 2009), 61. A study in 2012 found that the negative stereotyping of Latinos in the media, such as their portrayal as gardeners, maids, and criminals, negatively affects the attitudes of non-Latinos toward the former. "Latino Decisions," *The Impact of Media Stereotypes on Opinions and Attitudes Towards Latinos* (Pasadena, CA: National Hispanic Media Coalition, 2012).

23 Margaret Hunter, "The Persistent Problem of Colorism: Skin Tone, Status, and Inequality," *Sociology Compass* 1(1) (2007); Adriana Maestas, "Gang Members, Gardeners, and Maids: Media Portrayals Matter," http://politic365.com/2012/09/14/gang-members-gardeners-and-maids-media-portrayals-matter/. Indeed, darker-skinned Latinas have bitterly complained of the media tendency to portray, even on Spanish channels such as Telemundo, successful and sexy Latinas always with fair complexions, and reserving the unwanted or laborers to dark-skin portrayals. See, generally, Arlene Davila, *Latinos, Inc. The Marketing and Making of a People* (Berkeley, CA: University of California Press, 2001).

24 Melissa A. Johnson, Prabu David, and Dawn Huey-Ohlsson, "Beauty in Brown: Skin Color in Latina Magazines," in *Brown and Black Communication; Latino and African American Conflict and Convergence in Mass Media*, ed. Diana I. Ri_os and A. N. Mohamed (Westport, CT: Praeger, 2003), 165.

25 Ruben Navarrette Jr., "Why Isn't Disney's Princess Sofia Latino?" *CNN Opinion*, October 26, 2012, accessed January 2, 2013, http://www.cnn.com/2012/10/25/opinion/navarrette-disney-hispanics/index.html. A media uproar quickly followed, with Disney at first defending and later claiming that the characterization of the princess as Latina was a misstatement by a producer promoting the cartoon. Cindy Y. Rodriguez, "Disney Producer 'Misspoke': 'First Latina princess' Isn't Latina," *CNN Entertainment*, October 25, 2012, accessed January 2, 2013, http://www.cnn.com/2012/10/25/showbiz/disney-sofia-not-latina/index.html.

26 Bruce McClish, *Old World Continents: Europe, Asia, and Africa* (Chicago, IL: Heinemann Library, 2003), 14.

27 Jablonski, *Living Color*, 81.

28 Colorism, however, exists in other Asian countries, such as Vietnam, see, e.g., Rosalind Chou, *Asian American Sexual Politics: The Construction of Race, Gender, and Sexuality* (Lanham, MD: Rowman & Littlefield, 2012), and in Hong Kong, Malaysia, the Philippines, South Korea, and Taiwan, see, e.g., Thomas Fuller, "Glamour at a Price in Asia—Health & Science—International Herald Tribune," *New York Times*, May 1, 2006, accessed February 1, 2013, http://www.nytimes.com/2006/05/01/health/01iht-skin.1644457.html?pagewanted-all&_r=0.

29 Jablonski, *Living Color*, 107. Caste was "associated with the role an individual played in connection with communal sacrifice and was determined by concepts of taboo, pollution, and purification." Ibid., 108.

30 Ibid., 107, 108. In India, for example, "many of the supreme deities, including Shiva, Rama, and Krishna, were depicted as dark blue or black--colours [sic] that are said to symbolize the dark clouds that bring rain to the fields and, by implication, the prosperity that accompanies a plentiful harvest." *Encyclopædia Britannica Online*.

31 Jablonski, *Living Color*, 108.

32 *Encyclopædia Britannica Online*.

33 Ibid.

34 Amali Phillips, "Gendering Colour: Identity, Femininity and Marriage in Kerala," *Anthropologica* 46(2) (2004): 255.

35 Romila Thapar, "The Theory of Aryan Race and India: History and Politics," *Social Scientist* 24(1/3) (1996): 6.

36 Phillips, "Gendering Colour," 255.

37 Alma M. Garcia, *Contested Images: Women of Color in Popular Culture* (Lanham, MD: AltaMira Press, 2012), 175. In India, 61 percent of the dermatological market consists of skin-lightening products. World Health Organization, "Mercury in Skin Lightening Products," accessed February 1, 2013, http://www.who.int/ipcs/assessment/public_health/mercury_flyer.pdf.

38 Shantanu Guha Ray, "India's Unbearable Lightness of Being," *BBC News*, March 23, 2010, accessed January 2, 2013, http://news.bbc.co.uk/2/hi/8546183.stm.

39 "Can't Single Bollywood Out," *Times of India*, August 4, 2011, accessed January 10, 2013, http://articles.timesofindia.indiatimes.com/2011–08–04/edit-page/29846955_1_bollywood-preferences-smita-patil.

40 Mark Dummett, "India Facebook Users Urged to 'Appear Whiter,'" *BBC News*, July 14, 2010, accessed January 2, 2013, http://www.bbc.co.uk/news/world-south+asia-10634777.

41 Ibid. See also Rajini Vaidyanathan, "Has Skin Whitening in India Gone Too Far?" *BBC News*, June 5, 2012, accessed January 2, 2013, http://www.bbc.co.uk/news/magazine-18268914.

42 Rondilla and Spickard, *Is Lighter Better?*, 5; Eric P. H. Li et al., "Skin Lightening and Beauty in Four Asian Cultures," *Advances in Consumer Research* 35 (2008): 444; Hiroshi Wagatsuma, "The Social Perception of Skin Color in Japan," *Daedalus* 96(2) (1967): 407–443.

43 Nita Tewari and Alvin N. Alvarez, *Asian American Psychology Current Perspectives* (Hoboken, NJ: Taylor and Francis, 2012), 543.

44 Jablonski, *Living Color*, 167.

45 Ibid., 170.

46 Ibid., 167.

47 Margo DeMello, *Faces around the World: A Cultural Encyclopedia of the Human Face* (Santa Barbara, CA: ABC-CLIO, 2012), 42; Charles D. Benn, *Daily Life in Traditional China: The Tang Dynasty* (Westport, CT: Greenwood Press, 2002), 107.

48 *Encyclopædia Britannica Online.* See also Jablonski, *Living Color*, 168.

49 Wagatsuma, "The Social Perception of Skin Color"; Li, "Skin Lightening and Beauty."

50 Wagatsuma, "The Social Perception of Skin Color."

51 Li, "Skin Lightening and Beauty."

52 *Encyclopædia Britannica Online.*

53 See, e.g., Rondilla and Spickard, *Is Lighter Better?*, 3.

54 Sharon LaFraniere, "For Many Chinese, New Wealth and a Fresh Face," *The New York Times*, April 23, 2011, accessed January 2, 2013, http://www.nytimes.com/2011/04/24/world/asia/24beijing.html?pagewanted=all&_r=0.

55 International Society of Aesthetic Plastic Surgery, "ISAPS International Survey on Aesthetic/Cosmetic Procedures Performed in 2010," accessed January 2, 2013, http://www.isaps.org/files/html-contents/ISAPS-Procedures-Study-Results-2011.pdf. This is a very serious issue in South Korea as well. As Elizabeth King and Jinna Yun explain, "[b]ecause so many people in South Korea have undergone eyelid surgery, the country has the highest percentage of people with plastic surgery in the world." Elizabeth King and Jinna Yun, "Plastic Surgery for Eyelids Popular Among Asian Women," *Medill News Service*, June 8, 2005, quoted in Hunter, "The Persistent Problem of Colorism," 247–248. For those who cannot afford blepharoplasty, cheaper alternatives exist, such as thin strips of clear tape or glues that are commonly used to temporarily adhere the "pretarsal upper lid skin to preseptal skin, resulting in a [Western] palpebral fold." Ira D. Papel, *Facial Plastic and Reconstructive Surgery*, 3rd edition (New York: Thieme, 2009), 437.

56 Hong Chen, in discussion with Kimberly Norwood, in St. Louis, MO, August 19, 2012.

57 Roland G. Fryer Jr., "Guess Who's Been Coming to Dinner? Trends in Interracial Marriage over the 20th Century," *Journal of Economic Perspectives*, 21 (2007): 77.

58 Bonnie Berry, *The Power of Looks: Social Stratification of Physical Appearance* (Burlington, VT: Ashgate Publishing, 2008), 37.

59 Stuart Notholt, *Fields of Fire: An Atlas of Ethnic Conflict* (London: Stuart Notholt Communications, Ltd., 2008), chap. 6.18. The Spanish colonized the Philippines from 1565 to 1898. Ibid.

60 "Mestizo" in this instance refers to individuals of mixed Spanish, Filipino, and sometimes Chinese ancestry. Rondilla and Spickard, *Is Lighter Better?*, 54.

61 Ibid.

62 Ibid.

63 Princess Orig, "Kayumanggi Versus Maputi: 100 Years of America's White Aesthetics in Philippine Literature," in *Mixed Blessing: The Impact of the American Colonial Experience on Politics and Society in the Philippines*, ed. Hazel M. McFerson (Westport, CT: Greenwood Press, 2002), 99–100.

64 Fuller, "Glamour at a Price in Asia."

65 Hunter, "The Persistent Problem of Colorism"; Catherine Choy, "Asian American History: Reflections on Imperialism, Immigration, and the Body," in *Pinay Power: Peminist Critical Theory: Theorizing the Filipina/American Experience*, ed. Melinda L. Jesus (New York: Routledge, 2005), 81–98.

66 Mark McDonald, "Filipinos Debate Racism in a Men's Magazine," *International Herald Tribune*, February 28, 2012, accessed February 1, 2013, http://rendezvous.blogs.nytimes.com/2012/02/28/filipinos-debate-racism-in-a-mens-magazine/; Philip Caulfield, "FHM Philippines Magazine Pulls its March Cover Featuring Beauty Bela Padilla After 'Racism' Outcry," *New York Daily News*, February 27, 2012, accessed February 1, 2013, http://www.nydailynews.com/news/fhm-philippines-magazine-pulls-march-cover-featuring-beauty-bela-padilla-racism-outcry-article-1.1029331.

67 McDonald, "Filipinos Debate Racism."

68 Yaba Blay, "Skin Bleaching and Global White Supremacy: By Way of Introduction," *Journal of Pan African Studies* 4(4) (2011); Marita Golden, *Don't Play in the Sun: One Woman's Journey through the Color Complex* (New York: Anchor Books, 2005); Melanie Miyanji de Souza, "The Concept of Skin Bleaching in Africa and Its Devastating Health Implications," *Clinics in Dermatology* 26(1) (2008): 27; Evelyn Glenn, "Consuming Lightness: Segmented Markets and Global Capital in the Skin-Whitening Trade," in *Shades of Difference: Why Skin Color Matters*, ed. Evelyn Nakano Glenn (Palo Alto, CA.: Stanford University Press, 2009), 169; Christopher A. D. Charles, "Skin Bleaching, Self-Hate, and Black Identity in Jamaica," *Journal of Black Studies* 33(6) (2003): 711–728; Kelly M. Lewis, Navit Robkin, Karie Gaska, and Lillian Carol Njoki, "Investigating Motivations for Women's Skin Bleaching in Tanzania," *Psychology of Women Quarterly* 35(1) (2001): 29–37.

69 Nakedi Ribane, *Beauty: A Black Perspective* (Scottsville, South Africa: University of KwaZulu-Natal Press, 2006), 12.

70 Golden, *Don't Play in the Sun*, 166. Yaba Blay suggests that whiteness likely had negative connotations in traditional Ghanian culture because the word "white" is used both to describe color and someone with a sickly disposition. Yaba Amgborale Blay, "Yellow Fever: Skin Bleaching and the Politics of Skin Color in Ghana," PhD dissertation, Temple University, 2007, 334–335. Blay also suggests that because early European travelers frequently died of tropical diseases, whiteness was likely seen as a weakness. Ibid.

71 Glenn, "Consuming Lightness," 170.

72 See Yaba Blay, "Get Light or Die Trying," http://yabablay.com/get-light-or-die-trying/; Blay, "Skin Bleaching and Global White Supremacy"; World Health Organization, "Mercury in Skin Lightening Products." In Côte d'Ivoire, 87 out of 100 seemingly fair-skinned women use skin-whitening products on a regular basis. Blay, "Skin Bleaching and Global White Supremacy."

73 "Tanzania Counts Cost of 'White Skin,'" *BBC News*, November 23, 2004, accessed February 1, 2013, http://news.bbc.co.uk/2/hi/africa/4032837.stm.

74 Golden, *Don't Play in the Sun*, 155; Kelly M. Lewis et al., "Investigating Motivations," 33–34.

75 Golden, *Don't Play in the Sun*, 149–150.

76   Dr. S. Allen Counter, "Whitening Skin Can Be Deadly," *Boston Globe*, December 16, 2003, accessed February 2, 2012, http://www.boston.com/news/globe/health_science/articles/2003/12/16/whitening_skin_can_be_deadly/.

77   Pumza Fihlani, "Africa: Where Black is Not Really Beautiful," *BBC News*, December 31, 2012, accessed February 2, 2013, http://www.bbc.co.uk/news/world-africa-20444798.

78   Golden, *Don't Play in the Sun*, 155.

79   This section will focus on the origins of colorism in the United States and will discuss its impact as it relates to black Americans. This is in no way to suggest that colorism in the United States affects only black Americans. The preference for light skin over dark skin is infused within American culture, not only affecting black Americans but actually affecting *all* people who live in America. Colorism can even be traced to early Native American history—postcolonization of course. Bethany R. Berger, "Red: Racism and the American Indian," *UCLA Law Review* 56 (2009) 591. Native Americans adopted racial theories of white colonists. Ann McMullen, "Blood and Culture: Negotiating Race in Twentieth-Centure Native New England," in *Confounding the Color Line: The Indian-Black Experience in North America*, ed. James F. Brooks (Lincoln: University of Nebraska Press, 2002). 261–291. William J. Ware, "African/Native American Cherokees: The Politics of Ethnic Identity," PhD dissertatiion, Union Institute and University, 2006, 6–7. As colonists "disallowed Indian self-identification for individuals who appeared to have Black ancestors," and society was heavily prejudiced against black individuals, Native American reluctance to be associated with black individuals can be understood both as evidence of their changing attitudes as a result of socialization with white society and as self-advancement. The influence of white values on Native Americans was so pronounced that by the end of the nineteenth century light skin color was idealized. McMullen, "Blood and Culture," 266–267. See also Ronald E. Hall, *An Historical Analysis of Skin Color Discrimination in America: Victimism among Victim Group Populations* (New York: Springer, 2010), 94, 96–97, 101 (in school settings, Native American students with lighter complexion often teased full-blooded Native Americans who had darker complexions); Ware, "African/Native American Cherokees," 7. (In the Lumbee Native American community, they "divide themselves into white versus black Lumbees, where the white Lumbees could deny kinship or any cultural connection to the black Lumbees.").

80   For some insight into the reach of colonization, see, e.g., Charles W. Mills, *The Racial Contract* (Ithaca, NY: Cornell University Press, 1999); Paulo Freire, *Pedagogy of the Oppressed,* 30th anniversary edition (New York: Bloomsbury Academic, 2006); Frantz Fanon, *The Wretched of the Earth* (New York: Grove Press, 2005).

81   *Encyclopædia Britannica Online.*

82   Jablonski, *Living Color*, 145.

83   Ibid.

84   *Encyclopædia Britannica Online.*

85   Ibid. See also Jablonski, *Living Color*, 141.

86   Jablonski, *Living Color*, 136.

87   Ibid., 139.

88   *Encyclopædia Britannica Online.*

89   See, e.g., Joy DeGruy Leary, *Post Traumatic Slave Syndrome: America's Legacy of Enduring Injury and Healing* (Oakland, CA: Uptone Press 2005), 54–55 (discussion of the cognitive dissonance that occurs in the minds of slave owners to justify the horrors of slavery).

90   E. Franklin Frazier, *Black Bourgeoisie* (New York: Free Press Paperbacks, 1957), 136.

91   Margaret L. Hunter, "'If You're Light You're Alright': Light Skin Color as Social Capital for Women of Color," *Gender and Society* 16(2) (2002): 175–193.

92 Eduardo Bonilla-Silva and David R. Dietrich, "The Latin Americanization of U.S. Race Relations: A New Pigmentocracy," *Shades of Difference: Why Skin Color Matters*, ed. Evelyn Nakano Glenn (Stanford, CA: Stanford University Press, 2009).

93 See, e.g., Jennifer L. Eberhardt, Paul G. Davies, Valerie J. Purdie-Vaughns, and Sheri Lynn Johnson, "Looking Deathworthy: Perceived Stereotypicality of Black Defendants Predicts Capital-Sentencing Outcomes," *Psychological Science* 17 (2006): 383, 385. See also Jill Viglione, Lance Hannon, and Robert DeFina, "The Impact of Light Skin on Prison Time for Black Female Offenders," *The Social Science Journal* 48 (2011): 250–258.

94 Joni Hersch, "Skin Color, Physical Appearance, and Perceived Discriminatory Treatment," *Journal of Socio-Economics* 40 (2011): 671–678; Ronald Hall, "The Bleaching Syndrome: African Americans' Response to Cultural Domination vis-à-vis Skin Color," *Journal of Black Studies*, 26 (November 1995): 172–184; Verna M. Keith and Cedric Herring, "Skin Tone and Stratification in the Black Community," *American Journal of Sociology* 97(3) (November 1991): 775. For disparities in health care, see Vernellia Randall, *Dying while Black* (Dayton, OH: Seven Principles Press, 2006).

95 See, e.g., Philip Lee Williams, "Skin Tone More Important than Educational Background for African Americans Seeking Jobs, According to New Research from the University of Georgia," *Broward Times* (Coral Springs, FA), August 18–24, 2006, 4, available at http://proquest.umi.com/pqdweb?did=1134125241&sid=1&Fmt= 3&clientld=9108&RQT=309&VName=PQD. See also Travis Loller, "Study Says Skin Tone Affects Earnings," Associated Press, January 26, 2007, available at http://sfgate.com/cgi-bin/article.cgi?file=/News/archive/2007/01/26/national/ a135252S09.DTL. See also "Unemployed Black Woman Pretends to be White, Job Offers Suddenly Skyrocket," Techyville.com, November 15, 2012, http://www. techyville.com/2012/11/news/unemployed-black-woman-pretends-to-be-white-job-offers-suddenly-skyrocket/.

96 Nadra Kareem Nittle, "CNN's Don Lemon: 'Anchors of Color on Television are Light-Skinned,'" About.com, June 30, 2011, http://racerelations.about.com/b/2011/ 06/30/cnns-don-lemon-anchors-of-color-on-television-are-light-skinned.htm?p=1. See generally, Sharon Bramlett-Solomon, *Race, Gender, Class and Media: Studying Multiculturalism and Mass Communication* (Dubuque, IA, Kendall Hunt Publishing: 2012).

97 See, e.g., Robert M. Entman and Andrew Rojecki, *The Black Image in the White Mind: Media and Race in America* (Chicago, IL: University of Chicago Press, 2000). See also Tom Burrell, *Brainwashed: Challenging the Myth of Black Inferiority* (New York: Smiley Books, 2010).

98 Common leading ladies of color in Hollywood today include Halle Berry, Zoe Saldana, Paula Patton, Thandie Newton, and Jada Pinkett-Smith. So, while one can point to many famous and/or powerful black men who are dark in complexion, black women are not so lucky and indeed are sometimes even pitted against one another. Consider the debate within the black community over the casting of Zoe Saldana, the café au lait–colored Latina, to play Nina Simone, a dark chocolate woman who wore her African features prominently and proudly. See Tanzina Vega, "Stir Builds Over Actress to Portray Nina Simone," *The New York Times*, September 9, 2012, http://www.nytimes.com/2012/09/13/movies/should-zoe-saldana-play-nina-simone-some-say-no.html?

99 Russell, Wilson, and Hall, *The Color Complex*; Michael Hughes and Bradley R. Hertel, "The Significance of Color Remains: A Study of Life Chances, Mate Selection, and Ethnic Consciousness among Black Americans," *Social Forces* 68 (1990): 1116; Arthur H. Goldsmith, Darrick Hamilton, and William Darity, Jr., "From Dark to Light: Skin

Color and Wages among African-Americans," *Journal of Human Resources* 42(4) (Fall 2007), 701–738.

100 Darrick Hamilton, Arthur H. Goldsmith, and William Darity, Jr., "Shedding 'Light' on Marriage: The Influence of Skin Shade on Marriage for Black Females," *Journal of Economic Behavior & Organization* 72 (2009): 30–50.

101 See, e.g., "2009; Katie Stam," Miss America, accessed May 9, 2013, http://www.missamerica.org/our-miss-americas/2000/2009.aspx. See also *There She Is, Miss America: The Politics of Sex, Beauty, and Race in America's Most Famous Pageant*, eds Elwood Watson and Darcy Martin (New York: Palgrave Macmillan, 2004).

102 See generally, Solangel Maldonado, "Discouraging Racial Preferences in Adoptions," *University of California–Davis Law Review* 39 (2005–2006): 1415. International adoptions, from primarily Asia, Russia, and Guatemala, are the next highest ranking. Ibid.

103 See, e.g., Zanita E. Fenton, "In a World Not Their Own: The Adoption of Black Children," *Harvard BlackLetter Law Journal* 10 (1993): 39, 54; Solangel Maldonado, "Discouraging Racial Preferences in Adoptions," 1426. Family blending has been raised as an issue that comes up in this area. See generally, Elizabeth Bartholet, *Family Bonds: Adoption, Infertility, and the New World of Child Production* (Boston, MA: Beacon Publishing, 1993), 87. Only the adopting parent knows if the child's skin color preference was based on this reason although the data clearly demonstrates that people discriminate based on color without even realizing it and even *when believing that they are not*. See, e.g., Jerry Kang, "Trojan Horses of Race," *Harvard Law Review* 118 (2005): 1489, 1512. Even drug-exposed children are preferred over drug-free African American babies. See Ralph Richard Banks, "The Color of Desire: Fulfilling Adoptive Parents' Racial Preferences through Discriminatory State Action," *Yale Law Journal* 107 (1998): 875, 964 n. 20. This suggests that mere family blending is not always a motive.

104 See generally, Barbara Fedders, "Race and Market Values in Domestic Infant Adoption," *North Carolina Law Review* 88 (2010): 1687.

105 See, e.g., Perry, "Buying White Beauty," 608.

106 Boyce Watkins, "CNN Does Show on Colorism, But Are They Guilty of Colorism Themselves," YourBlackWorld.net, http://www.yourblackworld.net/2012/12/black-news/cnn-does-show-on-colorism-but-are-they-guilty-of-colorism-themselves/.

107 "Black or White: Kids on Race," CNN, http://www.cnn.com/SPECIALS/2010/kids.on.race/.

108 Ian F. Haney Lopez, "Is the 'Post' in Post-Racial the 'Blind' in Colorblind?," *Cardozo Law Review* 32 (2011): 807; Charles R. Lawrence III, "The Id, the Ego, and Equal Protection: Reckoning with Unconscious Racism," *Stanford Law Review* 39 (1987): 317, 333.

109 See, e.g., Jerry Kang and Kristin Lane, "Seeing through Colorblindness: Implicit Bias and the Law," *UCLA Law Review* 58 (2010): 465. I find the online data interesting in this area. While so many profess colorblindness, the data for online dating reveals very specific racial requests. See, for example, Randall Kennedy, *Interracial Intimacies* (New York: Pantheon Books, 2003), 27–37; Elizabeth F. Emens, "Intimate Discrimination: The State's Role in the Accidents of Sex and Love," *Harvard Law Review* 122 (2009): 1307; Russell K. Robinson, "Structural Dimensions of Romantic Preferences," *Fordham Law Review* 76(6) (2008): 2787–2819.

110 Po Bronson and Ashley Merman, *NurtureShock: New Thinking about Children* (New York: Twelve Books, 2009).

111 See, e.g., Leary, *Post-Traumatic Slave Syndrome*, 114–144; Maxine S. Thompson and Verna M. Keith, "Copper Brown and Blue Black," in *Skin Deep: How Race and*

Complexion Matter in the "Colorblind" Era, eds Cedrick Herring, Verna M. Keith, and Hayward Derrick Horton (Champaign, IL: University of Illinois Press, 2003), 47; Elizabeth A. Klonoff and Hope Landrine, "Is Skin Color a Marker for Racial Discrimination? Explaining the Skin Color-Hypertension Relationship," *Journal of Behavioral Medicine* 23 (2000): 329–338.

112 For information on wealth gaps, for example, see Rakesh Kochhar, Richard Fry, and Paul Taylor, "Wealth Gaps Rise to Record Highs Between Whites, Blacks, Hispanics," Pew Research, http://www.pewsocialtrends.org/2011/07/26/wealth-gaps-rise-to-record-highs-between-whites-blacks-hispanics/. In the land of *Shelley v. Kraemer*, 334 U.S. 1 (1948), St. Louis remains one of the most racially segregated cities in the country. See "Segregation Still Permeates St. Louis Area, Data Show," *St. Louis Post-Dispatch,* December 15, 2010, http://www.stltoday.com/news/national/segregation-still-permeates-st-louis-area-data-show/article_3a2a66a3-fc6a-5f1d-ab57-b64d3b57714f.html). Segregation in public schools remains. See Motoko Rich, "Segregation Prominent in Schools, Study Finds," *The New York Times*, September 19, 2012, http://www.nytimes.com/2012/09/20/education/segregation-prominent-in-schools-study-finds.html. Nationwide disparities based on race continue in mortgage lending and foreclosures, see "Lost Ground 2011: Disparities in Mortgage Lending and Foreclosures," http://www.responsiblelending.org/mortgage-lending/research-analysis/Lost-Ground-2011.pdf; Rakesh Kochhar et al., "Wealth Gaps Rise to Record Highs"; Kenneth Chang, "Black Scientists Less Likely to Win Federal Research Grants, Study Reports," *The New York Times*, August 19, 2011, http://www.nytimes.com/2011/08/19/science/19nih.html?_r=0. In the area of poverty, 37.4 percent of black children, 34.1 percent of Hispanic children and 12.5 percent of white non–Hispanic children were considered impoverished in 2011. U.S. Department of Health and Human Services' Office of the Assistant Secretary for Planning and Evaluation Issue Brief, "Information on Poverty and Income Statistics: A Summary of 2012 Current Population Survey Data," http://aspe.hhs.gov/hsp/12/povertyandincomeest/ib.shtml. The disparities in health care between blacks and whites remain troublesome. See Randall, *Dying while Black.*

113 See, e.g., Laura Ly, "Oberlin College Cancels Classes to Address Racial Incidents," CNN, March 5, 2013, http://www.cnn.com/2013/03/04/us/ohio-oberlin-hate-incidents; Mark Potok, "White Hot," *Southern Poverty Law Center Intelligence Report*, Spring 2012, http://www.splcenter.org/home/2012/spring/white-hot; "Put the White Back in White House T-shirt Spotted at Romney Rally Goes Viral," October 14, 2012, http://thegrio.com/2012/10/14/put-the-white-back-in-the-white-house-t-shirt-spotted-at-romney-rally-goes-viral/#s:offensive-anti-obama-tshirt. During the 2012 Republican National Convention a black female camerawoman had peanuts thrown at her by convention attendees and was called a monkey. Gene Demby, "CNN Camerawoman: Peanut-Throwing Incident At Republican Convention A 'Wake-Up Call," *Huffington Post*, August 30, 2012, http://www.huffington post.com/2012/08/30/cnn-camerawoman-peanuts-rnc_n_1843576.html; Seth Stephens-Davidowitz, "How Racist Are We? Ask Google," nytimes.com, June 9, 2012, http://campaignstops.blogs.nytimes.com/2012/06/09/how-racist-are-we-ask-google/; Sonya Ross and Jennifer Agiesta, "Polls Show a Majority Harbor Prejudice Against Blacks," *Huffington Post*, October 27, 2012, http://www.huffington post.com/2012/10/27/racial-views-new-polls-sh_n_2029423.html; Lisa Brown, "Study Notes Disparity in Lending to Blacks, Whites Here: Amid Subprime Crisis, Housing Loans Were Down for Blacks, Up for Whites," *St. Louis Post-Dispatch*, March 4, 2011, http://business.highbeam.com/435553/article-1G1–250618754/study-notes-disparity-lending-blacks-whites-here-amid; "Racial Discrimination in Jury Selection Remains Widespread, According to EJI Study Released Today," Equal Justice Initiative, June 22, 2010, http://www.eji.org/node/397.

114 "NAACP Chairman Julian Bond Says Racism Has Increased during Obama's Tenure," YourBlackWorld.com, http://www.yourblackworld.net/2013/03/black-news/naacp-chairman-julian-bond-says-racism-has-increased-during-obamas-tenure/.

115 Mark Potok, "The Year in Hate and Extremism," *Southern Poverty Law Center Intelligence Report*, Spring 2013, http://www.splcenter.org/home/2013/spring/the-year-in-hate-and- extermism. The irony, of course, is that the data shows major slips in all economic indicators for black Americans during the Obama Administration. Consider, e.g., "Ben Jealous: Black Americans 'Are Doing Far Worse' Under Obama Admin," available at http://www.yourblackworld.net/2013/01/black-news/ben-jealous-black-americans-are-doing-far-worse-under-obama-admin/; see also "The Gap Between Blacks and Whites is Larger Under Obama than Bush or Any Other President," January 5, 2013, http://www.blackbluedog.com/2013/01/news/the-gap-between-blacks-and-whites-is-larger-under-obama-than-bush-or-any-other-president/?utm_source=rss&utm_medium=rss&utm_campaign=the-gap-between-blacks-and-whites-is-larger-under-obama-than-bush-or-any-other-president.

116 See Frank Bass, "Nonwhite U.S. Births Become the Majority for the First Time," *Bloomberg*, May 17, 2012, http://www.bloomberg.com/news/2012–05–17/non-white-u-s-births-become-the-majority-for-first-time.html. For very interesting comments on this phenomenon by readers, see comments posted at "Census: Fewer White Babies Being Born—in America," CNN.com, May 17, 2012, http://inamerica.blogs.cnn.com/2012/05/17/census-2011-data-confirm-trend-of-population-diversity/.

117 Several scientists and scholars alike have advanced the idea that "race," as we have historically defined it, does not exist. See, e.g., Jefferson M. Fish, "The Myth of Race," in *Race and Intelligence: Separating Science from Myth,* ed. Jefferson M. Fish (Mahwah, NJ: Lawrence Erlbaum Associates, 2002), 114; Kwame Anthony Appiah, Amy Gutmann, and David B. Wilkins, *Color Conscious* (Princeton, NJ: Princeton University Press, 1998); Anil Ananthaswamy, "Under the Skin: Our DNA Says There's No Such Thing as Race. So Why Do Doctors Still Think It Matters?," *New Scientist* (April 20, 2002): 34; Ian F. Haney Lopez, "The Social Construction of Race," *Harvard Civil Rights-Civil Liberties Law Review* 29(1) (1994): 1–62.

118 Toni Morrison, *The Bluest Eye* (New York: Holt, Rinehart, and Winston, 1970).

119 Leonard Baynes, "If It's Not Just Black and White Anymore, Why Does Darkness Cast a Longer Discriminatory Shadow than Lightness? An Investigation and Analysis of the Color Hierarchy," *Denver University Law Review* 75 (1997–1998): 158–159.

120 Of course, even after the Civil War, the practices of sharecropping, peonage, convict leasing laws, and Jim Crow continued the degrading effects of slavery. See, e.g., Douglas A. Blackmon, *Slavery by Another Name: The Re-Enslavement of Black Americans from the Civil War to World War II* (New York: Anchor Books, 2009). Some scholars have critically demonstrated that these oppressive systems of old continue, differently disguised, today. See Michelle Alexander, *The New Jim Crow: Mass Incarceration in the Age of Colorblindness* (New York: New Press, 2010); Leary, *Post Traumatic Slave Syndrome*, 83–96.

121 Cheryl Harris, "Whiteness as Property," *Harvard Law Review* 106 (1993): 1707. See also Peggy McIntosh, "White Privilege: Unpacking the Invisible Knapsack," *Independent School* 49(2) (1990): 31–35; Tim Wise, *White Like Me: Reflections on Race from a Privileged Son* (Brooklyn, NY: Soft Skull Press, 2011); Paula Rothenberg, *White Privilege* (New York: Worth, 2011).

122 D. Channsin Berry and Bill Duke, *Dark Girls, Real Women. Real Stories*, video (2013); Kathy Sandler, *A Question of Color: Color Consciousness in Black America,* video (San Francisco, CA: California NewsReel, 1992).

2

THE ORIGINS OF COLORISM IN EARLY AMERICAN LAW

Paul Finkelman

Colorism in the United States began in the colonial and early national period. In early America, color was initially associated with Africans[1] who faced discrimination because they were not only a different color, but also because they were both foreigners and non-Christians. Most of this chapter focuses on Virginia, because it was the largest of the colonies, it was the first one to have Africans, and most of the Southern colonies adopted the rules and laws coming out of Virginia in this period.

Early seventeenth-century Virginia, where slavery became deeply rooted, was initially a triracial, multiethnic place. Most of the early English settlers in Virginia were neither racial nor ethnic egalitarians. They made distinctions between themselves and settlers from other parts of Great Britain or mainland Europe. The leadership of early Virginia brutalized white indentured servants, often savagely punishing them for infractions. Some English settlers married Indians—most famously the colony's secretary, John Rolfe, who married Pocahontas. The Englishmen in early Virginia also exploited Indians but did not enslave them, in part because the English had no experience with slavery and the very idea of slavery ran counter to English law and custom. By the mid-seventeenth century, however, the vast majority of Indians had been marginalized, slaughtered, or forced west, although some remained within the area settled by the English, including some who were married (or at least had children) with both Europeans and Africans.

The first Africans arrived in 1619 and were treated as indentured servants. Before 1650 most Africans were servants; some intermarried with Indians and Europeans. But, as the Indians were mostly gone, Virginia became an increasingly biracial society. Indian ancestry, however, would continue to affect personal status. In the late eighteenth and early nineteenth centuries, some slaves would claim Indian ancestry as a basis for freedom. But, after the late seventeenth century,

Indians themselves were increasingly separated from Virginia's legal and economic culture.

Seventeenth-century Virginia society had a clear pecking order, with white English Christians at the top and heathens (black and Indian) at the bottom; however, non-English, non-Anglican Europeans were hardly privileged. Although runaway servants—black and white—were severely punished with whippings, brandings, and extra service added to their indentures, Africans suffered more. For example, at least one runaway African servant was sentenced to lifetime servitude—a sentence never imposed on any Europeans.[2]

While Africans faced discrimination for their heathenness and their color, those who were acculturated and essentially became "black Englishmen" by learning the language, adopting Christianity, and acquiring land were able to rise far above indentured servants, black and white. Three early examples illustrate how some Africans were able to transcend their race and status in the seventeenth century.

In 1624, "*John Phillip* A negro Christened in *England 12* yeers" was allowed to testify in a civil law suit between whites. By the end of the century, black testimony would be rejected by most Virginia courts when whites were litigants or defendants. But, at this time, race was not the determining factor in whether testimony might be allowed. Surely, John Phillip's conversion, his experience with English life, and his ability to speak fluent English gave him a status more like that of a free white man than an indentured African. The fact that he had an English name and a last name underscored his acculturation, because many African slaves lacked one of these.[3] In 1641, one John Graweere, "a negro servant," fathered a child with an African woman owned by someone who was not Graweere's master. While Graweere had an African last name, he was acculturated enough to have an English (and Christian) first name and to understand how the Virginia legal system and economy worked. Thus, Graweere persuaded his master to let him raise hogs in his own time and, with the money earned from selling them, he was able to purchase the freedom of his son from the mother's master. Graweere "desired [that the child] should be made a christian and be taught and exercised in the church of *England*." Thus, he arranged for the court to record the freedom of his son and turn him over to the care of a white "godfather," who would "see [him] brought up in the christian religion as aforesaid."[4]

More dramatic in this early period is the record of the life of "Anthony, a Negro," who arrived in Virginia around 1619. He was initially treated as an indentured servant, but by the time of his death, Anthony Johnson, as he was now known, was a Christian, a landowner, and the owner of at least one African slave.[5]

By the time Johnson became a landowner, most blacks in Virginia were facing increased discrimination and greater likelihood of being held in slavery. Most blacks who came to British America before 1660 were indentured servants, although some were fully free people and a few others were treated as slaves.

Many of the indentured servants from this period eventually became free. Because the British did not have a system of slavery, they treated Africans as indentured servants, and many of them became free, and some, like Anthony Johnson, became property owners. From 1660 to the mid-1670s, the status of Africans in Virginia was confused and in flux. As late as 1672, for example, the Virginia General Court determined that "Edward Mozingo[,] a Negro man [who] had been and was an apprentice by Indenture," had served out his indenture; thus the Court ordered "the [s]aid Edw: Mozingo be and Remayne free to all Intents and purpo[s]es."[6] A year later the court ruled that "Andrew Moore[,] A Servant Negro," had also served out his indenture and would henceforth "bee free from his [s]aid ma[s]ter," and that the master had to give him freedom dues of "Corne and Clothes According to the Cu[s]tome of the Country and ffour hundred Pounds" of tobacco.[7] These examples and other scattered court records illustrate that the status of blacks was in flux in early British Virginia. The rules were unclear, and there was no certain definition of who was a slave. The legislature had passed a few laws recognizing slavery, but it was only gradually moving to define the status.

However, by the end of the century blacks were mostly associated with slavery. While in 1660 there were about 1,000 Africans in Virginia and most were indentured servants, by 1700 there were about 10,000 Africans and African Americans in Virginia; the overwhelming majority were slaves who had been recently imported from Africa.

After the 1660s, being black became a marker for status and nonfreedom, while whiteness denoted freedom, or at least indentured status that would lead to freedom. However, during this period a small class of mixed-race people—Afro-Europeans and Afro-Indians—emerged in the America. As this happened, shades of color became increasingly important. By the end of the seventeenth century, blacks were presumptively slaves. People of mixed ancestry, however, were not necessarily assumed to be slaves. After the Revolution, courts had to sort out the status of mixed-race people and determine where they fit in what had become a biracial society of whites and blacks. Before looking at the cases on race and colorism after the Revolution, it is necessary to see how Virginia developed a law of race and slavery in the seventeenth century.

I: Moving into Colorism and Slavery

Virginia never actually created a clear definition of race or slavery, either in the colonial period or later in its history. In the 1660s, the legislature passed a series of laws that provided guidance on who could be a slave, but there was never anything definitive. An act in 1659–60 allowed Dutch traders and other foreigners to bring "negro slaves" to the colony at a lower duty than other goods. This was the first formal recognition of slavery by the colonial legislature.[8] The law was clear that Africans imported as slaves could be held as slaves; however, the law did not say who else might be a slave, what the status of their children might be, or what the status was of Africans who came as indentured servants.

Even before Virginia formally recognized slavery, there were black servants and some black slaves. Like people in bondage everywhere, they resisted their masters. Most commonly, they ran away. That created a new problem. The standard punishment for runaway servants was whipping (and sometimes branding), followed by additional service beyond their indenture.[9] However, slaves could never have additional service added to their bondage. Thus, a year after its first statute on slave importation, the colonial legislature, the House of Burgesses, passed its first police regulation of slaves, which dealt with the problems of white indentured servants escaping with slaves. To discourage such interracial challenges to the regime, the law provided that whites would have to serve extra time for any slaves who ran away with them. The new law declared:

> [I]n case any English servant shall run away in company of any negroes who are incapable of making satisfaction by addition of a time, *it is enacted* that the English soe running away in the company with them shall at the time of service to their owne masters expired, serve the masters of the said negroes for their absence soe long as they should have done by this act if they had not beene slaves, every christian in company serving his proportion; and if the negroes be lost or dye in such time of their being run away, the christian servants in company with them shall by proportion among them, either pay fower [four] thousand five hundred pounds of tobacco and caske or fower [four] yeares service for every negroe soe lost or dead.[10]

This law not only provided compensation for masters whose slaves ran away with whites, but it also drove a wedge between black slaves and white servants.[11] It was the beginning of a formalization of race and color as a legal category, with blacks having limitations on their rights. It might also be seen as the first segregation statute in America, because it punished racial intermixing and actually punished whites for associating with black slaves. If captured, the whites who ran away with slaves could have more time added to their service. This would discourage interracial challenges to the planter class and might even lead to fewer escapes. Slaves, excluded from escape plots, would have an incentive to report such plots to their masters. On the other hand, without the help of English-speaking whites, slaves, almost all of whom at this point were native Africans, might have a more difficult time escaping.[12] Equally important, the law discouraged white servants from becoming friendly with their African coworkers. This too would strengthen the planters who dominated the colony.

By driving a wedge between white servants and black slaves, this law more firmly attached the chains of lifetime bondage to Africans in the emerging system of slavery. It also helped create a sense of entitlement for white servants by giving cultural value to whiteness, but punishing them more if they escaped with African slaves. The law also unambiguously acknowledged and affirmed that the evolving distinctions were racially based. Thus the statute noted that some "negroes" in Virginia were "incapable of making satisfaction by addition of a time."[13] Color now truly mattered as a marker of assumed status, although status was also being defined by ethnicity and religion.

The law began by talking about any "English servant" who might escape with "any negroes" who were incapable of having time added to their servitude. This language implied that some blacks had this status, but that other blacks did not have such a status. All blacks in the colony were clearly not slaves; only some of them were. Thus, while being a "negro" was clearly a marker of being a slave, all "negroes" were not slaves. The use of the term "English" was also unclear, because at the time there were white indentured servants who were Irish, Scottish, Dutch, and probably other nationalities as well. Yet surely, the legislation applied to them. Further confusion comes from the use of the term "Christian," with the law providing that, if a slave ran away with other servants, "every christian in company" would serve extra time for the loss of the slave's time.[14] This may have implied that Christians could not be slaves, and thus conversion might emancipate a slave. It would take a few years for the Burgesses to clarify this.[15]

Before the Burgesses could address how religion helped define slavery, the Virginia legislators faced a more pressing problem: how to classify the offspring of white men and African women. Under English common law, a child, even one born out of wedlock, followed the status of the father. If this rule applied to the children of slaves, then the mixed-race children of slave women would be born as free people. This would lead to the odd situation of slave mothers raising their freeborn children, while also creating a class of free mixed-race people.[16] Both of these issues were troublesome to the English in Virginia. In addition, because slaves could not be legally married, the mixed-race children of slave women were legally bastards. Under existing law, the Overseers of the Poor were obligated to help raise and educate all illegitimate children. Furthermore, authorities were obligated to track down the fathers of all bastard children to make sure they supported them. Applying these rules to the mixed-race children of slave women would lead to extensive social problems, as masters—and leaders of the community—might be prosecuted for illicit (and often adulterous) sex with their own slaves.

On the other hand, if the colonies abandoned the common law and instead adopted the Roman law rule of *partus sequitur ventrem, 17* all of these problems would disappear. This was the legal rule that applied to livestock and other domestic animals: that the offspring of a domestic animal belonged to the owner of the female who gave birth. Applying the law of domestic animals to the children of slave women resolved some tough legal issues, and at the same time had the added virtue—if the word applies here—of benefiting white men, who could now freely have sex with slave women without any legal consequences. Any children resulting from unions would be slaves who belonged to the owner of the mother. Thus, the local authorities would not need to institute an investigation, or bastardy proceedings, against the father because society would not be required to maintain or support the illegitimate child. That would be the responsibility of the owner of the mother, who usually would not mind the upkeep of the child because the child would also be his slave property. When subsequent statutes prohibited blacks from testifying against whites, the entire issue was taken out of the legal culture—there could never be bastardy proceedings or any rape prosecutions involving slave women, because a slave could never be a complaining witness against a free person. There would only be more slaves, albeit mulatto slaves. In a society with a huge gender imbalance, with far more men than women, this law was a great benefit to white men. Thus, in 1662, the white men in the House of Burgesses wrote a statute with far reaching implications: "WHEREAS some doubts have arrisen whether children got by any Englishman upon a negro woman should be slave or ffree, Be it therefore enacted . . . that all children borne in this country shalbe held bond or free only according to the condition of the mother."[18]

This law essentially left slave women vulnerable to all white men because the law simply would not take notice of sexual activity that resulted in mixed-race children of slave women. Masters were free to have sex with their slaves without facing any legal sanction. A non-slave owner might have been subject to a potential trespass suit from a master of a slave woman for having sex with her, but no such lawsuits appear to have been filed. The law helped define slaves by denying a slave woman the most fundamental right to control her own body or have any control over her children. By implication, the lack of control over children also applied to slave fathers. The law also led to a horrifying aspect of American slavery that would continue until final abolition: Throughout the South, masters would be the owners of their own children and would treat them as property, to be bought, sold, gifted, and used as collateral. This law reduced the children of all slave women to property and, perversely, led generations of white Southern men to treat their own children as property.

Five years after dealing with the status of the children of slave mothers, the Burgesses returned to the troublesome issue of slavery and baptism. From the first arrival of Africans, Virginians had been confused by the interrelationship of religion, race, and ethnicity. Early statutes often made a distinction between Africans (or Negroes) and "Christians."[19] One early justification for enslavement was that Africans were not Christians; however, at the same time, another justification for the African slave trade was that it brought Christianity to the heathens from Africa. Tied to this was a belief among some Europeans that it was wrong to enslave fellow Christians, and thus conversion would lead to emancipation. Some slaves apparently gained their freedom through conversion. In 1667, the Virginia legislature devised a solution to this dilemma with the following statute:

WHEREAS some doubts have risen whether children that are slaves by birth, and by the charity and piety of their owners made pertakers of the blessed sacrament of baptisme, should by vertue of their baptisme be made ffree; It is enacted . . . that the conferring of baptisme doth not alter the condition of the person as to his bondage or ffreedome; that diverse masters, ffreed from this doubt, may more carefully endeavour the propagation of christianity by permitting . . . [slaves] . . . to be admitted to that sacrament.[20]

Unlike the statute on the status of the children of slave women, which effectively treated the children of slave women as property, this law recognized the fundamental humanity of slaves, by acknowledging that they had souls that required attention. Ultimately, conversion would help fasten the chains of bondage onto slaves, as generations of Southern ministers taught slaves that obedience to their masters was the equivalent of obedience to God, and that the key to heaven began with proper deference to their earthly status. After the Revolution, Southern ministers would also defend slavery on the grounds that it was sanctioned by the Bible.[21]

The rules Virginia developed were almost entirely accepted by other colonies. Thus, by the eve of the American Revolution, the general American rules were that the children of slave mothers were slaves, even if the fathers were free blacks or white men; masters should baptize their slaves, but this would not affect their status. Color was a marker of servitude in a variety of ways. People who appeared to be wholly of African ancestry were presumptively slaves; people of mixed African and European ancestry might be free or slave, as might be people of mixed Indian and African ancestry.

II: Toward a Limited Colorism

The use of race as a marker for status began to crumble in the mid-eighteenth century. By the 1740s there were an increasing number of mixed-race people, some of whom did not look all that African. Some masters felt paternal instincts toward their mixed-race children and emancipated them, or simply allowed them to live free. There had also always been a small number of white women who had children with Africans. These children were free from birth because a child of mixed African ancestry followed the status of the mother. Thus, there was a small but growing population of free people of African ancestry who were often also of European ancestry. Presumptions of color and status were beginning to break down. In the first half of the eighteenth century, some religious opposition to slavery—among Quakers, Methodists, and some Puritans—led to a smattering of manumissions.[22] The only prerevolutionary census of free blacks, taken in Maryland in 1755, found that 80 percent of the free blacks in the colony were of mixed ancestry. Furthermore, 90 percent of the free blacks under age 16 were classified as mulattoes.[23] Most of these people were probably the children of white masters and their slaves, and they were manumitted by their fathers. Clearly, visible evidence of being mixed race was becoming a marker of not being a slave.

By the time of the Revolution, there was growing opposition to slavery in the North and to some extent in the South. During the war, slavery collapsed in New England and faced increasing hostility in the rest of the North. In New York, slave owners, such as John Jay, helped form that state's manumission society. In Pennsylvania, Benjamin Franklin terminated his relationship with human bondage and later helped found the Pennsylvania Manumission Society. In the South, there was no strong movement to end slavery, but numerous masters voluntarily manumitted their slaves. In 1782, Virginia passed a law specifically allowing for private manumission, with the newly created free person being allowed to remain in the state.[24] From 1782 to 1806 (when the law was modified to require emancipated slaves to leave the state), the free black population of the state grew from about 2,000 to more than 30,000.[25]

In this period some masters freed all their slaves, either out of devotion to the Revolutionary ideals or devotion to God. For example, Robert Carter, III (known as "Councillor" Carter) emancipated all his slaves in the 1790s, reflecting his Christian piety and his devotion to revolutionary principles. The Virginia Quakers—John Pleasants and his son, Jonathan—manumitted close to 200 slaves in their wills because of their religious beliefs. George Washington manumitted all of his slaves in his will in 1799. Some of the slaves manumitted during this period were undoubtedly of mixed ancestry, but most were not.

However, especially after 1800, most manumissions involved select slaves, and they were often the mixed-race relatives, in one way or another, of the master. Illustrative of this were the handful of relatives of Sally Hemings that Thomas Jefferson freed in his lifetime and in his will.[26] The increase of free blacks in the four decades after the Revolution was obvious from Maryland to South Carolina.

Thus, in the years after the Revolution, there were shifting notions of color based on a new reality that many people of mixed ancestry were free. In Maryland, a number of slaves sued for freedom on the grounds that they had a white grandmother or great grandmother, or even a great-great-grandmother. The evidence was never clear, and there was often no documentary evidence, but the Maryland courts accepted hearsay evidence, while at the same time used a visual standard: If the slaves claiming freedom looked like they had white ancestry, they were likely to gain their freedom.[27] In some parts of the South, such as Charleston, free blacks developed their own culture, community organizations, and institutions. By the 1840s, free blacks of mixed ancestry in Charleston saw themselves as distinct from black slaves and white people.[28] Similarly, in 1803 when the United States acquired Louisiana, about 80 percent of the 2,000 free blacks were of mixed ancestry.[29]

It is also important to understand that, as blacks, whites, and Indians had children with each other, color became a factor in determining status and created social presumptions. People who appeared to be completely of African descent were presumptively slaves, but people who were of mixed ancestry might not be slaves. Indeed, they might not even be considered "Negroes." In *Thurman v. State*, the Alabama Supreme Court held that the child of a mulatto and a white woman was *not* black and could not be prosecuted under the state's black code, which regulated the behavior of both free blacks and slaves. An outraged Alabama Supreme Court justice refused to accept the argument that someone who was *at most* one-quarter black could be prosecuted under a law designed to punish Negroes and mulattoes. He declared, "If the statute against mulattoes is by construction to include quadroons, then where are we to stop?"[30]

III: Mixed Ancestry as a Vehicle to Freedom

Slaves of mixed ancestry often asserted freedom based on their color, suing to end their servitude. People of mixed ancestry were far more likely to make freedom claims, and they were far more likely to win them. The vast majority of slaves never had any legal claim to freedom. They were born into slavery and died in slavery. There were, after all, only a few potential freedom claims. These included: residence in a free jurisdiction; manumission of a maternal ancestor; manumission of the individual claiming freedom; and a claim that the person had a white or Indian maternal ancestor and was thus not a slave because only the children of black women could be slaves. Except for residence in a free jurisdiction, most of the rest of these claims were more likely to be available to slaves of mixed ancestry. While some masters freed slaves indiscriminately, like "Councilor" Carter and George Washington, most masters who manumitted any slaves only freed "special" slaves—which would often include family members. Jefferson's willingness to free a handful of slaves who were related to his mistress illustrates this fact. All of these people were of mixed ancestry, because Sally Hemings and her siblings were the children of their master, John Wayles.[31] Some were Jefferson's own children, and he was related to most of them through his wife. Obviously, slaves who were partially or mostly white or Indian were in a better position to argue that they had a free maternal ancestor.

Two cases illustrate how courts in the early national period dealt with claims of freedom and color. These cases illustrate the very real advantage that people of mixed ancestry had over slaves who were of pure African ancestry.

A: Gobu v. Gobu

The facts of this case, as set out in the opinion of the court, are spare. When the defendant, a woman named Gobu, was 12 years old, she found a baby boy in a barn.[32] The baby was about eight days old. The young girl took this baby home and raised him as a slave. He was of mixed race, but also of undetermined race.

As an adult the young man, also named Gobu, sued for his freedom, arguing that his mistress had no legal proof that he was a slave.[33]

The North Carolina Supreme Court readily accepted the claim of the defendant that there was a "presumption of every black person being a slave." This was obvious to the Court, because "the negroes brought to this country were slaves, and their descendants must continue [as] slaves until manumitted by proper authority." A black slave claiming his freedom had to "establish his right to it by such evidence as will destroy the force of the presumption arising from his color."[34]

However, the Court declared that it was "not aware that the doctrine of presuming against liberty has been urged in relation to persons of mixed blood, or to those of any color between the two extremes of black and white." The presumption of slavery only applied to visibly black people. The Court explained why. People of mixed ancestry might "have descended from Indians . . . [or] they may have descended from a white parent in the maternal line or from mulatto parents originally free."[35] Given the "many probabilities . . . in favor of the liberty" for people like Gobu, the Court asserted that the plaintiff "ought not to be deprived" of his liberty "upon mere presumption," especially when the claim to the alleged slave could not be "satisfactorily proved." [36]

The case for the plaintiff was particularly strong because he "was of an olive colour, between black and yellow, had long hair and a prominent nose."[37] It is hard to know what these descriptions meant, other than that he was of very mixed ancestry and clearly not mostly African—or perhaps even African at all.

The court did not comment on the circumstances of the discovery of the baby. A baby left in a barn was probably born to a single mother—perhaps a white woman who had a child with a black or an Indian. If that were the case, then it would be wrong to hold him in slavery. This real-life analysis surely occurred to the Court.

Nevertheless, whatever the real-life issues, the court's doctrine was clear. In North Carolina, Negroes—people of unmixed African ancestry—were presumptively slaves. A Negro claiming freedom would need a strong case, even if the master had no paper trail of ownership, because of the strong presumption that people of pure African ancestry were slaves. However, if a person was of mixed and ambiguous ancestry—a "colored person" or a "person of color"—the legal presumptions would change. The common terms for such people included mulatto (half black and half white), quadroon (one-quarter black and three-quarters white), and octoroon (one-eighth black and seven-eighths white).[38] With someone like Gobu, who was "between black and yellow" and who "had long hair and a prominent nose,"[39] the master would have to *prove* an ownership claim.

B: Hudgins v. Wrights

In 1806 Virginia's highest court devoted considerable energies to setting out how color and appearance created certain presumptions about race. In *Hudgins v.*

Wrights,[40] Judge St. George Tucker had to determine if the parties before him were free or slaves. Three generations of Wrights claimed their freedom on the grounds that they were descended from an Indian woman named Butternut Nan. The trial court judge, Chancellor George Wythe, noted that they varied in color, with the youngest child being "perfectly white, and that there were gradual shades of difference in colour between the grand-mother, mother, and grand-daughter, all of whom were before the Court."[41] Chancellor Wythe found in favor of the mixed-race plaintiffs and the putative owner appealed.

When the case reached the Virginia Court of Appeals, Judge St. George Tucker pondered the question of race and status. He upheld the freedom claims of the Wrights, in part based on their color and appearance. To reach this conclusion, he considered the importance of race in understanding status. His long discussion of this issue is worth quoting in full:

> Suppose three persons, a black or mulatto man or woman with a flat nose and woolly head; a copper-coloured person with long jetty black, straight hair; and one with a fair complexion, brown hair, not woolly nor inclining thereto, with a prominent *Roman* nose, were brought together before a Judge upon a writ of *Habeas Corpus,* on the ground of false imprisonment and detention in slavery: that the only evidence which the person detaining them in his custody could produce was an authenticated bill of sale from another person, and that the parties themselves were unable to produce any evidence concerning themselves, whence they came, &c. &c. How must a Judge act in such a case? I answer he must judge from his own view. He must discharge the white person and the *Indian* out of custody, taking surety, if the circumstances of the case should appear to authorise it, that they should not depart the state within a reasonable time, that the holder may have an opportunity of asserting and proving them to be lineally descended in the maternal line from a female *African* slave; and he must redeliver the black or mulatto person, with the flat nose and woolly hair to the person claiming to hold him or her as a slave, unless the black person or mulatto could procure some person to be bound for him, to produce proof of his descent, in the maternal line, from a *free female ancestor.*—But if no such caution should be required on either side, but the whole case be left with the Judge, he must deliver the former out of custody, and permit the latter to remain in slavery, until he could produce proofs of his right to freedom. This case shews my interpretation how far the *onus probandi* may be shifted from one party to the other.[42]

Here was a clear statement about race and color. People who might have African ancestry, but looked to be white or Indian, were presumptively free. People who looked to be purely of African descent were presumptively slaves and could only counter that by evidence to the contrary.

In a concurring opinion, Judge Spencer Roane reached a similar conclusion:

> In the case of a person visibly appearing to be a negro, the presumption is, in this country, that he is a slave, and it is incumbent on him to make out his right to freedom: but in the case of a person visibly appearing to be a white man, or an *Indian,* the presumption is that he is free, and it is necessary for his adversary to shew that he is a slave.[43]

Like the North Carolina court, the Virginia court was sympathetic to freedom claims from slaves who appeared to be white or Indian. Neither court was particularly sympathetic to such claims from people who appeared to be fully or mostly of African ancestry.

IV: Color and Freedom

Gobu and *Hudgins* illustrate how color mattered in determining status. If you did not look black, you had a greater chance of claiming for your freedom. Certainly, there were many slaves of mixed ancestry, and there were some free people who were of pure African ancestry. Most of the free blacks in the South, however, were of mixed ancestry. Many were the children of white men, and often they were given some resources when they gained freedom.[44]

A full study of the social and economic advantages of mixed-race children within the antebellum and post-Civil War black community would require a book in itself. But, some general observations are obvious. Many mixed-race children of masters and slave women were given advantages that other slaves did not receive. Frederick Douglass, for example, was treated remarkably well by his owner (who was almost certainly also his father), and instead of being doomed to plantation labor he was sent to Baltimore, where he gained all sorts of urban skills (and literacy) that helped him gain freedom. His master did not want him to become literate, but when Douglass did learn to read he was not punished or exiled to plantation labor.

Other slave children of white masters were educated and manumitted. The successful cotton gin manufacturer William Ellison was the son of either his owner or his owner's father.[45] The light-skinned Ellison was manumitted by his owner and went on to be financially successful and to even own a number of black slaves himself. After gaining his freedom, Ellison changed his first name to that of his former master (and probably his father), William. Ellison traded on the advantages of his mixed-race status, his literacy, and the knowledge of the wider world he learned as a privileged slave. Ellison was apparently the *only* slave that his master ever manumitted.[46]

Thus, the message of the antebellum period was clear: Lighter-skinned blacks were more likely to be free and more likely to have some wealth than those who were mostly or fully of African ancestry. Some of the children of slave masters were more likely to become literate and educated—skills that would position them to succeed before the Civil War and after slavery. In addition, some free blacks of mixed ancestry had ties to powerful white families who were able to help them and sometimes protect them from the harshness of antebellum discrimination against free blacks and post-Civil War racism, violence, and discrimination. In postwar South Carolina, for example, people of mixed racial background with ties to elite white families—such as Archibald Grimké and Francis Lewis Cardozo—were able to use their family ties and other advantages to gain political office. Cardozo, for example, had been able to attend the University of Glasgow and seminars in Edinburgh and London before the war. This education helped him after the War. Similarly, the former slave Archibald Grimké had gained some advantages from his white father, and was later able to attend Harvard Law School through the intervention of his white aunts, Sarah Grimké Weld and Angelina Grimké.

The stories of Grimké, Cardozo, and Frederick Douglass are of course unusual and their successes were truly uncommon. But, their lives illustrate the point that the children of slave women and white fathers often had educational and economic advantages that most other slaves or free blacks did not have. These advantages —tied to money, skills, education, status, and color—led to greater success and prosperity for such people and to the perception that people of mixed race were "elite." These advantages, and the connection between them and "elite" status would continue well past the end of slavery.

Notes

1 In the colonial period, color was also a marker of being Indian, but, because of the nation status of Indians and the constant warfare between Europeans and Indians, the legal issues concerning Indians and race were quite different from those for blacks.
2 *In re John Punch,* in Minutes of the Council and General Court of Colonial Virginia 466 (H.R. McIlwaine ed., 1924) [hereinafter McIlwaine] (July 9, 1640). I have kept the original (archaic and sometimes creative) spelling and syntax for all of these early sources. I have not used "sic" because it would require multiple uses of that designation in almost every quotation.
3 *In re Sir Henry Maneringe,* McIlwaine, 33 (November 24, 1624).
4 *In re John Graweere* (1641), McIlwaine, 477 (March 31, 1641).
5 T. H. Breen and Stephen Innes, *"Myne Owne Ground": Race and Freedom on Virginia's Eastern Shore, 1640–1676* (New York: Oxford University Press, 1980), tells the story of Anthony Johnson, who eventually came to own land and even his own black slaves in Virginia.
6 McIlwaine, at 316 (emphasis omitted) (recording an entry for October 5, 1672).
7 McIlwaine, at 354 (emphasis omitted) (recording an entry for October 27, 1673 regarding the resolution of *Moore v. Light*).
8 An Act for the Dutch and all other Strangers for Tradeing to this Place, Act XVI, March, 1659–60 (1 Hening 540). [The dating of 1659–1660 is a function of the transition from the "old style" to the "new style" calendar.]
9 See generally, Paul Finkelman, *The Law of Freedom and Bondage* (New York: Oceana Publications, 1986), Chapter 1.

10 Act CII, 2 Laws of Va. 116, 116–17 (Hening 1823) (enacted March 1661–62).

11 On black–white relations in this period, see generally Edmund Morgan, *American Slavery, American Freedom: The Ordeal of Colonial Virginia* (New York: W.W. Norton, 1975). There is not a great deal of literature on runaways in the seventeenth century, but for the eighteenth century, see generally Gerald W. Mullin, *Flight and Rebellion: Slave Resistance in Eighteenth-Century Virginia* (New York: Oxford University Press, 1972).

12 Mullin notes that, in the eighteenth century, English-speaking, American-born slaves were more likely to successfully escape than native Africans. Mullin, supra note 13, at 91–92.

13 Act CII, 2 Laws of Va. 116, 116–17 (Hening 1823) (enacted March 1661–62).

14 Ibid.

15 Act III, 2 Laws of Va. 260, 260 (Hening 1823) (enacted 1667) (declaring that the "baptisme of slaves doth not exempt them from bondage").

16 William M. Wiecek, "The Statutory Law of Slavery and Race in the Thirteen Mainland Colonies of British America," *William and Mary Quarterly* 34 (1977) 258, 263 (reprinted in Paul Finkelman, ed., *Articles on American Slavery: Colonial Southern Slavery* [New York: Garland, 1989], 452, 457).

17 "Of all tame and domestic animals, the brood belongs to the owner of the dam or mother; the English law agreeing with the civil, that '*partus sequitur ventrem*' in the brute creation, though for the most part in the human species it disallows that maxim." William Blackstone, *Commentaries on the Laws of England*, vol. 2 (1766), 390. This rule, according to Coke, did not apply to swans because they were royal animals.

18 Act XII, 2 Laws of Va. 170, 170 (Hening 1823) (enacted 1662) (emphasis omitted).

19 For example, a statute of 1662 provided "that if any christian shall committ ffornication with a negro man or women, hee or shee soe offending shall pay double the ffines imposed by the former act." Negro women's children to serve according to the condition of the mother, 2 Laws of Va. 170 (Hening 1823) (enacted December 1662).

20 Act III, 2 Laws of Va. 260, 260 (Hening 1823) (enacted 1667) (emphasis omitted).

21 Examples of religious defenses of slavery are found in Paul Finkelman, *Defending Slavery: Proslavery Thought in the Old South* (Boston: Bedford/St. Martin's Press, 2003), 96–128.

22 See, for example, Arthur Zilversmit, *The First Emancipation: The Abolition of Slavery in the North* (Chicago, IL: University of Chicago Press, 1967).

23 Ira Berlin, *Slaves Without Masters: The Free Negro in the Antebellum South* (New York: Pantheon Books, 1974), 3.

24 An act to Authorize the Manumission of Slaves, Laws of Virginia, 1782, Chap. LXI.

25 For a summary of the Virginia legislation on manumission, see Finkelman, *The Law of Freedom and Bondage*.

26 For a discussion of manumission in this period, see Paul Finkelman, *Slavery and the Founders: Race and Liberty in the Age of Jefferson*, 2nd edition (Armonk, NY: M. E. Sharpe, 2001). On the Pleasants family, see Pleasants v. Pleasants, 2 Call (Virginia) 319 (1799).

27 Berlin, *Slaves without Masters*, 32–35. See also Mima Queen and Child v. Hepburn, 11 U.S. 290 (1813), which was based on Maryland law and Mima Queen's family history in Maryland, but because the case was brought in the District of Columbia, it reached the U.S. Supreme Court, where Chief Justice John Marshall held against Mima Queen, despite the fact that in Maryland a state court would probably have freed her.

28 Michael P. Johnson and James Roark, *Black Masters: A Free Family of Color in the Old South* (New York: W.W. Norton, 1984).

29 Berlin, *Slaves without Masters*, 32–35, 110–111.

30 Thurman v. State, 18 Ala. 276, 279 (1850).

31 See Finkelman, *Slavery and the Founders*, Chapters 6 and 7. John Wayles was also the father of Thomas Jefferson's wife, Martha Wayles Skelton. Thus, Sally Hemings was Jefferson's half-sister-in-law.

32 Gobu v. Gobu, 1 N.C. 188 (1802).

33 Ibid.

34 Ibid.

35 Ibid.

36 Ibid.

37 Ibid.

38 The definition of "white" changed over time, but before the Civil War most Southern states accepted a definition that people who were more than seven-eighths white were legally white. This led to the occasional situation of a legally "white" person being held as a slave. As late as 1983, the Louisiana Revised Statutes provided that, "In signifying race, a person having one-thirty second or less of Negro blood shall not be deemed, described or designated by any public official in the State of Louisiana as 'colored,' a 'mulatto,' a 'black,' a 'negro,' a 'griffe,' an 'Afro-American,' a 'quadroon,' a 'mestizo,' a 'colored person' or a 'person of color.'" La. Rev. Stat. Ann. § 42:267, repealed by Act No. 441, § 1, 1993 La. Acts 97.

39 Gobu v. Gobu, 1 N.C. 188 (1802).

40 Hudgins v. Wrights, 11 Va. (1 Hen. & M.) 134 (1806).

41 Ibid.

42 Ibid., at 140.

43 Ibid., at 142.

44 See Bernie Jones, *Fathers of Conscience: Mixed Race Inheritance in the Antebellum South* (Athens, GA: University of Georgia Press, 2009).

45 Johnson and Roark, *Black Masters*, 5.

46 Ibid., at 6.

3

THE RISE AND FALL OF THE ONE-DROP RULE

How the Importance of Color Came to Eclipse Race

Kevin D. Brown

Since the beginning of colonization of North America, the color of descendants of the soil of Africa was always crucial in determining the amount of social discrimination black individuals encountered. Throughout history, American society developed different ways to classify individuals based on race, but appearance, including color, was most important. For most of the twentieth century, Americans used the one drop rule to determine who was black. Under this rule, one-drop of black blood made a person black. Its use also made it easy to determine a person's race based on their skin color.

As the twenty-first century unfolds, America is witnessing the demise of the one-drop rule. This is happening as the dominant legal rationales that have justified the maintenance of racial classifications are also disappearing. This chapter will chronicle the rise and fall of the one-drop rule. Because the importance of the one-drop rule was that it provided the social and legal means by which to determine who was black, this chapter will also point out the historic legal reasons for maintaining racial classifications. With the demise of both the one-drop rule and legal rationales for race, race is losing its importance. As race loses its significance, American society is witnessing a reversal of the historic reality of race being more important than color.

A racially based system of slavery developed in the United States, even though the determination of the status of individuals as slave or free was independent of their race. Mixed-race individuals with some black ancestry, known as "mulattoes" for much of American history, threatened such a system. One of the first legal uses of race during the colonial period was to prevent miscegenation and, therefore, uphold the operation of a race-based system of slavery. For much of the colonial and antebellum periods, in the North and Upper South the race line was bimodal. Even though some places legally defined mulattoes as distinct from blacks, free mulattoes generally had the same legal rights as blacks. Thus, the legal racial line was drawn between either black/white or white/colored (with mulattoes treated the same as blacks). By contrast, in the Lower South, especially in the urban areas, society drew more of a distinction between blacks and mulattoes. The first part of this chapter will discuss the importance of race and its uses in the development and maintenance of a race-based system of slavery, including the enactment of antimiscegenation legislation during the colonial period. The Founding Fathers enshrined the importance of racial classifications in the Constitution. Race was used to allocate representation among the states in the House of Representatives, determine how many votes a given state would receive in the Electoral College, and the amount of direct taxation that the federal government levied on the states. Thus, this part will also discuss the primary ways in which the highest law of the land required the use of racial classifications. It will also address the black/mulatto color distinctions that existed during slavery in the major urban areas of the Lower South.

Because of the legal importance of race, by the 1800s the states had developed three different legal methods to determine a person's race: blood fractions, appearance, and associations. However, appearance provided the most important evidence of race. While the first mention of the one-drop rule occurred in the 1830s in the North, it would take time for it to replace these other means and ascend to national prominence. The beginnings of that process can be traced back to a scientific debate that started in the late 1830s about whether blacks and whites were different species. A new trend in scientific thinking disputed the traditional belief drawn from Genesis that all humans descended from Adam. This new trend viewed blacks and whites as different species. Therefore, the products of interbreeding of the two races were inferior to both. This scientific debate helped to lead to the inclusion of a "mulatto" category on the 1850 census. During the antebellum period, the primary legal justifications for racial classifications related to the maintenance of a race-based system of slavery; however, the end of the Civil War, abolition, and Reconstruction did not lead to a diminution of the social or legal significance of race. The Civil War generated the first mass studies of the physical differences not only of blacks and whites, but also mulattoes. Anthropological studies generated during the war tended to support the ante-bellum scientific hypotheses of the dangers of miscegenation. This evidence provided additional compelling support for the belief that the products of black/white interbreeding were physically inferior and, often, mentally or morally inferior to both full-blooded blacks and whites. The prevention of miscegenation was the strongest justification for keeping the races apart. For segregation to operate, legal rights had to depend upon racial classifications. Thus, race became legally important in order to support segregation. By the end of the nineteenth century, the country established the one-drop rule as the dominant way to determine who was black. The second part of this chapter will discuss the early nineteenth-century methods that were utilized to determine race, the scientific debate about the dangers of miscegenation that developed prior to the Civil War, the scientific evidence generated during the Civil War that reinforced the need to prevent miscegenation, and the rise of the one-drop rule.

During the segregation era, the primary legal uses of racial classifications were for the purposes of separation, exclusion, and discrimination directed at individuals from minority groups, especially blacks. Throughout the period of both slavery and *de jure* segregation, Americans presumed that racial differences were innate. As the 1930s unfolded, however, scientists increasingly came to believe that culture and social environment influenced intelligence more so than innate characteristics. Throughout the 1930s and 1940s, this position gained adherents among racial experts. Thus, by the 1950s, most social scientists believed that black people could be improved by enriching their social environment and assisting them in overcoming their deficit culture. The social environmentalist triumphed in the unanimous 1954 ruling by the Supreme Court in *Brown v. Board of Education.*[1] This opinion set off a dramatic fifteen-year period in which American society committed itself to desegregation and an attempt to address racial inequality in education, employment, housing, medical care, and voting rights. At the start of the desegregation movement, the one-drop rule functioned to make the race of individuals visible when they were present. There were two different aspects of the desegregation movement. One aspect used race as a means for determining and dismantling the effects of America's history of racial discrimination. In order to decide if discriminatory effects existed and to determine the beneficiaries of policies and programs to attenuate its effects, this aspect required the determination of the race of individuals. Thus, this aspect of the desegregation movement provided new legal rationales for the importance of race. The second aspect of the desegregation movement, however, sought to transcend considerations of race in favor of viewing, treating, and judging individuals with reference to the content of their character, not the color of their skin. This colorblind/individualist aspect of the desegregation movement sought to deemphasize the importance of race. Therefore, it was in conflict with the other aspect. The third part of this chapter will focus on the aspect of the desegregation movement that generated a continuing need for the use of racial classifications. Thus, it will discuss the Supreme Court opinions and policies and programs that reinforced the importance of race. Largely because of Supreme Court decisions and civil rights laws enacted during the period noted above, several federal agencies were collecting racial data by the early 1970s. This produced the federal government's first effort to standardize the collection and reporting of this data. In 1978, the federal government issued the *Statistical Policy Directive No. 15, Race and Ethnic Standards for Federal Statistics and Administrative Reporting* or "Directive 15" for short. Directive 15 implicitly accepted the one-drop rule and the view that race was a socially ascribed trait, not a product of self-identification. This part will also discuss the federal process that led to the adoption of Directive 15.

By the end of the twentieth century, it was apparent that the Supreme Court's interpretations of the Equal Protection Clause, for the most part, adopted the colorblind/individualist aspect of the desegregation movement. As a result, the Supreme Court has eliminated most legal justifications for employing racial classifications. From a legal perspective, race means less today than at any time since the early 1700s. At the same time that being black was losing its legal significance, America experienced its first wave of massive voluntary immigration from parts of the world populated primarily by people of color. New immigrants from Africa, Asian, Latin America, and the Middle East changed the face and complexion of American society. Because of immigration from other parts of the world, however, the one-drop rule has increasingly lost its ability to allow individuals to accurately determine the race of others based on their physical appearance. In addition, in October 1997, the Office of Management and Budget (OMB) issued the *Revisions to the Standards for the Classification of Federal Data on Race and Ethnicity* (hereinafter the "1997 Revised Standards"). The Standards changed the way racial and ethnic data is gathered and reported to the federal government. It embraced the position that self-identification was the preferred way to determine a person's race and required that the forms used to collect this data allow individuals to indicate all of the racial or ethnic categories that apply to them. The collection and reporting of this data for the 2000 and 2010 Censuses, generally, followed the 1997 Revised Standards. The Standards also required other federal agencies to modify their processes for gathering and reporting racial and ethnic data to conform to it, including the Department of Labor and the Department of Education. Thus, most public and private organizations, including employers and educational institutions that report this data to the federal government, must use forms that allow individuals to designate all of the racial or ethnic categories that apply to them. Anyone who indicates that they are Hispanic/Latino, including those who designate black as one of their racial categories, are reported by institutions to federal agencies as Hispanic/Latino. In addition, institutions do not report those self-identified non-Hispanic/Latinos who indicate black and at least one other racial category in aggregate counts of blacks. Rather, they are lumped in with other multiracial non-Hispanic/Latinos in counts of a new "Two or More Races" category. As a result, the federal government has abandoned the one-drop rule. From this new racial data, it is also clear that more and more people with some black ancestry are rejecting the one-drop rule and no longer identify themselves as only black. The younger the people with some black ancestry are, the more likely they (or their parents or guardians) are to identify with more than one race. With increasing rates of interracial marriages and cohabitations, the percentage of blacks who reject the one-drop rule will continue to rise for some time. The fourth part of this chapter will discuss these developments, which have led to the fall of the one-drop rule.

In short, the elimination of most legal justifications for racial classifications during the past thirty-five years has largely eliminated the legal importance of race. In addition, because of substantial immigration and the ability of individuals to self-identify their race, the one-drop rule can no longer provide an accurate way in which to determine who is black based on physical appearance. Also, the rise in mixed-race sexual relations involving blacks means that the percentage of those with some black ancestry who will reject the one-drop rule will continue to increase. The inescapable consequence of these factors is that race will continue to lose its significance. As this occurs, color will become far more important than race in American society.

The Importance of Racial Classifications During Slavery

Even though the determination of the status of individuals as slave or free was independent of their race, a racially based system of slavery developed. Not long after arriving on the shores of North America, the English colonists realized that they needed to import African slaves in order to make their new lands profitable. While economic motivations played a critical role in the selection of blacks as the labor force to develop and cultivate North America, the Europeans also developed race-based rationales to justify slavery. For centuries before significant contact with sub-Saharan Africans, Europeans held the divine word of the Almighty as sacrosanct. Thus, the original justifications for enslaving blacks were primarily drawn from interpretations of Christian doctrine. The first section of this part will address the religious justifications for enslaving blacks. English colonists understood that, because of their color, black Africans could easily be distinguished from whites. Mixed-race blacks, however, could undermine the slavery system. Thus, the racial character of American slavery combined with the religious sentiment against miscegenation to create a general antipathy in the English colonies to racial mixing.[2] The second section of this part addresses the efforts to contain the number of mixed-race blacks through the enactment of antimiscegenation statutes. Several provisions in the Constitution ratified by the Founding Fathers also made the determination of race important. The Constitution included provisions for using a population formula in order to determine state representation in the lower house of Congress and the Electoral College, as well as the amount of direct taxes levied on each state. This formula counted blacks as three-fifths of a person and required the country to conduct a national census every ten years. Thus, from the beginning, the census employed racial categories in counting people. The third section shall briefly discuss those provisions in the Constitution that made the use of racial classifications necessary. Before the Civil War, the determination of race in the North and Upper South (places like Virginia and Maryland) was bimodal. Though not employing the one-drop rule, distinctions were drawn between either white/black or white/colored (which included blacks and mulattoes). In contrast, in the Lower South, mulattoes were often valued and appreciated on their own. This was especially the case around the major urban areas of Charleston, South Carolina; New Orleans, Louisiana; and Mobile, Alabama.[3] Many mulattoes there were fathered by wealthy white males. Often these wealthy fathers recognized and supported their mixed-race offspring. As a result, whites tended to draw more of a distinction between mulattoes and blacks, especially the more affluent mulattoes, in the urban areas of the Lower South than the other parts of the country.[4]

Primary Religious Justifications for Enslavement of Blacks

By the time the first blacks walked off a slave ship in Jamestown, Virginia, in 1619, Europeans had been in contact with sub-Saharan Africans for 175 years. At the time of British colonization of North America, Christianity was the dominant religion of Europe. It also provided the intellectual boundaries of European and North American thought. Europeans knew that sub-Saharan Africa was a place where the divine light of Christianity had not yet penetrated. Many English colonists and Americans accepted the burden of instructing their slaves about Christianity. If blacks were not enslaved, then their chances for eternal salvation by following the heathen religious practices of their people in Africa were remote. Thus, many whites believed that slavery benefited black people because it provided them with the ability to reap the tremendous benefits of being exposed to the divine light of Christianity and the mercy of the Son of God.

When looking for justifications for slavery, European Christians naturally turned to the Bible. There they found plenty of support for the institution. Abraham, the grand patriarch of Judaism, Christianity, and Islam, owned slaves. In Chapter 25 of Leviticus in the Old Testament, God specifically authorized the Israelites to enslave the heathens among them, but not the descendants of Israel. Thus, as long as the Europeans were enslaving heathens, whom they considered the Africans to be, they were carrying out the will of the Almighty. Jesus was silent on the issue of slavery, however the letters of the Apostle Paul took slavery for granted.[5] Thus, the Europeans believed that slavery was not a sin against Divine law, because the Bible sanctioned the institution.[6]

There were two stories drawn from Genesis to justify the enslavement of blacks.[7] The primary religious justification for enslaving blacks, and blacks alone, was derived from the curse Noah placed on the descendants of Ham. According to Chapter 9 of Genesis, Noah became drunk one day and was lying naked in a stupor in his tent when he was discovered by his son, Ham. Ham saw the nakedness of his father and told his two brothers, Shem and Japheth. The other two brothers took a garment, laid it upon their shoulders, went backward, and covered Noah. They never saw their father's nakedness. When Noah awoke and discovered what had happened, he blessed Shem and Japheth, but cursed the descendants of Ham to be servants to Shem and Japheth. Both Christians and Muslims came to believe that the descendants of Ham had turned black. Oral stories of the Hebrews collected in the Babylonian Talmud from the second to the sixth century CE, also stated that the descendants of Ham were cursed by being black.[8] The Ham legend was generally accepted in Christian communities before the importation of slaves to the New World and was used to justify the argument that the enslavement of blacks was the result of a divine curse that no human had the right to alter.[9]

The second justification for enslaving blacks was derived from the Biblical story of the murder of Abel by Cain, which brought human death into the world. Cain was a tiller of the soil, and Abel was a keeper of sheep. Both brothers made sacrifices to God. Cain offered the fruit of the ground. But, Abel offered a young sheep. God did not respect Cain's offer of a sacrifice, but respected that of Abel. Angered by God's rejection, Cain slew his brother. In punishment, God placed a mark on Cain. As earlier Christian groups before them, some Christian groups in the United States, including the Southern Baptist, believed that the mark God placed on Cain was black skin; however, because the Cain story did not indicate that his descendants were to be enslaved, this story lacked the justification for placing blacks in bondage. Thus, these religious groups also asserted that a descendant of Cain married a descendant of Ham. Black people were, therefore, the descendants of the merging of these two blood lines.[10] As a result, black people took their color from the mark of Cain's descendant and the curse of being slaves from the descendant of Ham.

Enactment of Antmiscegenation Statutes

Since slavery was largely based on a distinction between blacks and whites, race mixing created a problem because it blurred the boundary lines between the races. Rigid racial lines were necessary for the seamless operation of slavery. In addition, most whites also believed that God did not approve of miscegenation. The story of the destruction of the Tower of Babel explained that God objected to the amalgamation of humanity.[11] Thus, God placed whites on one continent and blacks on another. These racial groups only came together on a continent populated by Native Americans because of mankind's desires. Whites also tended to object much more to white female relations with black men than the other way around.[12]

Since the African slave population was relatively small throughout most of the seventeenth century, English authorities dealt with issues generated by interracial unions on an *ad hoc* basis. For example, the first reference to an African in the Virginia legislature was the recorded punishment for Hugh Davis, a white man, who defiled *his* body because he lay with "a negro."[13] As the population of Africans grew, colonial governments enacted legal prohibitions against miscegenation. The Virginia House of Burgesses adopted the first antimiscegenation statute in 1662.[14] The Virginia law sought to discourage miscegenation by doubling the fine imposed for fornication if the act was committed between a black person and a white person. The law also specified that the status of a mulatto child of a free white father and a black mother would be slave or free based upon the condition of the mother.[15]

In 1691, Virginia adopted a statute that banished from the colony any free English or other white man or woman who married a Negro, mulatto, or Indian man or woman bound or free.[16] The preamble to the law made the rationale for the statute clear: "for the prevention of that abominable mixture and spurious issue which hereafter may increase in this dominion."[17] The purpose of the statute left no doubt that Virginians were motivated by a desire to suppress the numbers of mixed-race children. Over the years, Virginia increased the punishments for anyone complicit in the crime of intermarriage, eventually making it a capital crime.[18]

Virginia became the first colony to use the word "mulatto," which it took from the Spanish, to describe any blacks with mixed white ancestry.[19] From the time that Virginia started to distinguish mulattoes from blacks, however, its laws dealing with Negro slaves also included "and mulattoes." In 1705, Virginia passed the first blood fraction statute to define a person's race. This law defined a mulatto as the child of a white person and an Indian, or the child, grandchild, or great-grandchild of a Negro.[20] While Virginia law distinguished mulattoes from blacks, free mulattoes possessed the same legal rights as free blacks. For example, at the same time that Virginia passed the law defining who was a mulatto, it passed a law that prohibited blacks, Indians, and mulattoes from holding office in the colony. By 1723, Virginia denied free mulattoes the right to vote and limited their access to firearms.[21] From a legal point of view in Virginia, individuals with one-eighth or more black blood were treated as black, even if they were legally defined as mulatto.

Maryland—the other Chesapeake Bay colony—shared Virginia's negative views about miscegenation and mulattoes. Not long after Virginia adopted its first antimiscegenation law, the Maryland General Assembly passed a statute to discourage miscegenation.[22] From the beginning, miscegenation laws in Maryland were concerned with controlling the sexual proclivities of white women. The miscegenation statute stated that "Diverse freeborne Englishwomen [who were] forgetful of their free Condition and to the disgrace of our Nation doe intermarry with Negro slave."[23] At the time that Maryland passed its antimiscegenation statute, biracial children took their legal status from their mothers. Thus, if the mother was free, so was the child. The Maryland statute provided that children inherit their legal status from their father;[24] however, in order to discourage black male/white female miscegenation, the statute changed the status of the white females who married slaves to that of a slave for as long as the father of the child was a slave. As an ex-post facto punishment, the statute went on to declare that the children of freeborn women who were already married to slaves would serve the master of their parents until age 30.[25]

There were a couple of significant issues with Maryland's law that demanded attention. Since the Maryland law for determining the status of the child differed from that of Virginia, it created an incentive for interracial couples with African husbands and white wives to flee to Virginia. At the same time, interracial couples with white husbands and African wives in Virginia started to move to Maryland.[26] Another problem with Maryland's initial provisions to discourage miscegenation was that it encouraged economically motivated slave owners to marry their black male slaves to white female indentured servants.[27] In so doing, the slave owner would come to own the white female, as well as the children of these unions. Disturbed by this practice, Lord Baltimore, the founder of the colony, used his influence to have the law changed. In 1681, Maryland adopted a statute that said if the marriage of any freeborn English or white woman to a slave had the permission of the master, such woman and her issue would be free. Thus, Maryland took away the economic incentive that slave owners had to mate white women with black slaves.[28] Also, in the same year, Maryland adopted Virginia's rule that slave status depended on the status of the mother. Then, in 1692, Maryland also outlawed interracial marriage, by adopting a statute similar to Virginia's 1691 statute.[29]

Northern colonies also banned miscegenation. The New England colonies of Massachusetts, New Hampshire, Connecticut, and Rhode Island were settled primarily by farmers and artisans who arrived in the New World with families and strong religious convictions. They flocked to New England in order to create godly communities built on the centrality of the family.[30] In 1705, Massachusetts became the first northern colony to adopt an antimiscegenation law.[31] The following year, New York adopted such a statute. In 1725–26, Pennsylvania banned all interracial marriages, punished whites who engaged in the practice, and decreed that the mulatto children of white women became servants until the age of 31.[32] By the signing of the Declaration of Independence, twelve of the thirteen colonies had banned interracial marriage. South Carolina was the only exception.[33]

Constitution Makes Race Necessary for the Census

Even though the Founding Fathers artfully left out of the Constitution the words "slave" or "slavery," at least seven provisions addressed the institution.[34] Among those provisions were ones that required the need to employ racial classifications. Article I, Section 2, clause 3 states:

> [The House of] Representatives and direct Taxes shall be apportioned among the several States which may be included within this Union, according to their respective Numbers, which shall be determined by adding to the whole Number of free persons, including those bound to Service for a Term of Years, and excluding Indians not taxed, three fifths of all other Persons.[35]

Therefore, the Constitution effectively separated individuals into three racial classfications: free persons, who were whites; Indians, who were not counted; and three-fifths of other persons, generally understood to be the black slaves. The Constitution also used this formula to determine the number of electors in the Electoral College that each state received.[36]

The above clause in the Constitution also required the country to conduct an actual enumeration of the U.S. population within three years after the first meeting of Congress and every ten years thereafter.[37] Thus, at its beginning, the census had to employ racial categories.

Distinctions Based on Color of Blacks in the Lower South

Before the Civil War, the determinations of race in the North and Upper South (places like Virginia and Maryland) were bimodal. Distinctions were drawn between either white/black or white/colored (which included blacks and mulattoes). Since whites outnumbered black slaves by large numbers in the North and Upper South, whites did not need the assistance of mulattoes as allies in case of slave rebellions. In the Upper South, mulattoes also increased over the generations and tended to reside in rural areas. The white parents of mulattoes were more likely to be poor individuals who did menial work and who originally came to America as indentured servants. Because of this genealogy, elite whites were inclined to look down on the practice of miscegenation, disdained mulattoes, and, generally, recognized few distinctions between mulattoes and blacks.[38] As in Virginia, even when colonies or states provided different legal definitions for mulattoes from blacks, generally, the law assigned the same legal rights to both groups. As a result, for purposes of legal rights, mixed-race blacks were simply viewed as lighter-skinned blacks.[39]

In the Lower South, mulattoes were often valued and appreciated, especially around urban areas such as Charleston, New Orleans, and Mobile.[40] While there were fewer mulattoes in the Lower South, many of them were fathered by wealthy, white males who often recognized and supported their mixed-race offspring. Thus, there were many affluent free mulattoes in the Lower South. Elite whites tended to treat the more affluent mulattoes as a sort of third class, an intermediate class between black and white and slave and free.[41] The free mulattoes often dominated the free black communities, both in numbers and influence, until emancipation.

Charleston, South Carolina

In 1670, a permanent English colony was founded on the coast of the Atlantic Ocean near present-day Charleston. The attitudes about race mixing in South Carolina developed differently from the way they developed in the other British mainland colonies. Of the early white settlers in South Carolina whose origins were known, half came from the West Indies. Many of them, along with their slaves, migrated from Barbados. The Barbadians were also the richest and most influential whites in early South Carolina and dominated the economic, political, and social life. Between 1670 and 1730, for example, six of the governors of the Carolina colony were from Barbados.[42]

The settlers who came to the British mainland colonies came with families. In contrast, white male colonists immigrated to the West Indies alone. The far greater gender imbalances between white men and white women that existed in the British West Indies led to widespread miscegenation between white men and black women.[43] In addition, because Barbados was a constant military staging ground for British troops fighting against its European enemies, it was the one slave-based economy that did not need a white yeoman class to deal with servile insurrections.[44] Barbados developed a unique population of wealthy planters who had a large number of black slaves doing the work, with a small biracial group of free mulattoes in between. Thus, free mulattoes emerged as a separate class in Barbados, and whites held them in higher regard than black slaves.

Crossing of the color line in South Carolina was probably greater than any other place in the English-speaking part of the United States.[45] The children of black parents were often accepted into white society, especially if their parents were wealthy and their complexion was light enough. In addition, the perception of who was white shifted toward more of an African admixture in South Carolina. People whose color and other physical features placed them in the black category in, say, Massachusetts, might look physically white in South Carolina.[46]

Even though the color line was permeable, mulattoes did not occupy a separate legal category in South Carolina. Like other free blacks, they lost the right to vote in 1721. In 1740, the legislature enacted provisions that required newly manumitted slaves to leave the colony. But, South Carolina was the one colony that did not adopt an antimiscegenation statute before the Revolutionary War.[47]

Mulattoes continued to receive good treatment in South Carolina after the Revolutionary War. For example, the results of a legislative commission that investigated the failed insurrection plot of Denmark Vesey in 1822 demonstrated the high regard that whites had for mulattoes. Vesey, a free black man, recruited some 9,000 slaves to participate in what would have been the largest and most elaborate servile insurrection in U.S. history.[48] However, his potential uprising was exposed before it could be executed. The legislative commission that investigated the plot specifically noted the benefit and importance of mulattoes, who acted as a buffer between the whites and the masses of black slaves.[49]

New Orleans, Louisiana

The origins and history of Louisiana created the conditions for a greater mixture of people there than anywhere else in the United States.[50] France began colonizing Louisiana in 1699. At the time, Louisiana's territory included modern-day Alabama. The French founded New Orleans in 1718.[51]

Fourteen years before the French began to colonize Louisiana, King Louis XIV issued the *Code Noir* in order to deal with a number of issues involving slavery.[52] Through Article IX of the code, the French sought to encourage the creation of a mixed-race group that could serve as a buffer class between whites and blacks in order to reduce the possibility of servile insurrections.[53] Among the provisions of Article IX was the requirement that if an unmarried slave master had children by a slave woman, he must marry the slave, who, together with the children, would become free. By the middle of the eighteenth century, a tripartite racial division of blacks, whites, and mulattoes was firmly in place in New Orleans, and most people married within their respective racial group.[54]

The Seven Years' War, with the North American component known as the French and Indian War, came to an end in 1763. The war changed the fortunes of Louisiana and the North American territory controlled by France, Spain, and England. Before the war, France held vast colonial territories in the North America; however, with France on the verge of losing the war, in 1762, King Charles III of Spain and his cousin King Louis XV of France signed the Treaty of Fontainebleau. The Treaty divided France's territory in the New World into three parts. The Mississippi River split the French territories into the western and eastern parts. The area that France called the Isle of Orleans was carved out and treated as a third territory. While the British had shown significant interest in the French territories east of the Mississippi River, which France transferred to England after the end of the French and Indian War, the English had not expressed interest in the territories west of the River.[55] The Treaty of Fontainebleau transferred the French territories west of the Mississippi River and New Orleans to Spain. The French viewed these transfers as strategic measures to prevent the British from acquiring the land and safeguard these territories for later reacquisition.[56]

The Spanish did not take control of the French territories, including New Orleans, until six years after the treaty. Free blacks made up only 7 percent of the city of New Orleans' black population in 1769; however, by 1805 they were more than 37 percent of the black population.[57] A number of free blacks and mulattoes immigrated to New Orleans during Haiti's liberation struggle with France from 1791 to 1806.[58] But, the main reason for the dramatic increase in free blacks was that Spanish law made it easier for slaves to obtain their freedom than French law. Muslims from North Africa had ruled the Iberian Peninsula for seven centuries before Columbus sailed to America. African slaves were even imported into the Iberian Peninsula in order to replenish their populations that were devastated by wars between the Christians and the Muslims.[59] Thus, the Spanish had long intermingled with darker-skinned people. Therefore, the racial attitudes in Spanish North America were very different from those under English influence.

Napoleon Bonaparte reacquired the lands the French had transferred to Spain in 1800.[60] However, after the French failed to reconquer Haiti, Napoleon abandoned his hopes of reestablishing a French colonial empire in North America. He sold the French holdings to the United States in 1803.

When Louisiana was purchased by the United States, New Orleans still had a three-tiered racial division. The Colored Creole Community in New Orleans was different in terms of education, wealth, history, and social standing than any other community of free persons of color in the United States.[61] For example, the 1830 census revealed that nearly 1,000 members of the Colored Creole Community owned almost 4,400 slaves, 4 percent of the slaves in Louisiana.[62] Colored Creoles viewed themselves primarily as Afro-European (and, in some cases, also with Native American genes). They generally claimed the French language as their mother tongue, practiced Catholicism, and usually married others within their community.[63] These Colored Creoles were normally free persons, and many of them did not have slave parents.[64] In fact, New Orleans not only had "quadroon balls," which were popular dances limited to white men and free mulatto women, but also the institution of *placage*, where wealthy white men carried on long-term extramarital relationships with women of color.[65] Thus, in antebellum Louisiana, mulattoes enjoyed a presumption of free status, whereas blacks were presumed to be slaves.[66]

Mobile, Alabama

Even though the British took control of Alabama after the French and Indian War, most of Anglo Alabama was not open to white migration until the 1830s.[67] Half of the free blacks in Alabama resided in Mobile and Baldwin counties, the two most southwestern counties in Alabama, which bordered the western edge of the Florida panhandle, and the part of Alabama closest to Louisiana. The cultural heritages of these counties primarily stemmed from French and Spanish influences, as opposed to English.[68] Calculations made from 1860 census data showed that 78 percent of the free Negroes were mulatto, making Alabama's free black community second only to Louisiana in terms of products of miscegenation.[69] The free black population also appeared to be a much larger percentage of blacks living in Latin-influenced Alabama as opposed to the Anglo Alabama. For example, according to Gary Mills, who exhaustively studied the 5,614 free blacks in antebellum Alabama, the percentage of the black population that was free in Latin Alabama ranged from 15.3 percent in 1830 to 8.1 percent in 1860. In contrast, the percentage of blacks who were free in Anglo Alabama remained below one percent during that time.[70] There was also evidence from census records that the three racial groups generally married within their respective group. Mills noted that about half of their marriages were between men and women of similar racial composition, 13 percent were unions between mulattoes and blacks, and about a third were between blacks and whites.[71] Alabama's laws also distinguished between colored and black in such matters as intermarriage, association, civil rights, and public education.[72]

While Alabama defined Negroes or mulattoes as any person of mixed blood to the third generation inclusive, numerous free mulattoes who had obvious Negro physical features and well-remembered ancestries were permitted to cross the color line into white society.[73] In actual practice, both the Alabama judiciary and popular custom were more lenient when determining whether a person was white than the blood fraction expressed by the law.[74]

The Rise of the One-Drop Rule

The race of individuals affected a number of their legal rights during the antebellum period, including individuals' ability to vote, inherit property, institute legal proceedings, marry, or testify in court.[75] Because of race's legal importance, the states developed different legal definitions and ways to determine a person's race. The first mention of the one-drop rule occurred in the 1830s.[76] However, it would take some time before the one-drop rule would achieve national acceptance. The first section of this part discusses the methods employed to determine a person's race by the beginning of the nineteenth century. Starting in the late 1830s, a scientific debate about whether blacks and whites were different species generated another concern about the need to distinguish blacks from whites. A new scientific strain of thought disputed the traditional beliefs that all humans descended from Adam and that mixed-race blacks were superior to full-blooded blacks. Polygenesists argued that blacks and whites were different species. Thus, the products of interbreeding of the two races would be inferior to both their black and white parents. This debate contributed to the inclusion of a "mulatto" category on the 1850 census. With the exception of the years 1880 and 1900, a mulatto category was on census forms from 1850 to 1920.[77] The second section of this part will discuss this new scientific argument and the inclusion of a mulatto category on the 1850 census. With the end of the Civil War and abolition of slavery, the need for racial classifications to support a race-based system of slavery no longer existed; however, the Civil War generated the first mass studies of the physical differences of not only blacks and whites, but also mulattoes. Scientists argued that this evidence confirmed the belief that the product of black/white interbreeding produced individuals who were physically inferior and, often, mentally or morally inferior to both full-blooded blacks and whites. The prevention of miscegenation was the strongest justification for keeping the races apart. Therefore, the institution of legal segregation provided the new primary motivation for the maintenance of racial categories. The third section will discuss these Civil War studies and the conclusions that subsequent racial scholars drew from this evidence. Fueled by concerns about the dangers of miscegenation, the one-drop rule became the unwritten law for determining race by the end of the nineteenth century, and during the first three decades of the twentieth century it was codified into law. The final section will discuss the ascendency of the one-drop rule.

Methods for Determining Race and the Origin of the One-drop Rule Before the Nineteenth Century

Since most states tied some legal rights to race, by the start of the nineteenth century the states had developed three different legal methods to determine a person's race: Blood fractions, appearance, and personal associations.[78] States enacted a variety of blood fraction statutes to specify the quantum of blood that separated whites from blacks/mulattoes. The most common blood fraction for determining if a person was black was one-eighth or more Negro blood.[79] This remained the case up through the early part of the twentieth century and, by then, almost all states had adopted a statutory definition of race based on blood fractions; however, because slave masters did not allow their black property to build stable family relations, it was often impossible to determine a "black" person's blood fraction. Another problem with blood fractions was that they could contradict physical appearance. Thus, blood fraction laws tended to be used in conjunction with physical appearance. The third method used to determine race was a person's associations. Courts would sometimes give weight to the fact that a person only associated with whites as proof that the person was white, though this was normally combined with physical appearance.

The one-drop rule developed first in the North during the antebellum period. Before 1830, there was no mention of it.[80] Nor was there any mention of "white-looking black people," a concept that only makes sense when using something like the one-drop rule to determine a person's race. According to Frank Sweet, events such as the publication in 1829 of David Walker's *Appeal in Four Articles* that called for black violence against whites to end slavery and Nat Turner's 1831 revolt in Southampton County, Virginia, generated concern among white mainstream society that there might be black sympathizers secretly among them.[81] However, it would take some time before the one-drop rule would achieve national acceptance.

Scientific Theory of Polygenesis and Addition of the Mulatto Category to the 1850 Census

A scientific debate emerged in the 1840s that generated additional concerns about miscegenation. Up to that time, the dominant belief about the unity of the human races was derived from the Bible. According to the Book of Genesis, all humans descended from Adam and Eve. Differences that existed between the races in color, physical appearance, and personality characteristics, including intelligence, were the result of environmental factors as groups adapted to their geographic locations over the generations. As these monogenesists argued, though blacks may differ physically and mentally from whites, they were of the same species. South Carolinian Lutheran minister John Bachman, who was also a trustee and the first professor of natural history of the College of Charleston, summarized the position of these theological naturalists.[82] He noted that when different species of animals produced a hybrid, by art or accident, these hybrids became extinct in a very short period of time. As a result, no group of animals has ever developed from the commingling of two or more species. Consequently, the creation of the various species of animals is an act of Divine Power alone. The fact that all the races of mankind produce fertile progeny is one of the most powerful and undeniable arguments in favor of the unity of the races.[83]

The American School of Ethnology argued that humankind originated as the result of different acts of creation in several different places in the world. Thus, the differences among the human races were divisions of species, not varieties. As a result, blacks were a form of life altogether distinct from whites. While rejecting the position of the monogenesists, these polygenesists, nevertheless, preached the natural superiority of whites and the inevitability that the destiny of the white race was "eventually to hold every foot of the globe where climate does not interpose an impenetrable barrier."[84] The polygenesists would remain influential throughout the rest of the nineteenth century, until the Social Darwinists largely supplanted their debate with the monogenesists.[85]

Louis Agassiz, a Harvard professor who founded and directed the Museum of Comparative Zoology, and Samuel Morton, a Philadelphia physician, were the best known of the early polygenesists.[86] When asked if his theory of polygeny contradicted the account of creation of Adam in the Book of Genesis, Agassiz responded that the Genesis account spoke only of the creation of the Caucasian race.[87] Morton published three major works on the sizes of human skulls between 1839 and 1849. Based on his measurements of cranial capacity of current and ancient human skulls, Morton argued that the various human races had remained unchanged in terms of their physical and mental facilities since the time of their creation.[88] According to his work, Caucasians had the largest skulls, followed by Mongolians, American Indians, and then Africans.[89] Morton believed that these differences in the size of the skulls provided evidence that Caucasians had different origins than those of other racial groups. In addition, because intellectual superiority was tied to cerebral volume, Caucasians were also the most intelligent group.[90]

Josiah C. Nott was a Southern surgeon from Mobile, Alabama, who would figure prominently in the debate about the dangers of miscegenation. He followed up on the work of Morton and published a short piece in 1843 in the prestigious *Boston Medical and Surgical Journal*. Nott made the provocative claim that the mulatto was a hybrid. By "hybrid," what Nott meant was the offspring of two distinct species like a mule from a horse and a donkey.[91] Nott concluded that mulattoes were shorter-lived than either blacks or whites; mulatto women were more delicate and subject to many chronic female diseases; mulatto women were bad breeders because many of them would not conceive at all and a large portion of the children from those who did conceive would die at an early age; and when the two sexes interbred, they would be less prolific.[92] Nott went on to assert that each successive generation of mixed-race people would become more degenerate. Thus, his conclusions about blacks with 50 percent white blood applied with even more force when dealing with quadroons (blacks with 75 percent white blood).[93] Nott's piece challenged two of the dominant notions of the day. He asserted that hybrids could simply be less fertile and feebler than their parents, as opposed to sterile. In addition, mulattoes might actually be worse than full-bloodied blacks, not better.[94]

The controversy sparked by Nott's work coincided with debates about the results of the 1840 census. The census data showed that higher rates of physical handicaps and mental illnesses existed among the black population than among the white.[95] In addition, the rate of insanity of free blacks in the North was ten times higher than among slaves.[96] For proslavery advocates, this was strong evidence that freedom drove black people insane. Thus, slavery was the natural state for them. However, closer examination of some of the census results by Dr. Edward Jarvis, a physician and founding member of the American Statistical Association, revealed significant errors in the census data. Jarvis's work showed that on returns from several towns, the number of insane black people equaled the number in the town. In addition, on other returns, there were insane black people counted in towns without any blacks at all.[97]

Because of the controversies surrounding the 1840 census, Congress sought the advice of several social scientists in preparations for the 1850 census.[98] Congress created a special census board, which granted considerable authority to the new superintendent of the census, Joseph C. G. Kennedy. Kennedy implemented a number of changes in the way the census was conducted and sought advice from the leaders of the American Statistical Association and the American Geographical and Statistical Society.[99] As a result, the 1850 census was the first to benefit from scientific advice. It was far more detailed than any previous census. For example, where the 1830 census only had 7 questions, the 1850 one had 138. This census form was also the first one to add a "mulatto" category for mixed-race blacks/whites and blacks/Native Americans.[100] Congressional testimony about the 1850 census revealed that this category, and other questions about race, were added because of efforts by scientists and supportive legislators to gather information on mixed-race blacks.[101]

As the 1850s unfolded, the South's institution of slavery came under increased pressure from the North and foreign countries. One of the issues that the Southern slaveholders had to justify was the inconsistency between the rationales for slavery and the enslaving of those whose blood was predominantly white. The need to defend their enslavement required the rejection of distinctions among blacks based on mixed-race ancestry. Thus, tolerance for special treatment of mulattoes began to decline in the places in the Lower South that previously had recognized some distinctions between them and blacks. For example, in 1852, Alabama changed the law to allow for the punishment of those who solemnized the rites of marriage between free white persons and free persons of color.[102] Even though Louisiana legislature began to treat Colored Creoles as black earlier, the judiciary resisted these efforts until the 1850s.[103]

Nott continued his efforts to establish the belief that blacks and whites were separate species. In 1854, Nott published his coedited book the *Types of Mankind*, with G. R. Gliddon.[104] This 800-page defense of Morton's theory of polygenesis and white supremacy was a contemporary bestseller in the field of anthropology. Before the Civil War, Nott helped to get French aristocrat Count Arthur de Gobineau's book published in English.[105] Gobineau's book was highly regarded in the United States.[106] He asserted that all of the high civilizations of humanity were products of the white race. The white race had a peculiar racial characteristic that produced a people with reflective energy, energetic intelligence, feeling for utility, unusual perseverance, great physical power, extraordinary instinct for order, lovers of liberty and life, and haters of despotism. Among the other issues that Gobineau dealt with in his book were the laws that explain the rise and fall of civilizations.[107] Gobineau claimed that a society's abundance was based upon its ability to preserve the blood of the noble group that created it. When their blood is mixed with that of degenerate groups it, inevitably, leads to the destruction of that society.

Scientific Evidence that Supported the Continued Prevention of Miscegenation after Abolition

With the end of the Civil War and abolition of slavery, the need to maintain racial categories to support a race-based system of slavery no longer existed. However, the strongest justification for racial segregation was the fear of the consequences of miscegenation.[108] "From social amalgamation it is but a step to illicit intercourse, and but another to intermarriage."[109] Like a race-based slavery system, the legal rights accompanying the institution of segregation also required the maintenance of racial classifications. Thus, as slavery was abolished, the institution of segregation provided new legal motivations to continue to determine a person's race.

The passage of the Civil Rights Act of 1866 and the Fourteenth Amendment created questions about the continued validity of antimiscegenation statutes; nevertheless, most state courts that addressed the issue upheld their state's antimiscegenation statutes.[110] Even when courts did not champion the cause of black inferiority, many still believed that God disdained miscegenation. An opinion handed down by the Pennsylvania Supreme Court shortly after the end of the Civil War made this rationale clear.[111] The case addressed the actions of a train conductor, acting pursuant to a company rule, to compel a black female passenger to sit in an area of the carriage for blacks that in all respects was as comfortable, safe, and convenient as the area for whites. In upholding the conductor's action, the Court wrote:

Why the Creator made one black and the other white, we know not; but the fact is apparent, and the races distinct, each producing its own kind and following the peculiar law of its constitution. Conceding equality, with natures as perfect and rights as sacred, yet God has made them dissimilar, with those natural instincts and feelings which He always imparts to His creatures when He intends that they shall not overstep the natural boundaries He has assigned to them. The natural law which forbids their intermarriage and that social amalgamation which leads to a corruption of races, is as clearly divine as that which imparted to them different natures . . . But to assert separateness is not to declare inferiority in either; it is not to declare one a slave and the other a freeman—that would be to draw the illogical sequence of inferiority from difference only. It is simply to say that following the order of Divine Providence, human authority ought not to compel these widely separated races to intermix.[112]

The United States Supreme Court removed all doubt about the legitimacy of antimiscegenation statutes with its decision in *Pace v. Alabama*.[113] The Court upheld an Alabama law that made interracial adultery or fornication a much more serious crime than intraracial adultery or fornication. At least thirty-eight states eventually enacted antimiscegenation statutes.[114] Some states extended the prohibition against interracial marriage to cover whites who intermarried with Native Americans, Asiatic Indians, Chinese, Hindus, Japanese, Koreans, Malayans, and Mongolians.[115] All of the antimiscegenation statutes, however, proscribed black/white sexual relations.

The scientific evidence generated during the Civil War affirmed the notion that interracial breeding produced corruption of the races. Agencies of the U.S. government pioneered wide-scale measurements of soldiers during that time. The autopsies and anthropological studies carried out during the war were the first mass studies of physical differences of the races that also included mulattoes. The results of these studies were important because they helped to crystalize and substantiate earlier scientific concerns about miscegenation.[116] From these scientific measurements, surgeons and physicians generally concluded that mulattoes might be more intelligent than the full-blooded black; however, because of their physical infirmities and lack of morals, all things considered, mulattoes were worse than full-blooded blacks.

One of the federal agencies involved in the work of physical anthropologists was the U.S. Sanitary Commission. President Abraham Lincoln created the Commission to study the physical and moral conditions of federal troops in order to offer suggestions for how to improve army life. Dr. Sanford Hunt, a surgeon in the U.S. military during the war, prepared a report for the Sanitary Commission that discussed the results of 405 autopsies he had conducted on soldiers. In 1869, Hunt published the report as an article titled "The Negro as Soldier," in the prestigious London *Anthropological Review*. Nearly all subsequent late nineteenth-century studies on racial inferiority of blacks pointed to this report in order to justify their conclusions.[117]

At the time of the publication of Hunt's report, scientists recognized three methods to determine the mental capacities of the races.[118] One was by external measurements of the cranium. The downside of this method was that it could not account for the thickness of the skull. The second method, the one employed by Samuel Morton, was to measure the internal space of the skull; however, as those engaged in scientific investigations became more professionalized, the researchers who had studied the shapes and sizes of the skulls began to focus more attention on the weight of the brain. The previous work in this area had always assumed that intelligence correlated with the size of the brain. Thus, the weight of the brain was a direct, better, and more accurate measure of innate intellectual ability than the size of the cranium or the interior volume of the skull.

Hunt's article confirmed the implications from Morton's earlier findings: Whites had larger brains than blacks. Hunt, however, went further and classified the brains that he weighed based on the fraction of white blood of the soldiers that were autopsied. Thus, Hunt reported the average brain weights for full-blooded whites and those with three-fourths (quadroon), one-half, one-quarter, one-eighth and one-sixteenth white blood, as well as those who were full-blooded blacks. Hunt found that the average weight of the brain of the white solider was more than five ounces heavier than that of the average black. He also found that the average weight of the brains of quadroons was closest to that of the average white brain, only three ounces smaller. The mixed-race person who was 50 percent black and 50 percent white had a slightly heavier brain than the full-blooded black. However, Hunt also found that those with only one-quarter, one-eighth, or one-sixteenth white blood had smaller brains than the full-blooded black person.[119] Thus, Hunt concluded, "Slight intermixtures of white blood diminish the negro brain from its normal standard; but, when the infusion of white blood amounts to one-half, it determines a positive increase in the negro brain, which in the quadroon is only three ounces below the white standard."[120]

Hunt also found that "the percentage of exceptionally small brains is largest among negroes having but a small proportion of white blood."[121] Thus, his research "established" that blacks with at least 50 percent white blood were more intelligent than full-blooded blacks, but those blacks with less than this amount were not as intelligent as full-blooded blacks. Miscegenation by whites with any blacks, therefore, would prove to have negative consequences for generations to come.

Benjamin Gould performed several anthropometric studies of Civil War soldiers for the Sanitary Commission.[122] He also published his findings in 1869.[123] Gould discovered that the lung capacity of the black soldier was less than that of the white, but greater than that of the mulatto. Comparisons of the head size, weight, and height led Gould to conclude that mulattoes were physically inferior to both blacks and whites. In discussing mulattoes in his report, Gould stated:

The curious and important fact that the mulattoes, or men of mixed race, occupy so frequently in the scale of progression a place outside of, rather than intermediate between, those races from the combination of which they have spring cannot fail to attract attention. The well-known phenomenon of their inferior vitality may stand, possibly, in some connection with the fact thus brought to light.[124]

Another federal agency that published data on physical measurements conducted on troops during the Civil War was the Provost Marshal-General's Bureau. In 1875, the Bureau released its report on the records of the examinations of more than a million recruits, drafted men, substitutes, and enrolled men in military service during the Civil War.[125] Though its conclusions varied at times from that of the Sanitary Commission, the Bureau's findings generally corroborated those of the Commission, but on a much larger scale.[126] Part of the results of this report included a study of questionnaires sent to military medical doctors regarding their observations of black and mulatto recruits, including their physical builds, intellects, and abilities to perform military service. The answers of the doctors confirmed the belief that mulattoes were physically inferior and, thus, were less capable of enduring the hardships of military service than both black and white recruits.[127]

Nathaniel Shaler, one of the most prominent Harvard professors and dean of the university's Lawrence Scientific School, wrote extensively on race in the last quarter of the nineteenth century. Shaler argued that the anthropometric studies confirmed that not only was the black race a separate species from whites, but it had reached a point in its evolutionary development beyond which its further development could only result from imitating the master race, not from their own innate motives.[128] Shaler also noted that common opinion agreed that the products of unions between a pure black and a pure white, on average, had shorter life spans and were less fertile than those of the races of either parent.[129] Shaler argued that mulattoes grew up with disharmonic features. Their body frames were too large for their small hearts and kidneys, and their large teeth were tightly crowded into an undersized mouth. Shaler went on to say:

> The mulatto, like the man of most mixed races, is peculiarly inflammable material. From the white he inherits a refinement unfitting him for all work which has not a certain delicacy about it; from the black, a laxity of morals which, whether it be the result of innate incapacity for certain forms of moral culture or the result of an utter want of training in this direction, is still unquestionably a negro characteristic.[130]

Jospeh LeConte was a former student of Agassiz, a member of the faculty of several universities, including the University of California,[131] and a president of the American Association for the Advancement of Science.[132] He published two notable articles in 1879 and 1880.[133] LeConte noted that, while the mulatto was intellectually superior to the pure black, he did not retain the physical capacity of either the white or the black race. Building on work of earlier race scholars such as Josiah C. Nott, George R. Gliddon, and Sanford Hunt, LeConte concluded that the mulatto was an inferior breed that would eventually perish in the natural course of the race struggle.[134]

Writing in the 1890s, Frederick Hoffman, a noted scholar on the racial characteristics of blacks, argued that the product of black/white interbreeding possessed the least vital force of all the races. While Hoffman conceded that the mulatto was undoubtedly intellectually superior to the pure black, he noted this did not compensate for the deterioration in the physical and moral capacity. "Morally, the mulatto cannot be said to be superior to the pure black . . . most of the illicit intercourse between whites and coloreds is with mulatto women and seldom with those of the pure type."[135] Thus, miscegenation was a positive hindrance to the social, mental, and moral development of the black race. Hoffman went so far as to assert that the consequences of black/white interbreeding "demand race purity and a stern reprobation of any infusion of white blood."[136]

Herbert Hovenkamp accurately summarized the view of the biological scientists of the nineteenth century. For them, the "mulatto was an outcast in both worlds —too civilized to be comfortable with the black, but too primitive to live with the white without giving offense."[137] Even though the mulatto might be considered more physically attractive than the pure-blood black and, often more intelligent, he was considered to be constitutionally weak, prone to disease, and less fertile.[138] Thus, concluded Edward Youman, one of Herbert Spencer's devotees, mixing the northern European with the inferior races, including the black, would be extremely injurious.[139]

Ascendancy of the One-drop Rule

Fueled by concerns about the horror of miscegenation, the one-drop rule had become the unwritten law for determining race by the end of the nineteenth century.[140] In discussing the embrace of the one-drop rule, Booker T. Washington stated:

> It is a fact that, if a person is known to have one per cent of African blood in his veins, he ceases to be a white man. The ninety-nine percent of Caucasian blood does not weigh by the side of the one per cent of African blood. The white blood counts for nothing. The person is a Negro every time.[141]

The popular horror regarding miscegenation reached its apogee in the first two decades of the twentieth century. At this time, also, state legislatures began to codify the one-drop rule into statutory definitions of race. The first state to adopt the one-drop rule by statute was Tennessee in 1910, followed by Louisiana later that year and Texas and Arkansas a year later, then Mississippi (1917), North Carolina (1923), Virginia (1924), Alabama and Georgia (1927), and Oklahoma

(1931). In addition, eight other states—Florida, Indiana, Kentucky, Maryland, Missouri, Nebraska, North Dakota, and Utah—amended their blood fraction statutes to classify a person as black who had as little as one-sixteenth or one-thirty-second of black blood.[142] With the 1930 census, the Census Bureau finally abandoned its inclusion of any categories for mixed-race individuals. The instructions for that census form stated that a person "of mixed white and Negro blood should be returned as Negro, no matter how small the percentage of Negro blood."[143]

The Civil Rights Movement and the Continuing Need for Racial Classifications

As the 1930s unfolded, scientists increasingly began to believe that environment influenced intelligence more so than innate characteristics. Throughout the 1930s and 1940s, this position gained adherents and became the dominant one. Thus, by the 1950s, most social scientists believed that enriching their environment and assisting them in overcoming their deficit culture could improve black people. The social environmentalist triumphed in the unanimous ruling by the Supreme Court in *Brown v. Board of Education*.[144] The landmark ruling also sparked a fifteen-year period in which all three branches of the federal government contributed to addressing racial inequality in education, employment, housing, medical care, and voting rights.[145] Pursuant to the Equal Protection Clause, Supreme Court rulings in the 1950s and 1960s outlawed racial and ethnic discrimination by governmental entities. Congress passed several major pieces of civil rights legislation in the 1960s attacking discrimination in the private sector and the political process, including the 1964 Civil Rights Act, the 1965 Voting Rights Act, and the 1968 Fair Housing Act. During this same time period, selective higher education programs began to institute affirmative action admissions policies as a way to increase the number of underrepresented minorities on their campuses. Private and public employers created affirmative action hiring and promotion programs in order to increase the number of blacks and other minorities who were either in their workforces or in supervisory positions. Governmental units and private institutions also established a number of programs and policies to provide assistance for minority-owned businesses.

There were two different aspects of the desegregation movement's judicial decisions, legislation, and programs and policies. One aspect used race as a means for dismantling the effects of prior *de jure* segregation. As Justice Blackmun put it in his opinion in *Regents of the University of California v. Bakke*, "in order to get beyond racism, we must first take account of race."[146] For this aspect, it was important to employ racial classifications and generate racial statistics. However, rather than using racial classifications to exclude, segregate, and discriminate against individuals from minority groups, now these classifications were put in the service of including members of these groups, prohibiting the discrimination they encountered, and attenuating its effects on them. In addition, the rationale for the production of racial data changed. Instead of using this data to justify discrimination, now it was generated in order to demonstrate the existence of legally recognized discrimination, to prove that discrimination was systemic in nature, and to produce support for new laws and policies to address the effects of discrimination. As a result, even with the demise of segregation, new legal rationales evolved, justifying the need to continue to determine a person's race. The other aspect of the desegregation movement, however, involved the assertion of the need to transcend considerations of race. People should act as if they were colorblind and judge individuals based on the content of their character, not the color of their skin. Thus, the colorblind/individualist aspect of the desegregation movement sought to deemphasize the consideration of race in favor of treating people as individuals. As is obvious, the aspect of the desegregation movement that reinforced the importance of race was in considerable conflict with the colorblind\individualist aspect. The second aspect would eventually become dominant and help lead to the fall of the one-drop rule.

This part shall address the aspect of the desegregation movement that emphasized the importance of using race as a means in which to dismantle segregation and attenuate the effects that it had on people of color, particularly blacks. The second aspect of the desegregation movement, the colorblind/individualist aspect that emphasized the need to transcend race, will be discussed in the final part of this chapter, which addresses the fall of the one-drop rule.

The first section of this part focuses on some of the major court decisions, interpreting the equal protection clause and federal civil rights legislation, as well as policies and programs such as affirmative action in higher education that reinforced the importance of utilizing racial classifications. Because of court opinions and federal legislation in the 1960s, by the 1970s several federal agencies were collecting racial and ethnic data. This development led the federal government, for the first time, to standardize the collection and reporting of this data. The second section shall discuss the process that produced the federal government's standardized procedures for the collection and reporting of racial and ethnic data.

Supreme Court Opinions and Policies and Programs that Reinforced the Importance of Race

In *Brown v. Board of Education*[147] the Supreme Court concluded that state-imposed racial segregation of public schools deprives blacks of equal protection of the laws. By doing so, the Court struck down segregation statutes that existed in twenty-one states, which covered 40 percent of the nation's school children.[148] In one of the most quoted phrases from the opinion, the Court said, "[t]o separate [African American youth] from others of similar age and qualifications solely because of their race generates a feeling of inferiority as to their status in the community that may affect their hearts and minds in a way unlikely ever to be undone."[149] The Court went on to quote approvingly from the district court in Kansas:

> Segregation of white and colored children in public schools has a detrimental effect upon the colored children. The impact is greater when it has the sanction of the law; for the policy of separating the races is usually interpreted as denoting the inferiority of the negro group. A sense of inferiority affects the motivation of a child to learn. *Segregation with the sanction of law, therefore, has a tendency to (retard) the educational and mental development of negro children.*[150]

Chief Justice Earl Warren buttressed the conclusion that segregation in public schools inflicted psychological harm on African Americans by citing studies of social science in the (in)famous footnote no. 11.[151]

Much of the civil rights progress that occurred through the 1960s and early 1970s was predicated upon a special concern about assisting blacks to overcome the impact of historical discrimination. For example, in his landmark speech at the commencement ceremony at Howard University in June 1965, President Lyndon Johnson stated:

> You do not wipe away the scars of centuries by saying: Now you are free to go where you want, and do as you desire, and choose the leaders as you please. You do not take a person who, for years, has been hobbled by chains and liberate him, bring him up to the starting line of a race and then say, "you are free to compete with all the others," and still justly believe that you have been completely fair.[152]

In its 1968 opinion in *Green v. New Kent County*,[153] the Court rejected a freedom of choice plan implemented by a former *de jure* segregated school because the plan failed to produce enough racial balancing. The Court went on to decree that previously segregated school systems use racial classifications in order to produce racially integrated student bodies, faculties, and administrations. Thus, the Court placed an affirmative obligation on formerly dual school systems to treat individuals as members of racial groups in order to bring about the desegregation of public schools. The Court's only rationale for this was that *Brown I* required it. With opinions in cases such as *Brown I*, *Green*, and others,[154] the Supreme Court made racial classifications vital in the nation's efforts to desegregate the public schools.

In addition to school desegregation, the 1960s saw selective higher education institutions begin to employ racial classifications as a way to increase the number of blacks on their campuses. In the introduction to their groundbreaking book *The Shape of the River*, William Bowen and Derek Bok noted, "[I]t is probably safe to say . . . that prior to 1960, no selective college or university was making determined efforts to seek out and admit substantial numbers of African

Americans."[155] However, once selective higher education institutions started to employ special efforts to recruit black students, their numbers immediately increased. For example, in 1965, law schools began employing affirmative action admissions practices.[156] Within ten years, the proportion of black students enrolled in the nation's law schools jumped from about 1 percent to 4.5 percent.[157] The percentage of blacks enrolled in Ivy League colleges increased from 2.3 percent to 6.3 percent between 1967 and 1976.[158] In the 1968–69 academic year, only 2.2 percent of the nearly 36,000 medical school students were black, with almost 60 percent of them enrolled at the two historically black medical schools of Howard University College of Medicine and Meharry Medical College.[159] Seven years later, blacks constituted 6.2 percent of the nation's medical school students.

During the 1960s and 1970s, racial classifications and racial statistics were employed in a number of other areas in order to attenuate the effects of racial discrimination on minority groups. For example, many public and private employers created affirmative action programs to increase the number of black and other minorities who were in their workforces.[160] Various governmental units and private institutions created programs and policies to provide benefits to minority-owned businesses.[161] When President Johnson pushed for the enactment of the Voting Rights Act of 1965, he proactively attempted to change the public opinion of racial discrimination by granting blacks the opportunities to engage in the political process and to elect their own leaders.[162] Once the Act was passed, although they faced great opposition in doing so, blacks flocked to the polls to make their voices heard.[163]

In addition to the need to determine a person's race in order to decide if they should be a beneficiary of various policies and programs established to attenuate the effects of racial discrimination, race was also important in helping to define when discrimination existed under federal law. One of the provisions of the Civil Rights Act of 1964 was Title VII, which prohibited discrimination in employment. In *Griggs v. Duke Power Co*,[164] a landmark decision for years, the Supreme Court concluded that Title VII proscribed nonracial employment practices that have a disparate impact on black employees.[165] In concluding that employment practices of requiring a high school diploma or passage of an aptitude test could constitute discrimination, the Court noted that Title VII was directed at the consequences of employment practices not the motivation. In order to demonstrate the racially discriminatory effects of various employment practices or policies, it was necessary to employ racial classifications and generate racial statistics.[166] Another provision of the Civil Rights Act of 1964 was Title VI, which banned discrimination in federally funded programs. Specifically, Section 601 of Title VI "prohibits discrimination based on race, color, or national origin in covered programs and activities."[167] In the Supreme Court's 1974 opinion in *Lau v. Nichols*,[168] the Court held that a school system's failure to provide English language instruction to Chinese-speaking students denied them a meaningful opportunity to participate in the educational programs offered by the school district in violation of Title VI. In the opinion, the Court noted that the U.S. Department of Health, Education, and Welfare guidelines declared that "discrimination is barred which has that effect even though no purposeful design is present."[169] The language suggested that the Court was willing to conclude that minority plaintiffs, including black plaintiffs, could establish a *prima facie* case of discrimination under Title VI by demonstrating that a given policy or practice produced a racially disparate impact on them. The decisions of the Court in cases like *Griggs* and *Lau*, for a time, indicated that the Supreme Court might even conclude that blacks could prove at least a *prima facie* case of race discrimination against them under the Equal Protection Clause by using racial statistics. When interpreting the Voting Rights Act, the Court has clearly indicated that minorities could establish discrimination by showing that a change in voting legislation had a discriminatory effect. In *Beer v. United States*[170] for example, the Court interpreted Section 5 of the Act as implementing a standard of retrogressive effect. Similarly, under Section 2 of the Act as amended in 1982, plaintiffs may establish a violation of the law by making a showing of discriminatory effects.

Adoption of Directive 15

Before the 1970s, no federal standards existed for the collection of data on race and ethnicity that applied to all federal agencies.[171] Largely because of civil rights laws enacted during the 1960s noted above, several federal agencies were collecting racial data by the early 1970s. In addition, in its 1973 opinion in *Keyes v. School District No. 1*,[172] the Supreme Court addressed the issue of how to deal with Hispanics/Latinos for purposes of school desegregation. The Court stated, "There is also much evidence that in the Southwest Hispanos and Negroes have a great many things in common."[173] The Court went on to note that the District Court recognized that "though of different origins Negroes and Hispanos in Denver suffer identical discrimination in treatment when compared with the treatment afforded Anglo students."[174] Congress jumped into the issue of compiling statistics on Hispanics/Latinos in 1976 when it passed Public Law 94–311 in response to the undercount of Hispanics/Latinos on the 1970 census. That law required federal agencies to provide separate counts for the Hispanic population, in order to remedy discrimination against those of Hispanic origin.[175]

The need of so many federal agencies to collect data on racial and ethnic groups generated the federal government's first effort to standardize the collection and reporting of such information. Thus:

> The driving force for the development of the standards in the 1970s was the need for comparable data to monitor equal access, in areas such as housing, education, mortgage lending, health care services, and employment opportunities, for population groups that historically had experienced discrimination and differential treatment of race and ethnicity.[176]

The Federal Interagency Committee on Education created an ad hoc committee in 1974 to come up with terms and definitions to cover the major categories of race and ethnicity that all federal agencies could use to meet their particular data requirements. The ad hoc committee considered creating an "Other" category for use principally by individuals of mixed racial backgrounds.[177] However, a majority of the committee members opposed this because it would complicate the surveying and add to the costs of collecting data.[178] The committee did recognize that the use of an "Other" category might be appropriate when entities were collecting racial and ethnic data using a self-identification approach. If an "Other" category was used, however, the respondent should also be required to specify the group to which they identify. Thus, the ad hoc committee sought to provide the means to edit the responses of those who chose the "Other" category. This would help to keep the number of responses in the "Other" category as small as possible. When an entity used an observer identification method to gather data, however, the ad hoc committee viewed the "Other" category as undesirable.

After a period of testing by several different federal agencies, the Office of Management and Budget (OMB) made slight revisions to the categories and definitions initially adopted by the ad hoc committee and proposed them for agency comment.[179] OMB made no provision for an "Other" category. On May 12, 1977, the *Race and Ethnic Standards for Federal Statistics and Administrative Reporting* became effective for all federal government agencies and required that all existing data collections comply with its terms and definitions by January 1, 1980.[180] The final document rejected an "Other" category. Instead, with regard to mixed-race individuals, it stated, "The category which most closely reflects the individual's recognition in his community should be used for purposes of reporting on persons who are of mixed racial and/or ethnic origins."[181] Thus, these standards acquiesced to the one-drop rule and continued to view race as a socially ascribed trait, rather than a result of self-identification. In 1978, the standards went through a name change and were subsequently renamed the *Statistical Policy Directive No. 15, Race and Ethnic Standards for Federal Statistics and Administrative Reporting* or "Directive 15" for short.[182] Directive 15 listed the following five racial/ethnic categories and definitions:

a. **American Indian or Alaskan Native**. A person having origins in any of the original peoples of North America, and who maintains cultural identification through tribal affiliation or community recognition;

b. **Asian or Pacific Islander**. A person having origins in any of the original peoples of the Far East, Southeast Asia, the Indian subcontinent, or the Pacific Islands. This area includes, for example, China, India, Japan, Korea, the Philippine Islands, and Samoa;

c. **Black.** A person having origins in any of the black racial groups of Africa;

d. **Hispanic.** A person of Mexican, Puerto Rican, Cuban, Central or South
    American, or other Spanish culture or origin, regardless of race; and
e. **White**. A person having origins in any of the original peoples of Europe,
    North Africa, or the Middle East.

Thus, as the desegregation era unfolded, the legal motivation to continue to
determine a person's race and generate racial statistics was as strong as ever. The
difference was that now racial classifications and racial statistics were necessary in
order to dismantle discrimination and its effects on underrepresented minorities,
including blacks.

Fall of the One-Drop Rule

While one aspect of the desegregation movement reinforced the importance of
race, the other aspect deemphasized it. The other aspect urged individuals to be
colorblind, and thus transcend considerations of race when dealing with others.
This aspect views it as wrong, perhaps even immoral, to treat a person as a member
of a racial or ethnic group, even if it was for the purpose of dismantling the effects
of discrimination. This second aspect of the desegregation movement was in
considerable conflict with the first. Justice Anthony Kennedy noted this conflict
in his controlling opinion in *Parents Involved in Community Schools v. Seattle School
District No. 1*, which struck down the use of individual racial classifications in
voluntary school desegregation plans. In responding to the argument that if race
is the problem then race is the solution, Kennedy wrote:

> The idea that if race is the problem, race is the instrument with which to
> solve it cannot be accepted as an analytical leap forward. And if this is a
> frustrating duality of the Equal Protection Clause it simply reflects the duality
> of our history and our attempts to promote freedom in a world that
> sometimes seems set against it.[183]

As the twenty-first century unfolds, it is apparent that the Supreme Court's
interpretations of the Equal Protection Clause and most federal antidiscrimination
legislation have adopted the colorblind/individualist approach. As a result, from
a legal standpoint, race means less now than at any time since the early 1700s.
The first section of this part will address a number of major Supreme Court opinions
that deemphasized the importance of race. At the same time that being black was
losing its legal significance, the ability of Americans to determine who was black
based on their physical appearance was also fading. Until the last twenty or thirty
years, the one-drop rule functioned to make a person's race visible. Thus, skin
color marked a person's race for all to see. However, substantial immigration
from Africa, Asia, Latin America, and the Middle East has changed the face and
complexion of American society. Blacks with lighter complexions or less visible

African facial features increasingly encounter people who no longer can assume that they are black based on their physical appearance. The second section of this part will briefly discuss how immigration has changed the face and complexion of American society. In addition, in October 1997, the OMB issued the 1997 Revised Standards, which changed the way racial and ethnic data is gathered and reported to the federal government.[184] The preferred method to gather information about race and identity is self-identification. In addition, forms used to gather the information must allow individuals to designate all of the racial and ethnic categories that they believe apply to them. By allowing this, the federal government abandoned the one-drop rule. The primary motivation for the federal government to allow individuals to identify with multiple racial/ethnic categories was to respond to complaints by multiracials (or their parents or guardians), especially those with one black parent. They objected to government efforts that forced mixed-race individuals to identify with only one category. The collection and reporting of this data for the 2000 and 2010 censuses, generally, followed the 1997 Revised Standards.[185] The third section will discuss how the multiracial movement helped to lead the federal government to abandon the one-drop rule. When those with some black ancestry self-identify with more than one racial group, they are also rejecting the one-drop rule. Thus, from the 2000 and 2010 census data, it is clear that more and more people with some black ancestry no longer identify themselves as only black. And, the younger people with some black ancestry are, the more likely they (or their parents or guardians) are to identify with more than one race. Given this and increasing interracial sexual relationships involving blacks, the percentage of mixed-race blacks who no longer self-identify as only black will continue to increase. The fourth section of this part will discuss the increasing numbers of those with black ancestry who are now identifying with more than one race. As a result of the developments discussed in detail below, American society is experiencing the fall of the one-drop rule.

The Supreme Court's Opinions that Deemphasized Race

While a majority of the justices on the Supreme Court have not yet embraced a colorblind interpretation of the constitution, the Court's jurisprudence for interpreting the Equal Protection Clause and federal antidiscrimination legislation have traveled a long way toward this result. The Supreme Court's opinions in this area treat government as if it were an individual. Thus, the Court's jurisprudence presumes that the actions of government, like those of individuals, are motivated by its intentions. In addition, the Court's jurisprudence requires that government treat people as individuals, not as members of racial or ethnic groups. There are two different ways in which this colorblind/individualist aspect of the Court's jurisprudence is manifested. First, what is considered racial discrimination is determined by focusing principally on the actor's motivations, not the effects of their actions. Actions not motivated by racial considerations may have negative effects on members of certain minority racial or ethnic groups, including blacks. However, since it is the intent that determines whether race discrimination exists, minority individuals whose interests are harmed by actions motivated by nonracial concerns are often not viewed as victims of racial discrimination. Second, since government and private parties are to treat people as individuals, they should not develop policies and programs based on race or ethnicity, absent compelling justifications and means that are narrowly tailored to advance those justifications. Thus, the Court's opinions have prevented almost all efforts by governmental entities to employ racial classifications in policies and programs intended to attenuate the effects of past and present racial discrimination.

Deemphasizing the Importance of Race by Rejecting Disparate Impact as the Definition of Discrimination

Shortly after the Supreme Court's decision in *Brown I*, the Court applied the colorblind/individualist aspect and issued a series of *per curiam* opinions that struck down state statutes that mandated segregation in public parks,[186] beaches,[187] golf courses,[188] transportation,[189] and other public facilities.[190] In 1964, the Supreme Court struck down a Florida antimiscegenation statute that provided a greater punishment for a black/white interracial couple cohabitating than intraracial couples.[191] In so doing, the Supreme Court rejected the rationale it had accepted in its 1883 decision in *Pace v. Alabama*.[192] Three years later, the Court invalidated an antimiscegenation marriage statute in *Loving v. Virginia*.[193] At the time of the Court's opinion in *Loving*, antimiscegenation statutes were still on the books in fifteen other states.[194] All of the above statutes involved situations where government classified people based on race on the face of the legislation in order to exclude or discriminate against minority individuals, especially if they were black. As Chief Justice Warren noted in his opinion for the Court in *Loving*, these statutes that discriminate against blacks on their face are not justified by any purpose independent of invidious racial discrimination.[195]

The 1964 Civil Rights Act and the 1968 Federal Housing Act banned many forms of international discrimination by private parties in employment, federal government contracting, public accommodations, and the real estate industry. In addition, in the 1970s, the Supreme Court turned its attention to defining what constituted race discrimination under the Due Process Clause of the Fifth Amendment and the Equal Protection Clause, when racial classifications were not used on the face of the governmental statute or regulation.

As mentioned earlier, the Court's Title VII opinion of *Griggs v. Duke Power Co.* and Title VI case of *Lau v. Nichols* seemed to imply that the Court might be willing to also conclude that minorities could establish a *prima facie* case of race discrimination under the Constitution by demonstrating that a given governmental action produced a discriminatory effect. However, in *Washington v. Davis*[196] the

Court directly addressed the concept of discrimination under the Constitution when the government policy did not use racial classifications. In *Washington v Davis*, the black plaintiffs raised a claim of race discrimination similar to the one raised by the black plaintiffs in *Griggs*. The black plaintiffs used statistical evidence to document the racial disparities that existed in a job-related test used for prospective police recruits.[197] Specifically, the plaintiffs argued that the test excluded a disproportionate number of black applicants because white applicants passed the employment test at a much higher rate.[198] The Court rejected the plaintiffs' discriminatory effects argument. Instead, the Court concluded that, because the police department's use of the test was not the result of a racially discriminatory motive, its use did not violate the Constitution. Since *Washington v. Davis* involved a challenge to discrimination by the District of Columbia under the Fifth Amendment's Due Process Clause, a year later the Court extended this holding to the determination of discrimination under the Equal Protection Clause in the case of *Village of Arlington Heights v. Metropolitan Housing Development Corporation*.[199] Thus, the Court rejected discriminatory effects in favor of discriminatory intent as the basis for determining discrimination under the Constitution when dealing with governmental policies and programs that were racially neutral on their face. In so doing, the Court reduced the need for racial statistics because what is far more important in determining discrimination under the constitution is motive and not effect. Discriminatory motive would trigger a case of discrimination even if there is no disparate effect.[200] Using racial statistics might be helpful in demonstrating racially discriminatory motives, but, generally, would not suffice without more.

As for Title VI, the Court's 1978 opinion in *Regents of the University of California v. Bakke*[201] raised serious questions about the disparate impact holding in *Lau*. In *Bakke*, five members of the Court concluded that the standard for determining racial discrimination under Title VI was the same as the standard under the Equal Protection Clause. In the 1983 decision in *Guardians Association v. Civil Service Commission of New York City*,[202] the Court made it clear that Section 601 of Title VI forbade only intentional discrimination.[203]

Deemphasizing the Use of Race by Eliminating the Ability to Employ Racial Classifications in Programs to Dismantle the Effects of Discrimination

Bakke is also notable because it was the first time the Supreme Court addressed the issue of whether race-based governmental action designed to *benefit* minority groups should also be subject to the same strict scrutiny as measures that discriminated against them. Before *Bakke*, the Court had indicated that heightened judicial scrutiny applied when government used a suspect classification; however, the Court stated that the traditional indicators of suspectness dealt with whether the class was "saddled with such disabilities, or subjected to such a history of purposeful unequal treatment, or relegated to such a position of political power-lessness as to command extraordinary protection from the majoritarian political process."[204]

A majority of the justices on the Court have not yet embraced a colorblind interpretation of the Constitution.[205] But, *Bakke* starts the Supreme Court down that judicial road. Today the Court has rejected almost all efforts by governmental entities that would employ racial classifications in policies and programs intended to attenuate the effects of past and present racial discrimination.

Allan Bakke was a white male who was denied admission to the medical school of the University of California at Davis. He argued that the medical school violated Title VI and the Equal Protection Clause because it operated a separate admissions program that reserved 16 out of 100 admissions seats for members of minority groups. Four justices declined to reach the constitutional issue. For them, the separate admissions program violated Title VI.[206] Four other justices agreed that the test of discrimination was the same under both Title VI and the Equal Protection Clause. They rejected the application of strict judicial scrutiny and instead indicated that they would have upheld the admissions program under both by using a more lenient intermediate scrutiny test. These four justices upheld the admissions program.[207]

Justice Lewis Powell's opinion was the decisive swing vote. Powell agreed that discrimination under Title VI was co-extensive with discrimination under the Equal Protection Clause. In addressing the purpose behind the Equal Protection Clause, Powell noted that the original pervading purpose of the clause was "the freedom of the slave race, the security and firm establishment of that freedom, and the protection of the newly-made freeman and citizens, from the oppressions of those who had formerly exercised dominion over him."[208] However, this purpose was virtually strangled in its infancy by the Supreme Court's post-Civil War decisions. Powell went on to note that while the framers of the "Fourteenth Amendment conceived of its primary function as bridging the vast distance between members of the Negro race and the white 'majority,' the Amendment itself was framed in universal terms, without reference to color, ethnic origin, or condition of prior servitude."[209] Powell concluded that it was too late to hold that the Equal Protection Clause permits the recognition of special wards. Rather, the purpose is to assure that all individuals receive the equal protection of the laws.

Having decided that the Equal Protection Clause was to protect the rights of individuals, Justice Powell rejected the social justice rationales to support the taking into account of race in the admissions process. Powell concluded that the university's social justice arguments of "reducing the historic deficit of traditionally disfavored minorities in medical schools and in the medical profession . . . ; (ii) countering the effects of societal discrimination; [and] (iii) increasing the number of physicians who will practice in communities currently underserved"[210] were inadequate to justify the use of race in the admissions process. In the end, Powell found that only the educational benefits of diversity justified the taking account of race as one factor among many in an individualized admissions process.

The Supreme Court followed the logic of Powell's opinion in *Bakke* in several different opinions issued in the 1980s and 1990s. For example, in the Supreme Court's 1986 opinion in *Wygant v. Jackson Board of Education*,[211] the Court rejected the argument that providing role models of academic success for minority public school students justified protecting black teachers with less seniority than white teachers from layoffs. In the 1989 opinion in *City of Richmond v. Croson*,[212] for the first time, a majority of the justices agreed that under the Equal Protection Clause all uses of racial classifications, including uses in affirmative action programs intended to benefit minority groups, should be subjected to strict scrutiny. In the 1995 opinion of *Adarand Contractors, Inc. v. Pena*,[213] the Court extended the standard of review articulated in *Croson* to also apply to the federal government's use of racial classifications. In so doing, the Court reversed a decision that it handed down only five years earlier where it agreed that Congress, a co-equal branch of government, had more authority to legislate in this area than state and local governments.[214] In another 1995 opinion, *Miller v. Johnson*,[215] the Supreme Court struck down a redistricting plan adopted by the Georgia General Assembly as violating the Equal Protection Clause. The General Assembly took account of the race of people in drafting a redistricting plan that intentionally created three majority-minority legislative districts.

In its 2003 opinion in *Grutter v. Bollinger*,[216] the Supreme Court did uphold the use of racial classifications in the admissions process of selective higher education institutions in order to produce a critical mass of underrepresented minorities with a history of discrimination; however, the Court also rejected a mechanical process that awarded fixed points during the application process to applicants from underrepresented minority backgrounds in *Gratz v. Bollinger*.[217] The Court concluded that the mechanical admissions process in *Gratz* did not provide for enough individualized consideration that must be the core of a race-conscious admissions policy. As mentioned earlier, in the *Parents Involved* decision in 2007, the Supreme Court struck down the use of racial classifications as a means by which public schools could pursue voluntary school desegregation plans.[218] In so doing, the Court essentially struck down the very type of school desegregation plans that it had actually ordered public schools to institute with its decisions in the 1960s and 1970s.

Much of the Supreme Court's rhetoric on the harm of the government's use of racial classifications contained in the controlling opinions in cases such as *Bakke, Wygant, Croson, Miller, Adarand, Gratz,* and *Parents Involved* rests upon the idea that government should not treat people as members of racial and ethnic groups. Rather, race should be transcended in favor of treating people as individuals. As the Court stated in *Miller*, at the "heart of the Constitution's guarantee of equal protection lies the simple command that the Government must treat citizens as individuals, not as simply components of a racial, religious, sexual or national class."[219] And, as Chief Justice John Roberts stated at the conclusion of his opinion in *Parents Involved*, "The way to stop discrimination on the basis of race is to stop discriminating on the basis of race."[220]

At the time of this writing, the Supreme Court has not yet rendered its fourth major affirmative action decision in higher education in *Fisher v Texas*.[221] However, the Court is poised to potentially reduce the use of race in the admission process of selective higher education institutions. The Court has also agreed to hear a challenge to the constitutionality of Section 5 of the Voting Rights Act.[222] Because of the decisions the Supreme Court has already issued, it is clear that American society has moved into the postdesegregation or post-racial era. As the twenty-first century continues to unfold, the Supreme Court's interpretation of the Equal Protection Clause and federal antidiscrimination legislation is mostly colorblind. Thus, the Court has severely limited the ability of American society to employ racial classifications in order to dismantle the effects of discrimination on black people. As a result, race currently means less for purposes of determining legal rights and responsibilities today than at any time in the past 300 years.

Immigration Has Changed the Face and Complexion of American Society

According to the 1960 census, whites constituted 88.8 percent of all Americans, with an additional 10.6 percent classified as black.[223] The 1960 census did not include a classification for Hispanics/Latinos. Instead, they were classified based on their race, not their ethnicity. Given that 99.4 percent of the American population was white or black, at the beginning of the desegregation era, the one-drop rule functioned to allow Americans to determine the race of just about everyone based on their physical appearance.

Immigration during the past fifty years has brought to America individuals with an array of colors, facial features, and hair texture. In 2010, non-Hispanic Latino whites (which include those from the Middle East and North Africa) made up 63.7 percent of the population and non-Hispanic/Latino blacks made up another 12.6 percent.[224] Thus, those who were not simply black or white have increased from less than 1 percent of the population to more than 23 percent— almost double the percentage of blacks in the country.

Immigration has increased the difficulty of determining a person's racial identity based on appearance. There are plenty of people who, by the application of the one-drop rule, look black but who are from diverse places across the world such as South Asia, Latin America, Africa, or the Middle East. In addition, blacks with lighter complexions or less visible African facial features are increasingly interacting with people who no longer can assume that they are black based on their physical appearance. When others inquire about their race or ethnicity, these racially ambiguous individuals with some black ancestry often encounter the question, "What are you?" As a result, application of the one-drop rule is no longer reliable as a means to determine the racial identity of a substantial number of people of color.

The Multicultural Movement Leads the Federal Government to Abandon the One-Drop Rule

For much of American history, race was not a matter of personal identification, but a socially ascribed characteristic. Thus, a person had his or her race imposed upon them by society, not chosen as a matter of self-identification. With the one-drop rule firmly in place for much of the twentieth century, mixed-race blacks were treated as black regardless of how they would have identified themselves; however, in an effort to improve the accuracy of data gathered about nonwhites, the Census Bureau changed the process for gathering census data in 1960.[225] Up until that time, the Census Bureau hired enumerators who went out to people's homes to fill out the census forms. Enumerators were responsible for determining a person's race based on their visual acuity; however, for the 1960 census, more than 80 percent of American households received an advanced copy of the form that the head of the household was to fill out before the enumerators arrived.[226] The 1970 census form was the first one designed to be completed by respondents without any assistance from census enumerators.[227]

While the Census Bureau viewed the change to households filling out the census forms and identifying the races of those in the households as an improvement in terms of the accuracy of racial statistics, it also began the process of changing the meaning of racial identification. Instead of a census enumerator imposing a racial identity on the person, the requirement that individuals fill out the forms and send them to the Census Bureau on their own raised the issue of how a person identified his or her own race. Thus, rather than race being a socially ascribed identity, it raised the question of race being a matter of self-identification. Many mixed-race individuals (or their parents or guardians on their behalf) began to object to forms that required them to identify with only one racial/ethnic category.[228] For example, the instructions for the 1990 census form stated that individuals should check the one box that best described their race. Nevertheless, more than 500,000 people refused to abide by these instructions and selected more than one racial category.[229]

From 1993 to 1997, the federal government conducted an extensive review of the racial/ethnic categories and definitions stated in Directive 15.[230] According to the OMB, the most controversial and sensitive issue during these discussions dealt with how to address the classifications of individuals with parents of different races.[231] Individuals in black/white intermarriages and groups such as Project RACE (Reclassify All Children Equally) and the Association of MultiEthnic Americans spearheaded the effort to add a "multiracial" category to the 2000 census.[232] According to Kim Williams—who extensively studied the effort—about 3,500 adult members, excluding student groups, were involved.[233] Only about twenty leaders were responsible for the attempt to add a multiracial category.[234] "White, liberal, and suburban-based middle-class women (married to black men) held the leadership roles in most multiracial organizations."[235]

Multiracial advocates, generally, argued that mixed-race individuals viewed themselves as multiracial rather than belonging to a single racial or ethnic group. A "multiracial" designation was, therefore, a better reflection of the true understanding of the multiracial person's racial identity. They pointed to the inherent racism of the one-drop rule.[236] These groups also noted the psychological problems created for biracial children when they are forced to identify with one parent more than the other.

In October 1997, the OMB issued the 1997 Revised Standards.[237] In the end, the OMB rejected a multiracial category for individuals to select; however, it decided that self-identification would be the primary method to determine racial/ethnic identity, and when it is used, a method should be employed to allow individuals to check more than one racial or ethnic category from a list provided. Thus, with the adoption of the 1997 Revised Standards, the federal government—for the first time ever—allowed individuals to designate more than one racial category. The collection and reporting of racial and ethnic data for the 2000 and 2010 censuses, generally, followed the 1997 Revised Standards.

The 1997 Revised Standards required other federal agencies to modify their processes for gathering and reporting racial and ethnic data. Thus, other federal agencies,[238] including the Department of Labor in 2005 and the Department of Education in 2007, have revised the process that reporting institutions use to collect and report this data to them.[239] Instead of forms used to collect such data that forced prospective employees and applicants for school to choose only one racial/ethnic category, now these forms provide individuals with the ability to designate all of the racial or ethnic categories that apply to them. Those individuals who indicate that they are Hispanic/Latino—including those who designate black as one of their racial categories—are reported by institutions to federal agencies as Hispanic/Latino. In addition, institutions do not report those self-identified non-Hispanics/Latinos who indicate black and at least one other racial category to federal agencies in aggregate counts of blacks. Rather, they are lumped in with other multiracial non-Hispanic/Latinos in counts of a new "Two or More Races" category.[240] Thus, self-identified mixed-race people with some black ancestry are no longer included in the aggregate counts of blacks reported to these federal agencies. As a result, the federal government's procedures for public and private institutions to use in gathering and reporting date about blacks has abandoned the one-drop rule.

Increasing Numbers of Blacks Reject the One-drop Rule

Because individuals can self-identify with all of their racial categories, it is apparent that the number of those with some black ancestry who are self-identifying with more than one race is increasing at a significant rate. The percentage of those identifying with black and at least one other racial category increased from 4.8 percent in 2000[241] to 7.4 percent in 2010.[242] This is over two and a half times the 2.9 percent of the American population as a whole.[243] The younger blacks are, the larger is the percentage that identify with more than one race. By self-identifying with more than one racial/ethnic group, however, these individuals (or their parents or guardians on their behalf) are rejecting the one-drop rule. The percentage of mixed-race blacks between the ages of 15 and 19 was only 6.5 percent.[244] However, for those with some black ancestry between the ages of 10 and 14 it increased to 9.3 percent, for those between the ages of 5 and 9 to 11.9 percent and for those under the age of 5 was 13.7 percent.[245]

Given the increase in the acceptance of interracial marriages and cohabitations, the percentage of those with some black ancestry who identify with more than one race will likely continue to increase for the foreseeable future. According to a Pew Research Center report, almost all millennials accept interracial dating and marriage. The report notes that 92 percent of white and 88 percent of African American millennials say that they would be fine with a family member marrying someone outside of their group.[246] As acceptance of interracial marriages with blacks has increased, the number of such marriages has increased. Data from the 2000 census revealed that 9.7 percent of married black men and 4.1 percent of married black women reported having a spouse of another race.[247] Another recent Pew Center Research report also noted that interracial marriages make up a much larger percentage of new marriages by blacks, when compared to the total of blacks currently married. Thus, in 2010, 23.6 percent of black male and 9.3 percent of black female newlyweds married outside of their race.[248] Given the increasing interracial marriage rates of blacks, it is likely that the number of blacks who identify with more than one race will skyrocket in the future.

Conclusion

Historically, race has been more important in American society than color. From a legal standpoint, racial classifications were originally necessary in order to uphold a race-based system of slavery. Because of its importance during the antebellum period, American society developed methods for determining a person's racial classification, including blood fractions, appearance, and associations; however, a person's appearance was always the most important one. Thus, color helped to function as the primary way to determine a person's race. After abolition, the social and legal importance of racial classifications did not fade away. The first massive studies of physical differences of blacks, whites, and mulattoes, including differences in brain sizes, were conducted during the Civil War. This evidence provided additional support for the antebellum scientific hypothesis that the offspring of interracial mating were worse than both the black or white parents. Preventing miscegenation provided the most compelling rationale for segregation.

Therefore, during the latter part of the nineteenth century racial classifications became legally necessary in order to support segregation. By the end of the nineteenth century, the country established the one-drop rule as the dominant way to determine who was black. This acceptance was written into the laws of many states during the first three decades of the twentieth century.

During the periods of slavery and *de jure* segregation, American society presumed that racial differences were innate and either permanent or very slow to change. However, throughout the 1930s and 1940s, social scientists increasingly came to believe that cultural and social environmental factors influenced intelligence more so than innate characteristics. The view of the social environmentalist prevailed in the Supreme Court's 1954 ruling in *Brown v. Board of Education*, which struck down statutes segregating public school children.

Brown helped to initiate a fifteen-year period in which American society instituted several measures to address racial inequality in education, employment, housing, medical care, and voting rights. As the desegregation movement commenced, Americans' firm acceptance of the one-drop rule as the way to determine a person's race was at its zenith. Census figures for race were based on the judgment of census enumerators about a person's race, not an individual's self-identification. Since virtually all Americans were either black or white, the one-drop rule also functioned as a way to easily determine the race of a person based on physical appearance.

There were two different aspects of the desegregation movement. One focused on the importance of racial statistics and racial classifications as a means for determining and dismantling the effects of America's history of racial discrimination. From the standpoint of this aspect, racial statistics demonstrated the effects of racism and racial classifications were necessary in order to determine the beneficiaries of policies and programs to attenuate those effects. As a result, this aspect of the desegregation movement provided new legal rationales for the importance of racial classifications, even as the law rejected their use to support segregation. The second aspect of the desegregation movement, however, attempted to transcend considerations of race in favor of a colorblind view of people whereby everyone would judge and treat others as individuals, not as members of racial or ethnic groups. This colorblind/individualist aspect sought to deemphasize the importance of race. It not only rejected the use of racial classifications to support segregation, but it rejected their use to dismantle the effects of segregation as well. Thus, it was in considerable tension with the other aspect.

By the end of the twentieth century, it was apparent that the Supreme Court's interpretations of the Equal Protection Clause and federal anti-discrimination legislation, for the most part, adopted the colorblind/individualist aspect. Thus, the Supreme Court eliminated most legal justifications for employing racial classifications and uses of racial statistics. As a result, from a legal perspective, race means less today than at any time since the early 1700s. While racial classifications were losing their legal significance, for the first time in America's history the country experienced substantial voluntary immigration from parts of the world populated primarily by people of color. Thus, immigrants from Africa, Asia, Latin America, and the Middle East began to literally change the face and complexion of the American people. Thus, the application of the one-drop rule is no longer a reliable marker for determining the race of a substantial number of people of color. Also, in October 1997, the federal government changed the way it wanted racial and ethnic data to be collected and reported. In so doing, the federal government not only made it clear that self-identification is the preferred method for determining a person's race or ethnicity, but required institutions that gather this information to use forms that allow individuals to choose all of their self-identified racial and ethnic categories. Most public and private organizations must report to the federal government people who indicate that they are Hispanic/Latino, including those who designate black as one of their racial categories, as Hispanic/Latino. In addition, institutions do not report those self-identified non-Hispanics/Latinos who indicate black and at least one other racial category to federal agencies in aggregate counts of blacks. Rather, they are lumped in with other multiracial non-Hispanics/Latinos in counts of a new "Two or More Races" category. As a result, the federal government has abandoned the one-drop rule. From this new racial data, it is clear that more and more people with some black ancestry are rejecting the one-drop rule and no longer identify themselves as only black. The younger people with some black ancestry are, the more likely they (or their parents or guardians) are to identify with more than one race. With increasing rates of interracial marriages, the percentage of blacks who reject the one-drop rule is on the rise.

As the twenty-first century unfolds, race means less in terms of determining legal rights than ever before. Because of immigration and the ability of individuals to determine their own racial identity, Americans can no longer tell the race of many, if not most, people of color from their physical appearance. In addition, the continued rise of interracial sexual relations involving blacks means that the number of those with some black ancestry who identify with more than one race will continue to increase. The inevitable result of these developments is that with race losing its legal importance and Americans no longer able to reliably tell a person's race from their physical appearance, race will continue to lose its significance. As race loses its significance, American society is witnessing a reversal of the historic reality of race being more important than color.

Notes

1 Brown v. Bd. of Educ., 347 U.S. 483 (1954).
2 Peter W. Bardaglio, "Shameful Matches: The Regulation of Interracial Sex and Marriage in the South before 1900," in *Sex, Love, Race: Crossing Boundaries in North American History*, ed. Martha Hodes (New York: NYU Press, 1999), 113.
3 Joel Williamson, *New People: Miscegenation and Mulattoes in the United States* (Baton Rouge, LA: Louisiana State University Press, 1995), 14–15.

4 Ibid.

5 See, e.g., 1 Cor. 12:13; Titus 2:9–10; Philem.; Col. 3:22; Ephesians 6:5–6.

6 Anthony E. Cook, "Beyond Critical Legal Studies: The Reconstructive Theology of Dr. Martin Luther King, Jr.," *Harvard Law Review* 103 (1990): 1016.

7 See, e.g., David M. Goldenberg, *The Curse of Ham: Race and Slavery in Early Judaism, Christianity, and Islam* (Princeton, NJ: Princeton University Press, 2003), 178–181.

8 Thomas F. Gossett, *Race: The History of an Idea in America* (Dallas, TX: Southern Methodist University Press, 1963), 5; see also Winthrop D. Jordan, *White over Black: American Attitudes toward the Negro, 1550–1812* (Chapel Hill, NC: University of North Carolina Press, 1968), 18–19.

9 See Joe R. Feagin, *Racist America: Roots, Current Realities, and Future Reparations* (New York: Routledge, 2000), 74.

10 See e.g., Goldenberg, *The Curse of Ham*, 178–181.

11 Gen. 11:1–9.

12 Peter W. Bardaglio, "Shameful Matches," 113.

13 Virginia Council cn, Minutes of the Council and General court of colonial Virginia, 1622–1632, 1670–1676, with Notes and Excerpts from Original Council and General Court Records, into 1683, now lost, ed. H. R. McIlwaine (Richmond, VA: Colonial Press, 1924), 479; but see Frank Sweet, *Legal History of the Color Line: The Rise and Triumph of the One-Drop Rule* (Palm Coast, FL: Backintyme, 2005), 120 (pointing out that "Davis was caught 'lying with a negro,' not 'lying with a negress' " and, thus, his offense could have involved homosexuality).

14 See F. James Davis, *Who Is Black? One Nation's Definition* (University Park, PA: Pennsylvania State University Press, 1991), 33.

15 William Waller Hening, *The Statutes at Large; Being a Collection of All the Laws of Virginia, From the First Session of the Legislature in the Year 1619*, vol. 2 (New York: R. & W. & G. Bartow, 1823), 170.

16 Ibid., 86–87.

17 Carter G. Woodson, "The Beginnings of Miscegenation of the Whites and Blacks," *Journal of Negro History* 3 (October 1918): 335–353.

18 Sweet, *Legal History of the Color Line*, 125.

19 See Winthrop D. Jordan, "American Chiaroscuro: The Status and Definition of Mulattoes in the British Colonies," *William and Mary Quarterly* 19 (1962): 184.

20 Hening, *The Statutes at Large*, 252.

21 Williamson, *New People*, 9–10.

22 See Laurence C. Nolan, "The Meaning of *Loving*: Marriage, Due Process and Equal Protection (1967–1990) as Equality and Marriage, From *Loving* to *Zablocki*," *Howard Law Journal* 41 (1998): 247–248.

23 Jonathan L. Alpert, "The Origin of Slavery in the United States—The Maryland Precedent," *American Journal of Legal History* 14 (1970): 195.

24 William D. Zabel, "Interracial Marriage and the Law," *Atlantic Monthly* 216 (October 1965): 75–79.

25 See statute quoted Woodson, "The Beginnings of Miscegenation."

26 Sweet, *Legal History of the Color Line*, 124.

27 Arthur W. Calhoun, *A Social History of the American Family from Colonial Times to the Present* (New York: Barnes & Noble, Inc., 1945).

28 Woodson, "The Beginnings of Miscegenation."

29 Sweet, *Legal History of the Color Line*, 124–125.

30 John D'Emilio and Estelle B. Freedman, *Intimate Matters: A History of Sexuality in America* (Chicago, IL: The University of Chicago Press, 1997), 3.

31 Zabel, "Interracial Marriage and the Law," 75–79.

32 Williamson, *New People*, 9–10.

33 Sweet, *Legal History of the Color Line*, 128.

34 Donald E. Lively, *The Constitution and Race* (New York: Praeger, 1992), 4–5.
35 See U.S. Const. art. I, § 2, cl. 3.
36 U.S. Const. art. II, § 1, cl. 2 of the Constitution states: "Each State shall appoint, in such Manner as the Legislature thereof may direct, a Number of Electors, equal to the whole Number of Senators and Representatives to which the State may be entitled in the Congress: but no Senator or Representative, or Person holding an Office of Trust or Profit under the United States, shall be appointed an Elector."
37 "The actual Enumeration shall be made within three Years after the first Meeting of the Congress of the United States, and within every subsequent Term of ten Years, in such Manner as they shall by Law direct." U.S. Const. art. I, § 2, cl. 3.
38 But see, Howard Bodenhorn, "The Mulatto Advantage: The Biological Consequences of Complexion in Rural Antebellum Virginia," *Journal of Interdisciplinary History* 33 (2002): 21 (arguing that complexion differences were as important a determinant of socioeconomic status in the rural Upper South as in the urban Lower South).
39 See, e.g., Carl N. Degler, *Neither Black Nor White: Slavery and Race Relations in Brazil and the United States* (Madison: University of Wisconsin Press, 1971), 103.
40 Williamson, *New People*, 9–10.
41 Ibid.
42 Ibid.
43 Bodenhorn, "The Mulatto Advantage," 24.
44 Sweet, *Legal History of the Color Line*, 189–190.
45 Ibid., 187.
46 Ibid.
47 Davis, *Who Is Black*, 35.
48 See David M. Robertson, *The Buried Story of America's Largest Slave Rebellion and the Man Who Led It* (New York: Alfred A. Knopf, Inc., 2000), 4.
49 Davis, *Who Is Black?*, 35.
50 See Mark Golub, "*Plessy* as 'Passing': Judicial Responses to Ambiguously Raced Bodies in *Plessy v. Ferguson*," *Law and Society Review* 39 (September 2005): 568.
51 Kimberly S. Hanger, "Origins of New Orleans Free Creoles of Color," in *Creoles of Color of the Gulf South*, ed. James H. Dormon (Knoxville, TN: University of Tennessee Press, 1996), 4.
52 For an English translation, see "The Code Noir (The Black Code)," last visited January 30, 2013, http://chnm.gmu.edu/revolution/d/335/. Carter G. Woodson called the *Code Noir* "the most human of all slave regulations." Woodson, "The Beginnings of Miscegenation," 338.
53 Sweet, *Legal History of the Color Line*, 207.
54 Pierre Force, "The House on Bayou Road: Atlantic Creole Networks in the Eighteenth and Nineteenth Centuries," *Journal of American History* 100 (2012): 9.
55 Junius P. Rodriguez, *The Louisiana Purchase: A Historical and Geographical Encyclopedia* (Santa Barbara, CA: ABC-CLIO, Inc., 2002), xx.
56 Ibid.
57 Ira Berlin, *Many Thousands Gone: The First Two Centuries of Slavery in North America* (Cambridge, MA: Harvard University Press, 1998), 333.
58 Eric Foner, *Reconstruction: America's Unfinished Revolution, 1863–1877* (New York: Harper & Row, 1988), 47.
59 Dirk Hoerder, *Cultures in Contact: World Migrations in the Second Millennium* (Durham, NC: Duke University Press, 2002), 41.
60 David Otto, *Insiders' Guide to Shreveport* (Guilford, CT: Globe Pequot Press, 2010), 159.
61 Foner, *Reconstruction*, 47.
62 Williamson, *New People*, 81–82.

63   Hanger, "Ethnicity and Identity," 167.

64   Ibid.

65   Roger A. Fischer, *The Segregation Struggle in Louisiana, 1862–77* (Urbana, IL: University of Illinois Press, 1974), 15.

66   David C. Rankin, "The Impact of the Civil War on the Free Colored Community of New Orleans," *Perspectives in American History* 11 (1977–78): 381–382. See also Adele v. Beauregard, 1 Mart. (o.s.) 183 (1810).

67   Gary B. Mills, "Miscegenation and the Free Negro in Antebellum 'Anglo' Alabama: A Reexamination of Southern Race Relations," *Journal of American History* 68 (June 1981): 26.

68   Ibid., 19.

69   Ira Berlin, *Slaves without Masters: The Free Negro in the Antebellum South* (New York: Pantheon Books, 1974), 105.

70   See Mills, "Miscegenation and the Free Negro in Antebellum 'Anglo' Alabama," 33.

71   Ibid., 21.

72   For a brief survey of such laws in Alabama, see Virginia M. Gould, "The Free Creoles of Color of the Antebellum Gulf Ports of Mobile and Pensacola: A Struggle for the Middle Ground," in *Creoles of Color of the Gulf South*, ed. James H. Dormon (Knoxville, TN: University of Tennessee Press, 1996), 28–50.

73   Mills, "Miscegenation and the Free Negro in Antebellum 'Anglo' Alabama," 29.

74   Ibid.

75   The most authoritative legal decision authored by the Supreme Court expressing the constitutional view of blacks and their rights during the antebellum period was Chief Justice Taney's 1857 opinion in *Dred Scott v. Sanford*. 60 U.S. 393 (1857). In concluding that the slave and would-be free man, Dred Scott, could not sue in federal court to obtain his freedom, Chief Justice Taney found that people of African descent (slave or free) were not considered citizens within the definition of the Constitution.

76   Sweet, *Legal History of the Color Line*, 299–315.

77   To see the list of questions raised on the census, including those about race or color, see "U.S. Census Bureau, 1900 General Population Schedule," last visited January 31, 2013, http://www.census.gov/history/www/through_the_decades/index_of_questions/1900_1.html.

78   Sweet, *Legal History of the Color Line*, 169.

79   Zabel, "Interracial Marriage and the Law," 75–79.

80   Sweet, *Legal History of the Color Line*, 325–346.

81   Ibid., 328–336.

82   See John Bachman, *Selected Writings on Science, Race, and Religion*, ed. Gene Waddell (Athens, GA: University of Georgia Press, 2011), 1–20.

83   See John Bachman, *The Doctrine of the Unity of the Human Race Examined on the Principles of Science* (Charleston, SC: C. Canning, 1850).

84   See Josiah Clark Nott et al., *Types of Mankind: Or, Ethnological Researches, Based Upon the Ancient Monuments, Paintings, Sculptures, and Crania of Races, and Upon Their Natural, Geographical, Philological and Biblical History* (Philadelphia, PA: J. B. Lippincott, Grambo & Co., 1854), 80.

85   Melissa Nobles, *Shades of Citizenship: Race and the Census in Modern Politics* (Stanford, CA: Stanford University Press, 2000), 31.

86   Stephen Jay Gould, *The Mismeasure of Man* (New York: W. W. Norton & Company, 1981), 79.

87   Kevin Brown, *Race, Law and Education in the Post-Desegregation Era: Four Perspectives on Desegregation and Resegregation* (Durham, NC: Carolina Academic Press, 2005), 67.

88   Nancy Krieger, "Shades of Difference: Theoretical Underpinnings of the Medical Controversy on Black/White Differences in the United States, 1830–1870," *International Journal of Health Services* 17 (1987): 265.

89 The mean internal cubic capacity of Caucasian was 87, Mongolian 83, Malay 81, American Indiana 80, and Black 78. Samuel G. Morton, *Crania Americana; or, A Comparative View of the Skulls of Various Aboriginal Nations of North and South America: To Which is Prefixed An Essay on the Varieties of the Human Species* (Philadelphia, PA: London, Simpkin, Marshall & Co., 1839), 290.

90 For a critique of the work by Morton, see Stephen Jay Gould, *The Mismeasure of Man*, 82–101.

91 Josiah Clark Nott, "The Mulatto: A Hybrid: Probable Extermination of the Two Races If the Whites and Blacks are Allowed to Intermarry," *Boston Medical and Surgical Journal* 29 (1843): 29.

92 Nott rested his conclusions in part on an 1842 article, also published in the *Boston Medical and Surgical Journal*, by an author who only identified himself as "Philanthropist."

93 Nott, "The Mulatto," 29.

94 Krieger, "Shades of Difference," 265.

95 Jennifer Lee and Frank D. Bean, *The Diversity Paradox: Immigration and the Color Line in Twenty-First Century America* (New York: Russell Sage Foundation, 2010), 38.

96 Melissa Nobles, *Shades of Citizenship: Race and the Census in Modern Politics* (Stanford, CA: Stanford University Press, 2000), 32.

97 Ibid., 33.

98 Ibid., 32–36.

99 C. Matthew Snipp, "Racial Measurement in the American Census: Past Practices and Implications for the Future," *Annual Review of Sociology* 29 (2003): 566.

100 Ibid.

101 Nobles, *Shades of Citizenship*, 36–42.

102 For an extended discussion of Alabama law at this time, see Peter Wallenstein, "Race, Marriage, and the Law of Freedom: Alabama and Virginia, 1860s–1960s," *Chicago-Kent Law Review* 70 (1994): 377–389.

103 Sweet, Legal History of the Color Line, 205. Josiah Clark Nott et al., Types of Mankind, 80.

104 Nott et al., *Types of Mankind*, 80.

105 Count Arthur de Gobineau, *The Moral and Intellectual Diversity of Races, with Particular Reference to Their Respective Influence in the Civil and Political History of Mankind* (Philadelphia, PA: J. B. Lippincott & Co., 1856).

106 See Idus A. Newby, *Jim Crow's Defense: Anti-Negro Thought in America, 1900–1930* (Baton Rouge, LA: Louisiana State University Press, 1965), 9.

107 Ibid.

108 Zabel, "Interracial Marriage and the Law," 75–79.

109 State v. Gibson, 36 Ind. 389 (1871) (quoting W. Chester & P. R. Co. v. Miles, 55 Pa. 209 (1867)).

110 See, e.g., W. Chester & P. R. Co. v. Miles, 55 Pa. 209 (1867) (upholding a Pennsylvania anti-miscegenation statute); State v. Gibson, 36 Ind 389 (1871) (upholding an Indiana miscegenation statute); Kinney v. Commonwealth, 71 Va. (30 Gratt.) 858 (1878) (upholding a lower court's decision that the marriage between a black person and a white person conducted in Washington, DC, was void in the state of Virginia). The Alabama Supreme Court upheld an antimiscegenation statute in 1868. See Ellis v. State, 42 Ala. 525 (1868). This decision was handed down in June of 1868, before the 14th Amendment was certified on July 28, 1868. Thus, relying on the Civil Rights Act of 1866 and the 14th Amendment, four years later the Court reversed its decision in Ellis and declared that the state ban on interracial marriage was unlawful. Burns v. State, 48 Ala. 195, 197 (1872). However, in 1873, the Alabama Supreme Court reversed itself again and held that Congress did not intend the Civil

Rights Act of 1866 to overturn anti-miscegenation laws. Green v. State, 58 Ala. 190 (1877).
111 W. Chester & P. R. Co. v. Miles, 55 Pa. 209 (1867).
112 W. Chester & P. R. Co., 55 Pa. 209, 213.
113 Pace v. Alabama, 106 U.S. 583 (1883).
114 See also Rachel F. Moran, *Interracial Intimacy: The Regulation of Race and Romance* (Chicago, IL: University of Chicago Press, 2001), 17.
115 Ibid.
116 John G. Mencke, *Mulattoes and Race Mixture: American Attitudes and Images, 1865–1918* (Ann Arbor, MI: UMI Research Press, 1979), 39.
117 John S. Haller, Jr., *Outcasts from Evolution: Scientific Attitudes of Racial Inferiority, 1859–1900* (Carbondale, IL: Southern Illinois University Press, 1971), 21.
118 Sanford B. Hunt, "The Negro as a Soldier," *Anthropological Review* 7 (January 1869): 49–50.
119 Ibid., 51.
120 Ibid., 52.
121 Ibid.
122 Cedric J. Robinson, *Forgeries of Memory and Meaning: Blacks and the Regimes of Race in American Theater and Film before World War II* (Chapel Hill, NC: University of North Carolina Press, 2007), 120.
123 Benjamin Apthorp Gould, *Investigations in the Military and Anthropological Statistics of American Soldiers* (New York: Hurd and Houghton, 1869), 471.
124 Ibid., 319.
125 Jedediah H. Baxter, Statistics, *Medical and Anthropological, of the Provost-Marshal-General's Bureau: Derived From Records of the Examination for Military Service in the Armies of the United States During the Late War of the Rebellion of Over a Million Recruits, Drafted Men, Substitutes, and Enrolled Men* (Washington, DC: Government Printing Office, 1875).
126 Haller, Jr., *Outcasts From Evolution*, 29.
127 Ibid.
128 Nathaniel Southgate Shaler, *The Neighbor: The Natural History of Human Contacts* (Boston, MA: Houghton, Mifflin and Co., 1904), 135.
129 Ibid., 162.
130 Nathaniel Southgate Shaler, "An Ex-Southerner in South Carolina," *Atlantic Monthly* 26 (July 1870): 57. For further discussion of the Gilded Age perception of mulattoes, see generally Mencke, *Mulattoes and Race Mixture*.
131 Haller, Jr., *Outcasts from Evolution*, 30.
132 Joseph LeConte, *The Race Problem in the South* (New York: Appleton, 1892), reprint available at http://ia600504.us.archive.org/0/items/raceprobleminsou00lecorich/raceprobleminsou00lecorich.pdf.
133 Joseph LeConte, "The Genesis of Sex," *Popular Science Monthly* 16 (December 1879): 167; "The Effect of Mixture of Races on Human Progress," *Berkeley Quarterly* 1 (April 1880): 89–90.
134 Haller, Jr., *Outcasts from Evolution*, 161.
135 Frederick L. Hoffman, *Race Traits and Tendencies of the American Negro* (New York: Macmillan, 1896), 184.
136 Ibid., 206–207.
137 Herbert Hovenkamp, "Social Science and Segregation Before *Brown*," *Duke Law Journal* 34 (1985): 655.
138 Mencke, *Mulattoes and Race Mixture*, 38.
139 Haller, Jr., *Outcasts From Evolution*, 131.
140 Mencke, *Mulattoes and Race Mixture*, 37.

141   Ibid.
142   Sweet, *Legal History of the Color Line*, 318–319.
143   Nobles, *Shades of Citizenship*, 72.
144   Brown, 347 U.S. 483.
145   See Gary Orfield and Susan E. Eaton, *Dismantling Desegregation: The Quiet Reversal of Brown v. Board of Education* (New York: New Press, 1996).
146   Regents of the Univ. of Calif. v. Bakke, 438 U.S. 265, 407 (1978).
147   Brown, 347 U.S. 483.
148   At the time, seventeen states mandated segregation and four permitted segregation. Diane Ravitch, *The Troubled Crusade: American Education, 1945–1980* (New York: Basic Books, 1983), 127.
149   Brown, 347 U.S. 483, 493–494.
150   Brown, 347 U.S. 483, 494 (quoting Brown v. Board of Educ., 98 F.Supp. 797 [D. Kan. 1951]) (emphasis added).
151   Brown, 347 U.S. 483, 494 n. 11.
152   President Lyndon B. Johnson, *To Fulfill These Rights*, Commencement Address at Howard University (June 4, 1965).
153   Green v. Cnty. Sch. Bd. of New Kent Cnty., 391 U.S. 430 (1968).
154   See, e.g., Swann v. Charlotte-Mecklenburg 402 U.S. 1 (1971) and Keyes v. Sch. Dist. No. 1, 413 U.S. 189 (1973).
155   William G. Bowen and Derek Bok, *The Shape of the River* (Princeton, NJ: Princeton University Press, 1998), 4.
156   Ernest Gellhorn, "The Law Schools and the Negro," *Duke Law Journal* 17 (1968): 1077–1085.
157   Bowen and Bok, *The Shape of the River*, 5–6.
158   Ibid., 7.
159   Barbara A. Noah, "A Prescription for Racial Equality in Medicine," *Connecticut Law Review* 40 (2008), 698–699.
160   See, e.g., Steelworkers v. Weber, 443 U.S. 193 (1979) and Wygant v. Jackson Bd. of Educ., 476 U.S. 276 (1986).
161   See e.g., Fullilove v. Klutznick, 448 U.S. 448 (1980); Adarand Constructors, Inc. v. Pena, 515 U.S. 200 (1995); and Metro. Broad., Inc. v. F.C.C., 497 U.S. 547 (1990).
162   Chandler Davidson and Bernard N. Grofman, *Quiet Revolution in the South: The Impact of the Voting Rights Act, 1965–1990* (Princeton, NJ: Princeton University Press, 1994), 30.
163   Ibid., 25.
164   Griggs v. Duke Power Co., 401 U.S. 424 (1971).
165   Derrick Bell, *Race, Racism, and American Law,* 6th edition (New York: Aspen Publishers, 2008), 178.
166   The Court would later restrict the use of disparate impact under Title VII in Wards Cove Packing Co. v. Antonio 490 U.S. 642 (1989). Congress would partially restore the Griggs standard when it passed the Civil Rights Act of 1991. For a discussion of the Civil Rights Act of 1991, see Bell, *Race, Racism, and American Law*, 196–208.
167   Alexander v. Sandoval, 532 U.S. 275, 275 (2001).
168   Lau v. Nichols, 414 U.S. 563 (1974).
169   Lau, 414 U.S. 563, 568.
170   Beer v. United States, 425 U.S. 130 (1976).
171   See Katherine K. Wallman, Suzann Evinger, and Susan Schechter, "Measuring Our Nation's Diversity: Developing a Common Language for Data on Race/Ethnicity," *American Journal of Public Health* 90 (November 2000): 1704. Katherine K. Wallman directed the review of the standards.
172   Keyes v. Sch. Dist. No. 1, 413 U.S. 189, 198 (1973).

173   Keyes v. Sch. Dist. No. 1, 413 U.S. 189, 198 (1973). For an extensive treatment of Keyes and its relationship to equality of educational opportunity for Latinos, see Tom I. Romero, II, "La Raza Latina? Multiracial Ambivalence, Color Denial, and the Emergence of a Tri-Ethnic Jurisprudence at the End of the Twentieth Century," *New Mexico Law Review* 37 (2007): 263–270; see also Guadalupe Salinas, "Comment: Mexican-Americans and the Desegregation of Schools in the Southwest," *Houston Law Review* 8 (1971): 929; Gary A. Greenfield and Don B. Kates, Jr., "Mexican Americans, Racial Discrimination, and the Civil Rights Act of 1866," *California Law Review* 63 (1975): 692–693 n. 149.

174   Keyes v. Sch. Dist. No. 1, 413 U.S. 189, 198 (1973).

175   See Department of Education, "Final Guidance, on Maintaining, Collecting, and Reporting Racial and Ethnic Data to the U.S. Department of Education," *Federal Register*, 72, no. 202, 59266, 59270 (October 19, 2007).

176   See Wallman et al., "Measuring Our Nation's Diversity."

177   See Education Resources Information Center, "Report of the Ad Hoc Committee on Racial and Ethnic Definitions of the Federal Interagency Committee on Education" 8 (April 1975).

178   Ibid.

179   Rainier Spencer, *Spurious Issues: Race and Multiracial Identity Politics in the United States* (Boulder, CO: Westview Press, 1999), 42–43.

180   U.S. Census Bureau, "Directive No. 15 Race and Ethnic Standards for Federal Statistics and Administrative Reporting," as adopted May 12, 1977, http://wonder.cdc.gov/WONDER/help/populations/bridged-race/Directive15.html.

181   Ibid.

182   For a more complete retelling of the change of the name of Directive No. 15, see Rainier Spencer, *Spurious Issues,* 70–71.

183   Parents Involved in Cmty. Schs. v. Seattle Sch. Dist., 551 U.S. 701, 797 (2007).

184   Office of Management and Budget, "Revisions to the Standards for the Classification of Federal Data on Race and Ethnicity," 1997 (62 Fed. Reg. 58, 782), http://www.whitehouse.gov/omb/fedreg_1997standards.

185   The 1997 Revised Standards indicated that there should not be a "Some Other Races" category. However, the Census Bureau obtained a waiver of this provision for the purposes of the 2000 and 2010 census. The Bureau felt that Hispanics/Latinos were likely to use this designation. For purposes of the 2000 and 2010 census, individuals were not only required to respond to the question of whether they were Hispanic/Latino, but also allowed to designate all of the racial or ethnic categories that apply to them. The Census Bureau reported counts broken down by whether individuals were Hispanic/Latino or non-Hispanic and counts broken down by racial categories, including a separate category for those who marked more than one racial category. For a discussion of the 2000 census categories and counts, see Kevin Brown, "Should Black Immigrants Be Favored over Black Hispanics and Black Multiracials in the Admissions Processes of Selective Higher Education Programs?," *Howard Law Journal* 54 (2011): 283–285.

186   New Orleans City Park Improvement Ass'n v. Detiege, 358 U.S. 54 (1958) (per curiam).

187   Mayor of Baltimore v. Dawson, 350 U.S. 877 (1955) (per curiam).

188   Holmes v. Atlanta, 350 U.S. 879 (1955) (per curiam).

189   Gayle v. Browder, 352 U.S. 903 (1956) (per curiam) (buses).

190   Johnson v. Virginia, 373 U.S. 61 (1963) (per curiam) (courtrooms); Turner v. Memphis, 369 U.S. 350 (1962) (per curiam) (municipal airports).

191   McLaughlin v. State, 379 U.S. 184, 195–6 (1964).

192   Pace v. Alabama, 106 U.S. 583 (1883).

193 Loving v. Virginia, 388 U.S. 1 (1967). In 1924, Virginia adopted the Racial Integrity Act, which defined a person as white if they had "no trace whatsoever of any blood other than Caucasian; but persons who have only one-sixteenth or less of the blood of the American Indian . . . shall be deemed to be white persons." Virginia Act to Preserve Racial Integrity of 3/20/1924(1) ch. 371:535. A 1950 statute also defined as colored, anyone "in whom there is ascertainable any Negro blood." Va. Code §1–14 (1950) (repealed 2005).

194 The sixteen states were Alabama, Arkansas, Delaware, Florida, Georgia, Kentucky, Louisiana, Mississippi, Missouri, North Carolina, Oklahoma, South Carolina, Tennessee, Texas, Virginia, and West Virginia. Loving v. Virginia, 388 U.S. 1, 6 (1967).

195 Loving v. Virginia, 388 U.S. 1, 11 (1967).

196 Washington v. Davis, 426 U.S. 229 (1976).

197 Washington v. Davis, 426 U.S. 229, 260 (1976).

198 Washington v. Davis, 426 U.S. 229, 245 (1976).

199 Arlington Heights v. Metro. Hous. Dev. Corp., 429 U.S. 252 (1977).

200 Miller v. Johnson, 515 U.S. 900, 911 (1995) (striking down a redistricting plan motivated by a desire to maximize the number of majority minority legislative districts without discriminating against any individual white voter or whites as a group).

201 Regents of Univ. of California v. Bakke, 438 U.S. 265 (1978).

202 Guardians Ass'n v. Civil Serv. Comm'n, 463 U.S. 582 (1983).

203 Guardians Ass'n, 463 U.S. 582, 610–11 (Powell, J., joined by Burger, C. J., and Rehnquist, J., concurring in judgment); 463 U.S. 582, 612 (O'Connor, J., concurring in judgment); 463 U.S. 582, 642 (Stevens, J., joined by Brennan and Blackmun, J. J., dissenting). See also, Alexander v. Sandoval, 532 U.S. 275 (2001) (concluding that there are no private rights of actions to enforce the discriminatory effects regulations under Section 602).

204 See San Antonio Indep. Sch. Dist. v. Rodriguez, 411 U.S. 1, 29 (1973).

205 For example, selective colleges and universities are still able to use racial classifications in an individualized admissions process to obtain a critical mass of underrepresented minorities with a history of discrimination. Grutter v. Bollinger, 539 U.S. 306, 334 (2003) ("We find that the Law School's admissions program bears the hallmarks of a narrowly tailored plan"). In addition, the government can still employ racial classifications in an effort to remedy identified acts of discrimination. City of Richmond v. J. A. Croson Co., 488 U.S. 469, 493 (1989). In the summer of 2007, Justice Kennedy wrote the deciding opinion in Parents Involved in Community Schools v. Seattle School District No. 1, 551 U.S. 701, 782–98 (2007) (Kennedy, J., concurring in part and concurring in judgment) (accepting that school officials are free to devise various race-conscious measures that don't employ individual racial classifications in order to pursue integrated schools).

206 Regents of Univ. of California v. Bakke, 438 U.S. 265 (Stevens, J., Burger, C. J., Stewart, J., and Rehnquist, J., concurring in the judgment in part and dissenting in part).

207 Regents of Univ. of California v. Bakke, 438 U.S. 265, 397 (Brennan, J., White, J., Marshall, J., and Blackmun, J., dissenting).

208 Regents of Univ. of California, 438 U.S. 265, 291 (Powell, J.).

209 Regents of Univ. of California, 438 U.S. 265, 293 (Powell, J.).

210 Regents of Univ. of California , 438 U.S. 265, 306 (Powell, J.).

211 Wygant v. Jackson Bd. of Educ., 476 U.S. 276 (1986). This opinion was a plurality opinion written by Justice Powell and joined by Burger and Rehnquist. Justice O'Connor joined all but Section IV of the opinion and wrote a separate concurrence. Justice White made the fifth person in the majority. His separate opinion concurring

in judgment simply stated that the layoff policy was no different than discharging whites and hiring blacks until the suitable percentage of blacks in the workforce was achieved.

212   Richmond v. J. A. Croson, 488 U.S. 469 (1989).

213   Metro Broad., Inc. v. F.C.C., 497 U.S. 547 (1995).

214   See Metro Broad. Inc. v. F.C.C., 497 U.S. 547 (1990) (holding that the federal government's use of racial classifications for benign purposes only needs to satisfy intermediate scrutiny).

215   Miller v. Johnson, 515 U.S. 900 (1995).

216   Grutter v. Bollinger, 539 U.S. 306 (2003).

217   Gratz v. Bollinger, 539 U.S. 244, 270 (2003).

218   Parents Involved v. Seattle Sch. Dist., 551 U.S. 701 (2007).

219   Miller v. Johnson, 515 U.S. 900, 911 (1995).

220   Parents Involved in Cmty. Schs. v. Seattle Sch. Dist., 551 U.S. 701, 748 (2007).

221   See Fisher v Texas, 631 F.3d 213 (5th Cir.), cert. granted, 132 S. Ct. 1536 (2012).

222   Shelby Cnty. v. Holder, 679 F.3d 848 (D.C. Cir. 2012), cert. granted, (Feb. 2013) (No. 12–96, OT 2012 Term).

223   See Campbell Gibson and Kay Jung, "Historical Census Statistics on Population Totals by Race, 1790 to 1990, and by Hispanic Origin, 1970 to 1990, for the United States, Regions, Divisions, and States" (United States Census Bureau, Working Paper Series No. 56, 2002), http://www.census.gov/population/www/documentation/twps 0056/twps0056.html - intro. The instructions for those enumerators stated: Document3zzF27350110108"A person of mixed white and Negro blood was to be returned as Negro, no matter how small the percentage of Negro blood." Snipp, "Racial Measurement in the American Census," 568.

224   See Karen R. Humes, Nicholas A. Jones, and Roberto R. Ramirez, "2010 Census Briefs, Overview of Race and Hispanic Origin: 2010, 4 Table 1" (March 2011), available at http://www.census.gov/prod/cen2010/briefs/c2010br-02.pdf.

225   Margo J. Anderson and Stephen E. Fienberg, Who Counts? The Politics of Census-Taking in Contemporary America (New York: Russell Sage Foundation, 2001), 29–30.

226   Snipp, "Racial Measurement in the American Census," 569.

227   See Sharon M. Lee and Barry Edmonston, "New Marriages, New Families: U.S. Racial and Hispanic Intermarriage," Population Bulletin 60 (June 2005): 9, available at http://www.prb.org/pdf05/60.2NewMarriages.pdf.

228   See Wallman et al., "Measuring Our Nation's Diversity."

229   Wendy D. Roth, "The End of the One-Drop Rule? Labeling of Multiracial Children in Black Intermarriages," Sociological Forum 20 (March 2005): 35.

230   For a listing of the steps taken, see Office of Management and Budget, "Revisions to the Standards for the Classification of Federal Data on Race and Ethnicity," 1997 (62 Fed. Reg. 58, 782), available at http://www.whitehouse.gov/omb/fedreg_ 1997standards.

231   See Wallman et al., "Measuring Our Nation's Diversity."

232   This effort was opposed by black civil rights leaders, such as Jesse Jackson, Kweisi Mfume (representing the Congressional Black Caucus), and representatives of the NAACP. Civil rights groups were concerned that the addition of a multiracial category would increase the difficulty of collecting accurate data on the effects of discrimination and thereby undercut enforcement of discrimination laws. Kerry Ann Rockquemore and David Brunsma, Beyond Black: Biracial Identity in America (Thousand Oaks, CA: Sage Publications, 2002), 1. The American MultiEthnic Association was the product of an effort to provide a multiracial option on official forms, including census forms. For a comprehensive history of the movement, see Naomi Mezey, "Erasure and Recognition: The Census, Race and the National Imagination," Northwestern University Law Review 97 (2003): 1749–1752.

233 Kim M. Williams, *Mark One or More: Civil Rights in Multiracial America* (Ann Arbor, MI: University of Michigan Press, 2006), 15.

234 Ibid.

235 Williams, *Mark One or More*, 112.

236 Rockquemore and Brunsma, *Beyond Black*, 1–17.

237 Office of Management and Budget, "Revisions to the Standards for the Classification of Federal Data on Race and Ethnicity," 1997 (62 Fed. Reg. 58, 782), available at http://www.whitehouse.gov/omb/fedreg_1997standards.

238 The Department of Justice began to include counts of persons that self-identified in two or more racial categories in their data starting in 2001. The Department of Commerce, Department of Agriculture, and the Federal Reserve Board started to comply in 2002. And the Department of Health and Human Services and Defense changed its data collection process in 2003. Jennifer L. Hochschild, Vesla M. Weaver, and Traci R. Burch, *Creating a New Racial Order: How Immigration, Multiracism, Genomics, and the Young Can Remake Race in America* (Princeton, NJ: Princeton University Press, 2012), 58–59.

239 The Equal Employment Opportunities Committee submitted revisions to the EEO-1 report to OMB in November of 2005 and OMB approved it. See Agency Information Collection Activities, "Notice of Submission for OMB Review; Final Comment Request to the Equal Employment Opportunity Commission," 2005 (70 Fed. Reg. 71,294, 71,296). The Department of Education did so in 2007; see Department of Education, "Final Guidance, on Maintaining, Collecting, and Reporting Racial and Ethnic Data to the U.S. Department of Education," *Federal Register*, 2007 (Vol. 72, No. 202, 59266, 59270).

240 Under these federal requirements, those who indicate that they are Hispanic/Latino are not included in this "Two or More Races" category.

241 See CensusScope, "United States Multiracial Profile," last visited January 31, 2013, http://www.censusscope.org/us/print_chart_multi.html.

242 Humes et al., "2010 Census Briefs."

243 Ibid. In addition, another 3 percent of those who indicated black alone also indicated that they were Hispanic/Latino. There were 42,020,743 black alone reported on the 2010 census and 1,243,471 black alone individuals who also indicated that they were Hispanic/Latino (1,243,471/42,020,743 = 2.959 percent). Ibid.

244 Kevin Brown and Tom I. Romero, II, "The Social Reconstruction of Race & Ethnicity of the Nation's Law Students: A Request to the ABA, AALS, and LSAC for Changes in Reporting Requirements," *Michigan State Law Review 2011* (2011): 1174.

245 Ibid.

246 See Pew Research Center, "Almost All Millennials Accept Interracial Dating and Marriage," last modified February 1, 2010, http://pewresearch.org/pubs/1480/millennials-accept-interracial-dating-marriage-friends-different-race-generations.

247 Lee and Edmonston, "New Marriages," 12.

248 See Wendy Wang, "The Rise of Intermarriage: Rates, Characteristics Vary by Race and Gender," *Pew Social and Demographic Trends* (Washington: Pew Research Center, 2012), 9, http://www.pewsocialtrends.org/files/2012/02/SDT-Intermarriage-II.pdf. For black men, these represent substantial increases from the 15.7 percent figure in 2000 and 7.9 percent in 1980. While it also increased for black women, the increase went from 7.1 percent in 2000 and 3.0 percent in 1980. See Jeffrey Passell, Wendy Wang and Paul Taylor, "Marrying Out: One-in-Seven New U.S. Marriages is Interracial or Interethnic," *Pew Social and Demographic Trends* (Washington, DC: Pew Research Center, 2010), 11–12, http://pewresearch.org/pubs/1616/american-marriage-interracial-interethnic. With respect to blacks having a white spouse, more

recent statistics show a similar trend. In 2010, 8.5 percent of married black men had white spouses, an increase from 6.6 percent in 2005. U.S. Census Bureau, "America's Families and Living Arrangements," last visited January 31, 2013, http://www.census.gov/hhes/families/. On the other hand, only 3.9 percent of black women were married to white men, an increase from 2.8 percent in 2005. According to a *New York Times* article, intermarriage between blacks and whites "make up 1 in 60 new marriages today, compared with fewer than 1 in 1,000" a half a century ago. Sam Roberts, "Black Women See Fewer Black Men at the Altar," *The New York Times*, June 4, 2010, A12.

4

A DARKER SHADE OF PALE REVISITED

Disaggregated Blackness and Colorism in the "Post-Racial" Obama Era

Taunya Lovell Banks

The election of Barack Hussein Obama as the forty-fourth president of the United States suggests that conventional notions of blackness are being disaggregated. The old hypodescent rule has lost its power to define who is black and who is not, especially for light-skinned black Americans and individuals with some African ancestry and one white parent. Further, conventional racial designations today may be less important than factors such as skin tone, especially when combined with traditional tropes of high-status whiteness like elite education, stable family structure, high socioeconomic status, and "command of spoken English." Empirical research suggests the existence of a small group of light-skinned black elites that dates back to the antebellum era who were able to accumulate and pass on small amounts of wealth. The intergenerational transfer of even small amounts of wealth created opportunities for their descendants not available to most black Americans. Today, these descendants still benefit from the advantages created as a result of light skin tone and relative economic success. This group and the mixed-race children of one white parent are posed to move beyond unitary blackness into a middle group between white and most black Americans. The movement away from unitary blackness may result in a pigmentocracy that reinforces whiteness even as the country becomes less white. One byproduct of this change is that racial inequality between those raced as white and black will become more severe. Twentieth-century antidiscrimination laws that treat blackness as one-dimensional are ill equipped to combat more subtle race-based discrimination. This chapter explores whether skin tone, rather than racial classification or racial self-identification, will, in the near future, determine who gets better access to quality education, jobs, and real power in America; in other words, does color and socioeconomic status, more than old racial classification schemes, matter in the "post-racial" Obama era and, if so, what are the legal implications of this development?

Introduction

In 1961, writer and public intellectual James Baldwin, remarking on whether America would ever elect a black president, said that the more interesting question is "what kind of country he'll be president of."[1] Forty-seven years later Barack Hussein Obama, the son of a white woman from Kansas and a black man from Kenya, was elected the forty-fourth president of the United States. Thus, it seems appropriate to explore Baldwin's implicit question about the significance of race in the country President Obama now governs.

Ironically, Barack Obama was elected president of the United States at a time when the racial gaps in income and employment were increasing,[2] and these gaps continued through the third year of his presidency.[3] Still, the income gap between whites and blacks is narrower than it was in 1954 when the Supreme Court struck down racial segregation laws.[4] Nevertheless, a significant gap in black–white wealth persists. The racial inequality between black and white wealth is the result of the "continuing significance of racial discrimination,"[5] what some scholars call "smiling racism,"[6] which impacts some black Americans harder than others.[7] Yet suggestions for closing this gap that depend on class-based analyses or structural inequalities fail to factor in the correlation between wealth and race-related factors, such as skin tone bias, which continue to favor light-skinned black and multiracial Americans with some African ancestry.

In 2003 when the U.S. Supreme Court upheld the use of race in law school admissions to achieve racial diversity in *Grutter v. Bollinger,* Justice Sandra Day O'Connor wrote in her majority opinion, that "[r]ace-conscious admissions policies must be limited in time . . . [Adding, w]e expect that 25 years from now, the use of racial preferences will no longer be necessary to further the interest approved today."[8] She and other members of the Supreme Court were acutely aware of the glaring educational inequities in public education that dispropor-tionately affected nonwhite children and made meaningful racial diversity in race-blind admissions impossible in Michigan.[9] Nonetheless, Justice Ruth Bader Ginsburg, in her concurring opinion, wrote: "Despite these inequalities, *some* minority students are able to meet the high threshold requirements set for admis-sion to the country's finest undergraduate and graduate educational institu-tions."[10] Undoubtedly, most of those children come from the small class of elite blacks who, like their white counterparts, had the benefit of good schooling and comfortable homes. In failing to acknowledge the reasons for the historical advantages that distinguish this privileged group of black Americans from their less fortunate racial group members, Justice Ginsburg and the others effectively perpetuated race-based inequalities that date back to the slave era.

Given the dismal state of America's urban public schools where the poorest black (and Latina/o) children are educated,[11] it is highly unlikely that most of these children will be able to gain entry and afford to attend elite colleges or universities. Yet the laws addressing race discrimination fail to draw meaningful distinctions between race, skin tone, white parentage, and wealth, and they do not consider what the absence of these advantages means for the life chances of these children in this allegedly post-racial country.[12]

Today some scholars argue that traditional racial boundaries are fading[13] with the increasing numbers of multiracial individuals, the result of both growing rates of intermarriage, and migration from the Caribbean, Latin America, Africa, and Asia.[14] As a result, they argue, America will experience a kind of racial stratification similar to Latin American countries, where racial lines always appeared more fluid.[15] Unlike the past, having some African ancestry will not automatically result in an individual being raced as black. Instead, America will see "the development of race and racial categories . . . based on allocations of power and privilege."[16] If this is the direction in which public concepts of racial differences are moving, then racial discrimination will not disappear, but rather it will become more difficult to apply traditional legal standards. Thus closer examination of racial dynamics in the Obama era is warranted.

This chapter explores whether skin tone, coupled with high socioeconomic status, rather than traditional racial classification or self-identification, will determine who gets quality education, high-paying jobs, and access to real power in America and who gets left behind. In other words, whether color matters in the "post-racial" Obama era more than old racial classification schemes and, if so, what are the legal implications of this development in the quest for social justice. Proponents of the post-racial ideology see racial discrimination as a thing of the past and attribute persistent inequality to the failure of individuals to take personal responsibility for their lives. Absent more critical analysis of how skin tone differences among blacks advantages some and disadvantages others, more affluent black Americans who benefited because of light skin tone or white parentage will be used as the measures of black mobility in the United States. Their success will stand as proof that America is post-racial. The resulting economic and social consequences of this misperception may be severe for dark-skinned Americans.

Colorism: A Few Caveats

A few caveats are needed when discussing skin tone. Skin tone differences are relative. There may be significant disagreement about what constitutes skin tone difference, even within a racialized group. Skin tone measurement may be egocentric, in that a dark-skinned member of a racialized group may judge the skin tone of another member based on his or her own skin tone.[17] Thus, a dark-skinned black person might rate another as lighter than the rating given by a light-skinned black person. Further, in-group notions of skin tone may differ from the perceptions of people outside this group.[18]

Because "skin color measurement scales may be relative and self-referenced," social psychological research consistently demonstrates individual tendencies to understate variation among members of other groups with which they have limited experience.[19] The implications of these distinctions by outsiders can be significant. Consider, for example, the 1981 Title VII employment race discrimination claim brought by Carmen Felix, a mixed-race Puerto Rican, whom the federal district judge described as "a medium shade," whereas Ms. Felix described herself as "dark olive."[20] The trial judge ruled in Felix's favor, noting that Felix's maternal grandfather was black, and that her father "had the physical characteristics of a person with a partial African ancestry."[21] Had the judge accepted Felix's characterization of her skin tone, he may have treated her lawsuit as a dispute between two "white" Latinas/os. In discussing this case a decade ago, I wrote:

> The judge's characterization of Felix as of a medium shade suggests that her complexion is medium brown, and brown skin tone has a distinct racial connotation in the United States: it means nonwhite. However, the term "olive," used by Felix is often used to describe Southern Europeans like Italians or other European ethnic groups considered white in the United States.[22]

A final caveat: Colorism (the preference for light skin tones) explored in this chapter differs from situations where people classified as black "cover" or hide their blackness[23] or "whiten" their résumés.[24] Rather, the colorism practices discussed in this chapter focus on how *other people* see and react to black (and other nonwhite) people based on skin tone and phenotypical characteristics.

Changing Notions of Blackness in America: The Obama Example

Barack Obama has been widely touted inside and outside the country as its first "black" president; nevertheless, many Americans do not consider him black, in the historic sense of the term. Under the hypodescent or one-drop rule, President Obama is raced as black despite his mixed parentage, because historically any *known* African ancestry makes one black in the United States. Yet, according to a 2010 report on racial attitudes by the Pew Research Center,

> Americans tend to construct their own view of [President] Obama's race based on their backgrounds . . . 55 percent of black respondents said Obama is black, . . . a third said he is mixed race. Among whites, the pattern is reversed. Fifty-three percent said he is mixed race, . . . just a quarter said he is black. Hispanics were even more inclined than whites to see him as mixed race; 61 percent identified him that way.[25]

Yet the persistence of the hypodescent rule, at least among the power elite, is reflected in a comment about Obama's perceived racial identity attributed to Senate Majority Leader Harry Reid, a Democrat from Nevada. In their book

Game Change, about the election of then-Senator Obama to the U.S. presidency, journalists Mark Halperin and John Heilemann write that Senator Reid, while pushing Obama to run for the presidency, privately described him as a "light-skinned African American" "with no Negro dialect, unless he wanted to have one,"[26] someone who would appeal to white voters. Reid's comment seems to confirm a long-held suspicion of many black Americans that some whites prefer "light-skinned" blacks over their dark-skinned counterparts.

Despite Reid's characterization of Obama as black, and even though the President self-identified as black on the 2010 Census form,[27] barely a quarter of white voters in 2008 considered him black. Perhaps it is his interracial parentage that causes some white Americans to reject the black racial label. During the 2008 presidential race, readers of nationally syndicated columnist Clarence Page, a black American, wrote asking him to stop calling Obama "black" because of his interracial parentage.[28]

As several scholars and political observers suggest, blacks as a racialized group are becoming disaggregated, "separate[d] into component parts,"[29] at least in the minds of some nonblacks.[30] The old hypodescent rule is losing its almost-absolute power to define someone with even minuscule African ancestry as black. Today Barack Obama might be classified by others, including black Americans, as a black American, a light-skinned black American, or as a bi/multiracial individual—part of what sociologist Haywood Horton calls the *neo-mulatto* class.[31] President Obama also is free to self-identify in other ways as well.[32] In the words of historian Jacqueline Jones, "perhaps it is mainly the prejudices of whites, and not the self-identity of blacks, that makes 'race' today."[33] Nevertheless, as economist William Darity and his coauthors note: "[t]he construction of racial identity is the result of both intra- and inter-group interactions . . . [We] allow individuals to pursue either a racialist or an individualist strategy in social interactions . . . Individualists attempt to live as though they are race-free, even though their 'phenotype' is in fact observable and has consequences."[34]

The possibility of racial stratification in the United States means the decreased importance of ascribed traits such as race, ethnicity, and even religion, and the increased importance of "achieved traits (earned education, occupational status)" that reduce the social distance between whites and nonwhite groups or individuals.[35] Earned education, for example, is a more important signifier of "status exchange, where caste status is traded for class status" for black than for Asian Americans.[36] Thus some scholars suggest that racial stratification rather than racial difference is a better method to study racial inequality in twenty-first-century America.[37] In other words, twenty-first-century scholars need to study "how racial stratification produces disparate outcomes among racialized groups"[38] and subgroups.

One likely subgroup suggested by an unexamined subtext of Senator Reid's comment is self-identified black Americans with elite educational credentials and high socioeconomic class status, credentials that when combined with light skin tones sometimes reduce the social distance between them and whites in America. Political scientist Melissa Harris-Perry (formerly Lacewell) wrote that President Obama, by "displaying all [the] tropes of traditional whiteness [elite education credentials, stable family, and 'command of spoken English' during his presidential campaign,] . . . disrupted the very idea of whiteness."[39] The idea that an individual with visible and acknowledged partial African ancestry can disrupt the idea of whiteness suggests that Obama's election to the American presidency signals a generational shift that reflects how we as a nation "race" individuals with some African ancestry.

This generational shift in racial attitudes also is occurring in black America. In 2007 the Pew Research Center found that "nearly four-in-ten African Americans (37 percent) say that blacks can no longer be thought of as a single race" because of increasing diversity within that community.[40] Unsurprisingly, perceptions about the irrelevance of traditionally assigned or imposed racial identity are stronger among younger black Americans, particularly those born after *Loving v. Virginia*,[41] who are more likely than their older counterparts to report that blacks in America are no longer a single race.[42] This willingness of younger self-identified black Americans to reject the externally (and internally) imposed hypodescent rule in the racialization of people with some African ancestry is further complicated by reports that many young black Americans no longer see race as the primary focus of their life.[43]

Much as sociologist William Julius Wilson predicted more than thirty years ago in his provocative book *The Declining Significance of Race*,[44] younger black Americans may see socioeconomic class rather than racial classification as a more important determinant of life chances in the United States. Many scholars and political pundits wistfully refer to this new era as *post-racial*, a time when the racial problems of the past have been left behind.[45] But others quickly add "that the postracial perspective typically does acknowledge that racial discrimination still exists" and that the post-racial label "tends to trivialize and downplay its significance."[46]

Sociologist Eduardo Bonilla-Silva calls the election of President Obama "part and parcel of the new racism,"[47] a phenomenon he calls "color-blind racism."[48] Two decades earlier, legal scholar Neil Gotanda invoked this term to describe the U.S. Supreme Court's use of a constitutionally "colorblind" legal jurisprudence to promote an ideology of white racial dominance.[49] Bonilla-Silva agrees, explaining that colorblind racism "[d]espite its suave, apparently nonracial character . . . is still about justifying the various social arrangements and practices that maintain white privilege."[50] Therefore, looking at racial permutations in early twenty-first-century America is especially important.

Skin Tone, Racial Stratification and Wealth

Most twentieth-century literature on skin tone discrimination focuses on the intra-racial phenomenon, how skin tone differences among black Americans impact in-group social interactions.[51] Economist Howard Bodenhorn, using census data on free black marriages gathered during the 1850, 1860, and 1870 censuses, concludes that during the antebellum period a small number of light-skinned people with African ancestry were better able to accumulate wealth than their dark-skinned counterparts.[52] Most were free blacks who had greater access to education, more remunerative jobs, and higher rates of land ownership than other blacks.[53] This group tended to intermarry, some scholars speculate, to preserve their wealth.[54] These opportunities translated into economic advantages for free light-skinned blacks during the period.[55] This wealth differential, Bodenhorn concludes, "has profound social and economic ramifications for black economic advancement."[56] Further, he writes that it is naïve to believe that this "complexion-based preference . . . would have persisted without reinforcement from the white community."[57]

Colorism practices within the black community during the antebellum era undoubtedly reflected white preferences about black Americans.[58] This light-skinned preference with its advantages continued after slavery ended, even in the segregated South.[59] In 1944, the Swedish economist Gunnar Myrdal, in his classic study of blacks in the United States, wrote: "without a doubt a Negro with light skin and other European features has in the North an advantage with white people when competing for jobs available to Negroes,"[60] adding, "actual quantitative correlation between class and color is not known."[61] Today some quantitative evidence suggests that there is a strong correlation between skin tone and socioeconomic class. One study found that although "the wages of whites were statistically significantly higher than light-skinned blacks . . . the wages of dark-skinned blacks were statistically significantly lower."[62] Thus, a disproportionate number of light-skinned men with skills and small amounts of property or money, now as in the past, were able to accumulate modest wealth—how much you own minus how much you owe.[63]

This transfer of wealth, even in small amounts, over generations mounts up[64] and translates into a tremendous advantage for descendants of privileged light-skinned black Americans. Economists Darrick Hamilton and William Darity, Jr. write:

> Wealth is a paramount indicator of social well-being. Wealthier families are far better positioned to finance elite independent school and college education; access capital to start a business; finance expensive medical procedures; reside in higher amenity neighborhoods; lower health hazards, etc.; exert political influence through campaign financing; purchase better counsel if confronted with the legal system; leave a bequest; and/or withstand financial hardship resulting from any number of emergencies.[65]

Most dark-skinned blacks did not share in the opportunity that some light-skinned blacks had to accumulate wealth in the mid-nineteenth century through the mid-twentieth century. The result is stratification among black Americans based on skin tone *and* class.

During the late nineteenth and most of the twentieth century, the rule of hypodescent kept all individuals with *known* African ancestry in a single category. Thus, the dominant culture confined this small group of light-skinned elites to a largely black world, socially and economically. Today, however, the situation is more complex. Individuals such as President Obama may be seen either as a light-skinned black elite or a biracial individual with one white parent. Arguably both categories have access to greater privileges than most dark-skinned blacks, but for the moment at least each grouping is somewhat differently situated.

Light-Skinned Black Elites in the Post-Civil Rights Era

Pondering the meaning of race in the colorblind post-civil rights era, a group of social scientists observed that the "familial socioeconomic advantages among African Americans with lighter skin tones . . . transferred across generations . . . [and was] reinforced by the socialization of related racial attitudes."[66] Undoubtedly, however, some dark-skinned blacks are represented among those affluent Americans whose children meet the high threshold requirements for admission to elite institutions of higher education—the gateway to success. Increased educational and occupational opportunities for black Americans following the civil rights era produced a small class of affluent black Americans of various skin tones, capable of providing their children with elite educations, downpayments on homes, and the prospect of transmitting significant wealth upon their death. Hence, today "skin tone may not operate the same way among more affluent African Americans who benefited most from the civil rights movement as among those who continue to face persistent underclass poverty."[67]

But, if the growing empirical evidence of light skin tone advantage is correct, black Americans with light skin tones are likely to account for a disproportionate percentage of these affluent black Americans. It is their children who are more likely to possess the academic credentials and financial means to attend elite colleges and universities. They benefit from primary and secondary educations that are substantially better than the vast majority of black Americans. Their socioeconomic background and educational credentials mirror those of white elites. These advantages transfer to the labor market.

Legal scholars Devon Carbado and Mitu Gulati argue that employers today often use a "variety of mechanisms to pick the most racially homogenized outsiders . . . whose performance of their racial identity suggests that they will fit comfortably within a workplace that is homogenized by the overwhelming presence of insiders."[68] These racial outsiders are assimilated in that they mirror the backgrounds, experiences, and perspectives of most white decision makers.[69] These racially homogenized outsiders sound like the light-skinned black elites described above. Arguably, the attractiveness of these assimilated racial outsider applicants is enhanced if they also physically look more like the white decision maker.

Assuming Carbado and Gulati accurately capture this phenomenon, insufficient attention has been paid to the reality that light-skinned blacks are represented disproportionately among elite blacks, and that racial outsiders without these attributes may be seriously disadvantaged. When measuring racial discrimination, existing laws tend to use "assimilated" minorities as a baseline.[70] Thus, if assimilated blacks are well represented in an employer's workforce, courts will have difficulty finding unlawful race discrimination. As I have argued for more than a decade, this subtle form of race discrimination represented by colorism practices is not captured by contemporary antidiscrimination laws.[71]

For the moment at least, racial and ethnic consciousness as well as affinity remain strong among black Americans, regardless of socioeconomic status and skin tone.[72] But there are signs of cracks in black group unity. A few scattered studies over the late twentieth century suggest that light-skinned affluent blacks have more assimilationist attitudes than dark-skinned impoverished blacks, who have a stronger sense of black consciousness or identity.[73] Whether the growing gap between affluent and impoverished black Americans will diminish the sense of group loyalty remains to be seen. More data is needed to confirm whether there is a real division and, if so, to explore the political, legal, social, and economic implications.

The Rise of Neo-Mulattoes

The issue of group identity and loyalty is even more complex for individuals with some African ancestry and one white parent. First, there is the question of identity, whether bi/multiracial individuals self-identify as black.[74] Second, identity issues may be further complicated by skin tone. Skin tone privilege may be even more pronounced for light-skinned individuals with one white parent.[75] The significance of having white parents in contemporary America should not be underestimated. Evidence suggests that having one white parent confers racial privilege even on self-identified black Americans that is similar to skin tone privilege.[76] Whites generally have higher incomes and greater wealth than blacks; therefore, mixed-race individuals with one white parent may benefit from skin tone privilege and the increased financial advantages of their white parent. Thus, they may be even more advantaged than light-skinned blacks without mixed parentage.

Implications

There may be some serious consequences if the late twentieth-century studies reflect perceptions among some Americans about the connections between skin tone and degree of assimilation into the dominant culture—individuals with light skin tones are perceived as more affluent and assimilated[77] and dark skin tones are more closely associated with impoverishment and strong black consciousness or racial identity.[78] One group of social scientists, looking backward and forward, offered this gloomy prediction for the twenty-first century:

> Historically, those with light skin tones may have been provided class advantages over those with darker skin, and these advantages may continue to be transferred to new generations . . . these historical . . . disparities may increasingly manifest themselves in a polarizing class structure. In turn, growing disparities between the post industrial poor and the most affluent may increasingly differentiate their racial attitudes.[79]

More importantly, from a legal perspective, unlike overt and intentional twentieth-century race discrimination models, discrimination based on skin tone or mixed-racial ancestry is difficult to combat. The few litigants who challenge employment discrimination in the courts based on skin tone or mixed-racial ancestry have had mixed success.[80] If a small, but growing body of empirical studies is correct in positing that, like most contemporary racial bias, most skin-tone bias is not only unintentional but automatic, the problem may be even more difficult because most antidiscrimination laws require proof of intentional discrimination.

Unintentional Racism Based on Skin Tone

As the twentieth century was ending, social scientists began to examine interracial colorism practices—discrimination or bias based on skin tone by people of difference racial classifications.[81] This growing body of empirical evidence suggests that white decision makers in all areas engage in implicit or unconscious discrimination against dark-skinned black Americans based on their skin tone.[82] Implicit bias is a mental process that occurs outside the consciousness of an individual.[83] This process is a function of implicit mental attitudes, biases, and stereotypical associations.[84]

Using the Implicit Bias Test (IAT)[85] empirical studies of race and skin tone "have consistently shown implicit associations between Black (or dark skin) and Bad, compared to White (or light skin) and Good."[86] Thus, if, as Senator Reid's comments suggest, whites respond more favorably to light-skinned blacks, their preference may reflect implicit more than explicit racialized biases. This unconscious preference for light-skinned individuals applies to Latinos/as as well as blacks.[87] The racially biased decision making in these cases is not intentional; thus, these decisions cannot be classified as "racist." Nevertheless, the people favored by these implicitly biased decisions, whether based on race or skin tone, unfairly "benefit from a system that differentially rewards and punishes society's members based on race."[88] In other words, people traditionally raced as black in America do not always experience race-based discrimination the same way and to the same extent. They can be differently racialized.

Colorism Examples

Because of the continuing power and wealth imbalance between whites and most nonwhites in the United States, the interracial preference for light-skinned nonwhites more negatively affects the life chances of dark-skinned individuals. Thus, interracial colorism is a serious race-based problem. It also is a confusing problem because it can coexist alongside more conventional forms of race-based discrimination.[89]

An employer who discriminates in hiring, preferring white applicants over equally qualified nonwhite applicants, is engaged in traditional race discrimination. If the same employer occasionally decides to hire a nonwhite applicant but prefers applicants with light skin tones over equally qualified dark-skinned applicants, she is engaged in colorism. Both practices are unfair and should be illegal. The first practice clearly is illegal under existing antidiscrimination laws, but courts remain confused about colorism practices in employment.[90] As mentioned earlier, under the existing legal regime, an employer who only hired light-skinned black Americans might be able to successfully argue that she is not engaging in impermissible race discrimination because she does not discriminate against people classified racially as black.

One possible outcome is that well-educated, high-status, affluent, light-skinned blacks (and other nonwhites) in the United States will become a buffer group, mediating the social and economic distances separating dominant whites from dark-skinned nonwhites. In other words, as some scholars predict, race in twenty-first-century America will mirror the racial hierarchies in Latin American countries like Brazil.[91] Further, not only skin tone, but cultural, ethnic, and socioeconomic differences, will more openly influence how people with some African ancestry, recent or remote, are perceived and treated by the dominant culture in the United States.[92] This result is an example of the harmful effects of black racial dis-aggregation.

Two Unscientific Case Studies

This chapter ends with two incidents that illustrate the possible disaggregation of blackness. The first incident supports Eduardo Bonilla-Silva's thesis that the racial category "black" will be expanded to include other nonwhites who will become part of a "collective black" category. The second incident suggests that almost simultaneously elite light-skinned blacks and neo-mulattoes are being perceived as separate from collective blacks, although not quite white.

Collective Blackness: The Miller Valley Elementary School Incident

The 2010 controversy about a mural commissioned by the Miller Valley Elementary School in Prescott, Arizona, is an example of the new, more nuanced twenty-first-century racial bias. After a city councilman denounced the mural's "prominent portrayal of ethnic minorities," school officials asked the mural painter "to lighten the skin of children depicted."[93] The city council member, who was white, was especially distressed about the mural's "main figure, a dark-skinned boy." He complained publicly: "To depict the biggest picture on that building as a black person, I would have to ask the question, 'Why?'" Ironically, the painter intended the main figure to represent a Mexican-American child.

The council member's reaction, while telling, is subject to multiple inter-pretations. First, this might be an instance where race and colorism are conflated—dark skin seen as synonymous with blackness—the traditional racial category. But since the child portrayed in the mural was meant to be a Mexican American, the city council member's comments also could be interpreted to mean that blackness in America is no longer confined to persons with some African ancestry.[94] Rather, as Bonilla-Silva argues, blackness in the twenty-first century encompasses other dark-skinned nonwhites, who he calls "collective blacks."[95] He includes dark-skinned Latinas/os in this category.[96]

However one interprets the Miller Valley Elementary School incident, the council member's bias against individuals with dark skin tone reflects empirical studies suggesting that skin tone bias is a race-related problem that affects not only dark-skinned black Americans, but all individuals with dark skin tones, even whites (although to different degrees).[97] The Miller Valley Elementary School incident aside, today's racial designations for individuals classified as African American/Black, as defined by the U.S. Office of Management and Budget (OMB)'s Directive No. 15,[98] may be less important than factors such as skin tone, especially when combined with traditional tropes of high-status whiteness. As the next section suggests, light-skinned and bi/multiracial individuals with some African ancestry, recent or remote, are more likely to possess the traditional signifiers of high-status whiteness than their dark-skinned counterparts.

The New York Times Magazine *and Obama's (Black) People*

Since who is black may, as Bonilla-Silva suggests, be expanding to include members of previously nonblack racial minorities, it is important to get a better idea of which black Americans may be moving out of the traditional black group—in other words, which black Americans are more likely to possess the tropes of high-status whiteness and thus decrease their social distance to white Americans. As mentioned previously, black Americans of all skin tones benefited economically and educationally during and immediately following the civil rights era (1960s and 1970s). The black middle class grew, as wealth, home ownership, income, and educational differences between whites and blacks narrowed considerably. Yet the preference by white Americans for light-skinned black Americans who also possess the traditional credentials of high-status whites may be more important as the levels of nonwhite access to power, political and economic, increases. This section looks at one incident that indirectly raises this question.

The January 14, 2009, inaugural photo issue of *The New York Times Magazine* was titled "Obama's People."[99] The selection of the fifty-four people to be photographed, according to the photographer, Nadav Kander, "was never intended to be comprehensive, but, rather [designed] to give a snapshot of a presidency in the ascendant."[100] So the photographer *and The New York Times*, not President Obama, identified these key advisers and officials in the Obama administration.

Looking through the photo array searching for black faces, only two of the eleven black people pictured—Rep. James Clyburn, then Democrat majority whip, an elected official, and Reggie Love, the personal aide to the president[101]— had dark skin tones. The nine other black members of "Obama's People" ranged in skin tone from very light to medium brown.[102] Looking at the educational credentials of these individuals, all but three of the eleven—South Carolina Representative James Clyburn, Chief of Staff Mike Strautmanis, and Melody Barnes, director of the Domestic Policy Council—attended Ivy League or other elite institutions such as Stanford or Duke. Many often had two degrees from these schools.

Not pictured were other dark-skinned black members of the Obama administration, such as: Surgeon General Regina Benjamin; Deputy White House Counsel Cassandra Butts, a very close friend of the president; or Van Jones, then the White House Council on Environmental Quality's special adviser for green jobs; and of course, Michelle Obama, the president's dark-skinned wife. Except for Butts, the rest have at least one degree from an elite university, and Michelle Obama has two, from Princeton and Harvard.

Who was selected, photographed, and displayed reflects the conscious, or perhaps unconscious, decisions of the photographer and *The New York Times Magazine* editor. Assuming a goal was to encourage white Americans to accept the new presidential administration, a conscious decision to display the light-skinned members of the Obama administration may explain the striking visual photo array. If so, this is an example of explicit bias. But if, on the other hand, there was no conscious effort to project a more light-skinned group of black Obama advisers, then the photo choices may reflect implicit skin tone bias. Either way, given what we know about the persistence of skin tone bias, the visual message is troubling.

Conclusion

Discussions about race and the relevance of race in the Obama era raise interesting questions about the status of people traditionally classified as black in America. A similar question was raised more directly by sociologist Sidney Willhelm shortly after the civil rights era ended in the late 1960s in his gloomy book titled *Who Needs the Negro?*[103] He argued that, given the lack of employment opportunities in postindustrial America, black Americans were becoming expendable—pushed to society's margins. Willhelm predicted that "illegal drugs [would] turn the ghettoized Negro into a virtual invalid."[104]

Today, decades of high unemployment rates, poor public schools, and illegal drugs have decimated many heavily black inner-city neighborhoods across the country. But another segment of black America thrived during the 1970s and 1980s. These black Americans benefited from the opportunities created by the civil rights era. Thus, it is no longer possible to speak of black Americans in a collective sense, at least with respect to class and location.

In 2000, Harvard sociologist Orlando Patterson, wrote that "[t]he racial divide that has plagued America . . . is fading fast—made obsolete by migratory, sociological, and biotechnological developments that are already underway."[105] In his essay titled "Race Over," he predicted four regionally based groups that "together will reshape the nation as a whole," replacing concerns about race with increasing class consciousness.[106] Scholars such as Patterson argue that conventional notions of race in the United States have been "destabilized" as a result of "increases in immigration, intermarriage, and cross-racial adoptions."[107] But what many scholars overlook is the impact of skin tone as an alternative means of racialized sorting as hybridity increases. Socioeconomic status and skin tone are related factors in determining who succeeds in America.

Bonilla-Silva argues that "Obama has reached the level of success . . . in large measure because he . . . made a *strategic* move toward racelessness and adopted a post-racial persona and political stance."[108] As this chapter suggests, although America is far from being post-racial, or even postblack, it is in the process of redefining individuals who historically were classified as black. Thus, someone such as Barack Obama—with elite credentials, whether considered a light-skinned black American or biracial—is perceived and treated differently than most black Americans by power elites, and some whites.

The statements of Senator Reid and the Prescott city council member suggest that white Americans are more comfortable with light-skinned blacks (and nonwhites). Consciously or unconsciously, some Americans also may prefer that the positive public face of American blackness not be *too* dark. Because evidence suggests that skin tone (and white parentage) rather than racial classification or racial self-identification is a key determinant of which nonwhites get education, jobs, and access to real power in America, one wonders whether color more than old racial classification schemes matters in the "post-racial" Obama era.

My fear is twofold: first, that people formally classified as black in the United States will internalize this disaggregation in the same way they internalized the hypodescent rule, yet more uncritically undercutting efforts to eliminate all forms of race-based discrimination; and second, that colorism practices, if not thwarted, will result in the United States becoming a pigmentocracy, where whiteness is on the top, and blackness, broadly defined to include other dark-skinned non-whites, is on the bottom. In the middle will be a broad and changing group of nonwhites—light-skinned Asian, Latina/o, black, and bi/multiracial individuals —whose quest for whiteness will reinforce this country's persistent ideology of white privilege.

Notes

1 James Baldwin, *The Cross of Redemption: Uncollected Writings* (New York: Pantheon, 2010) (citing a 1961 talk Baldwin gave at an event sponsored by the Liberation Committee for Africa).

2 In November 2009, the unemployment rate was 10.2 percent, the highest in more than twenty-five years. *White House Task Force on the Middle Class, Annual Report of the White House Task Force on the Middle Class* (Office of the Vice President, 2010), 3; Amaad Rivera and Others, *State of the Dream 2009: The Silent Depression* (Boston, MA: United for a Fair Economy, 2009), accessed June 14, 2012, http://www.faireconomy.org/files/pdf/state_of_dream_2009.pdf. The median income for whites in 2008 was $65,000, $39,879 for blacks, and $40,466 for Hispanics. In contrast, the median income for Asians was $73,578. *Table 696. Money Income of Families—Median Income by Race and Hispanic Origin in Current and Constant (2008) Dollars: 1990 to 2008*, U.S. Census Bureau, accessed June 14, 2012, http://www.census.gov/compendia/statab/2011/tables/11s0696.pdf. Legal scholar Robert Suggs writes: "Between 1970 and 1990 median black household incomes hovered near 60% of median white incomes." Robert E. Suggs, "Poisoning the Well: Law & Economics and Racial Inequality," *Hastings Law Journal* 57(2) (2005): 255.

3 Arthur Delaney, "Unemployment Rate to Remain Above 9 Percent through 2011, Will Remain Above 'Natural Rate' Until 2016: CBO," *Huffington Post*, January 26, 2011, updated March 25, 2011, http://www.huffingtonpost.com/2011/01/26/cbo-unemployment-rate-above-9-2016_n_814275.html. In late spring 2010, *The New York Times* ran a front-page series on the "new poor." One story focused on the decline in socioeconomic status of blacks in Memphis, Tennessee. After rising for several decades, the median income for black Memphis homeowners, exacerbated by unemployment and mortgage foreclosures, has plummeted to "roughly half that of white Memphis homeowners." Michael Powell, "Blacks in Memphis Lose Decades of Economic Gains," *The New York Times*, March 31, 2010, http://www.nytimes.com/2010/05/31/business/economy/31memphis.html?_r=1&scp=1&sq=memphis&st=cse.

4 The median income for whites in 1954 was $4,338 and $2,416 for blacks, almost two to one. *No. HS-25. Money Income of Families—Median Income in Current and Constant (2001) Dollars by Race and Type of Family: 1947 to 2001*, U.S. Census Bureau, accessed June 20, 2012, http://www.census.gov/statab/hist/HS-25.pdf.

5 Eduardo Bonilla-Silva, *Racism without Racists: Color-Blind Racism and the Persistence of Racial Inequality in the United States*, 3rd edition (Lanham, MD: Rowman & Littlefield, 2009), 210. For discussion of this point in the context of antidiscrimination law,

see Daira Roithmayr, "Them That Has, Gets," *Mississippi College Law Review* 27 (2007–2008): 373.

6   Bonilla-Silva, *Racism Without Racists*, 210 (citing Roy Brooks, *Atonement and Forgiveness: A New Model for Black Reparations* [Berkeley, CA: University of California Press, 1996]).

7   Bowman et al. write: "Despite the fact that the White-Black income and wealth gap continues . . . between the 1970s and 1990s there has been a clear 'increase in both the number of Black millionaires as well as persistent Black poverty.'" Phillip J. Bowman, Ray Muhammad, and Mosi Ifatunji, "Skin Tone, Class, and Racial Attitudes among African Americans," in *Skin Deep: How Race and Complexion Matter in the "Color Blind" Era*, eds Cedric Herring, Verna M. Keith, and Hayward D. Horton (Chicago, IL: University of Illinois Press, 2004), 131.

8   Grutter v. Bollinger, 539 U.S. 306, 342–43 (2003).

9   Justice Ruth Bader Ginsburg, concurring, writes that despite a "strong . . . public [ ] desire for improved education systems . . . it remains the current reality that many minority students encounter markedly inadequate and unequal educational opportunities." *Grutter*, 539 U.S. at 346.

10   Ibid. (emphasis added).

11   See generally, Gary Orfield and Chungmei Lee, *Why Segregation Matters: Poverty and Educational Inequality* (Cambridge, MA: Harvard Civil Rights Project, 2005), http://bsdweb.bsdvt.org/district/EquityExcellence/Research/Why_Segreg_Matters.pdf.

12   Sumi Cho defines post-racialism as "a twenty-first-century ideology that reflects a belief that due to the significant racial progress that has been made, the state need not engage in race-based decision-making or adopt race-based remedies, and that civil society should eschew race as a central organizing principle of social action." Sumi Cho, "Post-Racialism," *Iowa Law Review* 94 (2009): 1594.

13   See Jenifer L. Bratter and Tukufu Zuberi, "As Racial Boundaries 'Fade': Racial Stratification and Interracial Marriage," in *White Logic, White Methods: Racism and Methodology*, eds Tukufu Zuberi and Eduardo Bonilla-Silva (Lanham, MD: Rowman & Littlefield, 2008), 251.

14   Around the same time that *Loving* was decided, Congress reformed immigration laws removing the national origin quotas. Pub. L. No. 89–236, 79 Stat. 911 (codified as amended in scattered sections of 8 U.S.C.). As a result, more people with some African ancestry have entered this country over the past forty years than at any other time in our history. Sam Roberts, "More Africans Enter U.S. Than in Days of Slavery," *The New York Times*, February 21, 2005, A1. Many of their multiracial children are reaching adulthood as well.

15   Bratter and Zuberi, "As Racial Boundaries 'Fade'," 251.

16   Ibid., 252.

17   Mark E. Hill, "Race of the Interviewer and Perception of Skin Color: Evidence from the Multi-city Study of Urban Inequality," *American Social Review* 67 (2002): 100.

18   Ibid., 99. According to a study by social scientist Mark Hill: "[w]hite interviewers reported the skin tones of black respondents as substantially darker than did black interviewers . . . [B]lack interviewers categorized the skin tones of white respondents as much lighter than did white interviewers." Ibid.

19   Ibid., 100.

20   Felix v. Marquez, No. 78–2314, 1981 WL 275, at 8 (D.D.C. Mar. 26, 1981).

21   *Marquez*, No. 78–2314, 1981 WL 275, at 2.

22   Taunya Lovell Banks, "Colorism: A Darker Shade of Pale," *UCLA Law Review* 47 (2000): 1740–1741. A recent historical study of Dominicans deported by the United States between 1953 and 2004 found that "United States officials are more likely to describe Dominican deportees as possessing a medium complexion, or a shade thereof. United States officials used the variations of the medium color/racial category

in 64% of cases documented by this data." Charles R. Venator Santiago, *Dominican Deportees: Some Available Data for Further Research* (Storrs, CT: University of Connecticut, 2008), 18. In contrast, "the Dominican Consular Offices are more likely to use the category *Trigueño* or black to represent deportees. It is likely that Dominican officials will translate the racial category of medium as black or *Trigueño* rather than as Mulatto." Ibid.,19.

23 See, Kenji Yoshino, "Covering," *Yale Law Journal* 111 (2002): 772 ("Covering means the underlying identity is neither altered nor hidden, but is downplayed.").

24 For a discussion of this practice, see Michael Luo, "'Whitening' the Resume," *The New York Times*, December 6, 2009, Section WK. Final edition.

25 Pew Research Center, *A Year After Obama's Election: Blacks Upbeat About Black Progress, Prospects* (June 12, 2010), 59, http://pewsocialtrends.org/assets/pdf/blacks-upbeat-about-black-progress-prospects.pdf). This finding was widely reported in the national press. See, e.g., Krissah Thompson, "Poll: Feeling of Progress Rises Among African Americans," *Washington Post*, January 12, 2010.

26 John Heilemann and Mark Halperin, *Game Change: Obama and the Clintons, McCain and Palin, and the Race of a Lifetime* (New York: Harper Perennial, 2010), 36.

27 Melissa Harris-Lacewell, "Black by Choice," *Nation*, April 15, 2010, http://www.thenation.com/doc/20100503/harris-lacewell.

28 Clarence Page, "Obama Will Be Put to Test, and So Will We," *Baltimore Sun*. January 19, 2007, 11A.

29 Merriam Webster Dictionary, s.v. "disaggregate," http://www.merriam-webster.com/dictionary/disaggregate.

30 See, e.g., Eugene Robinson, *Disintegration: The Splintering of Black America* (New York: Doubleday, 2010) (arguing that black Americans are divided into four distinct groups based largely on socioeconomic status).

31 Hayward Derrick Horton, "Racism, Whitespace, and the Rise of the Neo-Mulattoes," in *Mixed Messages: Multiracial Identities in the "Color-Blind" Era*, ed. David L. Brunsma (Boulder, CO: Lynne Rienner, 2005), 117–119.

32 Consider, for example, President Obama's half-sister, Maya Soetoro-Ng, who self-identifies as "hybrid," "half white," and "half Asian." Ellen Goodman, Op-ed, "Transcending Race and Identity," *Boston Globe*, January 25, 2008, A19.

33 Jacqueline Jones, "Black Like Whom? In Search of a Shareable African-American History," *Slate*, http://www.slate.com/id/2243536 (reviewing Ira Berlin's *Making of African America*).

34 William A. Darity, Jr., Patrick L. Mason, and James B. Stewart, "The Economics of Identity: The Origin and Persistence of Racial Identity Norms," *Journal of Economic Behavior and Organization* 60 (2006): 301.

35 Bratter and Zuberi, "As Racial Boundaries "Fade," 253.

36 Ibid.

37 Ibid.

38 Tukufu and Bonilla-Silva, "Telling the Real Tale of the Hunt: Toward a Race Conscious Sociology of Racial Stratification," in *White Logic, White Methods: Racism and Methodology*, eds Tukufu Zuberi and Eduardo Bonilla-Silva (Lanham, MD: Rowman & Littlefield 2008), 329.

39 Harris-Lacewell, "Black by Choice."

40 Pew Research Center, "Blacks See Growing Values Gap Between Poor and Middle Class: Optimism About Black Progress Declines" (2007) 4, 24, http://pewsocialtrends.org/assets/pdf/Race.pdf (this survey was conducted in association with National Public Radio). The survey included "a nationally representative sample of 3,086 adults . . . [and] included an oversample that brought the total number of non-Hispanic black respondents to 1,007." Ibid., i. Only 53 percent of non-Hispanic black Americans polled thought that "blacks can still be thought of as a single race." Ibid., 24.

41 Loving v. Virginia, 388 U.S. 1 (1967).

42 Pew Research Center, note 40, 24.

43 Ibid.

44 William Julius Wilson, *The Declining Significance of Race* (Chicago, IL: University of Chicago Press, 1978).

45 See, e.g., Paul Gilroy, *Against Race: Imagining Political Culture beyond the Color Line* (Cambridge, MA: Belknap Press of Harvard, 2000); Antonia Darder and Rodolfo D. Torres, *After Race: Racism After Multiculturalism* (New York: NYU Press, 2004).

46 Darrick Hamilton and William Darity, Jr., "Can 'Baby Bonds' Eliminate the Racial Wealth Gap in Putative Post-Racial America?," *Review of Black Political Economy* 37 (2010): 208.

47 Bonilla-Silva, *Racism without Racists*, 208 n. 5.

48 Ibid.

49 Neil Gotanda, "A Critique of 'Our Constitution Is Color-Blind,'" *Stanford Law Review* 44 (1991): 1.

50 Bonilla-Silva, *Racism without Racists*, 211 n. 5.

51 Verna M. Herring and Cedric Herring, "Skin Tone and Stratification in the Black Community," *American Journal of Sociology* 97 (1991): 760; Howard E. Freeman, David Armor, J. Michael Ross, and Thomas F. Pettigrew, "Color Gradation and Attitudes among Middle-income Negroes," *American Sociological Review* 31 (1966): 365.

52 See, e.g., Bodenhorn, "Colorism, Complexion Homogamy, and Household Wealth," 256 (arguing that light-skinned "mulattoes" during the antebellum period tended to intermarry to keep wealth within the family and this trend applied to both the Lower and Upper South).

53 Ibid., 256–257; Howard Bodenhorn and Christopher S. Ruebeck, "Colourism and African-American Wealth: Evidence from the Nineteenth-century South," *Journal of Population Economics* 20 (2007): 601–602.

54 Bodenhorn, "Colorism, Complexion Homogamy, and Household Wealth," 257 n. 2 (citing Mancus Olson, *The Rise and Decline of Nations: Economic Growth, Stagflation, and Social Rigidities* [New Haven, CT: Yale Press, 1982]). A few empirical studies suggest that, historically, black women seemed disproportionately affected by this practice because successful black men of every hue preferred black women with light skin tones. Mark E. Hill, "Color Differences in the Socioeconomic Status of African American Men: Results of a Longitudinal Study," *Social Forces* 78 (2000): 1437; William B. Gatewood, *Aristocrats of Color: The Black Elite, 1880–1920* (Fayetteville, AR: University of Arkansas Press, 2000); Michael Hughes and Bradley F. Hertel, "The Significance of Colour Remains: A Study of Life Chances, Mate Selection, and Ethnic Consciousness among Black Americans," *Social Forces* 68 (1990): 1105. A more recent study, using data from the *Multi City Study of Urban Inequality* (New York: Russell Sage Foundation, 1997), suggests that, as the number of marriageable men declines, skin tone and "superficial" characteristics become more important to men seeking high-status black wives. Darrick Hamilton, Arthur H. Goldsmith, and William Darity Jr., "Shedding 'Light' on Marriage: the Influence of Skin Shade on Marriage for Black Females," *Journal Economic Behavior and Organization* 72 (2009): 30.

55 Howard Bodenhorn, "The Complexion Gap: The Economic Consequences of Color among Free African Americans in the Rural Antebellum South," *Advances in Agricultural Economic History* 2 (2003): 41.

56 Bodenhorn, "Colorism, Complexion Homogamy, and Household Wealth," 260 n. 52.

57 Howard Bodenhorn, "The Mulatto Advantage: The Biological Consequences of Complexion in Rural Antebellum Virginia," *Journal of Interdisciplinary History* 2 (2002): 23.

58 In the 1950s black social scientist E. Franklin Frazier, in a study of the black middle class, wrote (E. Franklin Frazier, *Black Bourgeoisie* [New York: Simon & Schuster, 1957], 135):

> Since the Negro's black skin was a sign of the curse of God and of his inferiority to the white man, therefore a light complexion resulting from racial mixture raised a mulatto above the level of the unmixed Negro. Although mulattoes were not always treated better than the blacks, as a rule they were taken into the household or were apprenticed to a skilled artisan. Partly because of the differential treatment accorded the mulattoes, but more especially because of general degradation of the Negro as a human being, the Negro of mixed ancestry thought of himself as being superior to the unmixed Negro. His light complexion became his most precious possession.

Skin color, however, did not overcome the stigma of race. Frazier continues, "In some parts of the South [mulattoes] constituted a sort of lower caste, since no matter how well they might be economically, they always bore the stigma of Negro ancestry." Ibid., 137. Nevertheless, Frazier "viewed color as an indication of . . . opportunity, acculturation, education, and wealth." Gatewood, *Aristocrats of Color*, 149 n. 54 (citing Frazier, *Black Bourgeoisie*, 405–406).

59 Victoria E. Bynum, "'White Negroes' in Segregated Mississippi: Miscegenation, Racial Identity, and the Law," *Journal of Southern History* 64 (1998): 247.

60 Gunnar Myrdal, *An American Dilemma: The Negro Problem and Modern Democracy* (New York: Harper & Bros., 1944), 697. Commenting more broadly he wrote (ibid.):

> Mixed bloods have always been preferred by the whites in practically all respects. They made a better appearance to the whites and were assumed to be mentally more capable. They had a higher sales value on the slave market . . . Many white fathers freed their illegitimate mulatto offspring . . . , or gave them the opportunity to work out their freedom on easy terms. Some were helped to education and sent to the free states in the North. Some were given a start in business or helped to acquire land . . . [While] emancipation broadened the basis for a Negro upper class . . . blackness of skin remained undesirable and even took on an association of badness.

61 Ibid., 698.

62 Arthur H. Goldsmith, Darrick Hamilton, and William Darity, Jr., "From Dark to Light Skin Color and Wages among African-Americans," *Journal of Human Resources* (2007): 707 (using data from the *Multi City Study of Urban Inequality* [1997] and the *National Survey of Black Americans* [1979]). Using data from the 2002 Survey of Income and Program Participation some scholars estimate that the median household net worth for white families is approximately $90,000 as compared with $4,000 for black families. Hamilton and Darity, Jr., "Can 'Baby Bonds' Eliminate the Racial Wealth Gap in Putative Post-Racial America?," 210. Another estimate approximates the median white household wealth at $76,519 as compared with $10,329 for black households. Darity, Jr., Mason, and Stewart, "The Economics of Identity," 284 n. 7.

63 On a more fundamental level, Regina Austin defines wealth as "what is left over after the bills are paid." Regina Austin, "Nest Eggs and Stormy Weather: Law, Culture and a Black Woman's Lack of Wealth," *University of Cincinnati Law Review* 65 (1996–1997): 771.

64 For a discussion of this point see John H. Langbein, "The Twentieth-century Revolution in Family Wealth Transmission," *Michigan Law Review* 86 (1988): 722. Law Professor Palma Stand writes: "The wave of racialized wealth owned by the parents of the baby boom generation is currently washing over the baby boomers in an enormous intergenerational transfer of wealth." Palma Joy Strand, "Inheriting

Inequality: Wealth, Race and the Laws of Succession," forthcoming *Oregon Law Review* (2010), 4, http://works.bepress.com/cgi/viewcontent.cgi?article=1005&context= palma_strand (citing Melvin L. Oliver, Thomas M. Shapiro, and Julie E. Press, "'Them That's Got Shall Get': Inheritance and Achievement in Wealth Accumulation," in *Research and Politics in Society: The Politics of Wealth Inequality*, eds Richard E. Ratcliff, Melvin L. Oliver, and Thomas M. Shapiro (Greenwich, CT: JAI Press, 1995).

65 Hamilton and Darity, Jr., 210 n. 21.

66 Bowman, Muhammad, and Ifatunji, "Skin Tone, Class, and Racial Attitudes among African Americans," 149 n. 7.

67 Ibid., 131. "Blacks who occupy the top ten percent of income earners live lives that are, according to standard indicators, indistinguishable from those of the white middle class." Audrey G. McFarlane, "Operatively White? Exploring the Significance of Race and Class through the Paradox of Black Middle-Classness," *Legal & Contemporary Problems* 72 (2009): 183 (citing Karyn R. Lacy, *Blue Chip Black: Race, Class and Status in the New Black Middle Class* [Berkeley, CA: University of California Press, 2007], 73).

68 Devon Carbado and Mitu Gulati, "The Law and Economics of Critical Race Theory," *Yale Law Journal* 112 (2003): 1765.

69 Ibid., 1810–1811.

70 Ibid., 1757.

71 See Banks, "A Darker Shade of Pale," 1740–1741 n. 32.

72 Bowman, Muhammad, and Ifatunji, "Skin Tone, Class, and Racial Attitudes," 146.

73 Ibid., 149 (studies cited omitted).

74 For a discussion of this point, see David L. Brunsma and Kerry Ann Rockquemore, "The New Color Complex: Appearances and Biracial Identity," *Identity: International Journal of Theory & Research* 1 (2001): 225.

75 For an interesting study of mixed-race college students' attitudes about racial identity, see Nikki Khanna and Cathryn Johnson, "Passing as Black: Racial Identity Work among Biracial Americans," *Social Psychology Quarterly* 73 (2010): 380.

76 See, e.g., Margaret Hunter, "The Persistent Problem of Colorism: Skin Tone, Status, and Inequality," *Sociology Compass* 1 (2007): 237.

77 Bowman, Muhammad, and Ifatunji, "Skin Tone, Class, and Racial Attitudes," 149 n. 7 (study citations omitted).

78 Ibid.

79 Ibid., 150.

80 For a discussion of this point see, Trina Jones, "Intra-Groups Preferences: Problems of Proof in Colorism and Identity Performance Claims," *N.Y.U. Review of Law & Social Change* 34 (2010): 657 (exposing the unique challenges that plaintiffs face in proving intragroup claims and proposing some changes). Employers settled in two early twenty-first-century cases claiming race discrimination by biracial (black-white) employees. In EEOC v. Bolling Steel Co., Civ. Action No. 7:06–00586 (W.D. Va. April 25, 2007), the director of EEOC's Richmond Virginia office said: "The EEOC will actively enforce Title VII's prohibitions of discrimination on the often intersectional bases of race [black-white] and color [brown], especially as our society continues to evolve as a melting pot of people of mixed race and ethnicity." "Agency Lawsuits: Racial Harassment EEOC Sues Steel Contractor for Harassment of Biracial Worker," *EEOC Compliance Manual*, October 30, 2006, available on LEXIS. In EEOC v. Jefferson Pain & Rehabilitation Center, No. 03-cv-1329 (W.D. Pa. settled March 10, 2004) the employer refused to address complaints by a white-looking employee who was harassed by a coworker who learned that she was biracial (black-white). According to the complaint, the coworker said, among other things, "Well, Vicky, you don't look black and you don't act black. Why do you even tell people

that you are?" Jim McKay, "EEOC Charges 2 Firms with Bias: AK Steel, Jefferson Pain Center Named," *Pittsburgh Post-Gazette*, September 10, 2003, Section B1.

81 See, e.g., Joni Hersch, "Profiling the New Immigrant Worker: The Effects of Skin Color and Height," *Journal of Labor Economics* 26 (2008): 345; Jennifer L. Hochschild and Vesla Weaver, "The Skin Color Paradox and the American Racial Order," *Social Forces* 86 (2007): 643; Arthur H. Goldsmith, Darrick Hamilton, and William Darity, Jr., "Shades of Discrimination: Skin Tone and Wages," *American Economic Review* 96 (2006): 242.

82 See, e.g., Justin D. Levinson and Danielle Young, "Different Shades of Bias: Skin Tone, Implicit Racial Bias, and Judgment of Ambiguous Evidence," *West Virginia Law Review* 112 (2010): 308 (skin tone affects how jurors assess ambiguous evidence and innocence); Kristin A. Lane et al., "Implicit Social Cognition and Law," *Annual Review of Law and Social Science* 3 (2007): 435–437; Cindy D. Kam, "Implicit Attitudes, Explicit Choices: When Subliminal Priming Predicts Preference," *Political Behavior* 29 (2007): 345; Taunya Lovell Banks, "Multi-Layered Racism: Courts' Continued Resistance to Colorism Claims," in *Shades of Difference Why Skin Color Matters*, ed. Evelyn Nakano Glenn (Palo Alto, CA: Stanford University Press, 2009).

83 See Anthony G. Greenwald and Mahzarin R. Banaji, "Implicit Bias Social Cognition: Attitudes, Self Esteem and Stereotypes," *Psychological Review* 102 (1995): 4. More specifically, implicit bias is the result of "introspectively unidentified (or inaccurately identified) traces of past experience that mediate in favorable or unfavorable feeling, thought, or action toward social objects." Ibid., 8.

84 Anthony G. Greenwald and Linda Hamilton Kreiger, "Implicit Bias: Scientific Foundations," *California Law Review* 94 (2006): 946.

85 The most widely used measure of implicit racial bias is the Implicit Association Test that "basically measures the relative strength of associations between pairs of concepts." Jeffrey J. Rachlinski and Gregory S. Parks, "Implicit Bias, Election '08, and the Myth of a Post-Racial America," *Social Science Research Network* (August 17, 2009), 21, http://papers.ssrn.com/sol3/papers.cfm?abstract_id=1456509.

86 Levinson and Young, "Different Shades of Bias," 320 n. 81 (citing Brian Nosek et al., "Pervasiveness and Correlates of Implicit Attitudes and Stereotypes," *European Review of Social Psychology* 18(36) [2008]: 36).

87 See Christina Gomez, "The Continual Significance of Skin Colour: An Exploratory Study of Latinos in the Northeast," *Hispanic Journal of Behavioral Science* 22 (2000): 94; Edward Murguia and Edward E. Telles, "Phenotype and Schooling among Mexican Americans," *Sociology of Education* 69 (1996): 276; Edward E. Telles and Edward Murguia, "Phenotypic Discrimination and Income Differences among Mexican Americans," *Social Science Quarterly* 71 (1990): 682.

88 Hayward Derrick Horton, "Rethinking American Diversity: Conceptual and Theoretical Challenges for Racial and Ethnic Demography," in *American Diversity: A Demographic Challenge for the Twenty-First Century*, eds Nancy A. Denton and Steart E. Tolnay, (Albany, NY: State University of New York Press, 2002), 262.

89 Banks, "Colorism: A Darker Shade of Pale," 1740–1741 n. 22.

90 Ibid.; Banks, "Multi-Layered Racism"; Trina Jones, "Shades of Brown: The Law of Skin Color," *Duke Law Journal* 49 (1999): 1487; Trina Jones, "The Case for Legal Recognition of Colorism Claims," in *Shades of Difference*; Trina Jones, *Intra-Groups Preferences: Problems of Proof in Colorism and Identity Performance Claim*; Tanya Kateri Hernandez, "Latinos at Work: When Color Discrimination Involves More Than Color Claims," in *Shades of Difference Why Skin Color Matters*. Banks, "Multi-Layered Racism," 216–219 n. 82; Trina Jones, "Shades of Brown: The Law of Skin Color," *Duke Law Journal* 49 (1999): 1487; Trina Jones, "The Case for Legal Recognition of Colorism Claims" in *Shades of Difference*, 229–32 n. 82; Trina Jones, "Intra-Groups Preferences: Problems of Proof in Colorism and Identity Performance

Claims," ns 80, 19–20; Tanya Kateri Hernandez, "Latinos at Work: When Color Discrimination Involves More Than Color Claims" in Shades of Difference Why Skin Color Matters, note 82: 237–41.

91 See, Tanya Kateri Hernandez, "To Be Brown in Brazil: Education & Segregation Latin American Style", *N.Y.U. Review of Law & Social Change* 29 (2004–2005): 683.

92 For a discussion of the negative impact of these practices out in Latin America, see Tanya Kateri Hernández, *Racial Subordination in Latin America: The Role of the State, Customary Law and the New Civil Rights Response* (New York: Cambridge University Press 2012).

93 Hugh Collins, "Mural Ignites Debate on Race, Censorship in Arizona," *AOLNews*, June 5, 2010, http://www.aolnews.com/2010/06/05/school-mural-ignites-debate-on-race-censorship-in-arizona/.

94 Although there are Afro-Mexicans, some indigenous people in Mexico also have dark skin tones. See Taunya Lovell Banks, "Unreconstructed Mestizaje and the Mexican Mestizo Self: No Hay Sangre Negra, So There is No Blackness," *Southern California Interdisciplinary Law Journal* 15 (2006): 199.

95 Bonilla-Silva, *Racism without Racists*, 179 n. 20.

96 Ibid., 180. Other groups in Bonilla-Silva's "Collective Blacks" category include Vietnamese Americans, Filipino Americans, Hmong Americans, Laotian Americans, Blacks, New West Indian and African Immigrants and Reservation-bound Native Americans. Ibid.

97 See Irene v. Blair, Charles M. Judd, and Kristine M. Chapleau, "The Influence of Afrocentric Facial Features in Criminal Sentencing," *Psychological Science* 15 (2004): 674 (controlling for crime and prior criminal background, skin tone rather than race affects criminal sentences for dark-skinned whites, Latinos, and blacks).

98 The American Anthropological Association describes OMB Directive 15 as follows:

> The Statistical Policy Division, Office of Information and Regulatory Affairs, of the Office of Management and Budget (OMB) determines federal standards for the reporting of "racial" and "ethnic" statistics. In this capacity, OMB promulgated Directive 15: Race and Ethnic Standards for Federal Statistics and Administrative Reporting in May, 1977, to standardize the collection of racial and ethnic information among federal agencies and to include data on persons of Hispanic origins, as required by Congress.
>
> Directive 15 is used in the collection of information on "racial" and "ethnic" populations not only by federal agencies, but also, to be consistent with national information, by researchers, business, and industry as well.
>
> Directive 15 described four races (i.e., American Indian or Alaskan Native, Asian or Pacific Islander, Black, and White) and two ethnic backgrounds (of Hispanic origin and not of Hispanic origin). The Directive's categories allowed collection of more detailed information as long as it could be aggregated to the specified categories.

American Anthropological Association Response to OMB Directive 15: Race and Ethnic Standards for Federal Statistics and Administrative Reporting (Sept 1997), accessed July 6, 2010, http://www.aaanet.org/gvt/ombdraft.htm.

99 Nadav Kander, "Obama's People," *The New York Times Magazine: Special Inauguration Issue*, http://www.nytimes.com/packages/html/magazine/2009-inauguration-gallery/index.html.

100 These photographs, accompanied by a commentary, also were published by the UK's *The Guardian*. "Obama's People by Nadav Kander," *The Guardian*, August 29, 2009, http://www.guardian.co.uk/world/gallery/2009/aug/30/barack-obama-photography.

101 Although this position involves close access to the president, it is not a policy-making or policy-influencing position. A *New York Times* article describes a presidential

personal aide as a man "who shadows the senator and anticipates everything he needs—and everything he does not need. He is not a bodyguard (security is provided by the Secret Service), but rather the ultimate assistant, rarely more than a body length away from the candidate." Thus a presidential personal aide is analogous to a celebrity's personal assistant, a gofer. Ashley Parker, "On the Court and on the Trail, One Aide Looms Over Obama," *The New York Times*, May 27, 2008, http://www.nytimes. com/2008/05/27/us/politics/27reggie.html?pagewanted=all&_r=0).

102 The nine other blacks photographed were: Alabama Congressman Arthur Davis; Attorney General Eric Holder; Mona Sutphen, deputy White House chief of staff; Susan Rice, UN ambassador; Chief of Staff Mike Strautmanis; Melody Barnes, director, Domestic Policy Council; Desiree Rogers, White House social secretary; Valeria Jarrett, senior adviser; and Patrick Gaspard, political affairs director. "Obama's People," n. 99.

103 See, generally, Sidney M. Willhelm, *Who Needs the Negro?* (Cambridge, MA: Schenkman, 1970).

104 Ibid., 234. Willhelm speculated that "the Negro may very well come to be treated much as the American Indian: confined to reservations or perhaps eliminated through genocide." Ibid., 3. As the twentieth century ended, another sociologist, reflecting on Willhelm's prediction, opined that urban ghettoes operate much like reservations, only these sites are "controlled by increasingly heavy structures of repression." John Brown Childs, "Toward Trans-Community, the Highest Stage of Multiculturalism: Notes on the Future of African-Americans," *Social Justice* 20 (1993): 35.

105 Orlando Patterson, "Race Over," *The New Republic*, January 10, 2000, 6.

106 Ibid. In the far West, "[a] hybrid population, mainly Eurasian—but with a growing Latin element—will come to dominate the middle and upper classes . . . Lower-class Caucasians, middle-class racial purists, and most African Americans, under pressure from an endless stream of unskilled Mexican workers, will move away. Those African Americans who remain will be rapidly absorbed into the emerging mixed population." Ibid. The other systems include: the "Caribbean-American system" centered in Florida but with "colonies" along the Northeast, that is, primarily Afro-Latin and whose culture incorporates Latin notions of *blanqueamiento* (whitening by marrying lighter-skinned or white spouses as a means of moving up the social hierarchy); the "Atlanta" pattern in the Southeast, where whites and blacks will cling to old "notions of racial purity and . . . remain highly (and voluntarily) segregated from each other"; and the last system that Patterson characterizes as "the most problematic . . . emerging in the Northeast and [the industrial] Midwest . . . [where] the economic situation for all classes of African Americans and native-born Latinos is likely to deteriorate," and where lower-class white Americans will be similarly affected. The result will be class solidarity that transcends race along with intermarriage and miscegenation. Ibid.

107 For a discussion and critique of these arguments, see David Roediger, "The Retreat from Race and Class," *Monthly Review* 58 (July–August 2006), http://monthlyreview. org/0706roediger.htm.

108 Ibid., 219 (emphasis in the original).

5

COLORISM AND INTERRACIAL INTIMACY

How Skin Color Matters

Kellina M. Craig-Henderson

Introduction

In the past two decades, research in the social sciences has considered the unique way that interracial intimacy can serve as an important metric for the quality of race relations in society.[1] For example, among ethnic minorities, involvement in intimate interracial relationships has long been recognized as an indicator of their structural and political participation within society. Indeed, a historical analysis of immigration rates and assimilation for most ethnic and racial newcomers to the United States suggests that interracial intimacy that is institutionalized in "mixed marriages" represents an important strategy toward full participation and freedom within U.S. society.[2]

The present chapter focuses on interracial intimacy as an option for African Americans who have experienced the problem of colorism. It examines the impact of colorism in African American motives to establish interracial romantic relationships. Although there are many reasons why one chooses to marry out, this chapter focuses on at least two reasons why African Americans might pursue interracial intimacy. In addition to love, some African Americans pursue interracial intimacy because they prefer mates with lighter skin tones. In contrast, others pursue interracial intimacy because they wish to avoid the problems of colorism by disassociating from other African Americans. Very little empirical work has addressed the topics of colorism and interracial intimacy simultaneously, even though the general issue of color complexion would seem to be an obvious feature in African Americans' decisions to "cross the color line."

For some people, interracial intimacy represents an ideal way of avoiding the psychological baggage of race consciousness. These people wish to avoid any reference to color complexion and regard participation in interracial relationships as a way of doing so. For other African Americans, who have internalized the negative attitudes associated with colorism, interracial intimacy provides a salutary way of being with those they most prefer—people with lighter-skinned complexions. Drawing from the literatures in social psychology and sociology, the present discussion compares the "fit" of two distinct hypotheses for why black people might consciously elect to participate in interracial intimacy. The chapter concludes by suggesting several directions for future research on the relationship between colorism and interracial intimacy.

Overarching Impact of Skin Color in Racial Impressions

What is it about racial status and skin color that makes it such a powerful determinant of interracial intimacy? While there are any number of correlates to racial status that are likely to exert an influence on the likelihood of intermarriage, in particular, and interracial intimacy, more generally (e.g., cultural preferences, socioeconomic differences), the present discussion focuses on the *role of skin color* in either facilitating or inhibiting interracial intimacy for African Americans. Skin color is the most visible and noticeable aspect of racial status in the United States.[3] It immediately cues thoughts about ancestry and heritage, as well as it activating the perceiver's stereotypes and expectations about behavior and competency.[4] Skin color differentiates members of different racial groups from one another, and it also serves to distinguish among members within racial groups.[5] In order to advance understanding of the continuing significance of skin color within and among African Americans, this chapter focuses upon the experience of interracial intimacy among members of this group. In doing so, it delineates several research questions, which, when taken together, outline a fruitful course for research in this area.

Although immigration and intermarriage have occurred for many different groups of people over many different years, there has been relatively little scholarly attention devoted to the topic and far less analysis that examines its connections to one of America's earliest "immigrant" groups—namely, African Americans. Clearly, the process of assimilation for African Americans (and the more recently arrived immigrants who hail from Africa, Asia, and Latin America) has progressed differently from that which characterized the experience of European whites.[6] For African Americans and a number of those who make up the most recent immigrants to the United States, racial status distinguishes them from Europeans and apparently makes intermarriage far less likely than what occurred between the European immigrants and "native" whites.[7]

Although African Americans have the dubious distinction of being the most negatively stereotyped racial group,[8] there are reasons to believe that these negative stereotypes are on the wane.[9] Consider the fact that, although 66 percent of whites who were surveyed in 1990 rated whites as harder working than blacks, this percentage declined steadily until 2006, when the figure was 43 percent.

In addition, the belief that blacks are less intelligent than whites has also declined from 57 percent in 1990 to just more than 25 percent in 2006.

Of course, results of surveys like this show that, while there has clearly been a decline in the numbers of whites who harbor negative beliefs about African Americans, still nearly a quarter continue to do so. Moreover, even with the popularity of the mythologized notion that America has evolved to become a post-racial nation, there is evidence that more subtle measures of racial attitudes reveal more widely shared negative perceptions about African Americans.[10] In contrast to some of the survey work described above, this work suggests that negative stereotypes continue to influence people's thoughts about race and racial groups.[11] Research that employs subtle measures to effectively mine the content of individuals' beliefs about racial groups reveals that African Americans are viewed far less positively than other surveyed racial groups.

Importantly, to a large degree social science research conducted in the United States that systematically examines racial perceptions has focused primarily, though not exclusively, upon whites. We know most about the attitudes that white Americans have concerning other racial groups. This is a consequence of the fact that a majority of researchers who raise questions like this, and who pursue this line of research, are white and so are interested in their own social group.[12] In addition, we also know most about the racial attitudes that whites have relative to others because they comprised the overwhelming majority at the time that this type of research was first initiated early in the 1930s.[13] This state of affairs is changing and may account for a gradual increase in research that examines racial attitudes of other racial and ethnic groups.[14]

As far as attitudes about other ethnic groups go, what appears to have improved are the racial norms dictating what thoughts are acceptable to disclose rather than the content of those thoughts. Thus, because of prevailing social norms that advocate the absence of racial bigotry, public expressions of racial attitudes may at times be disingenuous. When asked about their racial attitudes, many people feel compelled to respond in ways reflecting either no or very little racial prejudice, even though they may in fact harbor negative racial attitudes or strong feelings of racial antipathy.

People's attitudes influence their behaviors and actions. Indeed, the various approach and avoidance motives resulting from our attitudes operate as strong predictors for whether we will decide to approach or avoid another person. It is in this way that attitudes about race in general and skin color in particular can be influential in determining whether a person pursues or participates in an interracial romantic relationship.

Interracial Intimacy and Marriage in the United States

Objective reports about the frequency of interracial intimacy in the United States are primarily limited to information about interracial marriages. Indeed, it has only been within the 2010 census that rates for those who are living together and who are not married have been recorded. The U.S. Census Bureau has recorded rates of black/white interracial marriages for most of the second half of the twentieth century, and before that time rates of interracial marriage can also be gleaned from as far back as the 1850 census.[15] In 1960, when every southern state had a law against interracial marriage, the U.S. census documented 51,409 black–white couples in the United States.

A cursory review of census reports reveals that the number of African Americans in these types of marriages has increased overall, although not consistently, since rates have been recorded.[16] The greatest increases in rates have occurred since the 1967 landmark Supreme Court ruling in *Loving v. Virginia*,[17] which struck down legal restrictions on interracial marriage. The U.S. census records reveal 310,000 interracial marriages in 1970, 651,000 in 1980, and 1,161,000 by 1992. In 2010, there were more than 4,000,000 couples married interracially across all recorded racial groups in the United States.[18]

It is worth noting that as a group African Americans participate in interracial marriages less frequently than most other racial groups in the United States. In addition, rates of involvement for African American men and women are very different. Although rates of involvement for both men and women have increased, black men have outpaced black women in terms of their participation in interracial intimacy.[19] More black men are in intimate interracial relationships than black women, and this is reflected in the rates of marriage recorded by the U.S. Census Bureau. For example, figures from the 2010 decennial census reveal that, whereas 168,000 marriages were reported to include an African American woman and a white man, there were 390,000 that included an African American man and a white woman. In the United States, black men are more than twice as likely to be in interracial marriages than are black women.

As suggested above, census records provide only a snapshot of the extent of interracial intimacy because they are limited to marriage reports and, more recently, rates of cohabitation. It was only in 2007 that the Current Population Survey of the Census Bureau began measuring rates of cohabitation directly. Thus, census records should be regarded as conservative estimates of the actual extent of interracial intimacy that occurs in the United States. Indeed, research suggests that the numbers of people who "date" interracially far exceed those who marry or live together.[20]

Interracial marriage, particularly when it involves blacks and whites, is more widely accepted in the United States than ever before, although it continues to be an "attention elicitor," and there are periodic news reports of brutality directed at interracial couples in the United States.[21] Most current surveys and polls of American attitudes toward interracial relationships reveal an increasing acceptance of them. According to Gallup, although fewer than half of Americans approved of interracial marriage as recently as 1994, a more recent 2011 poll revealed that 86 percent of those surveyed expressed approval of interracial marriages between blacks and whites.[22] To be sure, there has been a decline in the numbers of people who express rejection or disagreement with interracial marriage. Gallup has been surveying Americans about their reactions to interracial marriage for fifty years. Figures 5.1 and 5.2, provided by Gallup in 2011, show the observed trends in attitudes to interracial marriage. Figure 5.1 depicts the increase in approval over time, whereas Figure 5.2 shows the relative rate of increase over time for blacks and whites. There is very clearly an increasing acceptance of interracial marriage between blacks and whites, a type of pairing that has historically elicited the most contention.[23]

Researchers studying changes in acceptance of interracial marriage have also focused on racial differences in family reaction to the interracial marriage of their relatives. Not surprisingly, African Americans have historically responded more positively to interracial unions than whites. In my own research investigating the experiences of African American men who "marry out," with one exception I consistently found that the men's families overwhelmingly supported their decisions.[24] Whereas the African American families accepted the decision of their family members to be in an intimate relationship with someone from another racial group, the families of the women they married were not always supportive. Indeed, quite a few of the men that I spoke with acknowledged having little to

■ % Approve

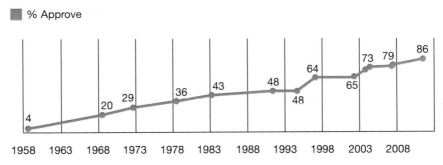

1958 1963 1968 1973 1978 1983 1988 1993 1998 2003 2008

FIGURE 5.1 Do you approve or disapprove of marriage between blacks and whites?

Percentage who approve

■ Blacks ▨ Whites

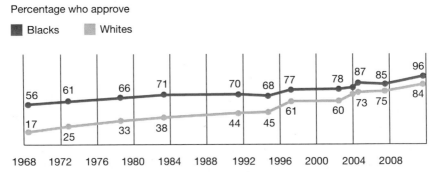

1968 1972 1976 1980 1984 1988 1992 1996 2000 2004 2008

FIGURE 5.2 Approval of marriage between blacks and whites, by race

no relationship with their in-laws. While this continues to be the case for many families, the trends as reflected in the figures above suggest that these differences between black and white families' reactions to interracial marriage are fading.

The Matter of Skin Color

Prejudicial or preferential treatment of others because of skin color or "colorism" is no stranger to the African American community.[25] African Americans have been consistently judged by white America on the basis of their status as "persons of African descent," and their skin color has served as the predominant "badge of [that] membership."[26] It has also comprised a significant part of African Americans' own collective identity because of its power in dictating relations among African Americans.

Moreover, there is ample evidence to suggest that the problem of colorism is not limited to African Americans,[27] as it exists throughout the global community in almost all countries with a history of European colonization.[28] For example, in Jamaica, Nicaragua, India, China, and Brazil, as well as various other countries in Africa and South America, there is a clear-cut preference for light skin complexions.[29] This preference for lighter complexions that most resemble European (i.e., white) people over darker complexions is consistent with early European preferences for lighter complexions among people of color. Europeans generally regarded people of color including Africans, who they called "blacks," as inferior and essentially less human. This type of perception would portend subsequent brutal treatment of Africans and other black and brown people by the Europeans. Indeed, prior to the sixteenth century, the *Oxford English Dictionary* provided the following definition of the color "black":

> Deeply stained with dirt; soiled, dirty, foul . . . Having dark or deadly purposes, malignant; pertaining to or involving death, deadly; baneful, disastrous, sinister . . . Foul, iniquitous, atrocious, horrible, wicked . . . Indicating disgrace, censure, liability to punishment, etc.[30]

It was not just the negative reaction to blackness that initiated European antipathy to Africans and people with darker complexions, but it was also a correspondingly high regard for "whiteness," and the belief in white purity, superiority, and virtue that served to infect subsequent global preferences for particular skin colors.

Although this tendency is indeed global, it is important to recognize the uniquely American character of this tendency. What makes America's preference for lighter skin colors distinctive from that which is apparent in other places in the world is the connection to a history in which a host of civil liberties and certain unalienable rights were legally and structurally linked to complexion. Prior to the latter part of the nineteenth century in the United States, the skin color an individual possessed determined their likelihood of freedom from bondage and treatment by whites.[31]

The remaining discussion examines the role of skin color in contemporary patterns of interracial intimacy among African Americans. Skin color is regarded as one of a constellation of factors that matter in the formation and maintenance of an interracial intimate relationship. This particular way of thinking about skin color—as an instigator or inhibitor of interracial intimacy—affords a certain value to skin color and treats it as more than a fortuitous consequence or antecedent to interracial intimacy.

In other countries, where the economic system historically was not based on chattel slavery, dark skin color was not the criteria for enslavement. In countries such as Egypt and India, for example, although there is ample evidence of the prevalence of the belief in superiority of whites and lighter complexions in general, these beliefs did not serve as a basis for a legalized system of racial slavery. It is the absence of this particular element in the history of other countries where slavery existed that makes interracial intimacy less of an issue elsewhere than in the United States.

In other parts of the world where African Americans can be found in large numbers, there is explicit recognition of this difference. For example, in France, a country to which African Americans have expatriated for many years, interracial relationships involving black people elicit little of the attention that characterizes them in the United States. Although few blacks in France would be willing to deny the presence of racism in the country, far more note the ease with which interracial intimacy occurs. I learned this firsthand in two interviews I conducted with African American expatriates who collectively have been living in France for more than forty-four years. Both individuals were emphatic about the freedom to engage in interracial intimacy in France without any regard to skin color.[32]

Skin Color and Interracial Intimacy

The tendency to use skin color as a moniker for other bases of judgment is so great that it may even be used independent of racial status.[33] Although it is true that most people are not accustomed to thinking of these concepts separately, it is worth mentioning their separateness here given the variability in skin color that exists within racial groups. For example, some African Americans with fair complexions can be "lighter" in skin color than some whites or Europeans with darker complexions.

Ironically, for some African Americans, making the decision to be in an interracial romantic relationship represents the culmination of a longstanding effort to move beyond what is perceived to be a black-centered obsession with lighter skin complexions. For those who share this perspective, there is resounding acceptance of the belief that African Americans as a group continue to be plagued by concerns with skin complexion. These concerns are manifested in preferential treatment for light-complexioned blacks and a corresponding disdain for darker-complexioned blacks.[34] Admittedly, these trends have diminished somewhat from earlier eras, but they nonetheless continue to be evident in many segments of the African American community.

The preference for light skin is so pervasive that it also influences the mainstream marketing of African American celebrities. Consider ongoing commentary about the advertising campaigns surrounding the light-brown complexioned pop star Beyoncé. In 2008, the cosmetics giant L'Oréal was accused of deliberately lightening the singer's complexion and, more recently, in an effort to promote her fourth album, the album's photo depicts her as a noticeably lighter, almost Caucasian, version of herself. A cursory review of Beyoncé's images online reveals a distinct difference: She is noticeably darker in impromptu pictures than she appears in the professional photos she uses for promotion.

Today, in the twenty-first century, many African Americans are reluctant to admit, or even acknowledge, the continued significance of skin color and its relation to European standards of beauty. This topic is regarded by some as passé and in some way not appropriate for mainstream discussion. Indeed, some ask the following questions: Haven't we gotten past this? Aren't we in a different era of black consciousness? Surely, black folks aren't still color struck? Questions like these are typically voiced by those who are most reluctant to engage in serious dialogue about the continuing problems associated with skin color preferences among African Americans.

At the other end of the spectrum are those who are aware of the problem of colorism and may actually work to call attention to its existence. As the author Richard Banks notes in his recent book *Is Marriage for White People?*, research conducted by a team of economists provides empirical evidence of the relationship between complexion and an African American woman's chances of being married.[35] In addition to finding that the lighter a woman's complexion the more likely she was to be married, they also found that women with lighter complexions married higher-earning African American men.[36]

Ironically, African Americans who are most sensitive to the problem of colorism may consciously opt to "cross the color line" in an effort to distance themselves from it. For these people, the possibility of having to confront other people's obsession with lighter complexions is so objectionable that they are willing—and even desirous—to affiliate with those for whom there is no possibility of this kind of in-group prejudice. Their obsession with these concerns taints any and all relationship prospects with other black people. This perspective is well captured by the film and television personality Yaphet Kotto, who happens to be dark complexioned. Consider his plaintive disclosure in describing the circumstances leading up to his interracial intimate encounters and subsequent marriage to a white woman:

> I was not able to attract a light-skinned black woman to my life, or even
> a black woman throughout the 1970s. They perceived me to be too ethnic
> looking and not Caucasian looking enough. My entire experience in my

20s was with Caucasian women. I never knew what it was to be dated by a black woman. I don't think Caucasian women care what race you are or how light you are. Black women do, and they let you know it.[37]

Kotto clearly attributes his involvement in interracial intimacy to his own desire to be with someone who he perceived to be unconcerned with skin color.[38]

Kotto sees white women as in some way preferable to black women because of the experiences he had with black women's rejection of him as a dark-complexioned black man. Ironically, what makes this particularly interesting, however, is the extent to which his disclosure belies his own ideas about skin complexion and highlights an alternative perspective that may well apply to other African Americans in interracial relationships. For some people, it may very well be a preference for lighter skin complexions that motivates their pursuit of interracial intimacy. Though not likely to be endorsed by most people who recognize that this type of a disclosure is unpopular today, it explains the motives of some cohort of African Americans who are involved in interracial intimate relationships or who are actively searching for this type of a relationship. Importantly, this type of motive fuels colorism and the problems associated with it.

As discussed above in relation to whites, today's cultural norms about race and racial attitudes among African Americans make certain types of pronouncements or disclosure unpopular. Like whites, African Americans are also sanctioned against appearing overtly racist, and this also means refraining from the expression of anti-black sentiments, as well as anti-white ones. Thus, those African Americans who are most aware of and sensitive to contemporary norms would not openly express their preferences for others with lighter complexions even though they may prefer them.

In this chapter, I wish to explore two very different types of psychological mechanisms (i.e., motives) for interracial intimacy among African Americans. The first mechanism is evident among African Americans who seek out interracial intimacy because of beliefs about what it will enable them to escape—namely the problems of colorism. The second type of mechanism involves the motive to affiliate with someone of another racial background because of beliefs or feelings about the superiority of that other skin color and corresponding background. For some African Americans, interracial intimacy serves a specific psychological or emotional purpose. That is, it is purposeful.[39] According to this perspective, both motives are based on the fact that a person will make the decision to be in an interracial relationship because they find it to be in some way satisfying.

While there are other explanations for the conscious decision to be involved in interracial intimacy, the two explanatory frameworks described here have their roots in concerns with skin color. In the first case, it ostensibly derives from a person's concerns about other people's problems with darker complexions and, in the second case, the interracial intimacy satisfies a person's own preferences for light complexions. Given their emphasis on skin color and the way that concerns about certain complexions may instigate—indeed motivate—the pursuit of interracial intimacy, the two mechanisms appear to be especially well suited for this volume's discussion of colorism.

Although it is not the case that all African Americans are saddled with the problem of colorism, many African Americans continue to struggle with their own self-perceptions, as well as treatment from outsiders because of their skin color. Those who are in intimate interracial relationships may be especially sensitive to concerns about skin color, given that these relationships may make the differences associated with skin color particularly salient. They are also more likely to elicit attention from outsiders than are same-race relationships and, as such, individuals in these relationships are likely to be reminded of the interracial nature of their relationship unpredictably. For example, consider the case of "Chester," a thirty-something, Midwest-based African American man who was in an interracial marriage. I interviewed Chester in an earlier study published in 2006 that examined the experiences of African American men in interracial relationships.[40] Chester described an incident that occurred one evening while he and his wife were out at a restaurant. Chester was clearly reminded of the interracial nature of their marriage.

> There was this one incident when we, my wife and me, went to a restaurant. We get there and they admit her, but separately from me. They didn't believe that I was with her . . . she had to come back and verify that we were together. It was crazy! It was like I had to prove to them that she was my wife or something.[41]

Similarly, another person I spoke with in a follow-up study that focused on African American women in interracial relationships also recounted her own experience with unsolicited reminders about the interracial nature of her relationship.[42] According to the 33-year-old New York–based "T.S.":

> To be honest with you, being with him, when we're out we might get stares, but most of the time no one ever says anything .. . . so, I don't know how someone can feel that it is okay for them to say anything or to even stare like that . . . In some cases, black men will feel like they have a right to dis my husband. I am not joking, they have walked right up to me when I am clearly with my husband and proceeded to throw some line at me![43]

Both comments make clear that interracial intimacy is not without its challenges in a society in which racial status and the corresponding skin complexion of one's partner is different from one's own.

Crossing the Color Line to Escape Colorism

For some African Americans, being in an intimate interracial relationship can provide a practical way of avoiding the problems of colorism. Individuals like Kotto who recount experiences contend that other African Americans have treated them (or those who are close to them) in undesirable ways *because* of their skin color. Their skin color may be dark or light; however, given our society's preference for lighter complexions, people with darker complexions are more likely to experience negative reactions from others.[44] Consequently, it seems likely that among those involved in interracial intimacy it is those with darker complexions more than lighter-complexioned African Americans who may be most motivated to avoid the problems of colorism and who therefore see interracial intimacy as a way of purposefully avoiding it.[45]

As African Americans, if they believe that others are treating them differently or negatively because of their complexion, then that is what matters. In this regard, whether perceptions are accurate matters less than what is believed to be true. The problem of colorism and the preference for lighter skin complexions among African Americans has had such a profound effect that even in the absence of negative reactions from others, if one anticipates such reactions and happens to have a dark complexion, one may purposefully refrain from establishing intimate relationships in order to avoid certain interactions with other African Americans. It is in this way that African Americans may adjust their preferences to fit with their expectations for what is likely to occur.[46]

Consider the following excerpt from an interview I conducted with an African American woman who frequently dated interracially.[47] In discussing the way that color continues to affect African American women and their esteem, "B.B." described her sister, who happened to be married to an African American man. She said:

> My sister, she is dark-skinned and she is married to a light-skinned man. And one day, she . . . expressed her insecurities to me. Her husband is attractive, but he is not gorgeous. And, she said that, she wonders if people think, "Why is he with that dark skinned woman?" And, that's . . . coming from the place of a person who was born in the '70s![48]

"B.B.," a 39-year-old D.C.-based graphic artist, concluded that the problem of colorism runs deep and had clearly affected her normally "level-headed" sister's self-esteem.

Unfortunately, her sister's disclosure is not all that unusual. In one focus group with African American women conducted in the study referenced above that focused on black women, I heard a popular explanation from multiple women that presumably underlies this type of concern. Although they may have used different words, I heard the following sentiment echoed by multiple women:

"Black men aren't interested in women that look like me." In settings where African American women felt safe in disclosing their concerns and private feelings, this sentiment—that black men find only certain types of black women to be attractive—was expressed. When it was articulated, it was often done as a euphemism for concerns about skin color and a preference for lighter skin complexions. Given that the preference for lighter skin complexions appears to continue to infect the African American community, black women who see themselves as not quite light enough may very well be correct in their assumptions about black men's interest (or lack thereof) in them.

For those African Americans who have had enough with the in-group distinctions that others make in order to distinguish among the different hues that exist among black people's skin complexions, being involved in an intimate relationship with someone who does not dally in such distinctions may seem like a welcoming remedy to a tiring predicament. No longer does one risk hearing such terms as "red bone," "yella' girl," or "cocoa brown." Rarely do white Americans use the types of terms that reflect recognition of and subtle distinctions in skin color familiar to most African Americans. For whites, in public discourse it is "white" or "black."

Importantly, and somewhat paradoxically, there does seem to be an almost visceral reaction that white Americans have to more overt differences in skin color among African Americans. This explains the willingness to include one or two people with lighter complexions in various cannons of beauty, judgments of humanity, and deliberations about innocence, as well as the reluctance to do so for darker-complexioned African Americans.[49] There is strong evidence from a variety of sources that indicates preferences among white Americans for African Americans who are lighter complexioned. Those with darker complexions are routinely excluded from national polls of beauty,[50] more often judged guilty and given longer sentences in legal arenas,[51] and least likely to be judged by whites as similar to themselves.[52]

Intersection of Race, Gender, and Skin Color

Given the way that skin complexion for African Americans is intertwined with perceptions of physical attractiveness, and given the relative importance of physical attractiveness for women as compared to men, the motive to cross the color line in order to escape the problems of colorism is likely to be stronger among African American women than men.[53] In the U.S. culture, perceptions of a woman's physical attractiveness are driven in part by perceptions about her skin color and racial status. In short, racialized perceptions of physical attractiveness are ubiquitous.[54]

Whether there are actually more African Americans who are darker complexioned than there are those with lighter complexions who are involved in interracial relationships because of concerns about colorism is an empirical question worthy of study. Similarly, whether this difference is most pronounced among women is also worth systematic analysis. Are African Americans with darker skin colors more likely to be in interracial relationships because of the problems of colorism among African Americans? Is this more often the case for darker-complexioned women than it is for men? Accurately answering any of these questions requires a careful analysis of the impact of this particular phenotypic trait within the relationship patterns of those engaged in interracial intimacy—a challenging activity. Moreover, given the taboo associated with admitting that skin color matters and that it constitutes a basis for decision making in the central domain of intimate relationships, it is hard to be optimistic about whether it will ever be possible to answer these questions accurately and completely. Nevertheless, research aimed at shedding light on some of these issues is certainly warranted.

As discussed here, some African Americans make the decision to establish an intimate relationship with someone who is not an African American in an effort to disassociate with other African Americans because of their own beliefs about prejudices toward skin color. By minimizing personal associations with their own racial group, and by actively making choices that diminish the possibility of associating with other African Americans, the people in this group effectively disassociate themselves from the larger community. This process of disassociation has been studied extensively in social psychology and has been found to have profound implications for a person's well-being and esteem.[55] This is because individuals define their self-concepts relative to their connections with social groups.[56]

Presumably, in this case, the concerns about colorism are so strong as to motivate an individual to seek intimacy with those outside of the group by retreating from potentially intimate associations with other African Americans. Those individuals perceive the African American community to be too infected with colorism. Of course, the potential cost of this strategy is that other African Americans may react negatively to the "retreatist." Yet, for the people who have already decided to disassociate themselves from other African Americans, this is not likely to represent a compelling enough reason to seek intimate connections with others. For the black person who has consciously decided to disassociate from other African Americans because of their belief that others are infected by colorism (i.e., they prefer those with light complexions), he or she is not likely to care much about what other African Americans think of them.

Satisfying Preferences for Lighter Complexions

In contrast to the dissociation motives resulting from beliefs about African Americans' colorism, there are some who are motivated by their own preference for lighter skin complexions and the features associated with it. Not surprisingly, this drives their pursuit of interracial intimacy. Because of the various changes in collective consciousness for African Americans that have transpired over the last fifty to sixty years, many African Americans are reluctant to admit to having a preference for lighter skin colors. For example, consider the outcry that erupted when it was determined that the late pop star Michael Jackson was purposefully lightening his skin color. Although he subsequently disclosed that he suffered from the debilitating skin disease vitiligo and that lightening provided a more even toned complexion, he had the misfortune of being the "poster child" for those of African descent who are obsessed with lighter skin complexions—a characterization with which he will likely always be associated.[57]

The motive to affiliate in intimate relationships with those who have a lighter skin color is not new in the African American community. Membership within the African American community includes the dubious privilege of personal acquaintance with, or at least firsthand knowledge of, African American preferences for lighter skin complexions. The history and experiences of African Americans in the United States has always involved an acute awareness of the differences in skin color and connotations with which they are associated.[58] Indeed, such biases are to be expected in a society that has been characterized by a racial caste system in which all of the variables associated with the quality of one's life were linked to skin color. Whites were the ruling class and blacks constituted the slave class. Exceptions included lighter-complexioned "blacks" who, though still in bondage, enjoyed somewhat better treatment than those who were dark skinned. Thus, the preference for lighter complexions among some African Americans is not new.

Yet what is perhaps more recent is the way that this higher regard for light skin complexions may underlie decisions of some African Americans to engage in interracial intimacy. After all, it was only after the 1967 Supreme Court decision in *Loving v. Virginia* that the *de jure* sanctions on interracial intimacy were lifted. Although various *de facto* prohibitions continued throughout the country (and occasionally today), African Americans were able to participate in intimate interracial relationships to a degree previously unknown.[59]

The notion that skin color and a preference for lighter complexions serves as a basis for pursuit and initiation of interracial intimacy is provocative. For African Americans today, the motive to affiliate intimately with someone of another race is often couched in terms of principles of "colorblindness." The person who engages in interracial intimacy because of his or her preferences for lighter skin complexions may opt to cloak those preferences in language that underscores the value of a *colorblind* or *multiracial* approach to intimacy. Such was the case with a number of the people I interviewed in the course of a study examining the experiences of African American men in intimate interracial relationships.[60] For example, according to the 31-year-old, California-based, medium-brown-complexioned African American man "M.B.": "My mother has white blood in her and she looks Spanish, so me being with a white woman is not really a problem. Besides I was taught to appreciate everyone. We're not prejudiced people, you know."[61]

Yet, because of his other comments and because of other behaviors he was engaging in,[62] I was well aware of his preference for a mate who was lighter than he was. Thus, I found his point about being colorblind to be somewhat disingenuous.[63]

Most apparent within this cohort are the problems associated with colorism as exemplified in the belief that lighter complexions are better than darker ones. Another man who was interviewed as part of the study articulated the most extreme example of this phenomenon. In providing his description of an attractive woman to me, "Brian"—a 51-year-old, brown-skinned attorney—noted his aversion to women of African descent. Instead, he preferred a woman "who doesn't look black."[64] For Brian it was skin color, hair texture, and the features more often associated with whites that were most appealing in the women with whom he was intimately involved.

Some African Americans who pursue intimate interracial relationships because of their preferences for lighter complexions may do so as a way of being close to what they see as superior; however, the motive to associate with those who have lighter complexions may be somewhat more complex than described thus far. Some African Americans may be driven to affiliate with someone who is not African American because they believe that doing so is in some way strategic. The status-caste exchange theory provides a useful framework for understanding this perspective.[65]

According to this theory as initially proposed,[66] the decision to engage in interracial intimacy is driven by processes much like those in any exchange relationship. Here, the market metaphor is used to explain and predict dating and mating behaviors. The theory says that African Americans of relatively higher socioeconomic status (SES) or educational background and whites with lower SES and education will marry in an exchange of racial caste position for economic resources and status. According to this perspective, marriage between high-status blacks and lower status whites represents a kind of informal exchange; that is, the higher SES of the African American spouse would directly compensate the white spouse for the loss of social standing that the white spouse would experience for having thrown his or her lot in with black society.[67]

Concluding Thoughts

It is consistent with the prevailing perspectives of contemporary intergroup relations theorists that some African Americans may opt out of same-race relationships because of the way that racial and cultural norms and preferences operate to privilege lighter complexions. For example, interracial intimacy that results from preferences for lighter complexions rather than darker ones among African Americans can be readily explained by the system-justification approach in intergroup relations.[68] According to this perspective, people internalize an ideology that justifies the existing social order, or status quo, even at their own expense, and this may be particularly apparent among those in disadvantaged groups.[69] For African Americans beset with the problems of colorism who prefer lighter complexions, interracial intimacy provides a ready way of demonstrating their willingness to endorse, uphold, and champion prevailing cultural norms that happen to privilege what is "white," or light, over what is "black," or dark.

Unfortunately, the same type of conclusion results from analysis of the other type of motive for interracial intimacy involving colorism. For those African Americans who pursue interracial intimacy because of their desire to avoid association with African Americans who may potentially be affected by colorism, the outcome is the same. However much their actions may belie their personal beliefs about the superiority of lighter complexions, their relationship unwittingly symbolizes an endorsement of social and cultural norms that elevate what is "white" and light over what is "black" and dark. Rather than fighting, or at least contradicting, the norms within mainstream American society and the African American community that privilege lighter complexions relative to darker ones, these African Americans have elected to make choices that ultimately validate the very system in which their own options may be limited and restricted. By deciding against any and all associations with other African Americans because of beliefs about their color consciousness, they have ruled out the possibility of affiliating with an African American who isn't infected by colorism.

In this chapter I have highlighted the way that concerns about skin color among African Americans are associated with participation in, and pursuit of, an intimate interracial relationship for some African Americans. The discussion included consideration of the unique way that race, gender, and concerns about skin color may intersect to influence judgments about, and interest in, interracial intimacy. As a result, several questions arise that represent fruitful lines of inquiry for empirical research in this area. First, are there more dark-complexioned African Americans who attribute their interracial relationships to the problems of colorism than light-complexioned African Americans in similar relationships? Second, is this type of motive more pronounced among women, for whom pressures to be consistent with societal definitions of physical attractiveness are likely to be strongest? Third, are there disproportionately more African Americans in interracial intimate relationships who readily admit to preferences for lighter complexions than among African Americans in same-race relationships? Each of the questions outlined here could be addressed by constructing a random probability sample composed of African Americans in interracial intimate relationships.

Deciding to engage in interracial intimacy can be a matter of avoiding the potential for interaction with others who may express preferences for those with lighter complexion; it may also be a matter of deliberately seeking out those with lighter complexions because of beliefs about the superiority of people with those complexions. This discussion draws from qualitative data obtained in two studies referenced earlier that included verbatim interviews with black men and women in intimate interracial relationships. Admittedly, not all African Americans involved in interracial intimacy will be influenced by the psychological weight of colorism, but hopefully this discussion can shed light on some of the ways that the problem of colorism continues to instigate behaviors among a segment of African Americans.

Notes

1 Glenn Firebaugh and Kenneth Davies, "Trends in Anti-Black Prejudice, 1972–1984: Region and Cohort Effects," *American Journal of Sociology* 94(2) (1988): 251; Carolyn Y. Fang, Jim Sidanius, and Felicia Pratto, "Romance Across the Social Status Continuum: Interracial Marriage and the Ideological Asymmetry Effect," *Journal of Cross-Cultural Psychology* 29(2) (1998): 290; Ewa A. Golebiowski, "The Contours and Etiology of Whites' Attitudes Toward Black-White Interracial Marriage," *Journal of Black Studies* 38(2) (2007): 268.

2 Barry Edmonston and Jeffrey S. Passel, eds., *Immigration and Ethnicity: The Integration of America's Newest Arrivals* (Washington, DC: Urban Institute Press, 1994); Milton M. Gordon, *Assimilation in American Life: The Role of Race, Religion and National Origin* (Oxford: Oxford University Press, 1964); Douglas Massey, "The New Immigration and Ethnicity in the United States," *Population and Development Review* 21(3) (1995): 631–652. During previous waves of immigration to North America and the United States involving the large-scale entry of European immigrants, there was substantial evidence of this type of intermarriage. For discussion, see Matthijs Kalmijn,"Trends in Black/White Intermarriage," *Social Forces* 72(1) (1993): 119–146. Intermarriage, also referred to as "exogamy," "out-marriage," or "marital assimilation" by some, can be regarded as an indicator of the social closeness or propinquity between groups. It is an indicator of propinquity in two ways. First, and most obviously, in order for it to occur, there must be some physical and spatial proximity between social groups. Large numbers of people from different social groups interact intimately with one another when they find themselves working in the same workplace settings, attending and studying in the same schools, or living in the same neighborhoods. Thus, rates of intermarriage signal the degree to which members of different ethnic groups interact with one another. The second way that intermarriage is related to the propinquity between groups has to do with the product of those marriages. When intermarriage occurs, offspring adopt multiple identities, and with successive generations this contributes to their assimilation into the social structures of society. Ultimately, this in turn leads to the eventual erosion of ethnic distinctiveness whereby formerly distinct and separate groups can evolve into a larger, more heterogeneous, group (Portes and Zhou, 1993). It is in this way that intermarriage can ultimately eliminate racial distinctions, distilling formerly distinct groups into one larger and more variable group.
Interracial, or *interethnic, intimacy* as experienced by the European immigrants who migrated in large numbers during the eighteenth and nineteenth centuries, represents one end of a continuum of intergroup relationships between ethnic outsiders and insiders, and in many cases results in "intermarriage." At the other end of the continuum are discordant intergroup relations where intimate interaction is forbidden and may even be unlawful. See Donald Horowitz, "Color Differentiation in the American Systems of Slavery," *Journal of Interdisciplinary History* 111(3) (1973): 509–526; Trina Jones, "Shades of Brown: The Law of Skin Color," *Duke Law Journal* 49 (2000): 1487–1557. Countries with large numbers of immigrants, such as the United States, tend to evidence every possible type of intergroup interaction along such a continuum.

3 Ronald E. Hall, "Bias among African-Americans Regarding Skin-Color: Implications for Social Work Practice," *Research on Social Work Practice* 2(4) (1992): 479–486; Clemmont E. Vontress, "Counseling Black," *Personnel and Guidance Journal* 48(9) (1970): 713–719.

4 Keith B. Maddox and Stephanie Gray, "Cognitive Representations of Black Americans: Reexploring the Role of Skin Tone," *Personality and Social Psychology Bulletin* 28(2) (2002): 250–259.

5 Michael Hughes and Bradley R. Hertel, "The Significance of Color Remains: A Study of Life Chances, Mate Selection, and Ethnic Consciousness among Black Americans," *Social Forces* 68(4) (1990): 1105–1120.

6 Barry Edmonston, Sharon M. Lee, and Jeffrey Passel, "Recent Trends in Intermarriage and Immigration and Their Effects on the Future Racial Composition of the U.S. Population," in *The New Race Question: How the Census Counts Multiracial Individuals*, ed. Joel Perlmann and Mary C. Waters (New York: Russell Sage Foundation, 2002), 227–255; Stanley Lieberson, *A Piece of the Pie: Blacks and White Immigrants since 1880* (Berkeley, CA: University of California Press, 1980).

7 Here native "white" refers to the superordinate grouping of people with predominantly European ancestry already present in the United States in large numbers with fair skin complexions. These whites tended to have arrived in the earliest waves of immigration from England, Ireland, Scotland, Germany, and some Scandinavian countries. Zhenchao Qian and Daniel T. Lichter, "Measuring Marital Assimilation: Intermarriage Among Natives and Immigrants," *Social Science Research* 30(2) (2001): 289–312.

8 Tom W. Smith, *Ethnic Images. GSS Topical report No. 19* (Chicago, IL: National Opinion Research Center, 1990); Daniel Solorzano, Miguel Ceja, and Tara Yosso, "Critical Race Theory, Racial Microaggressions, and Campus Racial Climate: The Experiences of African American College Students," *Journal of Negro Education* 69(1–2) (2000): 60–73.

9 Maria Krysan and Nakesha Faison, "Racial Attitudes in America: An Update," Institute of Government and Public Affairs: University of Illinois, accessed August 1, 2012, http://igpa.uillinois.edu/programs/racial-attitudes/detailed5.

10 John F. Dovidio et al., "On the Nature of Prejudice: Automatic and Controlled Processes," *Journal of Experimental Social Psychology* 33(5) (1997): 510–540; Bernd Wittenbrink, Charles M. Judd, and Bernadette Park, "Evidence for Racial Prejudice at the Implicit Level and Its Relationship with Questionnaire Measures," *Journal of Personality and Social Psychology* 72(2) (1997): 262–274.

11 Allen McConnell and Jill M. Leibold, "Relations among the Implicit Association Test, Discriminatory Behavior, and Explicit Measures of Racial Attitudes," *Journal of Experimental Social Psychology* 37(5) (2001): 435–442.

12 Nicole J. Shelton, "A Reconceptualization of How We Study Issues of Racial Prejudice," *Personality and Social Psychological Review* 4(4) (2000): 374–390.

13 David Katz and Kenneth Braly, "Racial Stereotypes of One Hundred College Students," *Journal of Abnormal and Social Psychology* 28(3) (1933): 280–290.

14 For examples, see Maddox and Gray, "Cognitive Representations of Black Americans"; Jennifer Richeson and Sophie Trawalter, "African Americans' Implicit Racial Attitudes and the Depletion of Executive Function After Interracial Interactions," *Social Cognition* 23(4) (2005): 336–352.

15 Aaron Gullickson, "Black/White Interracial Marriage Trends, 1850–2000," *Journal of Family History* 31(3) (2006): 289–312.

16 Sharon M. Lee and Barry Edmonston, "New Marriages, New Families: U.S. Racial and Hispanic Intermarriage," *Population Bulletin* 60(2) (2005): 1–40.

17 Loving v. Virginia, 388 U.S. 1 (1967).

18 Tavia Simmons, and Martin O'Connell, *Interracial Unmarried-Partner Households: How Do They Compare with Interracial Married Couple Households in Census 2000?*, accessed August 1, 2012, http://www.census.gov/population/www/socdemo/hh-fam/interracial-unmarried-partner.pdf.

19 See Ralph Banks, *Is Marriage for White People?: How the African American Marriage Decline Affects Everyone* (New York: Penguin, 2012). There are a number of ideas about why black men outpace women in interracial unions. For example, one explanation focuses

on the numbers by noting that there are far more eligible black women than men and black men consequently have more options. An alternative explanation for men's greater involvement hinges upon the importance of physical attractiveness in relationship initiation and black women's lower status on mainstream America's attractiveness hierarchy.

20 George Yancey, "Who Interracially Dates: An Examination of the Characteristics of Those Who Have Interracially Dated," *Journal of Comparative Family Studies* 33(2) (2002): 177–190.

21 As one example, in November of 2008 one married couple was tortured and brutally murdered in their home. The man, a member of the U.S. military was white and his wife was an African American. Although the district attorney charged with prosecuting the case continues to express reluctance in highlighting the racial aspects of the crime (the murderers were all black men and wrote racial epithets in the couple's home), it is the interracial nature of their relationship that appears to have invoked the ire of the killers.

22 Jeffrey M. Jones, "Record-High 86% Approve of Black-White Marriages: Ninety-Six Percent of Blacks, 84% of Whites Approve," *Gallup*, September 12, 2011, accessed July 5, 2012, http://www.gallup.com/poll/149390/record-high-approve-black-white marriages.aspx.

23 Martha Hodes, *White Women, Black Men: Illicit Sex in the Nineteenth-Century South* (New Haven, CT: Yale University Press, 1997).

24 See Kellina Craig-Henderson, *Black Men in Interracial Relationships: What's Love Got to Do With It?* (Piscataway, NJ: Transaction Publishers, 2006).

25 Jones, "Shades of Brown: The Law of Skin Color," Richard Seltzer and Robert Smith, "Color Differences in the Afro-American Community and the Differences They Make," *Journal of Black Studies* 21(3) (1991): 279–286.

26 Seltzer and Smith, "Color Differences in the Afro-American Community and the Differences They Make," *Journal of Black Studies* 21(3) (1991): 279–286.

27 Admittedly I have made the conceptual leap from explaining what colorism is to problematizing it. This is justifiable given the pervasiveness of negative consequences associated with it and the absence of positive outcomes.

28 Kathy Russell, Midge Wilson, and Ronald E. Hall, *The Color Complex: The Politics of Skin Color among African Americans* (New York: Anchor Books, 1993); Roger N. Lancaster, "Skin Color, Race and Racism in Nicaragua," *Ethnology* 30(4) (1991): 339–353; Christina Gómez, "The Continual Significance of Skin Color: An Exploratory Study of Latinos in the Northeast," *Hispanic Journal of Behavioral Sciences* 22(1) (2000*)*: 94–103.

29 Eric Uhlmann et al., "Subgroup Prejudice Based on Skin Color among Hispanics in the United States and Latin America," *Social Cognition* 20(3) (2004): 198–226.

30 James M. Jones, *Prejudice and Racism* (New York: McGraw-Hill, 1997), 475.

31 See Herbert Aptheker, *Herbert Aptheker on Race and Democracy: A Reader*, eds Eric Foner and Manning Marable (Urbana, IL: University of Illinois Press, 2010).

32 In 2011, I traveled to several countries in Europe and Asia to interview African Americans who had left the United States. The substance of these interviews serves as a basis for a current project exploring the experiences of black expatriates to be released in a forthcoming book. I met and spoke with two people in France, one in Paris, and one other in Toulouse.

33 Jones, "Shades of Brown: The Law of Skin Color," 1487–1557.

34 Ronald E. Hall, "The Bleaching Syndrome: African Americans' Response to Cultural Domination vis-à-vis Skin Color," *Journal of Black Studies* 26(2) (1995): 172–184; Margaret L. Hunter, "If You're Light You're Alright: Light Skin Color as Social Capital for Women of Color," *Gender and Society* 16(2) (2002): 175–193.

35 Banks, *Is Marriage for White People?*

36 Hamilton Darrick, Arthur Goldsmith, and William Darity, Jr., "Shedding 'Light' on Marriage: The Influence of Skin Shade on Marriage for Black Females," *Journal of Economic Behavior and Organization* 72(1) (2009): 30–50.

37 Yaphet Kotto, "Interview with Amanda Spake," *Salon Magazine*, November 12, 1995, http://www.salon.com/12nov1995/feature/kotto.html.

38 Of course, it should be noted that Kotto's belief in his potential white partner's lack of concern about skin color may well be dubious; however, it is worth mentioning in so much as it is different from his experiences with African Americans.

39 I recognize that it need not necessarily always be a matter of conscious deliberation, although the two mechanisms for interracial intimacy examined in the present discussion may well be conscious ones.

40 Craig-Henderson, *Black Men in Interracial Relationships*.

41 Ibid., 122.

42 Kellina Craig-Henderson, *Black Women in Interracial Relationships: In Search of Love and Solace?* (Piscataway, NJ: Transaction Publishers, 2010).

43 Craig-Henderson, *Black Women in Interracial Relationships*, 151.

44 Jennifer L. Hochschild and Vesla Weaver, "The Skin Color Paradox and the American Racial Order," *Social Forces* 86(2) (2007): 643–670.

45 For a similar point, see Banks, *Is Marriage for White People?*

46 William J. McGuire and Claire V. McGuire, "The Content, Structure, and Operation of Thought Systems," in *The Content, Structure, and Operation of Thought Systems: Advances in Social Cognition*, eds Robert S. Wyer, Jr. and Thomas K. Srull, vol. 4 (New York: Psychology Press, 1991), 1–78.

47 Craig-Henderson, *Black Women in Interracial Relationships*.

48 Ibid., 86.

49 Ibid.; Jennifer Eberhardt et al., "Looking Deathworthy: Perceived Stereotypicality of Black Defendants Predicts Capital-Sentencing Outcomes," *Psychological Science* 17(5) (2006): 383–386; Keith Maddox, "Perspectives on Racial Phenotypicality Bias," *Personality and Social Psychology Review* 8(4) (2004): 383–401; Russell, Wilson, and Hall, *The Color Complex*.

50 Russell et al., *The Color Complex*.

51 Eberhardt et al., "Looking Deathworthy."

52 Charles Judd et al., "Stereotypes and Ethnocentrism: Diverging Interethnic Perceptions of African American and White American Youth," *Journal of Personality and Social Psychology* 69(3) (1995): 460–481.

53 For a similar point, see Banks, *Is Marriage for White People?*

54 Russell et al., *The Color Complex*.

55 Naomi Ellemers, Paulien Kortekaas, and Jaap W. Ouwerkerk, "Self-Categorization, Commitment to the Group and Social Self-Esteem as Related But Distinct Aspects of Social Identity," *European Journal of Social Psychology* 28(2–3) (1999): 371–398; Claude Steele and Joshua Aronson, "Stereotype Threat and the Intellectual Test-Performance of African-Americans," *Journal of Personality and Social Psychology* 69(5) (1995): 797–811.

56 Dominic Abrams and Michael A. Hogg, "Social Identification, Self-Categorization and Social Influence," *European Review of Social Psychology* 1 (1990): 195–228; Roderick Kramer, "Cooperation and Organizational Identification," in *Social Psychology in Organizations: Advances in Theories and Research*, ed. Keith J. Murnighan (Englewood Cliffs, NJ: Prentice-Hall, 1993), 244–268; Henri Tajfel, "Social Identity and Intergroup Behavior," *Social Science Information* 13 (1974): 65–93.

57 More recently, in late 2009, Sammy Sosa, the former Chicago Cubs' baseball player who was brown skin-complexioned, received a great deal of media attention in reaction to his apparently lighter skin color. In response to questions about his skin's appearance, he said that, because of all the time he spent in the sun while playing baseball, he used a skin cream to soften his skin. He also said that it happened to have an additional effect

of lightening his complexion. He indicated that he was not able to stay in the sun very long when the cream was applied. In explaining his situation, Sosa offered: "I'm not a racist. I'm not like that. I'm just a happy person." Christian Red and Isaac Lopez, "Former Cubs Slugger Sammy Sosa Denies Suffering from Skin Condition That Plagued Michael Jackson," *New York Daily News*, November 11, 2009, accessed August 27, 2011, http://articles.nydailynews.com/2009–11–11/sports/17939619_1_dominican-republic-mark-mcgwire-dominican-born-sosa. Ironically, Sosa also wears colored contact lenses because, as he said, "I wanted to try something different. I'm not a superficial person."

58 Patricia Hill Collins, *Black Feminist Thought: Knowledge, Consciousness, and the Politics of Empowerment*, 2nd edition (New York: Routledge, 2000).

59 Hodes, *White Women, Black Men.*

60 Craig-Henderson, *Black Women in Interracial Relationships.*

61 Ibid., 103.

62 I was introduced to "M.B." by a female relative of his, who disclosed information about his "private" intimate relationship with an African American woman with whom she was acquainted. That relationship was cloaked in secrecy, presumably, according to his relative, because of his preference for appearing in public only with women who were white or at least lighter than himself.

63 See Cedric Herring, Verna Keith, and Hayward Horton, eds, *Skin Deep: How Race and Complexion Matter in the "Color Blind" Era* (Urbana, IL: University of Illinois Press, 2004), for further discussion about how the quest by many people of color to identify themselves as "other than black," ostensibly because of their multiracial ideals, reflects an overall system that privileges lighter complexions over darker ones.

64 Craig-Henderson, *Black Women in Interracial Relationships*, 95.

65 Kalmijn, "Trends in Black/White Intermarriage"; Robert Merton, "Intermarriage and the Social Structure: Fact and Theory," *Psychiatry* 4(3) (1941): 361–374.

66 Merton, "Intermarriage and the Social Structure."

67 Michael J. Rosenfeld, "A Critique of Exchange Theory in Mate Selection," *American Journal of Sociology* 110(5) (2005): 1284–1325.

68 John Jost and Mahzarin Banaji, "The Role of Stereotyping in System-justification and the Production of False Consciousness," *British Journal of Social Psychology* 33(1) (1994): 1–27.

69 John Jost, Mahzarin Banaji, and Brian Nosek, "A Decade of System Justification Theory: Accumulated Evidence of Conscious and Unconscious Bolstering of the Status Quo," *Political Psychology* 25(6) (2004): 881–919.

6

FRAGMENTED IDENTITY

Psychological Insecurity and Colorism Among African Americans

Vetta L. Sanders Thompson

This chapter discusses colorism, or skin color bias,[1] as a component of racism—particularly as it is practiced and experienced in the United States. The history of race in America has resulted in a psychologically fragile, albeit resilient, African American community that has adapted to a system that privileges white, light, or fair skin color. While I would like to believe that the color consciousness of the past has ended, recurring events suggest otherwise.

In my case, an elevator conversation provided an occasion for struggling with this issue. Two white colleagues were on the elevator engaged in a conversation that continued unabated when I entered. One said, "I am happy with the new person that we replaced her with; she is the right kind of black person, you know, light-skinned with nice, curly hair."[2] I have thought about these comments over the past six years. The remarks took me back thirty years when a college friend talked about her discomfort with a white male interviewer's remarks. The interviewer had essentially suggested that her status in society was assured by her "light skin color" rather than her intelligence or her effort.

As I reflected on my elevator experience, my first reaction was concern that there was minimal change in societal attitudes related to dark skin color. In addition, I was taken aback that my presence as a dark-skinned African American female with locs was insufficient to stifle the sentiment that somehow "light skin" was a positive and desirable trait of African Americans. I also wondered whether my colleagues were aware of how often similar sentiments were expressed within the African American community. Could they possibly believe that I might empathize with—or, worse, hold or espouse—similar opinions?

The realities of and reactions to experiences of racism and discrimination over centuries suggest the probable psychological insecurity of people of color who have developed strategies to cope with denigration, social isolation, and altered opportunities. One coping strategy used by people of color is to recognize and struggle against oppressive social structures and ideologies that provide the framework for a destructive system of race based on phenotypic features.[3] An important component of racist ideologies is the continued implication that social and cultural differences among individuals assigned to different racial groups are genetic.[4] Despite using social and political organization and struggle to dismantle the dichotomous social structure that privileges white racial group assignment, a substantial majority of people of color, whether consciously or unconsciously, seek the privileges of "white skin." Thus, while engaged in struggle and dialogue against racist ideologies and structures, communities of color also engage in an alternative coping strategy that relies on the pursuit of economic, social, and political advantage via approximations of the physical characteristics privileged in society. Plainly stated, communities of color often replicate and perpetuate privileging systems in their own communities via a social hierarchy based on skin pigmentation rather than race.[5]

This seemingly contradictory and largely unconscious behavior occurs because oppression encourages strategic and self-serving (whether economic, educational, legal, or social) decision making with respect to the enactment of identity. Identity decisions are made because they result in opportunities to support fragile egos, as well as meet real human needs, through success in the very system that oppresses all members of the group. In the context described, only certain elements of the identity are likely to be embraced at any given time—elements that are more difficult for those in the dominant community to discern or detect. Other aspects of the denigrated identity are minimized, suppressed and, in the case of skin color, altered to the extent possible. It must be clear that in the sociopolitical climate that supports white or light skin color preferences, there are occasional circumstances that privilege dark skin. The "Black is Beautiful" movement that emerged during the 1960s and extended through the 1970s highlights a time frame when dark skin enjoyed a level of acceptance and privilege,[6] at least that was the outward display. Dark skin may also be advantageous to the extent that light skin can provoke questions of "black authenticity," though there are any number of behaviors, activities, and sociopolitical attitudes that provoke questions of authenticity, in addition to skin color.[7]

I begin this chapter by summarizing what is known about the salience of skin color in racial/ethnic communities. I then discuss the salience of color among African Americans in the United States, linking colorism to social identity and the fragmentation of that identity and its implications. I end by discussing why colorism persists within the African American community—and by extension other communities of color—in what some would like to call a post-racial society.[8]

Definition of Colorism

Maddox and Gray defined colorism as "the tendency to perceive or behave toward members of a racial category based on the lightness or darkness of their skin tone."[9] Social science theorists and researchers consider colorism as a form of discrimination based on skin color, and in the social science literature in the United States it is more often discussed with reference to in-group dynamics among African Americans.[10] I discuss colorism as an African American in-group dynamic in this manner throughout most of this chapter, however, colorism operates in a broader context, with implications for how it manifests in any minority community. To place colorism in context, I provide the following as a brief summary of the issues that affect African American psychology as it relates to skin color preferences.

African American History and Skin Color

African American existence in the United States has consisted of sustained oppression and discrimination,[11] with those of African descent characterized as subhuman, irresponsible, lazy, and unintelligent. Deprivation of basic human rights, the reality of violent enforcement of slave status, and possible primary and secondary gains via submission to the demands of this system have assured internalization of this racist ideology in varying proportions by varying numbers of people of African descent. The emancipation of slaves brought only a brief period of relative freedom before people of African descent were again relegated to a system of oppression enforced by deprivation of political and human rights.[12] Rights were denied by law via a system of social norms and terror tactics that involved violence against property and person, including lynching.

There were only brief periods prior to the 1960s that directed community efforts toward pride and self-esteem,[13] thus inhibiting discussions of identity focused on positive images of the body or culture. The denigration of people of African descent and assertions of inferiority made during and after slavery laid the foundation for "color consciousness,"[14] as "slave" was associated with black and black became synonymous with inferior. Whatever one believes about the declining significance of race,[15] the associations between a black or African American identity and inferiority and the historical reality of racial discrimination have not diminished to the point that desire to avoid this stigmatized identity has been eliminated. As one interview participant noted, "[R]acism was practiced by our blacks same as whites. I had to be the great, greater, greatest achiever due to my skin color. To be black was a terrible experience."

However, lighter-skinned African Americans counter with the fact that they, too, are sometimes stereotyped. Interview participants noted that they were called "stuck-up, sell-outs, and Toms" and were perceived to have a range of negative personality traits. As one of the interview participants noted, "I had to fight just because girls were jealous of me because of my skin color. They thought that I believed that I was better than them, but I never felt that way. It wasn't true."

Expressions of Colorism

Colorism is observed in the United States just as it is observed among numerous nationalities and ethnic groups around the world. Physical features that suggest white ancestry are valued and result in the individual being viewed as more desirable, genetically superior, and worthy of higher social status and greater economic privileges.[16] Skin that is "too dark" is viewed as unattractive and belonging to the lower class,[17] creating pressure to lighten skin color to a more socially acceptable shade. Traditionally, there have been two ways to achieve lighter skin tones: skin lightening or makeup. R. Hall referred to skin lightening as the "bleaching syndrome."[18] Products such as skin bleaches and fade creams were developed with the intent of altering the skin tone to the preferred "light" shade.[19] African Americans continue to buy skin-lightening creams. This has also been observed in China and Japan.[20] And, as noted throughout the Caribbean, Central and South America, and South Asia, marriage options are often affected by skin color differences, with lighter skin tones resulting in better matches.[21]

Social and economic advantage

There is evidence that skin color matters in cross-racial and ethnic interactions. Numerous studies have indicated that variations in skin tone dictate differential life chances within the African American community.[22] Light skin is perceived as a valuable social resource, allowing the individual to receive preferential treatment in a variety of situations, including educational and occupational opportunities, income, and prominence within the community.[23]

African Americans generally experience an unemployment rate approximately twice that of whites.[24] However, data also suggest that individuals show a preference for lighter-skin candidates for employment when presented with employee profiles that differ only by the skin color portrayed in a photograph.[25] Harrison and Thomas noted that early in the twentieth century it was considered good business to hire lighter-skinned African Americans.[26] Harrison states:

> We found that a light-skinned black male can have only a bachelor's degree and typical work experience and still be preferred over a dark-skinned black male with an MBA and past managerial positions, simply because expectations of the light-skinned black male are much higher, and he doesn't appear as "menacing" as the darker-skinned male applicant.[27]

Hughes and Herte found that African Americans with lighter skin tones were likely to be better educated and to have higher salaries.[28] Subsequent studies have found that even when parental socioeconomic status is considered, socioeconomic advantages emerge for those with lighter skin.[29] Goldsmith, Hamilton, and Darity examined the affect of skin color on the wages of African Americans.[30] They noted that light-skinned African Americans earned wages similar to whites, wages declined as skin tone darkened, and darker African Americans earned less than whites. The researchers found that skin color association with wages held even as they accounted for union status, full- or part-time work, similarity of occupation, educational level, experience, and several other factors. Studies have also noted that dark-skinned African Americans are less likely to own homes and receive longer prison sentences for criminal convictions than their lighter-skinned counterparts.[31] Economic associations may explain skin color preferences in dating, marriage, and other close associations as people seek to optimize their social and economic positions and standing.

Perceptions of attractiveness

Historically, physical features, such as skin color, have played a major role in the lives of ethnic minorities in the United States, particularly African Americans. Lay theories of race inform attitudes related to skin color. Although race is now understood as a social construct,[32] studies suggest that physical characteristics perceived as having a biological basis are the strongest cues to group membership, even among African Americans.[33] The use of physiological characteristics to assign racial group membership focuses on skin color, hair texture, the shape of the nose and lips, and other physical attributes.[34] I propose that the development and use of these strategies of racial assignment reinforce colorism.

West has proposed that African Americans may be overwhelmed with the belief that their features are unacceptable in current society,[35] or that they have been labeled with certain characteristics because of stereotypical beliefs about people of African descent or dark skin. It has also been asserted that reactions to stereotypes of African Americans are so strong that topics associated with these portrayals (e.g., skin color, hair texture) are often issues in therapy with African Americans.[36] If true, the context color preference in the African American community is set.

Light skin has become synonymous with beauty, intelligence, morality, and virtually any other positive attribute,[37] and skin color has historically been used to justify racism, discrimination, and oppression. The preference for lighter skin tones is observed in many settings. Hall reported that African American college students preferred lighter skin,[38] and Ellison reported that study participants with lighter skin were described more positively than darker-skinned participants.[39] Similarly, judgments of attractiveness, intelligence, and suitability for dating and marriage are affected by skin colors, with lighter skin tones preferred.[40] Skin tone plays a role in perceived attractiveness of females by males and in dating and marriage.[41] Studies suggest that African Americans with darker skin tones are less likely to marry,[42] and Thompson Sanders has noted a continued preference for a lighter-skinned spouse among African American men.[43]

In my own research, even participants in their twenties have reported experiences of discrimination associated with skin color rather than purely race. One participant noted, "The white Roman Catholic nuns at my school favored the light-complexioned females by allowing them to try advanced math assignments that we [dark-skinned females] were not allowed to attempt." Another participant noted that "[I]t was hard for a dark-skinned girl to become a cheerleader."

The association of white features with beauty, goodness, and privilege are not only applicable to people; they are also applied to the icons of society. For example, while a white Santa Claus is considered acceptable for all children, regardless of race, ethnicity, or skin color, a black Santa in a predominantly European or white community would be considered ridiculous, and most children would reject his authenticity. This general response is replicated in the portrayal of religious icons and fictional superheroes. Jesus, for example, is described in the Bible as having caramel skin and hair made of wool, but the popular image universally projected of him as pale of skin and straight blond or light brown hair, and there are no sustained or commercially prominent black fictional superheroes.

Historically, research has suggested that lighter skin tones were more important for females within the African American community,[44] which Hill termed "gendered colorism."[45] Researchers have found that African American women who were less satisfied with the color of their skin also expressed less satisfaction with their overall physical appearance[46] and had lower self-esteem.[47] Regardless of their own skin tone, African American women perceive that African American men find light skin most attractive.[48] In addition, research suggests that the preoccupation with skin color results in personal dissatisfaction when an individual is on either end of the skin color continuum.[49]

Gendered colorism may explain why hair is often incorporated into discussions of colorism. Similar to dark skin color, coarse, tightly curled hair is seen as symbolic of an African connection, and hair texture, length, and style have made political and social statements. A quick Google search makes it clear that the term "good" hair is still in use in the African American community, although negative rather than affirmative reactions to the term's use are more prevalent. Historically, "good" hair has been defined as long and straight hair, similar to Caucasian hair.[50] Long, straight hair was idealized by women in the African American community and resulted in a higher social status within the community.[51] Again, examining Internet discourse on the topic suggests that loosely curled hair may now also qualify as "good hair," reflecting shifting community norms. Short, tightly curled African hair has been synonymous with "bad" hair[52] and viewed as a characteristic of those with dark skin.[53] It is estimated that 75 percent of African American women straighten their hair and that African Americans spend five times more money on hair care products than white women do.[54]

To be fair, there are ways in which dark-skinned African Americans can be privileged as a result of colorism.[55] Family members may become overprotective because of fears of the consequences their dark skin would bring. One female interviewed by Touré noted that her dark skin "became exoticized in a white world and [her] color was celebrated in weird ways."[56] In addition, there is some sense that black authenticity may be less subject to challenge among those whose skin is dark.

Colorism and Social Identity

Social identity theory suggests that group identity development is a cognitive process that uses social categories to define self.[57] Categories can be based on nationality, skin color, common history and oppression, and ancestry. Theoretically, social identities are based on the emotional significance and importance of group memberships for self-definition and their relevance to world view.[58] Salience affects when and how individuals access and use an identity, for example in integrated settings, on the job, and in child rearing.[59] Thus, the more stigmatizing the identity, the more likely it is that there will be variation in the strength of the identity among members and the greater the likelihood that members will identify with some and not all aspects of the identity.

Social identity can affect perception and response to the environment and when the content of the social identity is positive, it has been associated with an increase in frustration tolerance, sense of purpose, school achievement, and self-confidence.[60] Race serves as the basis for one of many social identities. Racial identification is considered important because of its ability to provide information on the relative positive or negative attitudes that an individual holds relevant to "their own racial or cultural group and their place in it."[61] Racial identity can be socially assigned or individually selected as desired, but racial identification is a continuous cognitive process of weighting social and personal needs and affective reactions against social and personal gains and costs. In this chapter, I discuss racial identity as the self-designation of group membership, and racial identification as the collection of attitudes the person holds as they relate to this designation, and the extent to which these attitudes inform an understanding of the self. As discussed below, racial identification is a multifaceted phenomenon, and the number of facets that must be explored and understood relate to the stigmatized nature of the identity.

Echoing Maslow's discussion of the need to belong,[62] Smith related racial identification to a sense of cultural identity and "peoplehood" or the sense of belonging and place that an identity can provide.[63] However, social identities may be stigmatized, leading to sensitivity to those components that are devalued and exposing individuals to marginalization and alienation from mainstream society. Reactions to the stigmatized aspects of identity result in fragmentation of the social identity and alter the way that the identity may be used to establish a functional, esteem-supporting sense of self. If membership in the black or African-descended racial group were not stigmatizing, we might assume the existence of a single, unified dimension of the racial identification construct; however, membership in the black/African-descended racial group is stigmatizing, while remaining socially relevant and retaining significant salience among a substantial segment of the population identified as black or African American. Thus, we expect racial identification to be fragmented and to result in a sense of fragmented peoplehood.

Zavalloni found evidence for the ability of individuals to accept a group identity without feeling compelled to accept or internalize all attributes typically associated with group membership.[64] Only certain aspects of the social identity need support the desired sense of acceptance and belonging achieved through association with the cultural or social identity under consideration. Thus, stigmatized identities result in fragmented social identities; fragmented identities with strong social relevance and high affective salience are not relinquished and can only result in a fragmented sense of peoplehood or belonging.

The line of reasoning proposed here does not assume that the fragmented identity is the single, absolute identity of the individual. It acknowledges the potential importance of other social identities, while also affirming the desire and need to embrace and celebrate a shared history and experience. The ability to embrace a historically important and shared identity can provide a strategy for socializing agents to instill a sense of pride and for individuals to enjoy a ready sense of community. Fragmentation problematizes fulfillment of the psychological need for belonging and peoplehood because there is shame associated with aspects of the identity in question.

A "fragmented" sense of racial identity militates against a strong sense of peoplehood. Individuals who have a fragmented sense of racial identification are often torn by competing models of the sense of peoplehood[65] or by what it means to be black/African American. Not all potential group members share an interest in the identity or identification and not all who share the identity and identification express that shared identity/identification in the same ways or with equal strength. In addition to prevailing attitudes and norms within the group itself, group members may look to the nongroup members for cues that suggest the advantageous components of an identity. While this phenomenon is often termed "black self-hatred," it is not a hatred of self or the group. It speaks to the complexities of identification in a society where one or more of a person's available social identities are stigmatized.

I prefer this notion of fragmented identity to notions of African American "self-hatred," because it removes African Americans from the tendency to attribute pathology to attitudinal and behavioral responses that are viable and understandable given a set of circumstances and a particular environment. As a clinician, I have encountered African Americans who were ambivalent about their identification with the group, including their response and reaction to skin color and other physical attributes, but they did not hate themselves, or African Americans as a group for that matter. This is not to say that individuals do not seek the material security or social status—the rewards and benefits that accrue from varied levels of privilege—associated with race and skin color. As a behavioral scientist I understand that, given the historical and social response to race and color, the best option is to address the environment that produces the privileging systems driving African American behavior rather than pathologize or cast aspersions on individuals.

Although this perspective on the discourse around racial identity/identification does not typically appear in the scholarly or popular discourse, there are several lines of research to support the fragmentation perspective. Williams was the earliest researcher in this area to suggest that African Americans might have varying group orientations coexisting in their repertoire of experiences.[66] Since African Americans incorporate various components of a racial identification into their self-systems, not all African Americans experience their blackness in quite the same way. Several theoretical models of racial identification assume that it is a multidimensional construct[67] and that variations in feelings and attitudes relate to aspects of this identity.[68] The literature is replete with analyses of these various aspects: physical,[69] sociopolitical aspects,[70] and psychological identification (awareness/group acceptance).[71]

Several researchers provide data that indicate the multidimensional nature of racial identification.[72] Hecht, Collier, and Ribeau noted the multidimensional nature of African American identification, in contrast to the one-dimensional nature of white racial identification.[73] Hilliard proposed, and Thompson Sanders demonstrated, the existence of four dimensions of racial identification that are relevant to the issue of colorism.[74] The proposed parameters reference: psychological aspects of identification, or the sense of belonging and commitment to the group experienced by the individual; cultural identification, or the level of awareness of group contributions to society as well as comfort with prevailing group norms related to dress, language, and artistic style; sociopolitical identification, or awareness or commitment to social, economic, and political well-being and progress of the group; and physical racial identification, the acceptance of the skin color, hair, and physical characteristics associated with the racial category assigned to those with dark or "black" skin. Physical racial identification, because of skin color's historical association with negative characteristics, is theoretically the dimension most vulnerable to the effects of fragmented identification.

My research has focused on the extent to which aspects of racial identification remain salient across psychological, sociopolitical, cultural and physical self-acceptance parameters. This work suggests that racial identification levels across parameters are highly variable.[75] Only 15 percent of participants held racial identification levels that were consistent across parameters, with 25.6 percent of participants having highly discrepant scores.[76] Psychological racial identification is the most likely aspect of racial identity to be embraced; plainly stated, most

African Americans admit to some ongoing sense of belonging and commitment to the group and the group's well-being and progress. Interestingly, the majority of participants, 44.6 percent, reported moderate levels of physical racial identification, and one-quarter of participants reported low levels of physical racial identification.[77] This suggests that most African Americans have some reservations related to the extent to which their physical presentation asserts an African or black identity, with one-quarter espousing strong reservations about a physical presentation that suggests African or blackness. Despite discussion of gendered colorism[78] or the differential pressure of skin color noted among men and women, there were no sex differences in levels of physical racial identification. These data suggest that the psychological reality of a people who live and work within a system that has made them vulnerable to denigration will continue to vacillate over the desirability of dark skin as well as associated physical attributes associated with the denigrated identity.

Fragmented peoplehood makes issues of physical self-acceptance among African Americans complicated, and the vacillation in physical racial identification is clearly evident when examining self-reported attitudes about physical attributes among African Americans.[79] My research suggests that African Americans currently report acceptance of a broad range of African physical features and attributes as evidenced by scores on a measure of physical racial identity; however, skin color preferences for mates and acceptance of African features, including the shape of lips and noses, received the lowest scores on the measure.[80] Nickens found that, while African American women freely reported African physical features as representative of their own body type, they were less likely to report these as ideal physical attributes or traits, suggesting continued belief that less African features are more attractive and more acceptable.[81] The data reported also indicate that the ability to accept a range of attributes was stronger among African American women compared with men. The strongest differences by sex were for shape of lips, African hairstyles, and spousal color preference. Young males with less income and male and female study participants with limited experience with discrimination appeared more likely to express a preference for more Caucasian features.[82]

Historical issues within the African American community may explain the role of demographic variables in explaining variation in physical racial identification. It is plausible that this phenomenon is associated with the historical use of skin color as an indication of status that is used when other avenues for status and self-image are unavailable.[83] Consistent with the discussion earlier in this chapter, African Americans continue to struggle against an ideology that privileges white and disadvantages black, but they recognize that light skin is associated in many ways with the American opportunity structure. Thus, low-income African American males, who may be unemployed or underemployed, may improve their self-esteem and image as a result of the ability to attract a lighter spouse, thus acquiring status.[84] Despite a recognition of racism, fragmented identification creates psychological space to accept behaviors that advantage some members of the community while disadvantaging others.

The chronic experience of discrimination is also a variable with implications for skin color preference. Data suggest that most African Americans have had some encounter with discrimination at some time in their lives.[85] African Americans with more experiences of discrimination express stronger group acceptance, pride, and cultural, sociopolitical, and physical racial identification, while those with minimal experiences of discrimination experience lower, more variable levels of consciousness, group acceptance, and pride.[86] Racism in the broader community suggests that those with darker skin will more often experience the levels of discrimination that heighten this pride and self-acceptance and limit fragmentation of racial identification. Individuals with limited experience of racial discrimination will experience greater fragmentation of identification and may be more willing to participate in a system that apportions privileges based on color due to the increased access to economic, social, and political opportunities it affords.

The work of Thompson, Sanders and Nickens also suggests that family norms, preferences, and pressures appear to be a strong influence on gendered colorism.[87] The patriarchal nature of society in general, and the African American community in particular, in conjunction with the racial identification process, likely encourages the use of female skin color and features as a means for men to acquire status, with secondary benefit to women and by extension their family. Although described here as an active socialization process, it is unlikely that the attitudes or messages are articulated directly and many may not be conscious. When a family recognizes the social and economic benefits that accrue to a woman due to skin color, parents and significant others provide subtle socialization messages aimed at increasing a woman's willingness to achieve the attributes that optimize social and economic opportunity—light or lighter skin color—through the processes available to lighten skin, alter eye color, lighten and lengthen hair, etc. Parents and significant others of the male provide socialization messages that encourage the selection of a mate who is likely to enhance his social status and, by extension, that of the family. This is true whether the man is of lower or higher socioeconomic status.

As African Americans observe the social and economic realities of access to the American opportunity structure based on skin color, dilemmas emerge. To what extent does any individual who feels that his or her skin color has produced an advantage related to employment, pay, etc. reject the benefits that accrue? Are individuals who are the recipients of these advantages in any way responsible for the disadvantage experienced by those who do not? And, finally, who is responsible for challenging this form of discriminatory behavior? The currently limited comment on and study of the role of skin color in our society can form the basis of new work in this area.

Colorism in Post-Obama America

Despite the election of the nation's first president of African descent, the issues of color remain. There are those who are willing to discuss the role that President Obama's lighter skin tone played in the ability of white America to consider voting for him.[88] America remains color-struck—black America definitely remains color stuck—because the aesthetics of white supremacy are so deeply embedded in so many of us.[89] And while it is true that white supremacy is embedded in our psyche, it is also true that colorism persists because the "structures of exclusion are still there," even if they are not as clear and explicit as they were in the past.[90]

Beyond current reactions to President Obama, we need look no further than the media to understand that the structures that reinforce colorism among African Americans persist even today. We need only examine the Twitter comments and posts expressing negative reactions to an African American actress being cast as Rue in the blockbuster movie *Hunger Games*. Fans also seemed disturbed that an African American actor was cast in the role of Cinna.[91] Comments ranged from disappointment to sadness and dismay that a sympathetic character, Rue, could be cast as an African American.[92] As has been historically true,[93] black actors do not equate to good, clever, and attractive characters among white American moviegoers. *These reactions emerged despite the fact that the book describes Rue as a person with "dark brown skin."* Americans read the book, but the subconscious allowed readers to block out the physical description and substitute the socially acceptable description. In another example of continued colorism in the broader society, an Acura Super Bowl commercial casting call listed an African American actor with the direction that the actor was "not too dark."[94] Color matters and, as illustrated in this example, skin color and skin tone may affect employment opportunities.

In addition to the persistence of colorism in the larger societal context, there are examples of this issue emerging among a new generation of African Americans. A recent *New York Times* article highlights the continued effects of the generations-old color consciousness found within the community as it affects today's youth. Seventh-graders at a New York school noted their experiences in a conversation on race:

> If you're darker, they'll call them burnt. Light-skinned ones get called white.
>
> The lighter-skinned girls think they're prettier. They say: "She's mad dark. Look at me, I'm much prettier."[95]

The psychological process of social weighting and balancing of the advantages and costs associated with blackness do not shift because discrimination manifests in different ways or because of the election of the first African-descended president of the United States. African Americans understand that color affects the ability to access economic, social, and political opportunities. For this reason, as racism seems to decrease, concerns about color intensify, as the odds that this physical feature will play a role in acceptance or rejection are based on imprecise statistical calculations. This process is a part of the dynamic racial identification equation. African Americans, like members of other racial/ethnic and identity groups, organize their understanding and expression of their social identities in order to minimize psychological, social, and economic harm and maximize access to the material and social opportunities available in the society. In fact as Glenn[96] notes, the racial hierarchy may be shifting to support a more subtle hierarchy based on skin pigmentation. Touré's dark-skinned interviewees noted changes in the extent to which dark skin was devalued, and Thompson Sanders' research suggests that there have been positive shifts in the extent to which colorism influences self-reported color preferences for a mate.[97] However, just as members of society learn ways of discussing race that can camouflage racist attitudes, we can discuss issues of skin color in ways that mask the lingering bias against individuals based on this stratification system.

Conclusions

This discussion highlights the importance of colorism as a component of racism and one of the most salient components of what I have previously called "fragmented peoplehood."[98] Fragmented peoplehood is a descriptive term for how people of color compartmentalize their identity, which allows them to resolve conflicting and contradictory attitudes about race and color. The history of race and color in the United States, and in other countries, has created a system that privileges white, light, and fair skin color, as well as other physical characteristics that suggest a background other than African heritage. This reality results in African Americans and other people of color seeking the privileges of "lighter skin," while at times creating tests of racial identity allegiance that can privilege those with darker skin over those with lighter skin. If color matters, then access to the American opportunity structure is restricted or optimized based on the extent to which an individual can approximate or secure relevant social relationships with those who have the requisite physical attributes.

Although African Americans are committed to the equality and advancement of the group as the primary concern,[99] they are also conscious of the need, on a personal level, to engage the larger society strategically. Situations and contexts are judged moment to moment and day to day to determine where the risks and benefits related to race—and, by extension, color—exist. When deemed necessary, our fragmented identity system permits strategic and self-serving (whether economic, educational, legal, or social) decisions. The decisions are made because they result in opportunities to advance, achieve success, and progress, sometimes at the expense of group members who are poorer, less well educated, and darker skinned. Thus, in order to maximize access to resources, power, and privilege, there is recognition of the advantages that a "lighter spouse" might provide, just as there is awareness of the ability to exploit the advantages associated with lighter skin tones. Similarly, dark skin can be exploited in situations where group support is linked to skin color as a litmus test to determine "black authenticity." This is not to say that love cannot cross racial, ethnic, or color lines, or that individuals with lighter skin tones are undeserving of their successes and those with darker skin tones are deserving of their triumphs; however, we cannot be blind to the realities of colorism, which derive from a history that privileges some based on a trivial physical feature such as skin color. The unequal burden of color must be addressed.

While this chapter has linked racism and colorism, they are distinct. The elimination of racism will not *ipso facto* eliminate colorism; in fact, the end of racism may mean the intensification of colorism. Until the end of racism occurs, those who encourage discussions of colorism may be viewed as disloyal or divisive within communities with high burdens of racism and colorism. There is, however, another plausible scenario.

The struggle for access to resources and opportunities is a major factor in human interaction. Race (executed based on skin color) and language have typically been the bases for stratifying groups in the United States; however, as darker members of recent immigrant communities acculturate, I believe that the impact of color will be more acutely felt. It is conceivable that members of diverse groups will recognize their common experience and the need to develop resources and strategies to address the insidious implication of color-based discrimination in our society. Voices across diverse racial and ethnic groups may strip away the concerns related to divisiveness in the struggle against racism and ethnocentrism and permit open examination of the uneven burden that these societal ills have generated.[100] The human need to acquire a sense of material security means that it is not easy to dismantle privileging systems; however, a first step is consciousness about what and who has been granted privilege. Once consciousness is secured, a conversation about healing fragmented psyches can begin.

Notes

1   Mark E. Hill, "Skin Color and the Perception of Attractiveness among African Americans: Does Gender Make a Difference?," *Social Psychology Quarterly* 65 (2002): 77.

2   Many interviews were conducted in confidentiality, and the names of interviewees are withheld by mutual agreement.

3   Lewis R. Gordon, "Racist Ideology," in *Turbulent Voyage: Readings in African American Studies,* ed. Floyd Hayes, III, 3rd edition (San Diego, CA: Collegiate Press, 1997), 505–509.

4   "Brief on Race and Genetic Determinism," Council for Responsible Genetics, accessed June 28, 2012, http://www.councilforresponsiblegenetics.org/ViewPage. aspx?pageId=.

5   Evelyn Glenn, introduction to *Shades of Difference: Why Skin Color Matters*, ed. Evelyn Glenn (Stanford, CA: Stanford University Press, 2009), 1–8.

6   Ernest R. Beck, "Black is Beautiful and It's History, Too," *Columbia News,* March 9, 2005, accessed September 13, 2012, http://www.columbia.edu/cu/news/05/03/black_artists.html.

7   See Kimberly Jade Norwood, "The Virulence of BLACKTHINK(tm) and How Its Threat of Ostracism Shackles Those Deemed Not Black Enough," *Kentucky Law Journal* 93(3) (2004–05): 143.

8   Beck, "Black is Beautiful and It's History, Too"; Nat Hentoff, "Post-Racial Society? Not Even Close," accessed July 10, 2012, http://www.cato.org/publications/commentary.

9   Keith B. Maddox and Stephanie A. Gray, "Cognitive Representations of Black Americans: Re-Exploring the Role of Skin Tone," *Personality and Social Psychology Bulletin* 28 (2002): 250.

10 Hill, "Skin Color and Perception," 77–91; Maddox and Gray, "Cognitive Representations," 250–259; Selena Bond and Thomas F. Cash, "Black Beauty: Skin Color and Body Images among African-American College Women," *Journal of Applied and Social Psychology* 22 (1992): 874–888; Kim S. Buchanan, "Creating Beauty in Blackness," in *Consuming Passions: Feminist Approaches to Weight Preoccupation and Eating Disorders*, eds Catrina Brown and Karin Jasper (Toronto: Second Story Press, 1993), 36–51; Mark E. Hill, "Color Differences in the Socioeconomic Status of African American Men: Results of a Longitudinal Study," *Social Forces* 78 (2000): 1437–1460; Michael Hughes and Bradley R. Hertel, "The Significance of Color Remains: A Study of Life Chances, Mate Selection, and Ethnic Consciousness among Black Americans," *Social Forces* 68 (1990): 1105–1120; Verna M. Keith and Cedric Herring, "Skin Tone and Stratification in the Black Community," *American Journal of Sociology* 97 (1991): 760–768; Kathy Russell, Midge Wilson, and Ronald Hall, *The Color Complex: The Politics of Skin Color among African Americans* (New York: Anchor, 1992), 2–8, 163–167; Richard Seltzer and Robert C. Smith, "Color Differences in the Afro-American Community and the Differences They Make," *Journal of Black Studies* 21 (1991): 279–286.

11 J. Blaine Hudson, "Democracy, Diversity, and Multiculturalism in American Higher Education: Issues, Barriers, and Strategies for Change," *Western Journal of Black Studies* 18 (1994): 222–226; Ian Robertson, *Sociology,* 3rd edition (New York: Worth, 1988), 298–300.

12 Hudson, "Democracy, Diversity," 222–226.

13 Robertson, *Sociology*, 299.

14 Angela M. Neal and Midge L. Wilson, "The Role of Skin Color and Features in the Black Community: Implications for Black Women and Therapy," *Clinical Psychology Review* 9 (1989): 323–333.

15 Julius Wilson, *The Declining Significance of Race: Blacks and Changing American Institutions*, 2nd edition (Chicago, IL: University of Chicago Press: J. 1978).

16 Neal and Wilson, "Black Women and Therapy," 323–333.

17 Touré, ed., *Who's Afraid of Post-Blackness? What It Means to Be Black Now* (New York: Free Press, 2011), 19–56.

18 Ronald Hall, "The Bleaching Syndrome: African Americans' Response to Cultural Domination vis-à-vis Skin Color," *Journal of Black Studies* 26 (1995): 172–184.

19 Buchanan, "Creating Beauty in Blackness," 36–51.

20 Hall, "Bleaching Syndrome," 172–184; Eugenia Kaw, "Medicalization of Racial Features: Asian American Women and Cosmetic Surgery," *Medical Anthropology Quarterly* 7 (1993): 74–89; Neal and Wilson, "Black Women and Therapy," 323–333.

21 Sarita Sahay and Niva Piran, "Skin-Color Preferences and Body Satisfaction among South Asian, Canadian and European-Canadian Female University Students," *Journal*

of Social Psychology 137 (1997): 161–171; Carlos H. Arce, Edward Murguia, and W. Parker Frisbie, "Phenotype and Life Chances among Chicanos," *Hispanic Journal of Behavioral Sciences* 9 (1987): 19–32; Roger N. Lancaster, "Skin Color, Race and Racism in Nicaragua," *Ethnology* 30 (1991): 339–353; Edward Murguia and Edward E. Telles, "Phenotype and Schooling among Mexican Americans," *Sociology of Education* 69 (1996): 276–289; Edward E. Telles and Edward Murguia, "Phenotypic Discrimination and Income Differences among Mexican Americans," *Social Sciences Quarterly* 71 (1990): 682–696; Frank F. Montalvo, "Surviving Race: Skin Color and the Socialization and Acculturation of Latinas," *Journal of Ethnic and Cultural Diversity in Social Work* 13 (2004): 25–43.

22   Hill, "Skin Color and Perception," 77–91; Hill, "Color Differences," 1437–1460; Hughes and Hertel, "Significance of Color," 1105–1120; Keith and Herring, "Skin Tone and Stratification," 760–768; Seltzer and Smith, "Color Differences," 279–286; Matthew S. Harrison and Kecia M. Thomas, "The Hidden Prejudice in Selection: A Research Investigation on Skin Color Bias," *Journal of Applied Social Psychology* 39 (2009): 134–168.

23   Hill, "Color Differences," 1437–1460; Hughes and Hertel, "Significance of Color," 1105–1120; Keith and Herring, "Skin Tone and Stratification," 760–768; Seltzer and Smith, "Color Differences," 279–286.

24   Harrison and Thomas, "The Hidden Prejudice in Selection," 134–168.

25   Ibid.

26   Ibid.

27   Matthew S. Harrison, "Skin Tone More Important than Educational Background for African Americans Seeking Jobs," accessed June 26, 2012, http://www.multi culturaladvantage.com/recruit/diversity/bias/Skin-Tone-More-Important-Than Educational-Background-African-Americans-Seeking-Jobs.asp.

28   Hughes and Hertel, "Significance of Color," 1105–1120.

29   Hill, "Color Differences," 1437–1460; Jennifer L. Hochschild and Vesla Weaver, "The Skin Color Paradox and the American Racial Order," *Social Forces* 80 (2007): 643–670; Arthur H. Goldsmith, Darrick Hamilton, and William Darity, Jr., "Shades of Discrimination: Skin Tones and Wages," *American Economic Review* 96 (2006): 242–245.

30   Goldsmith et al., "Shades of Discrimination," 244–245.

31   Hochschild and Weaver, "The Skin Color Paradox," 643–670.

32   American Anthropology Association, "AAA Statement on 'Race,'" *Anthropology Newsletter* 39 (1998): 3; Marshall H. Segall et al., *Human Behavior in Global Perspective: An Introduction to Cross Cultural Psychology,* 2nd edition (Boston, MA: Allyn and Bacon, 1999), 1–24.

33   Vetta L. Thompson Sanders and Maysa Akbar, "The Understanding of Race and the Construction of African American Identity," *Western Journal of Black Studies* 27 (2003): 80–88.

34   Janet Helms, *A Race is a Nice Thing to Have* (Topeka, KS: Content Communications, 1992); Philip C. Rodkin, "The Psychological Reality of Social Constructions," *Ethnic and Racial Studies* 16 (1993): 633–655.

35   Carolyn W. West, "Mammy, Sapphire, and Jezebel: Historical Images of Black Women and their Implications for Psychotherapy," *Psychotherapy* 32 (1995): 458–466.

36   Ibid.

37   Hill, "Skin Color and Perception," 77–91; Russell et al., *The Color Complex, 5.*

38   Ronald E. Hall, "Bias among African Americans Regarding Skin Color: Implications for Social Work Practice," *Research on Social Work Practice* 2 (1992): 479–486.

39   Christopher G. Ellison, "Are Religious People Nice People? Evidence from the National Survey of Black Americans," *Social Forces* 71 (1992): 411–430.

40 Hill, "Skin Color and Perception," 77–91; Thompson Sanders and Akbar; "The Understanding of Race," 80–88; Maxine S. Thompson and Verna M. Keith, "The Blacker the Berry: Gender, Skin Tone, Self-Esteem, and Self-Efficacy," *Gender and Society* 15 (2001): 336–357; Korie Edwards, Katrina Carter-Tellison, and Cedric Herring, "For Richer, For Poorer, Whether Dark or Light: Skin Tone, Marital Status, and Spouse's Earnings," in *Skin Deep: How Race and Complexion Matter in the "Color-Blind" Era*, ed. Cedric Herring et al. (Urbana, IL: University of Illinois Press, 2004), 65–81.

41 Hill, "Skin Color and Perception," 77–91.

42 Edwards et al., "For Richer, For Poorer," 65–81.

43 Thompson Sanders and Akbar, "The Understanding of Race," 80–88.

44 Hill, "Skin Color and Perception," 77–91; Maddox and Gray, "Cognitive Representations," 250–259; Bond and Cash, "Black Beauty," 874–888; Buchanan, "Creating Beauty in Blackness," 36–51; Neal and Wilson, "Black Women and Therapy," 323–333; Madeline Altabe, "Ethnicity and Body Image: Quantitative and Qualitative Analysis," *International Journal of Eating Disorders* 23 (1998): 153–159; Maya A. Poran, "Denying Diversity: Perceptions of Beauty and Social Comparison Processes among Latina, Black and White Women," *Sex Roles* 47 (July 2002): 65–72.

45 Hill, "Skin Color and Perception," 77–91.

46 Maddox and Gray, "Cognitive Representations," 250–259; Bond and Cash, "Black Beauty," 874–888; Jameca W. Falconer and Helen A. Neville, "African American College Women's Body Image: An Examination of Body Mass, African Self-Consciousness, and Skin Color Satisfaction," *Psychology of Women Quarterly* 24 (2000): 236–243.

47 Tracy L. Robinson and Janie V. Ward, "African American Adolescents and Skin Color," *Journal of Black Psychology* 21 (1995): 256–274.

48 Stephanie I. Coard, Alfiee M. Breland, and Patricia Raskin, "Perceptions of and Preferences for Skin Color, Black Racial Identity, and Self-Esteem among African Americans," *Journal of Applied Social Psychology* 31 (2001): 2256–2274.

49 Poran, "Denying Diversity," 65–72; Robinson and Ward, "African American Adolescents," 256–274; Coard et al., "Perceptions of and Preferences," 2256–2274.

50 Buchanan, "Creating Beauty in Blackness," 36–51; Hall, "Bleaching Syndrome," 172–184.

51 Beverly Greene, Judith C. White, and Lisa Whitten, "Hair Texture, Length, and Style as a Metaphor in the African American Mother-Daughter Relationship: Considerations in Psychodynamic Psychotherapy," in *Psychotherapy with African American Women: Innovations in Psychodynamic Perspective and Practice,* ed. Leslie C. Jackson and Beverly Green (New York: Guilford Press, 2000), 166–193.

52 Buchanan, "Creating Beauty in Blackness," 36–51.

53 Hall, "Bleaching Syndrome," 172–184.

54 Kamau Imarogbe, "Hair Misorientation: Free Your Mind and Your Hair Will Follow," in *African-Centered Psychology: Culture-focusing for Multicultural Competence,* ed. Daudi ya Azibo (Durham, NC: Carolina Academic Press, 2003), 201–220.

55 Touré, "Post-Blackness," 161–167.

56 Ibid., 164.

57 John C. Turner, "Towards a Cognitive Redefinition of the Social Group," in *Social Identity and Intergroup Relations,* ed. H. Tajfel (Cambridge, UK: Cambridge University Press, 1982), 15–40.

58 Sheldon Stryker, *Symbolic Interactionism: A Social Structural Version* (Menlo Park, CA: Benjamin Cummings, 1980), 51–55.

59 Sheldon Stryker and Anne Stratham, "Symbolic Interactionism and Role Theory," in *The Handbook of Social Psychology,* eds Gardner Lindzey and Elliot Aronson (New York: Random House, 1985), 311–378.

60 Vetta L. Thompson Sanders, "The Complexity of African American Racial Identification," *Journal of Black Studies* 32 (2001): 155–165.

61 Robert T. Carter and Janet E. Helms, "The Relationship between Racial Identity Attitudes and Social Class," *Journal of Negro Education* 57 (1988): 23.

62 Abraham H. Maslow, *Toward a Psychology of Being* (New York: Van Nostrand, 1962), 113–125, 172.

63 Elsie M. Smith, "Black Racial Identity Development: Issues and Concerns," *Counseling Psychologist* 17 (1989): 277–288.

64 Marissa Zavalloni, "Social Identity: Perspectives and Prospects," *Social Science Information* 12 (1973): 65–91.

65 Smith, "Black Racial Identity," 278.

66 Robert L. Williams, *Manual of Directions for Williams Awareness Sentence Completion* (St. Louis, MO: Robert L. Williams & Associates, 1976), 1–2.

67 Thompson Sanders, "The Complexity," 155–165; Smith, "Black Racial Identity," 278; Michael L. Hecht, Mary Jane Collier, and Sidney A. Ribeau, *African American Communication: Ethnic Identity and Cultural Interpretation* (Newbury Park, CA: Sage, 1993), 166–167; Hilliard Asa, "Parameters Affecting African American Racial Identification," paper presented at the Black Psychology Seminar, Duke University, Durham, NC, February 1985.

68 Thompson Sanders, "The Complexity," 155–165; Robert M. Sellers et al., "Multidimensional Model of Racial Identity: A Re-conceptualization of African American Racial Identity," *Personality and Social Psychology Review* 2 (1998): 18–39.

69 Kenneth B. Clark and Mamie Clark, "Racial Identification and Preferences in Negro Children," in *Readings in Social Psychology*, eds Theodore M. Newcomb and Eleanor L. Hartley (New York: Holt, Rinehart, and Winston, 1947), 169–178; Herbert J. Greenwald and Don B. Oppenheim, "Reported Magnitude of Self Misidentification among Negro Children: Artifact?" *Journal of Personality and Social Psychology* 8 (1968): 49–52; Joseph Hraba and Geoffrey Grant, "Black is Beautiful: A Re-examination of Racial Preference and Identification," *Journal of Personality and Social Psychology* 16 (1970): 398–402; Catherine Landreth and Barbara Johnson, "Young Children's Responses to a Picture and Inset Test Designed to Reveal Reactions to Different Skin Color," *Child Development* 24 (1953): 63–79.

70 Sellers et al., "Multidimensional Model," 18–39; Lafayette W. Lipscomb, "Parental Influence in the Development of Black Children's Racial Self-Esteem," PhD dissertation, University of North Carolina, 1974; Willie D. Smith, "The Effects of Racial Milieu and Parental Racial Attitudes and Rearing Practices on Black Children's Racial Identity, Self-Esteem, and Consequent Behaviors," PhD dissertation, Stanford University, 1974.

71 Williams, *Manual of Directions*, 1–2; Joseph A. Baldwin, "African (Black) Psychology: Issues and Synthesis," *Journal of Black Studies* 16 (1987): 235–249.

72 Hecht et al., *African American Communication*, 165–167; David H. Demo and Michael Hughes, "Socialization and Racial Identity among Black Americans," *Social Psychology Quarterly* 53 (1990): 364–374.

73 Hecht et al., *African American Communication*, 166–167.

74 Asa, "Parameters," unpublished lecture; Vetta L. Thompson Sanders, "A Multidimensional Approach to the Assessment of African American Racial Identification," *Western Journal of Black Studies* 15 (1991): 154–158. Vetta L. Thompson Sanders, "The Multidimensional Structure of Racial Identification," *Journal of Research in Personality* 29 (1995): 208–222.

75 Thompson Sanders, "The Complexity," 155–165.

76 Ibid.

77 Ibid.

78 Hill, "Skin Color and Perception," 77–91.

79   Asa, "Parameters," unpublished lecture; Thompson Sanders, "A Multidimensional Approach," 154–158; Thompson Sanders, "The Multidimensional Structure," 208–222.

80   Vetta L. Thompson Sanders, "African American Body Image: Identity and Physical Self-Acceptance," *Humboldt Journal of Social Relations* 30 (2006): 44–67.

81   Shannon D. Nickens, "Exploration of Ideal Body Image among African-American Women," PhD dissertation, University of Missouri-St. Louis, 2005.

82   Thompson Sanders, "African American Body Image," 44–67.

83   Touré, "Post-Blackness," 19–56; Keith and Herring, "Skin Tone and Stratification," 760–768.

84   Thompson Sanders and Akbar, "The Understanding of Race," 80–88; Thompson and Keith, "The Blacker the Berry," 336–357; Edwards et al., "For Richer," 65–81.

85   Hope Landrine and Elizabeth A. Klonoff, "The Schedule of Racist Events: A Measure of Racial Discrimination and a Study of its Negative Physical and Mental Health Consequences," *Journal of Black Psychology* 22 (1996): 144–168.

86   Vetta L. Thompson Sanders, "Factors Affecting African-American Racial Identity Salience and Racial Group Identification," *Journal of Social Psychology* 139 (1999): 748–761.

87   Thompson Sanders, "African American Body Image," 44–67; Nickens, "Exploration of Ideal."

88   Touré, "Post-Blackness," 184.

89   Ibid., 162.

90   Ibid., 151.

91   Christopher Rosen, "Hunger Games' Racist Tweets: Fans Upset Because of Rue's Race," *Huffington Post,* March 26, 2012, accessed July 9, 2012, http://www.huffingtonpost.com/2012/03/26/hunger-games-racist-tweets-rue_n_1380377.html.

92   Ibid.

93   Hill, "Skin Color and Perception," 77–91; Russell et al., *The Color Complex*, 135–136.

94   MSN NOW, "Casting Sheet for Acura Ad Called for 'Not Too Black' Actor," accessed June 9, 2012, http://now.msn.com/casting-sheet-for-acura-ad-called-for-not-too-black-actor.

95   N. R. Kleinfield, "Why Don't We Have Any White Kids?," *The New York Times,* May 11, 2012, accessed June 4, 2012, http://www.nytimes.com/2012/05/13/education/at-explore-charter-school-a-portrait-of-segregated-education.html.

96   Glenn, introduction to *Shades of Difference*, 1–8.

97   Thompson Sanders, "African American Body Image," 44–67.

98   Thompson Sanders, "The Complexity," 155–165.

99   Hochschild and Weaver, "The Skin Color Paradox," 643–670.

100   Ibid.

7

COLORISM AND BLACKTHINK

A Modern Augmentation of Double Consciousness

Kimberly Jade Norwood

[T]he Negro is a sort of seventh son, born with a veil, and gifted with second-sight in this American world,—a world which yields him no true self-consciousness, but only lets him see himself through the revelation of the other world. It is a peculiar sensation, this double-consciousness, this sense of always looking at one's self through the eyes of others, of measuring one's soul by the tape of a world that looks on in amused contempt and pity. One ever feels his two-ness,—an American, a Negro; two souls, two thoughts, two unreconciled strivings; two warring ideals in one dark body, whose dogged strength alone keeps it from being torn asunder.[1]

As a result of the history of the black experience in the United States from the early 1600s to the present, two very interesting practices have simultaneously grown and thrived in black America.[2] One practice deals with a strong skin tone preference among blacks for other blacks who are light in skin tone, or "colorism."[3] Although colorism is practiced worldwide,[4] its origins in the United States are uniquely linked to the way in which black people were introduced into this country. For centuries, enslaved black people came to understand that white and light skin were more valued than dark skin, and the results of this indoctrination persist today. Another practice, also connected to the historical black/white experience unique to the United States, is a practice I call "blackthink." Blackthink attempts to define what it means to be black and rejects anything that does not fit into that definition. Blacks who do not live as blacks are expected to are viewed as imposters or traitors to blackness and risk symbolic expulsion from the black community. Both practices discriminate based on the color of one's skin. In combination they pose a curious dichotomy: There is an adoration of light and white skin on the one hand but, on the other hand, practices that purportedly mimic whiteness, or that do not advance blackness, are abhorred.

Colorism in Black America

> There is no mystery as to why after all these years of black resistance to white racism, skin-color politics continues to be a negative force in our lives. White-supremacist thinking about color is so embedded in every aspect of contemporary life that we are daily bombarded in the mass media with images that suggest blackness is not beautiful.[5]

The preference for light skin over dark skin has existed in America since the country's beginning. Africans brought to the United States were enslaved and colonized by their white captors. The children born of the sexual unions between whites and blacks—and largely between enslaved African women and their white male captors—produced children, half black, half white, then commonly called mulattoes.[6] Because of the frequent lighter skin complexion of these children, they commonly held a different status relative to their nonmixed race and/or darker-skinned counterparts. There is evidence that these lighter-skinned individuals, who also often had hair closer in texture to the hair of whites—often called "good" hair[7]—were valued more by whites; for example, higher prices were paid for them on the auction blocks than for the darker-skinned counterparts.[8] The lighter-skin slaves often had a better quality of life.[9] Because they often worked inside the home of the slave owners, they were more familiar with, and thus comfortable around, the language, the speech, the culture, and the religious practices of the slave owners. Additionally, many were taught to read and write, taught trades and were hired out as craftsmen. Many were even freed by their slave-owning fathers and/or left property upon the father's death—property that in some cases included slaves of their own.[10]

Mulattoes ultimately became a buffer class between whites and blacks, and whites preferred to deal with them, believing them to be more intelligent and more culturally refined than Africans.[11] Many Africans, too, came to see mulattoes not only as their connection to white America, but better than them.[12] This created tension and disunity in the enslaved community:

> As color increasingly divided the slave community, frictions developed in the cabins. Light-skinned slaves returning home from their days in the "big house" imitated the genteel ways of upper-class white families, and the mulatto offspring of the master often flaunted their education. Many field hands both envied and resented the house servants.[13]

Some mulattoes actually did come to believe themselves better than their darker-skinned counterparts.[14] In fact, some associated so completely with their owners that they came to see themselves as one with their owners. Of this phenomenon, Malcolm X once famously noted: "If the master got sick, the house Negro would say, 'What's the matter, boss, *we* sick? He identified himself with his master, more than the master identified with himself.'"[15] Of course, not all mulattoes lived a better existence when compared with their darker-skinned brethren or wanted to escape their blackness. There is evidence, for example, that lighter-skinned females were more sexually exploited than their darker-skinned sisters.[16] There also is evidence of many in the mulatto class who dedicated their lives to the advancement of all blacks, their already privileged existence based on skin color notwithstanding.[17]

Slavery's end highlighted the differences between light-skinned and dark-skinned blacks. Many, if not most, mulattoes were already free by the end of the Civil War.[18] That group entered Reconstruction with more property, wealth, education, employment skills, and knowledge of the etiquette and culture of the white slave-owning class than their darker-skin slaves.[19] Even mulattoes who were not free by the end of the Civil War often entered Reconstruction with skills such as the ability to read, to write, to cook, to drive, to do carpentry work, and other valuable skills. All of these benefits, combined with the attributes of light skin and straight hair, became valuable capital for the mulatto class. Whites were more comfortable around them and they were thus preferable to darker-skinned blacks. The preferences led to employment, access to housing, and ultimately income and assets that were passed down to children and grandchildren. They became the elite of the black classes.[20] Even Dr. W. E. B. Du Bois's Talented Tenth, who he hoped would uplift the masses of black people, were, with one exception, all mulattoes.[21]

By the beginning of the twentieth century, it was clear in black America that the lighter one's skin, the greater the societal and communal bestowed/received/obtained benefits. The elevation in success and status based on white blood was so clear and unequivocal that the mulatto group almost always socialized and married people whose skin tone matched their own or was lighter. Aside from actual assimilation via the phenomenon of "passing,"[22] mulattoes who elected not to pass often created their own communities, segregated from their darker-skinned brethren. This included separate neighborhoods, churches, and schools.[23] Law Professor Trina Jones found that not only were there separate schools based on color, but even the curricula differed: Mulattoes were exposed to a broader liberal arts curriculum, while darker-skinned blacks received the lower-paying vocational education tracks.[24] The self-segregation included invitation-only social networks that required invitees to pass the ruler test or brown paper bag test—your skin had to be lighter than a ruler or lighter than a brown paper bag for admission[25]—or one had to be able to show clearly visible blue veins under pale skin as required by the so-called "blue vein societies."[26]

Today, the preference for light skin over dark skin is completely sown into the American fabric.[27] In the United States, people with light skin have higher annual earnings and wealth, live in more affluent neighborhoods, are more educated, have higher status jobs, and marry higher status spouses than their darker-skinned counterparts. The data for darker-skin blacks is not only the polar opposite in these categories, but darker-skin blacks also suffer at greater percentages in the criminal justice system and even in health.[28] As is true in society at large, the benefits of lighter skin within black America are undeniable and clear. Consider the following:

- Within black family members, it is not uncommon to have family members who not only favor the lighter children in the family over the darker siblings but who also visibly discriminate against the darker-skin children.[29] This often causes the darker-skin children to despise the lighter-skin children and creates hatred and envy.[30]
- Dark-skin blacks have been vilified by other blacks for their dark skin with names such as "buckwheat," "jigaboo," "darkie," "blackie," "tar baby," "burned," "baboon," and "skillet blonde."[31] It is not unheard of even today to hear kids say: "Yo mama so black, she . . ." "Get your black ass over here!" "Why you so black?"[32] Nappy hair makes the hatred even more intense. Naturally wooly hair is often looked upon with ridicule and scorn.[33] At some historically black colleges and universities (HBCUs), black hair in its natural state, despite cleanliness and neatness, is considered unacceptable, unprofessional, and unwelcomed.[34] Some elementary and secondary schools have effectively banned all natural hair choice options for girls, including locs, braids, twists, Afros, and Afro-puffs.[35]
- Some black parents tell their sons not to bring home "dark girls" and to marry light in order to lighten up the race."[36]
- Some black mothers have been heard thanking God that their newborn babies are not dark-skinned.[37]
- When seeking to adopt, many black women "come in and ask for . . . a 'Cadillac' description: Light-skinned, gray-green eyes, good hair, musically inclined."[38]
- Young black girls are told that they are "pretty to be so black" or hear "she's dark but she's pretty."[39]
- Little girls in showers (and even in public pools) have been caught scrubbing their skin incessantly, hoping to wash the black off.[40] Artwork documents this practice.[41]
- Little light-skin girls have told their darker sisters to stay away from them for fear of the black taint rubbing off on them.[42]
- Leaders of black political and social organizations—including governors, mayors, federal and state legislatures, those in the Obama inner circle, the NAACP, the Urban League, fraternities and particularly sororities, black social organizations like the Links, Jack & Jill of America, 100 Black Men, 100 Black Women, and past and current presidents at HBCUs—are often fair in skin tone.
- Light-skin females are the preferred mates of successful black males of any skin color[43] and are more likely to be married.[44] Those who also have European facial features and good hair are more valued.[45]

- Light-skin females are more likely to appear in, and be the love interest in, music videos of famous black music artists.[46] Dark-skin women are rarely considered for music video roles unless they offer something more than their pretty faces.[47] So, despite statements to the contrary,[48] ethnic beauty is the new "it" factor only so far as the ethnic or exotic beauty is not too dark and has good hair.
- In twenty-first-century doll tests, young black girls almost unanimously attach positive associations with light-skin images; similarly, they almost unanimously attach negative feelings to the images of children with dark skin.[49]
- Some dark-skin women in the twenty-first century are ashamed of their skin color.[50]
- Successful black women are often portrayed in the media as lighter than they actually are.[51]
- Light-skin parties and "battle of the complexions" contests still take place in nightclubs across America.[52]

Beauty in America is defined by European ideals.[53] This largely explains the gender divide we see in colorism as well: Dark-skinned women are not received, anywhere, with the same openness that dark-skinned males are. Dark-skin males do complain of discrimination against them in favor of their lighter-skin counterparts as well. Yet, because beauty is gendered, dark skin women feel the brunt of rejection at greater percentages than dark-skin men.[54] The seeds of colonization have grown and thrive, playing a role here, too, in the black consciousness of what is beautiful, what is worthy, what is successful, and what is valuable. This perfect storm informs what valued black women look like. Glancing at the centerfolds and covers of many black magazines makes the point clearly that "[i]n the eyes of many, including black people, beauty is to be seen only in women who have an infusion of Caucasian blood."[55] No wonder little black girls, with tears in their eyes, beg God to wash their black skin away. They know, as young as 3 and 4 years old, that lighter skin brings love, attention, and acceptance—that it represents access to a better life. And they think: Surely I want that.[56]

Blackthink

"Black," in our political and social reality, means those descended from West African slaves. Voluntary immigrants of African descent (even those descended from West Indian slaves) are just that, voluntary immigrants of African descent with markedly different outlooks on the role of race in their lives and in politics. At a minimum, it can't be assumed that a Nigerian cabdriver and a third-generation Harlemite have more in common than the fact a cop won't bother to make the distinction. They're both "black" as a matter of skin color and DNA, but only the Harlemite, for better or worse, is politically and culturally black, as we use the term.[57]

As we have seen, colorism, as practiced in the black community, is a behavioral pattern that preferences light-skin blacks over dark-skin blacks. It values people based on the color of their skin. It is not the only custom within black America, however, that discriminates based on skin color. Consider a doctrine I call blackthink. Blackthink, too, is a form of discrimination based on skin color, or, perceived blackness. It is an attempt to determine who is really black and who is not black enough, and it makes these determinations based on certain criteria. Being black is not simply a matter of DNA (drops of blood), who your parents are, how you look, how you categorize yourself or your thoughts, beliefs, or practices. Rather it includes additional markers, as defined by the guardians of black identity, once famously labeled the "Soul Patrol,"[58] of black authenticity. Fraudulent perpetrators are not *really* black.[59] They are imposters who deserve to be stripped of their black identity, as if blackness were a garment. Labeled sellouts, Uncle Toms, house niggers, Oreos, or racial traitors, they are often verbally assailed, publicly humiliated, and symbolically banned from association and/or affiliation with "real" black people.[60]

Interestingly, the blackthink analysis is only applied to those people who the accusers believe actually *are* black. Consider: President Obama has been accused of not being black enough, as well as Colin Powell, Condoleezza Rice, and Clarence Thomas. These are all people, who, if you look at them you would easily label them as black. Not true, for example, of George W. Bush, Hillary Clinton, and Antonio Scalia. They are not black, in perception at least. Nor would you hear someone criticizing them for not being black enough. You see the point. Those who are charged with not being black or black enough are somehow actually perceived as being black but are not accepted culturally or politically as black. In other words, merely being black in the biological or phenotypical sense is a start but not conclusive. Cultural and political blackness are the key criteria for true genuine blackness.

Who Is Black?

There is no definitive, universal definition of who is black; indeed, defining who is black is complex.[61] It is largely believed today that there is no such thing as biological races, as the genetic markers between any two given black people, for example, could be more varied than those between a given black person and white person.[62] Thus, many scientists and scholars assert that race is more a social construct.[63] There are phenotypical characteristics within groups of people, to be sure, but the idea of race as we refer to it today—black, white, yellow—is traced by historians to origins in the eighteenth century.[64] And, since that time, who qualified as black has been defined, variedly in quantity, by the one-drop rule: One drop of black blood made one black.[65]

Today the one-drop rule is losing significance. With the category changes in the 2010 census, society saw more black people *rejecting* black designations based on the one drop of black blood and choosing, instead, different identities.[66] This transition affecting racial classifications has complicated the question of who is black. For purposes of this chapter, though, we can rely on a fairly simple definition: A person is black if based on skin color and/or phenotype, the person is perceived by others as black. So, for example, this definition does not include those actually defined as black but who are not perceived as black. Susie Phipps in Louisiana, who was raised as white, looked white and lived her life as a white woman. It was only after applying for her passport as an adult that she learned that she was classified as black on her birth certificate.[67] Based on skin color and perception, Ms. Phipps would not be perceived as a black (and thus would never be ridiculed as a traitor). On the other hand, this chapter rightly includes people like Tiger Woods, who, although he has rejected a black classification, are perceived as black.

Once a person is *perceived* as black, certain rules, expectations, and stereotypes apply. No questions asked. Many people, at many different times and for many different reasons, engage in this labeling. Some people, for example, automatically apply racist stereotypes against black people. Take, for example, the fairly universal presumptions that blacks are lazy, poor, criminal, and uneducated. These are negative stereotypes that are automatically applied to black people. There are exceptions to the rules, and many white people have been known to point to one or two black friends who do not fit the stereotypes, but overall these are the general types of negative stereotypes associated with black people. This chapter does not deal with these types of stereotypes. Rather, I refer to another group of stereotypes that relies on another set of "criteria" to separate real black people from fraudulent perpetrators.

What Are the Defining Criteria of Blackness?

The Soul Patrol believes, based on unclear and unidentified criteria, that they are qualified to identify real black people. Interestingly, there is no process involved to become such a guardian. One may not even realize he or she is a member of the Soul Patrol until a given situation presents itself. I have seen black people criticize the policing of blackness but occasionally police blackness themselves. Moreover, one's identity as a guardian is not static. One might be a member of the Patrol one day but not the next. Professor Michael Eric Dyson has, as a guardian of blackness, vehemently accused other blacks of not really being black.[68] Recently, however, he has questioned the practice of judging blackness.[69]

Another wrinkle here is the fact that Soul Patrol members do not themselves have to be black, however defined. My own authenticity was once challenged by a white colleague.[70] President Obama's blackness has been challenged by a professed member of Al-Qaeda![71] The race or ethnicity of the guardian seemingly is irrelevant. The focus is on the target: Legitimate black people think certain thoughts, pursue certain political paths, and live certain lives. If you fall outside of this expectation, you are not really black and anyone can challenge your authenticity.

Now, although it is not always clear who the guardians are or how one becomes a guardian of blackness, there apparently are rules on *how* to be black. Biological blackness, the who is black biologically question, is nearly impossible to delineate. Yet, *how* to be black, *i.e.*, are you "*culturally*" black, has not only been defined but in many cases has become *the* litmus test for determining one's black authenticity. Falling outside of expectations can be eyebrow-raising at a minimum, expulsion from the "community" at the extreme. Examples of suspect characteristics, activities, or conduct include the following:

- failure of biracial (part black and part white) individuals to identify as black
- talking *proper*
- living in the suburbs
- dressing, walking, dancing like white people
- listening to "white" music
- marrying a white person
- *acting white* by excelling in school—attending school, doing homework, performing well on tests, participating in the class discussion, taking advance placement (AP) courses, etc.
- failure to trace one's ancestry to slavery in America, which, in President Obama's case, has also morphed into the failure to trace one's ancestry to West Africans enslaved in America
- voting Republican or being a political conservative (this includes the often related taboos of failing to support a liberal or progressive agenda, failing to stand up for issues deemed imperative to the black community, and the failure to support affirmative action)
- immutable characteristics of having light skin and/or good hair.

I have elaborated on all of these categories in earlier work,[72] but I provide a few examples below. Take the first marker on the list: the failure of a biracial person to identify as black. Focusing on a traditionally biracial (product of black and white parents) child, many biracial individuals tell stories of the pressure to identify as black or risk communal ostracism.[73] Tiger Woods found himself tangled in this web back in 1997, when he declared himself to be not black but rather "Cablinasian."[74] There was tremendous anger within the black community for Woods' failure to proclaim his blackness. Yet, he spoke the truth. He was not *only* black but also many other things. By and large, though, Mr. Woods' refusal to choose a black identity caused wide-scale offense within black communities across the country. A different response holds for those biracial adults who either hold themselves out as being black or who otherwise fully embrace their black side. They are welcomed in the black community with open arms. Consider: Newark Major Corey Booker, former NAACP President Benjamin Jealous, singers Mariah Carey and Alicia Keys, and actress Halle Berry. These are examples of biracial individuals who have embraced a black identity. They are rewarded with open arms, a loving wink to their decision to claim blackness. Pressured to choose, and choosing black, allows unfettered access into the black community. Ironically, this demand of all or nothing has direct ties to the one-drop rule, a rule used historically to oppress in a different context.[75]

Another marker relates to the phenomenon known as *acting white*. This is a charge leveled, primarily although not exclusively,[76] in the context of black students who want to perform well in school and/or who are performing well in school. My own life experiences and my prior survey of black students across the country revealed that black students who attended school on a regular basis, who turned in their homework, who raised their hands and participated in class, who performed well on tests, and who signed up for honors and advance placement classes were often accused by other blacks as "acting white."[77] While some scholars have questioned the reality of this practice, I know it exists—as one who was so accused and as one who has interviewed scores of other black students taunted for their academic strength. This is not just a matter of being teased for being a geek. Geeks still are left with their racial identities untouched and intact. Not true for those accused of acting white, who are metaphorically stripped of their blackness because being smart is equated to whiteness. This practice is ironic given the very strong black historical pursuit of education in this country.[78] If striving to do one's best in school means acting white, then what is acting black?

Another interesting behavioral taboo is the marginalization of those who are considered political conservatives, Republicans, those who oppose affirmative action, and those who do not appear to support issues deemed important to the larger black community. Supreme Court Justice Clarence Thomas falls into this category. Justice Thomas is the product of two black parents, and he also is a descendant of slaves from *West* Africa, something President Obama has been faulted for lacking.[79] Justice Thomas present himself as a black man, has the skin color phenotype of a black man, and believes his work on the Supreme Court is in the best interest of black people. Yet, because of his extreme conservatism, his accusers have challenged his blackness. He is not really black, his challengers allege, because of the way that he intellectualizes on social issues.[80] He has been called a racial traitor (and worse) who should be expelled from the black community.[81]

President Obama occasionally finds himself in this predicament as well. America, and indeed the world, looks upon him as a black man.[82] He has made history for being America's first African American president.[83] He, too, sees and portrays himself as black. He "looks" black in skin tone and phenotype. Put a hoodie on him and he would have the same problems catching a taxicab in New York City just as any other black male. Yet his blackness has been questioned on multiple levels: 1) He is not the descendant of enslaved people brought to

America from West Africa, nor has he lived the experience of native-born blacks in America;[84] 2) he has refused to declare himself the president of "black" America, and he has failed to give voice to race and issues most negatively impacting black Americans. The accusations bantered about between prominent black voices in this area have become toxic at times.[85]

Other markers, such as living in the suburbs and marrying outside of the race, are perplexing. A significant part of the civil rights struggle went to secure the rights of all people, to live where they want, and to marry who they wanted.[86] Exercising these hard-won gains still raises the eyebrows of some black gate-keepers.

Another marker includes a category of *immutable* characteristics. Consider the allegations hurled at black people as not really being black because they have light skin and/or good hair. Many light-skin blacks tell stories of being called "half-breed," "high yella," "white bitches," "wannabes," "redbone," and "light, bright and damn near white." The taunts are reportedly often worse for those who also have good hair. The venom is hurled at light-skin blacks, of both genders, by other blacks based solely on *the color of their skin*. They are labeled as uppity and bourgeois snobs. They are accused of thinking that they are better than their darker-skinned counterparts. Countless stories exist for the many who are hated as soon as they enter a room:

> "I'm gonna sneak inside your cabin when you go to sleep," the girl seethed, "and cut off your ponytail!" Hate roiled in her onyx eyes; malice rouged the rich, dark chocolate hue of her cheeks . . . While the girls in bunks around me giggled about cute boys and told scary stories, my 10-year-old heart hammered with terror for another reason: Hate from my own race.
>
> Because I was born on the terrain within the African-American community marked LIGHT, and that girl entered the world in the zone classified as DARK, she hated me for no other reason.
>
> And so she launched a verbal assault that officially enlisted me in the centuries-old war that Black people wage daily against each other's minds, bodies and spirits.
>
> While my long, curly hair survived the night, her hostility scarred my psyche: Would my appearance always inspire "hate at first sight" from dark-skinned people?
>
> Three decades later, sadly, too many situations affirm that anxiety; . . . icy glares from strangers . . . evil eyes . . . And recently, in exercise class, a half-dozen Sisters actually heckled me.[87]

I recently discussed this very issue with a mother of a light-complected boy one afternoon. The mother, a very fair-skinned biracial black female with long straight hair, told me that her very fair, straight-haired son did not fare well at all at an all-black elementary school. The mother had to withdraw her son from the school because, during his long and difficult year at the school, he was bullied daily by darker-skinned children. While being called a white boy, he was often physically assaulted, an ironic twist on a hate crime. The bullies in this case were *7 and 8 years old.* These children verbally and physically attacked other children based solely on the color of their skin: The black child masquerading in white skin is deemed white, too light, not black enough, and thus unacceptable.

These examples of marginalization, and in some cases ostracism, occur because of *immutable* characteristics: taunts, teases, slurs, and hatred hurled at black Americans simply because they are born with a light or fair complexion and/or because they have straight hair. There are even cases involving blacks who are taunted and ridiculed for having light-colored eyes. My husband and I are guardians for my young cousin, who not only has light skin but who also has hazel-colored eyes. He is adored by many, adults and children, black and white, because of his eyes. Yet, young dark-skinned black boys have occasionally walked up to him making jabbing motions toward his eyes. I think we can agree that this is a sign of hate. And it is based on an immutable characteristic.

Excoriation based on light-colored eyes, straight hair, and/or light skin not only borders on lunacy, but it replicates the very discrimination historically hurled by white Americans against black Americans—hatred based on immutability of skin color. In some ways this represents an example of the oppressed oppressing others, a historically common and still haunting practice.[88]

What Drives Blackthink?

Attempts to deny people of their claim to blackness are not always meant to be permanent. In the case of the behavioral markers for blackness, for example, the name-calling is largely meant to shame the alleged violator back on the path of black authenticity. By and large, those throwing the stones *want* the violator to correct his or her behavior and return to true blackness. The act of ostracizing and name-calling is, in some measure, a type of tough love. There is a strong sense in the black community that blacks must stick together or group disintegration (and, ultimately, extinction) will occur. Sticking together means a lot of different things, including supporting causes and issues that disproportionately affect black Americans. Indeed, there was a time not terribly long ago when virtually every black person in America shared the same goals: freedom from enslavement; citizenship; the right to vote; the end of convict leasing, peonage and Jim Crow laws; ability to marry who you wanted and to live where you wanted; and the right to an education. These rights have been secured, at least on paper. But, for the masses of black Americans, the results of these secured rights still have not trickled down. Drug abuse, incarcerations, unequal and inadequate education, lack of access to adequate health care, joblessness, inadequate housing, and continued societal and systemic discrimination all continue to weigh heavily on black people. Despite these still real problems for black Americans, there are some blacks who do not believe that these concerns are their concerns.[89] This divide of perceived communal interests, some believe, is weakening the whole. The black community clearly is no longer one cohesive group of people with communal interests, but rather it is a splinter of various groups with various interests, each interested in maintaining its separateness.[90]

Blackthink serves as a mechanism for preventing further and complete disintegration. It is also a way of keeping people grounded to their true selves, in other words, of reminding people who they are and where they came from. It purports to keep a lid on arrogance and uppitiness. It is, in some ways, an attempt to remind individuals that, no matter the perception of individual success, there remain voluminous and serious issues that continue to disproportionately affect the whole and, unless collective unified goals are pursued, the group will suffer. To the extent the person refuses to heed the message, guardians of black authenticity conclude that he or she rightly should be ostracized from the community or, as I have defined elsewhere, de-blacked. As Harvard Law Professor Randall Kennedy once stated: "Religions impose excommunication. Nations revoke citizenship. Parents disown children. Children disown parents. Why, as a matter of principle, should blacks be disallowed from casting from their community those adjudged to be enemies of it?"[91]

Although there are legitimate concerns about the need for a collective mass to focus on issues contributing to the genocide of black America, blackthink remains a troublesome practice. First, from a pure biological standpoint, if you are black, you are black. Period. There is no disowning you, as a parent might do with a child or a country might do of its citizen. Legally those methods can be accessed, but, as far as blackness is concerned, no amount of marginalization, name-calling, shaming, or outright expulsion removes the fact that when all is said and done, you are still black. Second, it clearly makes no sense to bully, marginalize, or expel people on the basis of immutable characteristics such as skin color, texture of hair, or eye color. The bullying here, often tied to some concern that the light-skin person believes that he or she is better than the rest, extracts allegiance at a heavy emotional price. Did not black America already learn the emotional price of discrimination based on the color of one's skin?

Third, practices that stifle free thought and free speech are troublesome. If I do not believe in affirmative action, I should be free to express that viewpoint. Certainly people have the right to disagree with me, but it should not be the case that I am somehow white—or, worse, colorless—because I don't believe as the accuser does. Nor should I have to support or vote for a person solely based on the color of their skin. For me there is discomfort, too, with the strange bedfellowing of policing thought and oppression. The modern-day use of allegiance based on skin color to oppress has some parallels to the centuries-old use of racial differences to oppress. Moreover, it is hypocritical to demand that one not be judged by the color of his or her skin and yet judge others by the color of their skin.

The schizophrenic nature of the way in which blackness is monitored also is riddled with holes. Consider the following examples. President Obama is accepted and celebrated as black when it comes to celebration and recognition of him as the first African American president in the nation, but because of his perceived failure to stand up for black causes his black authenticity is questioned. More interestingly, the moment he decides to change his thinking and actions, he becomes black again. The parameters of this transformation are unclear although seemingly possible, at least for some. Such a transformation likely would not be as easy for Justice Clarence Thomas. Moreover, for those able to transform, the newly anointed real black person can now himself become a guardian of blackness. Harry Belafonte is an example of one who not only successfully regained the right to be black, but who then went on to judge the authenticity of other blacks. Belafonte always married fair-skinned black and white women. He also was teased for acting white because of his own skin color and his speech. Yet, he was absolved from these "violations" with his commitment to civil rights during the 1960s.[92] With his blackness secured, he then went on to judge blackness in others.[93]

Schizophrenic application also abounds in cases where a person is simultaneously judged a traitor but yet applauded for the *identical* quality or conduct. In other words, a single criterion for marginalization can be *simultaneously* hated and revered. Take, for example, the stories of light-skinned wives paraded by their black husbands to others as valuable prizes and yet physically abused in private because of their light skin.[94] In my own experience, childhood friends would formerly target me as a wannabe white girl because I was a strong student academically. These same people would sometimes be heard proudly referring to me as the one who was going to make it. Notice the examples here are not of *one* group of black people who attack a given characteristic while *a different* group praises the identical characteristic. Rather I am speaking of the *same* individual who simultaneously despises, covets, and adores the identical characteristic at issue. And this occurs, seemingly without any sense of the inherent conflict.

My final concern with the practice of blackthink as implemented goes back to where this blackthink discussion began. Who or what is black? Are there really definitive markers for when the line has been crossed? How do you distinguish legitimate criteria from illegitimate ones? Should any black who joins the Republican Party be expelled from the black community? A Tea Partier? What if a black person does not believe in affirmative action? Should all black conservatives be ostracized? What if a black person lives life without making any outward attempt to help other blacks? Or, worse, what if the person acts as a Judas, all the while trying to pull down and/or sabotage other blacks, like crabs in a barrel? What about blacks who marry outside of the race or who don't want to be black? What if you hate dark skin or nappy hair? What is the scope of racial treachery? Who gets to decide?

Concluding Thoughts

The average black person in America still must deal with societal and systemic racism. Moreover, the additional burdens of colorism and blackthink weigh on the person's psyche. You may be despised by other black people just because of the color of your skin or, rather, may be showered with more privilege for the same reason. Or maybe your blackness is judged and assessed on a regular basis. Who are you married to? Where do you live? What's your sociopolitical position? What kind of music do your children listen to? How do they talk? Are you really black? Not black enough?

In my view, the intersection of colorism and blackthink, particularly when they overlap in one person, is an example of *dis*-ease. You revere white and light—white skin, light skin (and straight hair). On the other hand, there is not only a rejection of those very features—the mocking and ridicule of light-complected blacks based on their "light, bright, or damn near white" skin tones —but there is also this call for complete allegiance to blackness, though poorly defined.

Does not this practice represent an irreconcilable conflict? People are both hated and loved, in the same space and at the same time, for the same quality. Consider the spectrum of black people who have taunted, teased, and hated other blacks solely because of their light skin. Yet, look at the leaders black America routinely elects to political office or to head their political and social organizations, black universities and colleges. The hatred of light skin on the one hand while simultaneously adoring it on the other is mind-bending. It is, as one contributor to this book referenced earlier, clear evidence of a fragmented identity. Indeed, preferring light skin and other European beauty markers in your mate while policing blackness under blackthink is a modern augmentation of double consciousness. It reflects "two souls, two thoughts, two unreconciled strivings; two warring ideals in one dark body."[95] This is neither healthy nor normal.[96]

How do we come to grips with this? Clearly colorism has no place in any society, but what of blackthink? Is there a valid place for this type of accountability within black America? Journalist Thomas Chatterton Williams once noted that, "[a]t a moment when prominent, upwardly mobile African-Americans are experimenting with terms like 'post-black,' and outwardly mobile ones peel off at the margins and disappear into the multiracial ether, what happens to the core of black people who cannot or do not want to do either?"[97] This sentiment is the impetus for blackthink. If the sense of community is gone, if the sense of accountability is not there, then what happens to those who cannot help themselves? Yet, I still am left to wonder whether the additional mental toll used to extract conformity is worth it.

The verbal attacks hurled by blacks against other blacks, whether based on actual skin color, thoughts, or beliefs, all tear at the soul in unhelpful ways.[98]

Racism, colorism, and blackthink are taking their toll on the physical and mental well-being of the whole, individually and collectively.[99] It is time to lift this heavy weight.[100]

The way to resolution is through healing. The way to healing is through therapy. The way to therapy is through conversation. Conversation is the only way to get past this place of color-coded existences.[101] How else can one heal from wounds inflicted based on race and color discrimination? How else can one continue the process of believing, in fact, that black *is* beautiful and deserves to exist, unabashedly and proudly, unless and until colorism is confronted?

Dr. Du Bois famously predicted that the problem of the twentieth century would be the problem of the color line. That prophesy has come to pass. Indeed, far from a post-racial existence, we are in the throes of some of the most intense racial backlashes in recent memory.[102] Surprising, though, not only is the color line still a problem in the twenty-first century, but now that color line has expanded and is no longer just between black and white. It has morphed, and now includes tensions between black, brown, and beige. Black, beige, and brown people will soon be a majority in the United States. It is imperative, then, that we do not replicate the past. We have to start talking. Our children deserve that and more.

Notes

1 W. E. B. Du Bois, *The Souls of Black Folks Three Negro Classics* (New York: Avon Books 1965), 214–215.

2 At various points in this chapter, I will refer to black America, the black community, and black communities, as a collective. This reference is not to suggest that blacks are a monolith. Indeed, I have argued elsewhere that they are not. See Kimberly Jade Norwood, "The Virulence of BLACKTHINK™ and How Its Threat of Ostracism Shackles Those Deemed Not Black Enough," *Kentucky Law Journal* 93(3) (2004–2005): 143. The reality is, however, that, for the purposes of this topic, overwhelmingly large percentages of blacks throughout the United States are very familiar and intimate with, indeed struggle with, the practices of colorism and blackthink.

3 Alice Walker, "If the Present Looks Like the Past, What Does the Future Look Like?," in *In Search of Our Mothers' Gardens* (New York: Harcourt Brace Jovanovich, 1983), 290.

4 For examples of the international scope of colorism, see the following: Tanya Katerí Hernández, *Racial Subordination in Latin America: The Role of the State, Customary Law, and the New Civil Rights Response* (New York: Cambridge University Press, 2012); Evelyn Nakano Glenn, ed., *Shades of Difference: Why Skin Color Matters* (Stanford, CA: Stanford University Press, 2009); Ronald E. Hall, ed., *Racism in the 21st Century: An Empirical Analysis of Skin Color* (New York: Springer Science & Business Media, LLC, 2008); Joanne L. Bondilla and Paul Spickard, *Is Lighter Better?: Skin-Tone Discrimination among Asian Americans* (Lanham, MD: Rowman & Littlefield Publishers, 2007); Marita Golden, *Don't Play in the Sun: One Woman's Journey through the Color Complex* (New York: Anchor Books, 2005); Edward E. Telles, *Race in Another America: The Significance of Skin Color in Brazil* (Princeton, NJ: Princeton University Press, 2004).

5   bell hooks, *Sisters of the Yam: Black Women and Self-Recovery* (Boston. MA: South End Press, 2005), 70.

6   E. Franklin Frazier, *Black Bourgeoisie* (New York: Free Press Paperbacks, 1957), 136. Adrienne Davis has maintained that sexual abuse and reproductive exploitation so saturated southern slavery that she has denominated it "a sexual political economy." Adrienne D. Davis, *"Don't Let Nobody Bother Yo' Principle": The Sexual Economy of American Slavery, Sister Circle: Black Women and Work* (ed. S. Harley) (2002); Adrienne D. Davis, *Slavery and the Roots of Sexual Harassment, Directions in Sexual Harassment* (eds. C. MacKinnon & R. Siegel) (2003); Adrienne D. Davis, *The Private Law of Race and Sex: An Antebellum Perspective*, 51 Stan LR 222 (1999) (showing how inheritance cases reinforced enslaved women's sexual subordination).

7   "Good" hair is hair that is the same texture as Caucasian hair, and the straighter the better. See Ayana D. Byrd and Lori L. Tharp, *Hair Story: Untangling the Roots of Black Hair in America* (New York: St. Martin's Griffin, 2001), 19. It is not kinky, nappy, excessively curly, or woolly. It is "real to the roots" as some rap lyrics suggest. See, e.g., *Complexion Obsession*, a film by http://www.joydaily.tv, on file with author.

8   Byrd and Tharp, *Hair Story,* 19.

9   See, e.g., Joy Leary, *Post Traumatic Slave Syndrome, America's Legacy of Enduring Injury and Healing* (Oakland, CA: Uptone Press, 2005), 140.

10 Kathy Russell, Midge Wilson, and Ronald Hall, *The Color Complex: The Politics of Skin Color among African Americans* (New York: Anchor Books, 1992), 15, 18; see also Ronald E. Hall, *An Historical Analysis of Skin Color Discrimination in America: Victimism among Victim Group Populations* (New York: Springer, 2010), 112; Frazier, *Black Bourgeoisie*, 12–13.

11 Trina Jones, "Shades of Brown: The Law of Skin Color," *Duke Law Journal* 49 (2000): 1487, 1508–1509.

12 Russell et al., *The Color Complex,* 15.

13 Ibid., 18.

14 Hall, *An Historical Analysis of Skin Color Discrimination,* 112–113; Lawrence Otis Graham, *Our Kind of People: Inside American's Black Upper Class* (New York: Harper Perennial, 1999), 7; Jones, "Shades of Brown," 1510. There is evidence that some of this thinking still exists among light-skin blacks in the twenty-first century. See *Complexion Obsession*, film by http://www.joydaily.tv, on file with author.

15 "History is a Weapon: Message to the Grassroots," http://www.historyisaweapon.com/defcon1/malcgrass.html. Compare, too, Frazier's observations about the interest in many mulattoes to become one with white America in *Black Bourgeoisie,* 113–14.

16 Byrd and Tharp, *Hair Story,* 19.

17 Hall, *An Historical Analysis of Skin Color Discrimination,* 125.

18 Frazier, *Black Bourgeoisie,* 14 ("In 1850, mulattoes or mixed-bloods constituted 37 per cent of the free Negro population but only 8 per cent of the slave population.").

19 Ibid.; Graham, *Our Kind of People,* 9.

20 Hall, *An Historical Analysis of Skin Color Discrimination,* 113.

21 Russell et al., *The Color Complex*, 31. For the text of "The Talented Tenth," see W. E. B. Du Bois, "The Talented Tenth," in *The Negro Problem: A Series of Articles by Representative Negroes of To-day* (New York, 1903).

22 Hall, *An Historical Analysis of Skin Color Discrimination,* 119–124; see also Shirlee Taylor Haizlip, *The Sweeter the Juice: A Family Memoir in Black and White* (New York: Touchtone, 1994).

23 Jones, "Shades of Brown," 1515–1516.

24 Ibid. Historically, black schools often showed preferences for light-skin students. Howard University had a reputation for admitting more light-skin applicants than darker-skinned applicants into its university; photographs required as part of the application package assured such results. Audrey Elisa Kerr, *The Paper Bag Principle:*

Class, Colorism, and Rumor and the Case of Black Washington, D.C. (Knoxville, TN: University of Tennessee Press, 2006), 89–94. Some of the best black high schools also screened children based on skin color. Ibid., 82–87.

25 Ibid.

26 http://www.urbandictionary.com/define.php?term=blue veins. See also Cedric Herring, Verna M. Keith, and Hayward Derrick Horton, eds, *Skin Deep: Race and Complexion in the "Color-Blind" Era* (Chicago, IL: University of Illinois Press, 2004), 5; Russell et al., *The Color Complex*, 24–30.

27 Lighter *hair* is apparently better as well. See, e.g., Carole Jahme, "Why Do Men Find Blonde Women So Very Attractive?," http://www.guardian.co.uk/science/2010/jun/04/men-blonde-women-attractive. The benefits of being blonde have even taken some already successful women of color by storm. Beyoncé, one of the most famous singers in the world, recently appeared on the cover of her 2012 album demonstrably lighter in skin tone and blonde. See Julee Wilson, "Beyoncé Accused of Skin Lightening in New Album Promo Ad," http://www.huffingtonpost.com/2012/01/17/beyonce-skin-ligthening-ad_n_1210377.html. Again, on the cover of April 2012 *People Magazine* and there crowned the most beautiful woman in the world, she is lighter is skin tone and is sporting a blonde hairdo. See http://www.people.com/people/package/article/0,,20360857_20589758,00.html. Pop icon Rihanna, too, has gone lighter in skin and hair: http://colorlines.com/archives/2011/10/rihanna_has_gone_white_and_blonde_on_the_cover_of_vogue_uk.html.

28 For quality of life, wage data, see, e.g., Ronald Hall, "The Bleaching Syndrome: African Americans' Response to Cultural Domination vis-à-vis Skin Color," *Journal of Black Studies* 26 (November 1995): 172–184; Verna M. Keith and Cedric Herring, "Skin Tone and Stratification in the Black Community," *American Journal of Sociology* 97(3) (1991): 775; Travis Loller, "Study Says Skin Tone Affects Earnings," Associated Press, January 26, 2007, available at http://sfgate.com/cgi-bin/article.cgi?file=/News/archive/2007/01/26/national/a135252S09.DTL; Philip Lee Williams, "Skin Tone More Important than Educational Background for African Americans Seeking Jobs, According to New Research from the University of Georgia," *Broward Times* (Coral Springs, FL), August 18–24, 2006, 4, available at http://proquest.umi.com/pqdweb? did=1134125241&sid=1&Fmt=3&clientld=9108&RQT=309&VName=PQD; Arthur H. Goldsmith, Darrick Hamilton, and William Darity, Jr., "From Dark to Light: Skin Color and Wages among African-Americans," *Journal of Human Resources* 42(4) (Fall 2007): 701–738. In the criminal justice area, see Jill Viglione, Lance Hannon, and Robert DeFina, "The Impact of Light Skin on Prison Time for Black Female Offenders." *Social Science Journal* 48 (2011): 250–258; Joni Hersch, "Skin Color, Physical Appearance, and Perceived Discriminatory Treatment," *Journal of Socio-Economics* 40 (2011): 671–678; Jennifer L. Eberhardt, Paul G. Davies, Valerie J. Purdie-Vaughns, and Sheri Lynn Johnson, "Looking Deathworthy: Perceived Stereotypicality of Black Defendants Predicts Capital-sentencing Outcomes," *Psychological Science* 17 (2006): 383, 385. Finally, there are strong indicators linking dark skin color and stressors like high blood pressure and the like. See, e.g., Leary, *Post Traumatic Slave Syndrome*, 114–144; Thompson and Keith, "Copper Brown and Blue Black," in *Skin Deep: How Race and Complexion Matter in the "Colorblind" Era*, eds Cedrick Herring, Verna M. Keith and Hayward Derrick Horton (Champaign, IL: University of Illinois Press, 2003), 47; Camille A. Nelson, "Of Eggshells and Thin-skulls: A Consideration of Racism-related Mental Illness Impacting Black Women," *International Journal of Law and Psychiatry* 29 (2006): 112–136; Camille Nelson, "Considering Tortious Racism," *DePaul Journal of Health Care Law* 9 (2005): 905; Elizabeth A. Klonoff and Hope Landrine, "Is Skin Color a Marker for Racial Discrimination? Explaining the Skin Color-Hypertension Relationship," *Journal of Behavioral Medicine* 23 (2000): 329–338.

29 See, e.g., *A Question of Color*.

30 Russell et al., *The Color Complex*, 95–96.

31 See, e.g., *A Question of Color*.

32 Listen up at playgrounds, schoolyards, bus stops, train stops, malls, supermarkets, barber shops, and beauty shops just to name a few. This is happening in 2013.

33 See Chris Rock's documentary: *Good Hair*; see also Byrd and Tharp, *Hair Story*.

34 In 2012, Hampton University famously banned braids and locs for men in certain business school programs. See Julee Wilson, *Hampton University's Cornrows And Dreadlock Ban: Is It Right?* August 23, 2012, http://www.huffingtonpost.com/2012/08/23/hampton-university-cornrows-dreadlock-ban_n_1826349.html. This issue of black hair in its natural, nonchemicalized state also plagues campus queens at HBCUs. See, e.g., Chandra R. Thomas, "Scared Straight: At some HBCUs, Administrators and Campus Queens are Clashing Over Natural Hair," *Essence Magazine* 40(7) (November 2009): 126. Of course, outside of the black community, natural black hair continues to be a source of conflict. See Julee Wilson, "Rhonda Lee Fired: TV Station Responds to Meteorologist's Claim She Was Fired For Facebook Comments About Her Natural Hair," http://www.huffingtonpost.com/2012/12/11/rhonda-lee-fired-natural-hair-comments_n_2279950.html. Compare Robert M. Entman and Andrew Rojecki, *The Black Image in the White Mind: Media and Race in America* (Chicago, IL: University of Chicago Press, 2000), 179 (*Vogue* magazine editor Anna Wintour once observed: When it comes to fashion magazines, "it is a fact of life that the color of a model's skin (or hair for that matter) dramatically affects newsstand sales.").

35 *Schools criticized for bans on dreadlocks, Afros*, Sept. 25, 2013, http://www.stltoday.com/news/national/schools-criticized-for-bans-on-dreadlocks-afros/article 20f129ef-5413-5bd7-b17f-e42f51eOOe32.htmi#.Ukj9VCQLRmA.email.

36 See, e.g., Kathy Sandler, *A Question of Color: Color Consciousness in Black America,* video (San Francisco, CA: California NewsReel, 1992).

37 D. Channsin Berry and Bill Duke, *Dark Girls, Real Women. Real Stories,* video (2013).

38 Chris Levister, "No Equity in Adoption for Black Children," February 2, 2011, http://www.blackvoicenews.com/news/45680-no-equity-in-adoption-for-black-children.html. See also John Blake, "Single Black Women Choosing to Adopt," July 20, 2009, http://www.cnn.com/2009/LIVING/07/01/bia.single.black.women.adopt/index.html.

39 Adrienne P. Samuels, "Two Sides: Do Light-Skinned Black People Have an Advantage? Yes. They are likely to Get Hired First and May Earn More Money," *Ebony* (February 2008): 165.

40 Interview with Elaine Lee, program director of Girls, Inc., in St. Louis, July 30, 2012. Ms. Lee also told me stories of beautiful dark-skinned black girls who hated looking at their dark skin in the mirror and who refused to even play with dark-skinned dolls.

41 At the Portfolio Gallery in St. Louis, Missouri, there is on display a work by Rick Fager entitled *It's still clear*. The captivating black-and-white image shows a little dark-skinned girl taking a shower. With sad, haunting eyes, she appears to scrub her skin to no avail. As the author says, the black will not go away. The water is still clear.

42 Samuels, "Two Sides," 165.

43 See, e.g., http://www.ballerwives.com; see also http://www.afieldnegro.com. A substantial percentage of the black men in the images are paired with white women. Recent data also suggests that although interracial marriages in the United States are slowing down, blacks were much more likely than any other group to marry whites. See "Interracial Marriages in US Slow Down," *Shanghai Daily*, May 27, 2010, A11. Moreover, black men are more likely to marry white women than black women are to marry white men. Ralph Richard Banks, *Is Marriage for White People? How the African American Marriage Decline Affects Everyone* (New York: Dutton Adult, 2011), 117. "From

1970 to 2000, black men increased their rate of marrying white women almost six fold, so that by 2007, nearly 6% of black men were married to white women. Fewer than half as many—approximately 2.9% of—black women were married to white men." Elizabeth F. Emens, "Intimate Discrimination: The State's Role in the Accidents of Sex and Love," *Harvard Law Review* 122 (2009): 1307, 1320 (footnotes omitted). Many consider light skin the next best thing to white skin. See, e.g., Sandler, *A Question of Color*.

44   Darrick Hamilton, Arthur H. Goldsmith, and William Darity, Jr., "Shedding 'Light' on Marriage: The Influence of Skin Shade on Marriage for Black Females," *Journal of Economic Behavior & Organization* 72 (2009): 30–50; Michael Hughes and Bradley R. Hertel, "The Significance of Color Remains: A Study of Life Chances, Mate Selection, and Ethnic Consciousness among Black Americans," *Social Forces* 68(4) (1990): 1105–1120.

45   The black hair industry—weaves and extensions—exceeds *half a trillion* dollars annually. See, e.g., "What Spending A Half A Trillion Dollars on Hair Care and Weaves Says About Us," http://sdvoice.info/what-spending-a-half-a-trillion-dollars-on-hair-care-and-weaves-says-about-p1005–101.htm. For excellent commentary on good hair, see Chris Rock's documentary, *Good Hair*. Even Olympic gold medalist gymnast Gabby Douglas was scolded by *black women,* during her Olympic debut, for her nappy hair. See Dahleen Glanton, "Our Hair-Brained Obsession," http://articles.chicagotribune.com/2012–08–25/news/ct-perspec-0826-hair-20120825_1_hair-black-women-african-american-women, August 25, 2012, Douglas now sports a long, straight weave. See "Gabby Douglas Graces the December Issue of ESSENCE," http://www.essence.com/2012/11/02/gabby-douglas-graces-december-issue-essence/. Black women who value black hair in its natural state sometimes get weaved into the good hair trap. For example, w*hile donning an eighteen-inch weave,* Chris Rock's wife explained to audiences the importance of making a film that exposed the ugliness of the good hair debate so that their own daughter would begin to love her own natural hair. See Tom Burrell, *Brainwashed: Challenging the Myth of Black Inferiority* (New York: Smiley Books, 2010), 79.
     While the correlation between light skin and good hair is quite high some black men have expressed a willingness to date a dark-skinned black woman *if* she had long, straight hair. See, e.g., *Complexion Obsession* (Rapper Pusha of the Clipse, in response to questions about why so many men prefer light skin, says, "I actually don't know why they tend to prefer that. Umm, me personally, I like all types of women but umm, ain't nothing like some good, good chocolate skin with a good, good, good perm."). The infatuation many black Americans, male and female, have with good hair and with straight hair is beyond the scope of this work. Because of the strong correlation between good hair and light skin, however, the topic cannot be avoided.

46   See, e.g., "Where Are All the Dark Skinned Women in Music Videos," http://www.urbaneperspectivemag.com/2010/09/28/where-are-all-the-dark-skinned-women-in-music-videos/; D. Channsin Berry and Bill Duke, *Dark Girls, Real Women. Real Stories* (2013); *Complexion Obsession* film; "Sean Combs Angers Many with 'Only Light-Skinned' Black Women Remark," *Style News Wire*, April 6, 2009, http://www.stylemagazine.com/sean-combs-angers-many-with-%E2%80%9Conly-light-skinned%E2%80%9D-black-women-remark/ ("In issuing the call for women to participate in [a vodka commercial with the hiphop mogul], Combs specifically said that only 'White, Hispanic and Light-skinned African American women' need apply.")

47   As one in the music industry recently shared with JoyDaily.TV:

     Light skin women, the way the light hit they face, the way they show up from far away, the way they look from far away, you could see the prettiness in their face, you could see how they face shaped, you could see their facial expressions a lot better. When a dark skin woman try to do it from far away, it's kinda hard to get her facial expressions and the faces that she's making and the (interviewee starts moving to imaginary music) so that's why they tend to focus on the dark skin's woman's body. That's why a dark skin woman, when she gets in the video, she gotta have a crazy fat ass or some titties busting out or something that stick out so they can focus on that [as] opposed to her face.

See *Complexion Obsession* film.

48 See, Liane Membis, "Is Ethnic Beauty the New 'It' Factor," September 13, 2010, http://articles.cnn.com/2010–09–13/living/ethnic.beauty_1_ethnic-beauty-ethnic-cultures-etcoff?_s=PM:LIVING.

49 "Black or White: Kids on Race," http://www.cnn.com/SPECIALS/2010/kids.on. race/; *A Girl Like Me* documentary, http://www.kiridavis.com/index.php?option= com_content&task=view&id=17&Itemid=88888953.

50 Julee Wilson, "Kelly Rowland Didn't Like Her Dark Skin Color, Says Beyoncé's Mom Helped Her Embrace 'Chocolatiness,'" March 7, 2013, http://www. huffingtonpost.com/2013/03/07/kelly-rowland-dark-skin-color-beyonces-mom-embrace-chocolatiness_n_2831583.html.

51 See, e.g., Ernest Owens, "Beyoncé, Colorism, and Why All of This Needs to End in 2013," February 14, 2013, http://www.huffingtonpost.com/ernest-owens/ beyonce-colorism-and-why-_b_2687029.html.

52 See, e.g., "Light-skinned vs. Dark-skinned African-American Beauty Complexion Pageant Causes Outrage," February 12, 2012, http://www.dailymail.co.uk/news/ article-2106322/Racist-African-American-Battle-Complexions-causes-outrage.html; Ayanna Guyhto, "Light Skinned Vs. Dark Skinned: The Battle Continues," August 12, 2009, http://voices.yahoo.com/light-skinned-vs-dark-skinned-battle-continues-3970606.html.

53 Deborah L. Rhode, *The Beauty Bias: The Injustice of Appearance in Life and Law* (New York: Oxford University Press, 2010).

54 Rhode, *The Beauty Bias*, 30; Imani Perry, "Buying White Beauty," *Cardozo Journal of Law & Gender* 12 (2006): 579.

55 Trellie Jeffers, "The Black, Black Woman and the Black Middle Class," *Black Scholar* 12 (1981): 48. Light skin is a form of capital for women. Hamilton et al., "Shedding 'Light' on Marriage"; Margaret L. Hunter, "If You're Light You're Alright": Light Skin Color as Social Capital for Women of Color," *Gender and Society* 16(2) (April 2002): 178.

56　　　　Ironically, much of what I've learned about color I've learned because I have a mixed-race child. Because she is lighter-skinned, straighter-haired than I, her life,—in this racist, colorist society—is infinitely easier. And so, I understand the subtle programming, I, my mother, and my grandmother before me fell victim to. Escape the pain, the ridicule, escape the jokes, the lack of attention, respect, dates, even a job, any way you can. And if you can't escape, help your children to escape. Don't let them suffer as you have done. And yet, what have we been escaping to? Freedom used to be the only answer to that question. But for some of our parents it is as if freedom and whiteness were the same destination, and that presents a problem for any person of color who does not wish to disappear.

Walker, "If the Present Looks Like the Past," 290.

57 Debra J. Dickerson, "Colorblind: Barack Obama Would Be the Great Black Hope in the Next Presidential Race—If He Were Actually Black," January 22, 2007, http://www.salon.com/2007/01/22/obama_161/.

58   Back in the 1990s, news writer John Blake coined the term "Soul Patrol." The "Soul Patrol" represents, as Mr. Blake defined, those "legions of black people who impose their definition of blackness on other black people. They scorn and reject those who don't act 'black enough.'" John Blake, "The Soul Patrol Demanding Conformity, It Scorns Blacks Who Don't Act 'Black Enough,'" *Atlanta Journal-Constitution*, March 15, 1992, D1.

59   I have elsewhere detailed the practice of blackthink. See Norwood, *The Virulence of BLACKTHINK,* 143.

60   "Oreos," "Uncle Toms," "house negroes," and "sellouts" are names used to describe blacks who the labelers believe do not act black, do not support "black" issues, and, who maybe really want to be white. Similar derogatory slurs have been leveled against other groups of people of color. For example, the term "banana" is used to label Asian Americans who are yellow on the outside, white on the inside. Deborah Work, "Herbert Defenders Crumble Oreo Label," *Fort Lauderdale Sun-Sentinel*, January 19, 1998, 1B. Hispanics who are alleged to be inauthentic are coconuts; allegedly unauthentic Native Americans are called "apples." Ibid.

61   See generally F. James Davis, *Who is Black?* (1991).

62   Jefferson M. Fish, ed., *The Myth of Race, in Race and Intelligence: Separating Science from Myth* (Mahwah, NJ: Lawrence Erlbaum Associates, 2002), 114; Joy Leary, *Post Traumatic Slave Syndrome*, 22–23; Anil Ananthaswamy, "Under the Skin: Our DNA Says There's No Such Thing as Race. So Why Do Doctors Still Think It Matters?," *New Scientist* (April 20, 2002): 34.

63   Ian Haney Lopez, "The Social Construction of Race," *Harvard Civil Rights-Civil Liberties Law Review* 1 (1994): 29.

64   Nell Irvin Painter, *The History of White People* (New York: W. W. Norton & Co. 2010), 42.

65   See Davis, *Who is Black?,* 4–5; Beverly Daniel Tatum, *Why Are All the Black Kids Sitting Together in the Cafeteria? And Other Conversations About Race* (New York: Basic Books, 1997), 168–172. Under the one-drop rule, then, America likely has had a black president before. See, e.g., Kwaku Person-Lynn, "Were There Any Black US Presidents?, available at http://www.stewartsynopsis.com/Black_presidents.htm. See Karen R. Humes, Nicholas A. Jones, and Roberto R. Ramirez, "2010 Census Briefs, Overview of Race and Hispanic Origin: 2010, 4 Table 1," last modified March 2011, http://www.census.gov/prod/cen2010/briefs/c2010br-02.pdf.

66   Ibid.

67   Yaba, "Susie Guillory Phipps, the State of Louisiana, and the One-Drop Rule," October 3, 2011, http://1nedrop.com/susie-guillory-phipps-the-state-of-louisiana-and-the-one-drop-rule/.

68   Professor Michael Eric Dyson has referred to Condoleezza Rice and Colin Powell as the "White House Negros." See Tavia Evans, "Hip Hop Prof Raps to Crowd at UMSL," *St. Louis American*, February 12, 2004, A3.

69   See Touré, *Who's Afraid of Post-Blackness? What It Means to Be Black Now* (New York: Free Press, 2011), 5. There, Professor Eric Michael Dyson explores some of the many different ways to be black:

> There's been an exponential increase in both the modes and methods of Blackness, . . . and the ways in which Black people are allowed to be legitimately Black. It used to be much narrower. When I hear Black people tell me 'Black people don't' fill in the blank—scuba dive or be gay in Africa or whatever—I think, you're ignorant.

70   Norwood, The Virulence of BLACKTHINK.

71   Mark Whittington, "Al-Zawahri Calls Barack Obama a 'House Negro,'" November 19, 2008, available at http://voices.yahoo.com/al-zawahri-calls-barack-obama-house-negro-2225650.html.

72   See, Norwood, *The Virulence of BLACKTHINK*. For more on black authenticity and related doctrine, see Randall Kennedy, *Sellout: The Politics of Racial Betrayal* (New York: Vintage Reprint, 2009); Christopher Alan Bracey, *Saviors or Sellouts: The Promise and Peril of Black Conservatism, from Booker T. Washington to Condoleezza Rice* (Boston, MA: Beacon Press 2008); John McWhorter, *Authentically Black: Essay for the Black Silent Majority* (New York: Gotham Books, 2003).

73   See Norwood, *The Virulence of BLACKTHINK*; Kerry A. Rockquemore, "Between Black and White: Exploring the 'Biracial Experience,'" *Race & Society* 1 (1998): 197–212.

74   Woods defined "Cablinasian" to be a mixture of Caucasian, Black, Indian, American, and Asian. See "Woods Stars on Oprah, Says He's Cablinasian," *Lubbock Avalanche-Journal*, http://lubbockonline.com/news/042397/woods.htm.

75   Norwood, The Virulence of BLACKTHINK.

76   See, e.g., Devon W. Carbado and Mitu Gulati, *Acting White? Rethinking Race in Post-Racial America* (New York: Oxford University Press, 2013).

77   Kimberly Jade Norwood, "Blackthink's(tm) Acting White Stigma In Education and How It Fosters Academic Paralysis In Black Youth," *Howard Law Journal* 50(117) (2007): 735–742.

78   See, e.g., *Remembering Slavery: African Americans Talk About Their Personal Experiences of Slavery and Emancipation,* eds Ira Berlin, Marc Favreau, and Steven F. Miller (New York: The New Press 1996). After the Civil War's end, newly freed blacks pursued education with relentless vigor. See, e.g., "American Experience: Reconstruction: The Second Civil War." That fight for the right to an education continued well into the twentieth century. See, e.g., *The Road to Brown*, DVD.

79   Dickerson, "Colorblind: Barack Obama Would Be the Great Black Hope."

80   For some outlook on this, see John O. Calmore, "Airing Dirty Laundry: Disputes Among Privileged Blacks—From Clarence Thomas to 'The Law School Five,'" *Howard Law Journal* 46 (2003); Stephen F. Smith, "The Truth About Clarence Thomas and the Need for New Black Leadership," *Regents University Law Review* 12 (2000): 513; A. Leon Higginbotham, Jr., "An Open Letter to Justice Clarence Thomas From a Federal Judicial Colleague," *University of Pennsylvania Law Review* 140 (1991): 1005; Cynthia Tucker, "Clarence Thomas Would Kick Away the Ladder He Climbed," *Los Angeles Daily Law Journal*, July 26, 1991; Jack E. White, "Uncle Tom Justice," *Time*, June 26, 1995, 36; "Justice Clarence Thomas: Earns Buckwheat Award," June 24, 2003, http://www.thenorthstarnetwork.com/news/opinion/182027–1.html.

81   See Randall Kennedy, "The Fallacy of Touré's Post-Blackness Theory," August 11, 2011, available at http://www.theroot.com/print/54971.

>   Previously I have criticized Thomas' performance as a jurist—his complacent acceptance of policies that unjustly harm those tragically vulnerable to ingrained prejudices; his naked Republican Party parochialism; and his proud, Palinesque ignorance. But I have also chastised those who labeled him a sellout. I was a sap. Blacks should ostracize Thomas as persona non grata. Despite his parentage, physiognomy and racial self-identification, he ought to be put outside of respectful affiliation with black folk because of his indifference or hostility to their collective condition. His conduct has been so hurtful to and antagonistic toward the black American community that he ought to be expelled from membership in it.

82   Despite the fact that President Obama has embraced all of his ethnic identities, he is still accused by whites of hating whites. See, e.g., Glenn Beck: "Obama is a Racist," http://www.cbsnews.com/2100–250_162–5195604.html.

83   Brent Staples, "The Real American Love Story: Why America is a Lot Less White Than it Looks," http://www.slate.com/articles/news_and_politics/hey_wait_a_minute/1999/10/the_real_american_love_story.html (1999).

84 See, e.g., Ta-Nehisi Paul Coates, "Is Obama Black Enough," *Time Magazine*, February 1, 2007. Of course, President Obama actually has more *African* blood running through his veins than any of his black attackers. Yet the percentage of African blood or lineage to some special part of the continent also is not the real test of legitimacy.

85 See, e.g., Jarvis DeBerry, "Cornel West and Tavis Smiley upset Barack Obama isn't Martin Luther King," January 22, 2013, available at http://www.nola.com/opinions/index.ssf/2013/01/cornel_west_and_tavis_smiley_u.html; Michael Arceneaux, "Is Cornel West Fighting for Poverty or Ego?," November 13, 2012, available at http://newsone.com/2080898/cornel-west-obama/; Dr. Boyce Watkins, "Harvey's 'Uncle Tom' Remark to Cornel and Tavis Disrespects the Nation's Poor," August 11, 2011, available at http://www.huffingtonpost.com/dr-boyce-watkins/steve-harvey-uncle-tom-cornel-tavis_b_924247.html; Amir Shaw, "Tom Joyner Rips Tavis Smiley and Cornel West for Their Hatred Toward President Obama," July 4, 2011, http://rollingout.com/politics/tom-joyner-rips-tavis-smiley-and-cornel-west-for-their-hatred-towards-president-obama/.

86 Shelley v. Kraemer, 334 U.S. 1 (1948); Loving v. Virginia, 388 U.S. 1 (1967).

87 Elizabeth Atkins, "Two Sides: Do Light Skinned Black People Have an Advantage? No. We Face a Different Form of Racism," *Ebony* (February 2008): 164.

88 Paulo Freire, *Pedagogy of the Oppressed*, 30th anniversary edition (New York: Bloomsbury Academic, 2006), 45. Of course, it is not uncommon for formerly oppressed peoples to become oppressors in some capacity themselves. As Freire once observed: "[T]he oppressed, instead of striving for liberation, tend themselves to become oppressors, or sub-oppressors. The very structure of their thought has been conditioned by the contradictions of the concrete, existential situation by which they were shaped."

89 See, e.g., Eugene Robinson, *Disintegration: The Splintering of Black America* (New York: Random House, 2010): 227.

90 Ibid., 5–6. The author identifies four groups of African Americans who largely appear entrenched in maintaining their separateness: (i) mainstream middle-class; (ii) a large, abandoned minority steeped in poverty; (iii) a small transcendent elite with unlimited privileges; and (iv) an immigrant or mixed race community that exemplifies the fluidity of race and the multiple meanings of blackness.

91 Randall Kennedy, "The Fallacy of Touré's Post-Blackness Theory."

92 Harry Belafonte and Michael Shnayerson, *My Song: A Memoir* (New York: Alfred A. Knopf, 2011).

93 In 2002, Harry Belafonte called Colin Powell a "yassuh boss" and a disappointment to the black race. See interview by Larry King with Harry Belafonte (October 15, 2002), available at http://www.blackcommentator.com/14_belafonte.html. More recently, he has leveled accusations against Jay-Z and Beyoncé for not doing more to help black Americans. Alexis Garrett Stodghill, "Harry Belafonte: Jay-Z, Beyoncé 'Have Turned Their Back on Social Responsibility,'" http://thegrio.com/2012/08/08/harry-belafonte-jay-z-beyonce-have-turned-their-back-on-social-responsibility/. Consider also Touré, *Who's Afraid of Post-Blackness?*, 5. (Dr. Eric Michael Dyson, who once questioned the blackness of people such as Condoleezza Rice, now believes people can be black in any way they want to be.)

94 Russell et al., *The Color Complex*, 110.

95 Du Bois, *The Souls of Black Folks*, 215.

96 Leary, *Post Traumatic Slave Syndrome*, 166.

97 Thomas Chatterton Williams, "As Black as We Wish to Be," *The New York Times*, March 18, 2012, 5.

98 See, generally, Leary, *Post Traumatic Slave Syndrome*.

99 Ibid., 114–144; see also Camille A. Nelson, "Of Eggshells and Thin-Skulls: A Consideration of Racism-related Mental Illness Impacting Black Women," *International Journal of Law and Psychiatry* 29 (2006): 112–136; Camille Nelson, "Considering Tortious Racism," *DePaul Journal of Health Care Law* 9 (2005) 905; Elizabeth A. Klonoff and Hope Landrine, "Is Skin Color a Marker for Racial Discrimination? Explaining the Skin Color-Hypertension Relationship," *Journal of Behavioral Medicine* 23 (2000): 329–338.

100 See, generally, Burrell, *Brainwashed*; Na'im Akbar, *Breaking the Chains of Psychological Slavery* (Tallahassee, FL: Mind Productions, 1996).

101 See, generally, Leary, *Post Traumatic Slave Syndrome.*

102 Mark Potok, "The Year in Hate and Extremism," *Southern Poverty Law Center Intelligence Report*, Spring 2013, http://www.splcenter.org/home/2013/spring/the-year-in-hate-and-extremism; Mark Potok, "White Hot," *Southern Poverty Law Center Intelligence Report*, Spring 2012, http://www.splcenter.org/home/2012/spring/white-hot; "Duke Professor Mark Anthony Neal Discusses Racism After Obama: Has It Gotten Worse?" Yourblackworld.com, http://www.yourblackworld.net/2012/11/black-news/duke-professor-mark-anthony-neal-discusses-racism-after-obama-has-it-gotten-worse/; "NAACP Chairman Julian Bond Says Racism Has Increased During Obama's Tenure," Yourblackworld.com, http://www.yourblackworld.net/2013/03/black-news/naacp-chairman-julian-bond-says-racism-has-increased-during-obamas-tenure/.

8

THE IMPLICATIONS OF SKIN COLOR VIS-À-VIS DISCRIMINATION

Revisiting Affirmative Action

Ronald E. Hall and Adrienne Johnson

Introduction

Investigations pertaining to skin color illustrate a form of discrimination in the workplace that affirmative action policies were in fact intended to eliminate. Affirmative action policies as litigated, however, have failed to meet the formidable demands of skin color discrimination because of a preference for race in common discourse. When circumstances prove actionable, the defining criteria for discrimination have historically limited adjudication by race as black or white rather than by skin color or skin tone. Affirmative action, as originally intended, was utilized to address a history of workplace disparities where race became the single most critical complaint. As a historically tenacious iniquity, the power imbalance that exists in the workplace still fosters an "us against them" mentality. This mentality may have contributed significantly to workplace discrimination, both then and now, based not only on race but also on skin color—as suggested by Frances Cress Welsing in her book *The Cress Theory of Color-Confrontation and Racism*.[1] Discrimination recapitulates at every level of the workplace, including the hiring of, raises for, and the promotion of black and other nonwhite workers. These workers often find themselves alienated and isolated in a white-dominated occupational environment.

The degree of workplace discrimination against black Americans based on skin color or tone is a historical form of oppression that has not been adequately addressed commensurate with the extent of its historical existence. Discrimination by skin color has been all but ignored by mainstream scholars because its historical existence operates outside of the more dramatic racial context.[2] Despite a significant lack of interest on the part of mainstream scholars, discrimination by skin color may affect every phase of the workplace environment involving black

Americans.[3] As such, a well-known aspect of discrimination among white administrators is a continuing preference for hiring only white or light-skinned black
employees. Skin color remains a relevant factor in the workplace despite today's
emphasis on diversity as a fundamental aspect of the workplace ethos.

As a result of the continued preference for lighter skin color, the demographic
profile of a white or light-skinned American is germane to the history of
workplace discrimination.[4] Often individuals who are not born with preferred
skin color traits continue to be effectively banished from the possibility of
employment at certain levels. Despite an environment dominated by race, skin
color discrimination in the workplace remains an unspoken yet critical taboo. In
support of this taboo, empirical evidence compiled by F. J. Sciara[5] shows that
first-year college students, absent provocation, continually devalue people having
dark skin. Additionally, the rank ordering of mean test scores indicates a strong
pattern of negative appraisal assigned to dark-skinned black men in particular,
which is not irrelevant to the percentage of dark-skinned people hired within a
prestigious workforce. There is little reason to assume these beliefs would not
affect the ability of black Americans to overcome discrimination in the workplace today, regardless of gender. The predominance of racial obstacles makes
their attempts all the more subject to failure.

In a post-affirmative action era, the lesser regard for skin color in traditional
acts of workplace discrimination means that cases continue to be litigated on the
basis of race rather than color. The objective of this treatise, in contrast, is to
document the impact of skin color as a seldom acknowledged vehicle of workplace
discrimination.

Historical evidence of the social and cultural preferences for light skin will
substantiate the need to revisit affirmative action as a means to institutionalize
fair and equitable employment practices. This evidence will rationalize the
subjugation of race by skin color as the most realistic trek to a just and civil society.
Therefore, of particular concern is the negative perception of dark-skinned
workers who must overcome numerous stereotypes associated with their color.
Not to acknowledge and seek to address those stereotypes will diminish their
potential, without the opportunity to prove themselves and their occupational
skills accordingly. This reality further provides a rationale for revisiting affirmative
action policies that have been overturned by various judicial bodies around the
country. By reviewing the evidence presented herein, courts and policy makers
will have means at their disposal to solve the problem and will provide a representation of facts without subjective opinions, political whim, and racial preference.
Ultimately, by revisiting affirmative action with an eye toward skin color rather
than simply race, we will facilitate a glimpse into the future, where skin color
and all other demographic categories will be irrelevant in the workplace, to the
emerging masses of a diverse, racially indistinct human population. A tenacious
historical impediment will additionally be laid to rest in the process.

Some Historical Context of Skin Color in the United States

In the early twentieth century, and having greater opportunities both in the workplace and elsewhere, light-skinned "Talented Tenth"[6] black intellectuals— including W. E. B. Du Bois, William Monroe Trotter, James Weldon Johnson, A. Philip Randolph, and Walter White—dominated the upper classes of African Americans who were educated, owned businesses, and were in positions to assume leadership roles. While they believed themselves to be superior, many pledged their good fortunes in service to the black community. They were light skinned but suffered from the same oppressions that were directed at their darker-skinned brethren by whites. Despite opportunities to "pass,"[7] such blacks elected to be loyal to the black community, devoting the totality of their personal resources to this end as well. Their efforts unified the black community in a way that the antebellum white plantation class had not intended. Thus, unlike during the antebellum, twentieth-century dark-skinned blacks and their light-skinned ethnic counterparts formed alliances based upon a common oppression. What could be perceived among blacks as a version of skin color racism was complicated by classism, which many blacks were willing to ignore. Southern racism and Jim Crow attitudes forged notable light-skinned "Talented Tenth" intellectuals, who advocated publicly and forcefully for the black community. Their efforts unified the black community, as their demands for black liberation endeared them to the most jaded of dark-skinned blacks.

In large numbers, the first advocates for freedom and justice from the black community included light-skinned mulattoes[8] who chose to not pass for white. They did not celebrate their mixed-race superiority or workplace advantage. These light-skinned mulattoes seems to have dominated the ranks of the "Talented Tenth" as well, perhaps due to appearance, racial origin, or because it was believed that white ancestry implied superiority. Their commitment to the black community contradicted the antebellum and forged a unity among the black masses that would prove useful in the coming era.[9]

Shortly after the "Talented Tenth" era, overt verbal hostilities regarding skin color in the black community largely subsided. However, the association of light skin with physical beauty and superiority remained intact and actually became more accepted over time.[10] At one point, on black college campuses it was almost impossible for a dark-skinned student to join a sorority or fraternity. Various social events, such as school dances, required the "brown-paper-bag test" as a condition of admission: Those blacks whose skin was darker than a brown paper bag were assessed an admission fee; those who were lighter skinned were admitted free of charge.[11]

The idealization of light skin via the stigmatization of dark skin, by both whites and blacks, belongs to a tenacious history that has prevailed into the modern era. For example, as a result of the white power structure created after mass European migration to the Americas, light skin became an ideal, even for racial minorities.[12] Known as the "bleaching syndrome," studies have shown that there is a trend of dark skin tone as a vehicle of denigration and a correlation between dark skin and lower socioeconomic class. Those who have darker skin tones, therefore, often idealize light-skinned members of the population and believe that their skin color is associated with a better quality of life.[13] The bleaching syndrome and its effects suggest that discrimination is germane to American society because it is so deeply rooted in American history. Africans were brought to the New World in bondage and were forced to survive within an oppressive system that denied their humanity by using race and its characteristic traits. The most dramatic of such traits was skin color, which was used as a racial designate. In discourse, "race" was the preferred term. In acting out race, skin color was the vehicle that imposed no less upon blacks than on whites in the perceptions of the light skin ideal. Subsequently, regardless of racial heritage, light skin operated to the advantage of those so characterized. The white community saw no need to acknowledge the implications of skin color in its racial discourse, because it had no need for differentiations between race and color. Therefore, until recently case law involving workplace discrimination was contingent primarily upon race, although skin color was mentioned in the various stages of policy. Regarding skin color, "All white was all right."

Statutory Support for Color Claims

Though the occurrence of color discrimination is well documented in history, and its effects are often present in both the personal and professional lives of African Americans, the law has been slower to respond to color-based discrimination than it has been in its response to race-based discrimination. Those seeking statutory relief and legal remedy for color discrimination often have to turn to the same statutes used to combat race discrimination and attempt to argue that the discrimination the statute seeks to curtail includes discrimination on solely the basis of skin color.

When confronted with discrimination on the basis of skin color, plaintiffs generally look to two statutes for relief: either Section 1981 of the Civil Rights Act of 1866 (hereinafter, Section 1981) or Title VII of the Civil Rights Act of 1964 (hereinafter, Title VII). Section 1981 guarantees all people the same rights as white citizens. While the statute makes no specific reference to race or skin color beyond its mention of white citizens, courts have held that Section 1981 is properly asserted where discrimination on the basis of skin color is alleged.[14] However, it appears that, when a plaintiff asserts a claim based on color discrimination, courts would often use ethnicity and skin tone as surrogates for race if the plaintiff's race is unclear, and would ignore the impact of skin tone and ethnicity when the plaintiff's race is clearly identified.[15]

Title VII prohibits discrimination in employment on the basis of race, color, sex, and national origin.[16] Although the statute does specifically prohibit discrimination on the basis of color, the statute does not define its meaning and leaves courts free to determine its definition.[17] As a result, district courts often look to Section 1981 cases for guidance, because Section 1981 is thought to be the historical predecessor to Title VII.[18]

Often, under both Section 1981 and Title VII, courts and litigants treat race and color synonymously and fail to articulate how the two concepts differ. The relevant case law suggests that, although courts have allowed claims under Section 1981 and Title VII on the basis of color discrimination rather than race discrimination, very few courts have afforded the distinction much attention in their opinions. Instead, they conflate race and color or, at best, neglect to articulate what makes a color claim distinct from a claim based on race.[19] This is particularly problematic because, although employers have hired blacks into positions of prominence and authority at higher rates since the enactment of Title VII, these individuals are usually light-skinned blacks. This suggests that although employers may be willing to hire black employees, there may still be some discrimination and preference based on skin tone.[20]

Blacks and Workplace Discrimination

Some among Western lexicologists refer to discrimination as an ability to differentiate on the basis of selected criteria. In this context, discrimination may be harmless and, indeed, a necessary practice in everyday life. Universities discriminate in college admissions to enable the selection of the brightest students. Employers discriminate at the workplace ideally to enable the selection of the most qualified applicants. Even ordinary people discriminate for reasons related to matrimony as a way to ensure the selection of the most suitable spouse. Such manifestations of discrimination are ethically sound and germane to civilization; however, discrimination in the workplace, as with skin color discrimination, is unethical and refers to unfair practices attributed to the idealization of light skin relative to the denigration of dark-skinned people. In America, although discrimination discourse has been dominated by race and discriminatory comments and actions are often attributed solely to whites, skin color discrimination is enacted by and against blacks and other victims without respect to race, gender, or ethnic origin.

Skin color, as a crux of workplace discrimination, is a social byproduct of Western civilization, including the American antebellum era. Put forth by the once-called science of eugenics, "white racism" purports the superiority of Caucasian race groups and the subsequent idealization of light skin.[21] White racism extends from slavery, colonization, and the antebellum South, and necessitated the denigration of dark skin by light-skinned whites and their light-skinned mulatto (black) offspring, because separation of the masses was necessary to maintain white control of the workplace. Yet blacks and other darker-skinned people of color have not been immune to the impact of this event as it pertains to workplace discrimination: African Americans have not dismantled, and sometimes even perpetuate, the discrimination traditionally done by whites in housing, law, politics, and other areas of life as if they are immune to such acts themselves.[22] Consequently, the issue of skin color—associated with the antebellum period —has, for all intents and purposes, replaced race, becoming central for black Americans in their struggle to end various forms of discriminatory practices at home and abroad.

No doubt, the single issue of skin color discrimination does not exist independent of other factors that contribute to workplace disparities. Today, the myth of white supremacy and the idealization of light skin via the nineteenth-century "mulatto hypothesis"[23] is no longer accepted in polite society. The mulatto hypothesis postulates that having higher amounts of white blood in one's ancestry leads to more intelligence. Such skin color myths, however, while shattered in the scholarly literature and banished from the circles of polite society, remain largely intact among oppressed populations: The lighter the skin, the greater likelihood of assumed or expected superior workplace performance. While blacks are no longer legally banished professionally, workplace discrimination by skin color has been introduced into the state and federal legal annals.

Perhaps the first workplace skin color discrimination case brought by blacks is *Walker v. Secretary of Treasury, I.R.S.*,[24] in Atlanta Federal District Court in 1989. The plaintiff, Tracy L. Walker, was a permanent clerk typist in the IRS's Atlanta office. She is a light-skinned African American, while her supervisor —an employee of the defendant—was Ruby Lewis, a dark-skinned African American. Following her termination, an African American replaced the plaintiff, therefore arguably eliminating a potential claim for race discrimination. However, according to the record, the working relationship between the plaintiff and the defendant was strained from the very beginning of her employment. The plaintiff believed that this tension was a result of color discrimination rather than race discrimination as it is traditionally understood. The plaintiff further contended that the defendant singled her out for close scrutiny and reprimanded her for many things that were false or unsubstantial.

In an effort to initiate legal action, the plaintiff met with the U.S. Equal Employment Opportunity Commission (EEOC) program manager for the IRS's Atlanta district to discuss the problems she was having with her manager. Two weeks later, following the plaintiff's conversation with the EEOC and pursuant to the manager's recommendation, the plaintiff was terminated. The reasons given for termination were tardiness, laziness, incompetence, and attitude problems. The plaintiff believed that the true reason for her termination was the defendant's personal hostility toward the plaintiff because of the plaintiff's light skin. While the plaintiff did not present any direct evidence that the defendant was prejudiced against light-skinned black Americans, there was evidence that the defendant might have harbored resentful feelings toward "white" people; therefore, by inference, those feelings were possibly directed toward light-skinned black people.

The district court found that, under Title VII, race is distinct from color and that claims alleging discrimination on the basis of color were actionable under the statute. The court reasoned that it would be difficult to adjudicate claims on the basis of color but that it was nonetheless an issue that should be determined by a fact finder. This case was the first of its kind involving two African Americans; however, since this case was adjudicated in 1990, numerous cases have been filed on the basis of skin color discrimination in the workplace. Because the court found that skin color discrimination in the workplace by and among blacks is a valid claim and is a matter of fact, the decision in the *Walker* case opened the door for numerous subsequent cases filed to obtain a judgment.

While the *Walker* case addresses skin color discrimination among blacks, it is not the first case to address skin color discrimination. Ten years earlier, *Felix v. Marquez*[25] addressed skin color discrimination between Latinos and was decided in 1981 by the U.S. District Court of the District of Columbia. The case involved discrimination among Puerto Ricans and was brought by a dark-skinned plaintiff, Carmen Felix, versus a lighter-skinned defendant, Joaquin Marquez. Both the plaintiff and defendant were employees of the Washington Office of the Commonwealth of Puerto Rico (OCPRW). The plaintiff alleged that the defendant did not promote her on the basis of skin color discrimination.

The evidence at trial showed that the plaintiff's employer awarded promotions in grade based upon criteria that were neutral with respect to skin color. Employees whose color was as dark or darker than the plaintiff's were given promotions in grade, while many other employees who were lighter than the plaintiff were given infrequent promotions, or no promotions at all. Similar neutrality with respect to skin color was evident in the promotions in grade among employees throughout the entire agency. The court found that the OCPRW did not discriminate against the plaintiff on account of her color in failing to recommend her for a promotion in grade; however, despite being decided in favor of the employer, *Felix v. Marquez* helped to establish that skin color discrimination was actionable.

A recent case involving skin color discrimination in the workplace is *Willis v. Sears Holding Management Corporation*.[26] The plaintiff contended that, because of her dark skin, she was subjected to a stressful working environment, induced by the defendant. For example, the plaintiff, who had twenty-one years of relevant experience, was hired into the lowest position in the department with a guarantee that she would receive a promotion in one year. The plaintiff, however, never received this promotion and in fact was terminated despite a lack of economic necessity. Instead, male, nonblack attorneys with less experience were promoted over the plaintiff. Subsequently, the plaintiff claimed that such a stressful working environment contributed to her hypertension disease. The plaintiff, Jill Willis, is a dark-skinned, middle-aged, African American woman, and a graduate of the University of Chicago School of Law, one of the top five law schools in the country. She earned an undergraduate degree from the esteemed Wellesley College in Massachusetts, and a Master's degree from the Ivy League's Columbia University in New York City. Despite this educational background, the defendants stated that they were not "favorably impressed" by the plaintiff. It is arguable that the defendants developed that attitude because the plaintiff's physical attributes put her outside of categories associated with the workplace ideal: Not light, not young, not male. This kind of stereotyping would have put Willis in a constant position of being accorded less for doing more.

According to the mulatto hypothesis, dark-skinned African Americans who are intellectually gifted are often immediately assumed to be "uppity." Additionally, dark-skinned African Americans are often considered less intelligent—the most inferior within an assumed inferior race category. This creates instantaneous obstacles for dark-skinned African Americans in particular, upon being hired with both lesser credentialed, working-class whites and lesser-credentialed, lighter-skinned blacks. Such people must rationalize their lower professional status with the higher professional status of a racially lower-ranked and dark-skinned African American colleague. These realities were likely in operation in the *Willis* case.

One of the key factors in the *Willis* case is that Willis' supervisor is described as a light-skinned, African American male. After a review of his credentials, he is arguably less impressive than the dark-skinned plaintiff Willis. Although younger and a graduate of an Ivy League school, he is much less experienced as a trained litigator than the plaintiff. Additionally, the plaintiff is a graduate of two Ivy League institutions and the alumna of a prestigious undergraduate institution. That someone with lesser qualifications, such as the defendant operative, would assume supervision of someone more qualified, such as the plaintiff Willis, would appear to contradict the normal standards of prudent corporate management. That is, in comparing qualifications, prudent corporate management would not place, without motive, personnel in positions of supervising workers whose academic credentials and years of experience exceed their own. Not only is this cause for immediate conflict between worker and supervisor, but also this would deride the reputations and quality of work of all involved. Conversely, the plaintiff was placed in a position below her abilities, given her work history and educational background. Subsequently, one can easily posit that the discrimination suffered by the plaintiff Willis was not at all due to lack of competence, but it was a contrived effort motivated by longstanding cultural traditions aimed at dark-skinned African Americans whose intellect is questioned, consciously and unconsciously, on skin color. At present, a settlement has yet to be reached in this case.

Affirmative Action

According to the Congressional Record, after its inception in the 1930s the concept of affirmative action was initially applied for the benefit of nonunionized, white males who sought redress for discrimination at the hands of industrial employers. One of its primary sponsors was a New York senator, Robert F. Wagner.[27] Wagner's 74th Congress declared that discrimination against an employee by an employer shall require "such person to cease and desist from such unfair labor practice and to take such affirmative action, including reinstatement of employees with or without back pay, as will effectuate the policies of this act."[28] In what is formally known as the National Labor Relations Act and commonly referred to as the Wagner Act, Congress approved affirmative action on July 5, 1935.

As the nation sought to address its problems with race and racism, politicians and activities worked to construct policies to address discriminatory practices in the workplace. Among the most controversial of these policies is affirmative action. Some form of affirmative action can be traced as far back in American history as 1866 after the passage of the 13th, 14th, and 15th Amendments.[29] The modern understanding of the phrase, however, comes from President John Kennedy, who borrowed the term from the text of the 1935 Wagner Act. The Wagner Act empowered the National Labor Relations Board (NLRB) to "take such affirmative action, including the reinstatement of employees with or without back pay." However, President Kennedy used the term to create and encourage aggressive recruitment of minority employees by federal contractors. In 1967, President Lyndon Johnson signed Executive Order No. 11246 that required racial compensation in the workforce to be a factor in awarding government contracts. President Richard Nixon followed suit and resurrected Johnson's executive order in 1969 as a result of the nondiscrimination policies of the 1960s failing to adequately address institutional discriminatory hiring practices. The Supreme Court also weighed in on affirmative action when it decided *Griggs v. Duke Power* and held that employers could violate Title VII if they were engaging in neutral employment practices that disproportionately affected the hiring of minorities. Since this decision, the Court has continually decided cases based on affirmative action without ever truly endorsing or striking down the practice. It became clear from its history that one of the objectives of affirmative action is to engage in various compensatory acts to balance historical racial discrimination encountered by blacks in the workplace and society at large. The attempt to assign blacks to a protected class encountered strong resentment from the white community, which eventually led to the demise of affirmative action.

Affirmative action policy was originally intended as a legal tool to address workplace discrimination, which most will agree continues to exist. Unfortunately, it became a political issue consumed by the polarizing effects of race. Revisiting affirmative action in a context devoid of race will allow for its expansion across and within racial boundaries. Skin color pertains to all races and does not eliminate any potential plaintiff by race category. Therefore, accusations of reverse discrimination will be less plausible because the generalizations of race category will be irrelevant. An emphasis on skin color will then facilitate litigation on the basis of individual merit in each case.

It was only after 1964 that the United States government began to prohibit discrimination in the workplace "based on race, color, religion, sex or national origin,"[30] which served adjudication of the aforementioned cases; however, many people are still of the opinion that race and skin color are identical concepts and that those who are victimized by discrimination in the workplace must be of a different race than the alleged perpetrator. This opinion is problematic, though, because lawsuits that allege interracial discrimination (for example, when a black plaintiff brings suit against a white defendant) do not account for instances of workplace intraracial discrimination (for example, when a dark-skinned black plaintiff brings suit against a light-skinned black defendant). "Much of [intraracial discrimination] . . . goes unreported because people simply don't know that such a distinction is covered by the law," comments Joan Ehrlich,[31] who works as an EEOC district director in San Francisco. In an effort to ensure a fair work environment, she instructs her staff "to more carefully screen and question [complainants] to determine if color played a role in the alleged discrimination." Interestingly, skin color discrimination in this context is unlike what Dr. W. E. B. Du Bois envisioned. [32] Dr. Du Bois hoped his "Talented Tenth," a group comprised primarily of light-skinned blacks, would *uplift* the race as a whole.[33] The pitting of light versus dark and dark versus light occurring today, as highlighted by Joan Ehrlich above, often contributes to the opposite result and goes unnoticed (or unaddressed) by the legal system. At present, however, twenty-first-century colorism does not have uplift as its goal. As such, skin color is a necessary factor when revisiting affirmative action, particularly in response to the following definition:

> Affirmative action is the process of a business or governmental agency in which it gives special rights of hiring or advancement to ethnic minorities to make up for past discrimination against that minority. Affirmative action has been the subject of debate, with opponents claiming that it produces reverse discrimination against Caucasians. Affirmative action programs are governed by a number of overlapping laws. A common principle is that whether for admissions or employment, affirmative action programs such as targeted recruitment and goals are encouraged to remedy past effects of discrimination; quotas are disfavored. Affirmative action in American employment law has evolved through a series of governmental proclamations, court decrees, and voluntary programs instigated by employers in the private sector. Private employers who receive no public funding are not required to adopt affirmative action policies. Affirmative action policies are enforced by the entities adopting them if they are voluntary, while

affirmative action policies required by government mandates can be enforced through the legal system.[34]

Steeped in controversy, affirmative action programs were eventually overturned by the judiciary, as in the case of Allan Bakke.[35] Bakke, a white male, filed suit for what he concluded was an unfair policy, a suit that came to be infamously known as the Bakke decision. Bakke held that a Caucasian applicant to medical school had been unjustly excluded by an affirmative action admissions policy. The Court decided that affirmative action goals are in fact permissible, but using quotas in the attainment of such goals is not allowed.[36] The result is a decision that has left a blemish on the ethical sobriety of American jurisprudence. How to achieve the former without necessitating the latter escapes presently known rational systems of logic. Indeed, it is argued that Allan Bakke personally did nothing to discriminate against blacks or other members of oppressed populations. That he should be held accountable for circumstances beyond his control begets the very injustices upon which affirmative action was founded. Yet, but for his lawsuit, Bakke would have been denied a medical education at the University of California, Davis based solely upon race. Bakke scored within the requirements of the medical school admissions criteria, yet a certain number of the entering class positions that year were reserved for oppressed population applicants, and Allan Bakke was of dominant racial heritage—the basis of this infamous reverse discrimination. His was a case that ultimately contributed to a return to antebellum-like workplace disparities and "white privilege," for which affirmative action was intended to eliminate.[37] As with the Bakke case, race—being among the five categories of discriminatory attributes and as written into affirmative action law—unfairly disserves whole groups within the population from consideration for various programs in education.

Affirmative Action Revisited

The language of the Wagner Act avoided discrimination against blacks, women, and other oppressed populations. The central theme was that it is not enough to just cease and desist from the commission of a discriminatory act; the consequences of historical injustices require deliberate action to be corrected. The reversal of affirmative action, enabled by the Bakke decision, is based primarily on the fact that, unlike in 1935, affirmative action is hotly contested today on the basis of race without consideration for the utilization of less polarizing and more race neutral terminology. Restrictions pertaining to racial discourse and the elimination of affirmative action policies have served workplace discrimination by black Americans who offend on the basis of color. Their offenses would be otherwise less possible, because utilizing skin color for revisiting affirmative action would be more inclusive of both race and skin color attributes, enabling plaintiffs to bring suit on the basis of merits via a less charged racial environment.

Based upon "white privilege" and the Bakke case, race—as written into affirmative action law—now does a disservice to whole groups within the population. For this reason, affirmative action policy has become divisive and counterproductive, which politically, and thus legally, limits its application. Considering an alternative that moves beyond race is a hiring study completed by Andreana Holmes Kennedy at Rice University,[38] wherein Kennedy concludes that dominant-race citizens tend to give more favorable ratings to light-skinned members among people of color who are applying for jobs.[39] Dominant-race people are not alone in their discrimination. Perhaps as a consequence, people of color, under similar circumstances, give more favorable hiring ratings to darker-skinned job applicants. Thus, both whites and blacks discriminate on the basis of skin color in different ways. These kinds of discriminatory practices are also of the type that affirmative action policies were attempting to redress; however, the current policies erroneously emphasize race rather than both race and skin color.[40] In order to successfully address the discriminatory practices that affirmative action seeks to end, it is necessary to reimagine affirmative action. It should be more inclusive. It should include skin color. Reimagining the policy in this way should cause decision makers to see the landscape that results when color, and not race, is the focus. Law Professor Trina Jones came to a similar conclusion many years ago:

> [I]t is unacceptable for Whites to employ disproportionately those individuals who appear closer to White. The goal must be to nudge Whites beyond their ears and prejudices by encouraging them to consider the full array of Black individuals . . . a similar admonition may be directed to those individuals who, either consciously or subconsciously, discriminate against other Blacks on the basis of skin color.[41]

This nudging, a spotlight, should lead to more conscious, informed goals, targets, and outcomes relevant to unbiased decision making.

Conclusion

Empowerment has been defined as a process in which people become strong enough to take part in, share control of, and influence direction of critical institutions[42] that affect their employment and, therefore, their quality of life. An empowered person believes in his or her ability to act; however, a challenge for litigants, activists, and social scientists, in their conviction to empower workplace populations who must be evaluated fairly, is how that empowerment will be facilitated. Simply encouraging empowerment in the broader sense without direction is pointless.

In an effort to both empower and provide direction, affirmative action was one of a number of policies designed to deter discrimination and enhance quality of life on the basis of race, in particular for black Americans, historically oppressed by both race and skin color.[43] Before the Bakke decision, however, affirmative action was passively enforced by conservative political administrations and in jeopardy of eventual elimination.[44][45] Its existence compromised white workplace domination. Critics contend, as did Mr. Bakke, that affirmative action violated equal protection under the law and sets up a process of "reverse discrimination."[46] Subsequently, and destined for dismissal, affirmative action was arguably the most contested legislation by white male conservatives, such as Utah senator Orrin Hatch. Hatch contended that mere debate about affirmative action cannot take place without the perception of malice on the part of proponents, who have just reason to be suspect given the circumstances of American history.[47] These proponents believed that Senator Hatch and his cohorts intended to dismantle affirmative action—as they eventually did—without proposing any alternative for correcting past injustices, which all agree prevail.[48] Whether or not whites benefit unfairly in the workplace, critics continually ignore the complex web of issues— such as power and tradition—that are not only irrelevant to individual efforts but are frequently assigned to those in a Caucasian race category and also those having light skin.[49]

For proponents of fair employment, the idea of affirmative action remains an effective and necessary tool in combating employment differentials that extended from historical traditions of racism.[50] Moreover, many employers discriminate by race and color out of convenience. According to testimony given before the U.S. Senate Committee on the Judiciary,[51] for example, word-of-mouth recruiting by white male managers is a common practice. It perpetuates a statistically obvious tendency to favor white males, who are the largest in number of managers throughout America.[52] The noble intent of affirmative action policy was to create employment mechanisms that compensate for these workplace advantages, which consistently favor power groups by race and facilitate discrimination by skin color.

Both critics and proponents of affirmative action policy would be served by revisiting its application on the basis of skin color. In objections to affirmative action, the most heated debates are by white male conservatives who are frequently misinformed or uninformed, not only about race but the implications of skin color as well.[53] Their lack of reasoning takes a psychological toll on both black and white Americans, where workplace discrimination has extended beyond race to prevail because workplace equity is irrelevant consequent to white male entitlement motivations. Subsequently, all workers are subject to workplace discrimination because equity is unfortunately secondary to white male advantage.

As Americans, everyone feels a sense of entitlement—including the less powerful—that the trains should run on time. The entire nation takes for granted certain services, but may not be enthused about policies that equalize its operations personnel. As white Americans, they rely on the axis of race to bring forth desired outcomes because it is a longstanding unspoken tradition. That tradition extends from the genesis of Western civilization, which celebrates whiteness by using light skin as the superiority standard that has assumed the force of fact. Black Americans submerged in the depths of such a workplace fallacy have been predisposed to its directives. Through the mulatto hypothesis, the bleaching syndrome, and the "Talented Tenth" era, blacks also acknowledge white superiority. Revisiting affirmative action with a focus not on race but rather on skin color would do much to compromise the resulting workplace discrimination and depolarize its racial implication. Unfortunately, the American power structure, extended from racism, has led white males in particular to have an increased sense of racial entitlement, thus ensuring that a workplace free of discrimination is less likely to happen without deliberate actions.[54] When issues such as affirmative action arise, confrontations continuously proceed from racial issues. Thus, it will be incumbent upon black Americans of all skin tones to unify, as was done during the "Talented Tenth" era, and reintroduce affirmative action into the mainstream of political and legal discourse. Among challenges will be helping white males to distinguish what they are legitimately entitled to, as equal members of the American citizenry. That includes their status, not only as Americans but the fabric of humanity, and what they must surrender to society at large as just resolution. Replacing race or racial labeling with a heretofore less polarizing skin color will do much to accomplish such a goal. In the aftermath, revisiting affirmative action with colored lenses will accommodate a more just judiciary where the existence of workplace discrimination can be more easily challenged and fairly resolved.

Notes

1 Frances Cress Welsing, *The Cress Theory of Color-Confrontation and Racism (White Supremacy)* (Washington, DC: C-R Publishers, 1970).
2 Carel Germain, *Human Behavior in the Social Environment: An Ecological View* (New York: Columbia University Press, 1991).
3 Clemmont E. Vontress, "Counseling Blacks," *Personnel and Guidance Journal* 48 (1970): 713–719.
4 Willard B. Gatewood, *Aristocrats of Color, 1880–1920* (Bloomington, IN: University of Indiana Press, 1990).
5 Frank J. Sciara, "Skin Color and College Student Prejudice," *College Student Journal* 17 (1983): 390–394.
6 W. E. B. Du Bois, "The Talented Tenth," from Booker T. Washington, W. E. B. Du Bois Paul, and Laurence Dunbar, *The Negro Problem: A Series of Articles by Representative Negroes of To-day* (New York, 1903). TeachingAmericanHistory.org. Accessed October 5, 2012, http://teachingamericanhistory.org/library/index.asp?document =174.
7 Historically, to "pass" was to use one's light complexion or mixed heritage to assimilate into the white majority.
8 "Mulatto" is a term used to describe an individual of mixed black and white ancestry.
9 William Julius Wilson, *The Declining Significance of Race: Blacks and Changing American Institutions* (Chicago, IL: University of Chicago Press, 1980).

10 Ronald E. Hall, "Bias among African Americans Regarding Skin Color: Implications for Social Work Practice," *Research on Social Work Practice* 2(4) (1992): 479–486.

11 Ronald E. Hall, "The Projected Manifestations of Aspiration, Personal Values, and Environmental Assessment Cognates of Cutaneo Chroma (Skin Color) for a Selected Population of African Americans," PhD dissertation, Atlanta University, 1989.

12 Ronald Hall, "Bias among African Americans Regarding Skin Color: Implication of Skin Color for Human Behavior in the Social Environment," *Journal of Human Behavior in the Social Environment* 13 (2006): 19–31.

13 Ibid.

14 Taunya Banks, "Colorism: A Darker Shade of Pale," *UCLA Law Review* 47 (2000): 1705–1746.

15 Ibid.

16 Trina Jones, "Shades of Brown: The Law of Skin Color," *Duke Law Journal* 47 (2000): 1487–1556.

17 Banks, "Colorism."

18 Ibid.

19 Jones, "Shades of Brown."

20 Ibid.

21 Joel Kovel, *White Racism: A Psychohistory* (New York: Columbia University Press, 1984).

22 Harry H. L. Kitano, *Race Relations* (Englewood Cliffs, NJ: Prentice-Hall, 1985).

23 Hall, "The Projected Manifestations."

24 Walker v. Secretary of the Treasury, IRS. 1989. 713 F. Supp. 403. United States District Court, N.D. Georgia, Atlanta Division. May 11, 1989, accessed October 5, 2012, http://www.leagle.com/xmlResult.aspx?xmldoc=19891116713FSupp403_11038.xml&docbase=CSLWAR2–1986–2006.

25 Felix v. Marquez. 1981. WL 242, 24 Empl. Prac. Dec. Para 31, 279 (D.D.C., Sept. 11, 1980) (NO 78–2314).

26 Willis v. Sears Holding Management Corporation. 2011. United States District Court, Northern District of Illinois, 10 CV 2926, September 30, 2011, http://law.justia.com/cases/federal/districtcourts/illinois/ilndce/1:2010cv05926/247625/47.

27 U.S. Congress (74th). 1935. U.S. Statutes at Large (July 5, 1935). National Labor Relations Act (Wagner Act), Sess 1, ch. 372, 49 Stat. 449. Washington, DC: Government Printing Office.

28 Ibid.

29 Lara Hudgins, "Rethinking Affirmative Action in the 1990s: Tailoring the Cure to Remedy the Disease," *Baylor Law Review* 47 (1995): 815.

30 [EEOC]. 1964. "Title VII of the Civil Rights Act of 1964." Accessed 5 October 2012, http://www.eeoc.gov/laws/statutes/titlevii.cfm.

31 Marjorie Valbrun, "EEOC Sees Rise in Complaints Involving Intrarace Color Bias," *Wall Street Journal*, August 7, 2003, accessed October 5, 2012, http://online.wsj.come/article/0,,SB106021029773940900,00.html.

32 Du Bois, "The Talented Tenth."

33 Ibid.

34 U.S. Legal, Inc. 2012. "Affirmative Action Law & Legal Definition." Accessed May 5, 2012, http://definitions.uslegal.com/a/affirmative-action/.

35 Regents of the University of California v. Bakke, 438 US 265 (1978).

36 Ibid.

37 Peggy McIntosh, "White Privilege: Unpacking the Invisible Knapsack," *Independent School* 49(2) (1990): 31–35.

38 Timothy O'Neill, *Bakke and the Politics of Equality* (Scranton, PA: Wesleyan University Press, 1985).

39 Ibid.

40 Ibid.

41 Jones, "Shades of Brown," 1487–1557.

42 Elizabeth Torre, "Drama as a Consciousness-raising Strategy for the Self-empowerment of Working Women," *AFFILIA: Journal of Women and Social Work* 5(1) (1990): 49–65.

43 Howard J. Karger and David Stoesz, *American Social Welfare Policy* (New York: Longman, 1990).

44 Patricia Reid-Bookhard, "Blacks in Higher Education: A Study of Some of the Perceived Side-effects of Affirmative Action Policy Implementation on Designated Beneficiaries," PhD dissertation, University of Pennsylvania, 1984. [CD-ROM]. ProQuest (Dissertation Abstracts Item: 1075).

45 Karen D. Stout and William Buffum, "The Commitment of Social Workers to Affirmative Action," *Journal of Sociology and Social Welfare* 20(2) (1993): 123–135.

46 Wilson, *The Declining Significance of Race.*

47 Margaret Gibelman and Philip H. Schervish, "Pay Equity in Social Work: Not!," *Social Work* 40(5) (1995): 622–629.

48 Ibid.

49 Herman Schwartz, "In Defense of Affirmative Action." [CD-ROM]. ProQuest (Dissertation Abstracts Item 731) 1984.

50 Lawrence E. Gary, "African Amerian Men's Perceptions of Racial Discrimination: A Sociocultural Analysis," *Social Work Research* 19(4) (1995): 207–217.

51 U.S. Senate Committee on the Judiciary, Subcommittee on the Constitution. 1981. Affirmative Action and Equal Protection: Hearings on S. J. 41, 97th Cong. 1st Sess., May 11, June 18, and July 16, 1981.

52 Carol Kleiman, "Heavy Load of Diversity Falls on Employees Too," *Chicago Tribune*, November 24, 1993.

53 Richard J. Hernstein and Charles Murray, *The Bell Curve* (New York: Free Press Paperback Books, 1994).

54 Chester M. Pierce, "Entitlement Dysfunctions," *Australian and New Zealand Journal of Psychiatry* 12 (1978): 215–219.

9

A NEW WAY FORWARD

The Development and Preliminary Validation of Two Colorism Scales

Richard D. Harvey, Kira Hudson Banks, and Rachel E. Tennial

Introduction

Variations between skin tone gradients have been noted as a criterion of within-group differentiation and stratification among people of color, black Americans in particular. This phenomenon is generically labeled *colorism* across a wide range of disciplines. According to Meghan Burke, "*Colorism* is the allocation of privilege and disadvantage according to the lightness or darkness of one's skin."[1] The implications of colorism extend across multiple levels of analyses for black Americans, from the intrapersonal,[2] to the interpersonal,[3] to the intragroup,[4] and ultimately to the intergroup.[5] It is important to note that at the root of these implications is the notion that individuals (both within and without communities of color) do, in fact, embrace the ideology of colorism. That is, these implications hinge on the degree to which people actually assign significance and meaning to differences in skin tone gradients. To date, most of the evidence that people do assign significance and meaning to differences in skin tone come from experimental manipulations of skin tone salience[6] rather than from direct assessments from the people.

The purpose of this chapter is twofold. First, we discuss the development of two scales designed to assess the degree to which people assign significance and meaning to skin tone gradients. One scale could be used to assess such significance and meaning on the part of those inside a community of color and the other for those outside of it. This endeavor reflects a shift in the predominant approach to the way that colorism is often analyzed. For the most part, the analysis of colorism has been heavily focused on three primary poles: inequality and socioeconomic mobility, attraction, and racial socialization of children.[7] These topics reflect a structural-political level of analysis in that they point to the role of colorism in the larger social context. Within this larger context, colorism serves as a social stratification mechanism that typically pits lighter-skinned group members on the top and darker-skinned group members on the bottom across a number of outcomes. What appears to be notably absent from this analysis is an approach that recognizes that the significance or meaning associated with skin tone gradients might vary from person to person. Thus, the degree to which colorism is likely to be evoked in a given situation will depend upon the degree to which people in the situation, whether explicitly or implicitly, believe that skin color variations matter. An approach that attempts to capture the degree to which individuals embrace colorism reflects a psychosocial level of analysis. The current endeavor reflects this latter approach.

The second purpose of this chapter is to provide the reader with some guidelines on how these scales might be utilized in practical settings. One direct usage of these scales would be in research on the topic of colorism as discussed above; however, we suggest that these scales may have important practical applications for the workplace, schools, and community forums. To this end, we discuss how the scales may be used as catalysts for intrapersonal development, interpersonal dynamics, and institutional analyses for multiple stakeholders within each of these forums.

The Nature of Colorism

A psychosocial approach to the study of colorism reflects the individual level of analyses. At this level, the perceived significance and meaning associated with skin tone variation is the primary focus. Across the literature on colorism, there are four primary areas in which colorism has been perceived to hold significance and meaning: self-concept, impression formation, attraction/affiliation, and upward mobility.

Self-Concept

Perhaps the most paramount implications of colorism are its impact on how black Americans define and evaluate themselves. The preference for light skin that was a product of slavery has over time embedded itself into the definitive core values of African-American culture.[8] With respect to self-evaluations, early research found that black children's self-evaluations were based a good deal on their skin tone, with higher self-evaluations being linked to lighter skin.[9] Furthermore, Robinson and Ward[10] found a relationship between self-esteem and self-reported skin tone among adults as well. Thus, the idea that a person's self-concept is likely to be influenced by the significance placed on skin tone is well supported in the extant literature.

Impression Formation

The idea that the skin tone of a black person might convey important information about the character of the person is rooted in slavery. Within slavery, black Americans were differentiated on the basis of their perceived intelligence, skillfulness, and monetary worth in favor of light over dark skin tone.[11] Research has found that these early distinctions between people of light and dark skin tone have maintained their course such that the impressions that people form of black Americans are still heavily dependent on their skin tone.[12] As a recent and practical example, Viglione, Hannon, and DeFina found that dark-skin female criminals received harsher sentences than their lighter-skin counterparts, suggesting differing perceptions of the criminality of skin tones.[13] These findings suggest that skin tone may be an important factor when forming impressions of people of color.

Attraction/Affiliation

A great deal of the literature on colorism has focused on varying attractiveness of skin tones. Preference for a mate with a lighter skin tone has been found in a number of studies.[14] Furthermore, familial socialization can include admonitions for being out in the sun and getting darker, choosing a mate of dark skin tone, and encouragement to find a mate of light skin tone.[15] Even beyond romantic attraction, lighter skin tone is rated as more generally attractive than darker skin tone by black and white Americans.[16] In a study of adjectives used to describe people of various skin tones, the term "attractive" was more likely to be attributed to pictures of people with light skin tone, and "unattractive" was more likely to be assigned to people with dark skin tone.[17] This association between attraction and skin tone appears to be stronger when judging black American women versus black American men.[18]

Affiliation in the context of colorism more broadly speaks to the desire to be connected to or socialize with others based on skin tone. Historically, there has been a tendency for African Americans of lighter skin tone to be favored as social companions. Increased educational and occupational attainment[19] and access to social clubs and organizations[20] are examples of privileges afforded to black Americans with lighter skin tone. These factors could be seen as proxies for white Americans' desire to affiliate with African Americans of lighter skin tone and lighter-skin-toned African Americans' desire to create spaces where they affiliate with other African Americans of similar skin tone.

Upward Mobility

The driving force behind much of the research on colorism has been the notion that skin tone plays a significant role in shaping the life chances and experience of black Americans.[21] This has been most notable in those studies that have explored the wealth inequality that results from differing social privileges and opportunities afforded to some skin tones over others. Several studies[22] have suggested that skin tone variations have important implications for occupational status, income, and level of educational attainment. Thus, there seems to be a widespread explicit and/or implicit belief that skin tone could be used as a gateway to upward mobility on these traditional indicators of socioeconomic success.

Given that skin tone variation appears to hold significance across these four areas, and perhaps others, colorism can be said to be multidimensional in nature. Thus, any approach to the analysis of it must also be multidimensional. In so doing, an allowance is made for the complexity that is likely to exist in the relationships both among the various dimensions of it and between those dimensions and other important constructs.

Colorism vs. Racism

Given the fact that both terms hold implications for people of color, it is nevertheless important to distinguish colorism from racism. While the definitions of racism vary considerably, the common denominator between the various definitions is that racism is the belief that some race or races are superior or inferior to others. Thus, racism may be considered an *intergroup* phenomenon in that it involves a social comparison between two or more racial groups. While colorism does, in fact, have its roots in the intergroup distinction between free whites and enslaved blacks in the United States, it is much more of an *intragroup* phenomenon. That is, it reflects biases toward certain variations (e.g., lighter skin) within racial groups rather than between them. Of course, these biases might be held by either those outside or those inside the focal group. Hence, while connected in their origin, racism and colorism are not dependent upon each other for their modern existence. Thus, a decrease or even annihilation of racism does not preclude the existence of a colorism problem, since colorism can exist independent of an intergroup context.

Previous Measures

In our review of the extant literature on colorism, we could not find a single self-report scale that explicitly measures the significance and meaning that an individual places on skin tone variations. This is not totally unexpected, due to the level at which colorism has most typically been conceptualized. As discussed earlier, for the most part colorism has been considered a macro-level structural-political phenomenon. Thus, the unit of analysis has been at the societal level, and the indicators for its existence have also been societal indicators (e.g., discrimination rates, wealth inequality estimates, marital rates, etc.). At this level, whole societies are judged on the degree to which colorism is present. Attempts to examine colorism at the relatively more micro-individual level are sparse. This level allows for individual variation in the degree to which colorism is embraced and thereby locates colorism within the psyche of the individual more so than within the climate of the society.

Most of the research on colorism at the psychosocial level has focused mostly on assessing the skin tone of participants and then examining the association between their skin tones and important outcomes such as indicators of subjective well-being.[23] These measures of participant skin tones are, at best, indirect measures of the significance and meaning of skin tone, in that the significance of skin tone is only established to the degree to which correlations are found between skin tone and the particular outcome under study. Moreover, because they focus more on the participants' own skin tones rather than their perceptions of others' skin tones, they are limited to establishing the significance on only one of the four dimensions identified earlier, namely self-concept.

There is, however, an implicit measure of skin color bias that could be used to assess the significance that one might place on skin tone variations among black Americans in particular. Project Implicit represents a collaborative research effort between researchers at Harvard University, the University of Virginia, and University of Washington. The website of Project Implicit features a Skin-tone Implicit Association Test (IAT) among eleven other IAT tests. The accumulated results of participants who have been visiting the website and taking the test has revealed a general automatic preference for light skin relative to dark skin. This skin tone test, as with all IAT tests, measures implicit or unconscious processes believed to be associated with skin tone preferences. Thus, theoretically, such a measure could be used to reveal the salience of colorism for participants when making stereotypic judgments; however, it does not allow for probing the complex ideology of colorism because the IAT appears to be measuring colorism as unidimensional rather than multidimensional. Thus, it could be indicative of *significance* but not necessarily *meaning*. A purposeful attempt to explore colorism must take into consideration the complex multidimensional nature of colorism in order to best understand both its structure and its relationships with other important phenomena.

Scale Development and Validation

We utilized Simms' guidelines[24] on scale construction in order to develop and validate two scales of colorism: The In-group Colorism Scale (ICS) and the Out-group Colorism Scale (OCS). The ICS was developed to assess the significance and meaning of skin color variations on the part of those inside a community of color. While this particular version was developed for evaluation on African Americans, it is our contention that this scale could be modified and used for virtually any group, minority groups in particular. In comparison, the OCS was developed to assess the significance and meaning of skin color variations on the part of those outside of the focal community of color. This particular version was developed for evaluation on European Americans; however, as with the ICS, we contend that it may also be modified and used for any out-group population relative to a focal group.

The process of development and then subsequent validation for these scales are chronicled in a forthcoming manuscript by the authors. Simms' model[25] is based upon Loevinger's seminal model of scale construction,[26] and it integrates the three mutually exclusive approaches to scale construction: rational-theoretical, empirical criterion keying, and factor-analytic/internal consistency. Thus, Simms' model reflects an eclectic and comprehensive approach to scale development and validation. Considerable detail is covered in this forthcoming manuscript that is not entailed in this chapter; however, we will provide a brief overview of the development and validation activities for each of these scales, separately, before discussing the scales' practical utility.

In-Group Colorism Scale (ICS)

As a first step, subject matter experts (SMEs) were enlisted to develop and then subsequently review and edit potential items for the ICS scale. A subsequent empirical study involving a national sample of more than 500 male and female black American participants of various ages, socioeconomic statuses, and educational levels were then used to both explore and then confirm the dimensionality of the overall scale and each of its five subscales, namely, *self-concept, impression formation, affiliation, attraction*, and *upward mobility* (see Table 9.1 for a list of items). Both the overall scale and each of the subscales proved to have high psychometric quality (i.e., high reliability and high structural validity).

The empirical study included measures of other well-known phenomena that should have been theoretically related to colorism. Several significant relationships were found between the colorism scales and the other measures. Higher *self-concept colorism* scores were significantly correlated with higher racial centrality and nationalist racial ideology. Furthermore, higher scores were correlated with higher racial socialization, lower self-esteem, and darker skin tones. Higher *impression formation colorism* scores were significantly correlated with lower racial centrality, lower racial private regard, higher desires to be a lighter and darker skin tone, lower self-esteem, and darker skin tones. Higher *upward mobility colorism* scores were significantly correlated with lower racial private regard, higher nationalist racial ideology, higher racial socialization, lower self-esteem, and higher desires to be a lighter and darker skin tone. Higher *attraction colorism* scores were significantly correlated with lower racial private regard, higher nationalist racial ideology, lower self-esteem, and higher desires to be a lighter and darker skin tone. Finally, *higher affiliation* colorism scores were significantly correlated with lower racial private regard, higher nationalist racial ideology, lower

TABLE 9.1 Items of In-Group Colorism Scale (ICS) Subscales

Items

Self-Concept

My skin tone is an important part of my self-concept.

My skin tone is an important component of who I am.

My skin tone affects my self-esteem.

My skin tone is a big part of my identity.

Impression Formation

You can tell a lot about a person by their skin tone.

Blacks with lighter skin tone tend to be more pleasant people to deal with.

Dark-skinned people are more difficult to work with.

There are real differences between light-skinned and dark-skinned people.

Affiliation

I'm usually uncomfortable being around people who are a certain skin tone.

Most of my friends tend to be the same skin tone.

I usually choose who I'm going to be friends with by their skin tone.

The majority of my current friends are the same skin tone as me.

Attraction

I'm primarily attracted to people of a certain skin tone.

I prefer light skin over dark complexion skin when choosing romantic interests.

I prefer a romantic partner who has the same skin tone as me.

Lighter skin tone makes others more attractive.

Upward Mobility

Even if you work really hard, your skin tone matters most.

Skin tone plays a big part in determining how far you can make it.

Skin tone affects how much money you can make.

If you want to get ahead, you have to be the right skin tone.

Note: Responses to items were measured using a 7-point Likert-scale format (*Strongly Agree* to *Strongly Disagree*).

self-esteem, higher desires to be a lighter and darker skin tone, and darker participant skin tones. Thus, each of these scales proved to be valid predictors of various important phenomena.

Outgroup Colorism Scale (OCS)

The development and validation procedures utilized for the OCS were virtually identical to those discussed earlier. That is, SMEs were used for initial scale item development and review. Furthermore, a subsequent empirical study was conducted to examine the validity of the OCS. This study involved a national sample of 383 male and female white American participants of various ages, socioeconomic statuses, and educational levels. With the exception of the self-concept dimension, which is arguably irrelevant for an out-group population, the same dimensions in the ICS were developed and tested in the OCS: *impression formation, attraction, affiliation,* and *upward mobility.* As with the ICS, both the overall scale and each of the subscales proved to have high psychometric quality.

Several important relationships were discovered between the OCS and other theoretically related phenomena (see Table 9.2). Higher *impression formation colorism* scores were significantly correlated with higher scores on the institutional and blatant discrimination subscales of the Color Blind Racial attitudes scale, higher racial identification, higher racial socialization, and lower childhood neighborhood diversity. Higher endorsement of *upward mobility colorism* scores were significantly correlated with higher scores on the institutional and blatant discrimination sub-scales of the Color Blind Racial attitudes scale, higher racial identification, higher racial socialization, and lower childhood neighborhood diversity. However, higher awareness of upward mobility colorism scores were significantly correlated with higher scores on the racial privilege subscale of the Color Blind Racial attitudes scale (and not the institutional and blatant discrimination subscales), higher racial identification, and higher racial socialization. Higher *attraction colorism* scores were significantly correlated with higher scores on the institutional and blatant discrimination subscales of the Color Blind Racial attitudes scale, higher racial identification, higher racial socialization, and lower childhood neighborhood diversity. Finally, higher *affiliation colorism* scores were significantly correlated with higher scores on the institutional and blatant discrimination subscales of the Color Blind Racial attitudes scale, higher racial identification, and higher racial social-ization. Thus, there was a sufficient pattern of correlations between the OCS colorism scales and the other measures.

Application of the Colorism Scales

The scales can be used as a catalyst for intrapersonal development, interpersonal and intergroup dynamics, and institutional analyses. Bias is conceptualized to occur at multiple levels: intrapersonal, interpersonal, cultural, and institutional.[27]

TABLE 9.2 Items of the Out-Group Colorism Scale (OCS) Subscales

Items

Impression Formation

You can't really tell anything about a black person just by looking at their skin complexion.

There are important differences between light complexion and dark complexion black people.

A black person's skin complexion should not be a determining factor when making judgments about him or her.

The perceptions that I form about a black person have nothing to do with their skin complexion.

Upward Mobility

Endorsement

The upward mobility of blacks in the workplace has nothing to do with the lightness or darkness of their skin complexion.

Skin complexion should not be an important factor when evaluating black job applicants.

Skin complexion should not determine who should be leaders in the black community.

Awareness

The personal progress of many blacks depends on their skin complexion.

When conducting business with black people, I have no preference for one skin complexion over another.

Lighter complexion blacks tend to be more successful than darker complexion blacks.

Attraction

Blacks with lighter skin complexions tend to be more pleasant people to deal with.

Light complexion skin looks healthier than dark complexion skin among black people.

I have no preference for a particular skin complexion when deciding whether I like a particular black celebrity.

Lighter-complexioned black people are more physically attractive than darker-complexioned black people.

Affiliation

I have no preferences for light over dark complexion skin when choosing black friends.

My comfort level has nothing to do with the lightness or darkness of their skin complexion.

In general I prefer to have lighter complexioned black people as coworkers.

I prefer dark over light complexion skin when choosing black associates and friends.

Note: Responses to items were measured using a 7-point Likert-scale format (*Strongly Agree* to *Strongly Disagree*).

Therefore colorism, a particular form of bias, can also occur on these levels. An example of intrapersonal colorism would be an individual holding a negative self-concept on the basis of his or her skin tone because of negative socialization messages. Interpersonal colorism could involve an individual refusing to be friends with or associate with someone based on the potential friend's skin tone. Cultural colorism might occur when a group of people with a less desirable skin tone is negatively portrayed in the media or, conversely, the common representations of beauty are consistent with the more desirable skin tone. Finally, an example of institutional colorism is an organization or school using skin tone as a factor in admittance and being unwilling to allow individuals of an undesirable skin tone into the organization. Each of these examples is consistent with the way in which colorism has been enacted historically. The individual dynamics (i.e., intrapersonal and interpersonal) are most reflective of the ICS and OCS presented within the chapter.

While bias can happen on all of those levels, and it is important not to conflate the complexities, it is also important to keep in mind that the scales only measure an individual's self-report of their beliefs. Therefore, the data reside on the individual level. Yet the effective use of such data can have implications for larger work, which might address the cultural and institutional manifestations of colorism. The use of the scales should also take into consideration the racial makeup within and across group dynamics of the institution. Those examinations will lead to the consideration of other constructs that might be important to assess via quantitative measures of qualitative interviews.

As the scale is utilized within black communities or other communities of color, it is worth considering constructs such as racial identity, internalized racial oppression, and racial socialization. Internalized racial oppression or internalized racism is conceptualized as the ways in which people in oppressed groups take on and reproduce the negative beliefs about their group, which can result in feelings of self-doubt, disrespect, and disgust.[28] It has been examined as an important link in understanding the experience of targeted groups.[29] Acknowledging other within group differences, skin tone bias is thought to work differently for African American men and women[30] and has been found to correlate with self-esteem for African American women but not for African American men.[31] However, recent research has suggested that skin color is not as important as personal mastery for African American women.[32] Skin tone has positive effects on self-efficacy for African American men and women.[33]

Within predominantly white spaces, the era of colorblind rhetoric predominates. The hope of many is that we are "beyond" race, or that, if we would just stop talking about race, skin color, or difference, that they would cease to be of concern. It might seem counterintuitive to some to need or to utilize a colorism scale. As the scale is used within white communities, constructs such as colorblind racial attitudes, racial identity, and racial beliefs and attitudes could be assessed. Colorblindness, the assertion that race no longer matters, has a long history but has more recently been used as a tool to actually perpetuate racial inequality.[34] Increased endorsement that race is no longer relevant has been found to significantly correlate positively with a greater level of unconscious/implicit and conscious/explicit bias.[35] The more individuals are conscious of the ways in which race continues to play a role in access and experiences, the more positive the sense of racial identity[36] and the lower the levels of white guilt and white empathetic reactions to racism.[37] It remains unclear how these constructs would overlap with colorism.

Below, we will discuss examples of how this scale might be incorporated into various contexts. Within these various circumstances, there are varied opinions about how to move forward with initiative and engagement in such an assessment. Some believe you should start from the top down; others believe it should be a grassroots effort, beginning with those who "get it." Organizational theory would suggest that the buy-in from leadership, who set the tone and shape policy, is at some point necessary for the work to be institutionalized.[38] However, it is also the reality that buy-in across level is necessary for the work to not be perceived as top-down. There is no one way to proceed. Reflection on the dynamics within the organization, the relationship between management and line staff, and the history of related work previously embarked upon would all inform the structure of the engagement.

School

Schools are socializing agents for children and help shape their self-concept and how they evaluate others. Research has consistently conveyed that children as young as preschool have the ability to evaluate which groups of people are viewed as preferable.[39] The popular documentary "A Class Divided" portrays the power one elementary teacher had in teaching the children about fairness and justice. Recent studies suggest that the way in which schools teach about difference can have an impact on what children use to analyze situations.[40]

A recent study found that colorblindness can impede children's ability to detect and convey incidents of racial inequity.[41] Researchers exposed 8- to 10-year-old children from the United States (N = 51 white and 9 Asian American) to two versions of a book: one from the colorblind approach and the other from the value-diversity perspective. When students were subsequently provided with vignettes that conveyed racial discrimination, the students taught from the colorblind approach were significantly less able to identify discrimination when it was ambiguous and blatant. When these students described the events, the explanations inspired significantly less need for intervention by teachers. These findings hold implications for the real world in that, if people are taught not to attend to race, they likely are be less able to analyze situations effectively, particularly where race is a contributing factor. Similarly, being aware of how teachers and students assign meaning to skin color appears to be useful information.

These studies suggest that schools are a prime institution within which to examine and begin to deconstruct colorism. This is particularly true given recent data suggesting that parents, particularly white parents who are concerned with bringing attention to race, are less inclined to raise the matter of race and/or skin color with their children. As that data reveals not openly discussing these issues does not make the elephant that the children clearly see in the room go away and in fact impedes racial harmonization. Unless actively addressed, children retain a default message: White is good and black is bad.[42]

Schools serve as the primary context in which children and adolescents construct images of out-groups, in-groups, and their own self-concepts. Thus, the core components of colorism (i.e., *self-concept, impression formation, attraction, affiliation,* and *upward mobility*) are directly relevant to the development of positive images of others. And, for students of color, having positive images of their racial in-group and their own self-concepts have been intricately linked to the subject of colorism. To that end, the colorism scales could be used in conjunction with anti-bias curriculum as development tools in addition to part of a self-assessment. The tool could be used to reflect on the assumptions and judgments we make about teachers, students, and families of a certain skin tone. Even within predominantly white spaces, it is important to reflect on the assigned value of skin tone.[43] It is particularly important in integrated spaces as to foster interactional diversity across lines of difference.[44]

Key Stakeholders

It would be important to include administrators, teachers, support staff, students, and parents. If it is a small school or school district, the school board would also be essential to consider. Even in large districts, the support of the superintendent has proven to be leverage for getting people on board and validating the examination of bias.

Tips for Implementation

Think about the separate layers but also how you can share across groups. For example, the reflection and debriefing might look different for students, teachers, parents, and administration; however, there will be some overlap. Perhaps consider having the students or their parents give a presentation to teachers, hosting dialogues over potlucks, and allocating time during staff meetings.

Workplace

Addressing issues of bias within the workplace has become more common over the past two decades. Increasingly, companies understand the link between eliminating bias and improving the bottom line in the form of profits, employee satisfaction, and engagement. Awareness of bias can emerge from any direction, but it is often the case that people in power are less aware of incidents of bias, whereas groups who are marginalized are quite aware of unfair treatment. This dynamic can be attributed to issues of power and privilege, yet those concepts can be controversial and touchy to broach.[45] An accessible analogy that can be used is that of a mouse and an elephant.[46] In the workplace, it is often the overtly powerful and assertive capabilities of elephants that are encouraged, rewarded, and promoted. Yet, in reality, it is oftentimes useful to employ the agile, observant nature of the mouse. The dynamics between the two is that elephants take up so much room, literally and figuratively, that they can at times literally trample the mouse, unaware of their disregard for the mouse's tendencies or well-being. The mouse, on the other hand, is aware of the elephant's whereabouts and habits as a matter of survival. He or she most likely has studied the elephant and understands the actions that follow the swish of the tail or twitch of the ears. The mouse is able to not only anticipate the movement of the elephant, but the mouse must also conform to the tendencies of the elephant to succeed, be promoted, and to prosper. In the context of colorism, the groups that are marginalized are quite aware of how they must attempt to overcome negative assumptions and expectations that others have about them. Meanwhile, the privileged group has advantages that often remain invisible to them. Even beyond the topic of colorism, this analogy could prove useful as a template to look for social stratifications and power inequities within an organization.

Because colorism is more implicit than explicit, its presence within an organization is also likely to be more implicit than explicit. As with more institutional forms of discrimination, it is likely to be embedded within institutional mental models that impact day-to-day human resource practices. For example, it could potentially preference certain skin tones over others during selection processes. One of the core components of colorism was impression formation. Forming impressions is the central task of the interviewer during a job interview. Moreover, it might also impact opportunities for training and professional development. Another core component of colorism was the notion of upward mobility. Thus, some might believe implicitly and/or explicitly that certain skin tones are more associated with professional success. Organizational analysts would need to intentionally look for and address these types of colorism patterns. For example, it could be that only people with light skin tone are being chosen as mentees within a mentorship program. Or, perhaps, there might not be any executives within the organization who have darker skin tones.

Research suggests that constructs such as job strain and social stress are important factors when understanding the experience of bias in the workplace. High job strain is conceptualized as the extent to which a workplace has high emotional demands and low control.[47] Social stress is generally the exposure to common stressors that are not linked to any specific groups yet also can put individuals at increased risk for negative outcomes. Given the increase in racial diversity in the labor force, the skin tone of employees is bound to increase in variability and color. That shift, coupled with the reality that over time bias in the workplace persists and reduces the quality of labor force participation,[48] frames bias in the workplace as worth tackling. Employers are likely to discover that even beneath the layer of social stress due to intergroup racial/ethnic biases is a layer of social stress due primarily to intragroup colorism biases.

Key Stakeholders

It would be important to engage executive management, management, employees, and community partners. Within those categories, it would be helpful to include new hires and individuals who have tenure at the institution. Varying the groups by race would help ensure that there is variability across experiences. Knowledge of the extent to which individuals have self-awareness, awareness of the experience of others, and awareness of intergroup dynamics would be helpful, especially at the beginning of such a journey.

Tips for Implementation

Many current diversity programs already target race-based prejudice and discrimination; however, as we argued at the beginning of this chapter, racism and colorism are not synonymous nor are they interdependent. Thus, colorism can still be a problem even when race-based prejudice and discrimination are not. Including a discussion and the two scales introduced herein would be an important supplement to any race or ethnic diversity program. Just as important, having a discussion about how they might be linked could prove helpful. For example, it might be that there are a few notable minority "success" stories within the organization, which might seem to suggest that there is no real racial bias within the organization. However, upon closer inspection, it might be discovered that all of those success stories tend to be of one skin-tone hue. This might suggest a somewhat complex interaction between intergroup racial bias and within-group skin tone bias. Be mindful of power dynamics. It is unfair to have lower level employees sharing solutions when upper management is in total control. Also, look for ways you can model communication across levels. Consider one of the ready-made trainings and workshops (e.g. Crucial Conversations or Diversityinc) as a complement to the specific work on colorism.

Communities

Community settings can include families, places of worship, nonprofit agencies, neighborhood associations, and other groups connected by some common cause. Research on colorism has consistently highlighted the importance of family and other socializing agents as sources of learning and reinforcing ideas about skin color.[49] Such family and community socialization have been frequently linked to increased self-esteem[50]—however, not always.[51] They have also been associated with increased racial centrality.[52] Many of the constructs mentioned in schools and in the workplace are relevant here, because in many ways community organizations are certainly socializing agents similar to school systems, yet a number of them function as workplaces for staff. Therefore, colorism could be operating in many of the same and overlapping ways. For example, an agency might have a staff of individuals with fair skin tone whose target area is predominantly individuals with dark skin tone. The dynamics could involve people of the fairer skin tone making conscious or unconscious negative assumptions about the darker-skinned individuals. Alternatively, the individuals of darker skin tone could internalize such messages, exacerbating feelings of being judged for receiving services or feeling helpless to advocate for themselves.

Key Stakeholders

Involvement will vary based on the scope and collaborations but might include community/religious leaders, community organizers, community members, and agency leaders and staff. Places of worship, neighborhood dialogue groups, and community-building workshops are examples of where you might begin if your desire is to engage in a community assessment or reflection. Again, it is essential to be aware of or inquiring about dynamics of the relationships within and external of the organization.

Tips for Implementation

Even though engagement is important in every setting, it is particularly important in community projects. Schools and workplaces represent captive audiences to a large degree, whereas individuals can leave community organizations quickly and with little or massive aftermath. Depending on the structure, the alliances could be clear or less explicitly drawn. There are organizations particularly suited at providing resources and support for community work (i.e., Crossroads Anti-Racism Organizing and Training, Everyday Democracy).

Next Steps

Once you have decided the context and possibly correlated constructs you want to measure, it is important to get approval from the institution and the individuals you will be assessing. Be clear about what you are asking from individuals. It often helps to clarify the purpose and that there are no right or wrong answers. Perhaps you are hoping to simply get a baseline and plan to assess the average responses over a period of time and after a series of programs. You might be interested in comparing the average scores of people in different positions. Share your plans for the data with the participants, and they will be more likely to provide honest answers. Reiterate that no one answer will be pulled out for identification. Aggregate responses and share the range of scores to give people a broad idea of the data. Refrain from grouping or comparing if the numbers are small and could likely "out" members (e.g., if there are only three teachers of color, it would not be fair to report their data). Remain in communication with leadership so that it feels a part of the discovery and a part of the understanding of the results and related implications.

Conclusion

In this chapter, we first discussed the development of two scales that could be used to measure the significance and meaning of colorism for both members of groups of color (i.e., ICS) and those who are not (OCS). Using technically sophisticated methods of scale development, we developed scales that were proven to be both reliable and valid. Thus, we believe that these scales will prove highly useful in future research on the topic of colorism. Second, we set out to provide guidelines on how these same scales might prove useful on a more practical level within three distinct settings: school, workplace, and community. For practitioners, focusing on colorism can prove highly useful as an extension of conversations that might already be underway on the topics of discrimination and/or diversity. Because colorism is a related but distinct issue from racial biases, its inclusion in the discussion helps to both extend our understanding of racial biases and, at the same time, complicate our understanding of them. Institutions that don't necessarily show between-race bias may nonetheless demonstrate within-race skin tone biases that ultimately preference certain skin tone hues over others. An even more complicated notion is that colorism might even create double standards among skin tone hues within the same racial category. Thus, the racial bias of the institution is expressed more in the fact that their racial minority success stories all tend to have hues that are closer in proximity to the majority group. This could explain the often lack of homogeneity among the reports of minorities as to the degree to which they feel accepted within the institution.

As a parting nod to practitioners, anyone serious about facilitating a discussion on colorism might consider the use of social media as a catalyst. There have been both motion pictures and documentaries that could serve as lead-ins for group discussions. Spike Lee's 1988 comedy *School Daze* is roughly about colorism in a fictional black college, as exemplified by the dark-skinned sorority and fraternity members referred to as the "Jigaboos" and the light-skinned sorority and fraternity members called the "Wannabees." A recent documentary directed by Bill Duke and D. Channsin Berry titled *Dark Girls* explores the lives of different black women and their perspective on how their skin color has affected their life and their self-image.

Colorism dynamics play out in various institutions, and some would say it is futile to resist it, or that, in fact, we should simply wait for the older generation to die. Yet, it is important to remind ourselves that change is the only guarantee. A closer analysis of colorism on the intrapersonal, interpersonal, cultural, and institutional levels will reveal that the bias is embedded and interwoven to the point that it is not only interpersonal dynamics that need to be addressed. Thus the passing of a generation of people will not remedy this construct. Indeed, preschoolers today are color-struck.[53] The intrapersonal and cultural, as reflected by ICS and OCS, in addition to the institutional, hold relevant keys for our society to unlock skin tone bias. Research suggests that bias can impair peer relationships[54] as well as affect mental and physical health.[55] The deleterious outcomes of bias are worth minimizing. Using the proposed scales and assessing colorism is a small piece of doing that work.

Notes

1   Meghan Burke, "Colorism," in *International Encyclopedia of the Social Sciences,* ed. W. Darity, Jr. (New York: Macmillan Library Reference, 2008), 17.
2   For *self-esteem*, see Richard D. Harvey et al., "The Intragroup Stigmatization of Skin Tone among Black Americans," *Journal of Black Psychology* 31 (2005): 237–253.
3   For *romantic pairings*, see M. Hill, "Skin Color and the Perceptions of Attractiveness among African Americans: Does Gender Make a Difference?," *Social Psychology Quarterly* 65 (2005): 77–91.
4   For *familial socialization*, see JeffriAnne Wilder and Colleen Cain, "Teaching and Learning Color Consciousness in Black Families: Exploring Family Processes and Women's Experiences with Colorism," *Journal of Family Issues* 32 (2011): 577–604.
5   For *social inequality,* see Linda M. Burton, Eduardo Bonilla-Silva, Victor Ray, Rose Buckelew, and Elizabeth H. Freeman, "Critical Race Theories, Colorism, and the Decade's Research on Families of Color," *Journal of Marriage and Family* 72 (2010): 440–459.
6   Keith B. Maddox and Stephanie Gray Chase, "Manipulating Subcategory Salience: Exploring the Link between Skin Tone and Social Perception of Blacks," *European Journal of Social Psychology* 34 (2004): 533–546; Keith B. Maddox and Stephanie A. Gray, "Cognitive Representations of Black Americans: Reexploring the Role of Skin Tone," *Personality and Social Psychology Bulletin* 28 (2002): 250–259.
7   See Burke, "Colorism"; Burton et al., "Critical Race Theories."
8   Stephanie I. Coard, Alfiee M. Breland, and Patricia Raskin, "Perceptions of and Preferences for Skin Color, Black Racial Identity, and Self-Esteem among African-Americans," *Journal of Applied Social Psychology* 31 (2001): 2256–2274.
9   Phillip Jordan and Maria Hernandez-Reif, "Reexamination of Young Children's Racial Attitudes and Skin Tone Preferences," *Journal of Black Psychology* 35 (2009): 388–403.
10 Tracy L. Robinson and Janie V. Ward, "African-American Adolescents and Skin Color," *Journal of Black Psychology* 21 (1995): 256–274.
11 Maddox and Gray, "Cognitive Representations of Black Americans"; Coard et al., "Perceptions of Preferences for Skin Color."
12 Maddox and Gray, "Cognitive Representations of Black Americans"; Maddox and Gray Chase, "Manipulating Subcategory Salience"; Dawn S. Chin-Qee, "Impressions of the

Light, Medium, and Dark-Skinned: A Portrait of Racial and Intraracial Stereotypes,"
unpublished PhD dissertation, University of Virginia, 1993.

13 Jill Viglione, Lance Hannon, and Robert DeFina, "The Impact of Light Skin on Prison
Time for Black Female Offenders," *Social Science Journal* 48 (2011): 250–258.

14 Harvey et al., "The Intragroup Stigmatization of Skin Tone"; JeffriAnne Wilder,
"Revisiting Color Names and Color Notions: A Contemporary Examination of the
Language and Attitudes of Skin Color Among Young Black Women," *Journal of Black
Studies* 41 (2010): 184–206; Wilder and Cain, "Teaching and Learning Color
Consciousness."

15 Ibid.

16 Hill, "Skin Color and the Perceptions of Attractiveness."

17 Maddox and Gray, "Cognitive Representations of Black Americans."

18 Hill, "Skin Color and the Perceptions of Attractiveness"; Maxine S. Thompson and
Verna M. Keith, "The Blacker the Berry: Gender, Skin-tone, Self-esteem and Self-
efficacy," *Gender and Society* 15 (2001): 336–357.

19 Michael Hughes and Bradley R. Hertel, "The Significance of Color Remains: A Study
of Life Chances, Mate Selection, and Ethnic Consciousness among Black Americans,"
Social Forces 68 (1990): 1105–1120.

20 E. Franklin Frazier, *Black Bourgeoise: The Rise of the New Middle Class* (New York: Free
Press, 1957).

21 Wilder, "Revisiting Color Names and Color Notions."

22 Arthur M. Goldsmith, Darrick Hamilton, and William A. Darity, Jr. "From Dark to
Light: Skin Color and Wages among African Americans," *Journal of Human Resources*
4 (2007): 701–738; Hill, "Skin Color and the Perceptions of Attractiveness"; Hughes
and Hertel, "The Significance of Color Remains"; Verna M. Keith, and Cedric Herring,
"Skin Tone and Stratification in the Black Community," *American Journal of Sociology*
97 (1991): 760–778.

23 e.g., Self-esteem; Harvey et al., "The Intragroup Stigmatization of Skin Tone";
Thompson and Keith, "The Blacker the Berry."

24 Leonard J. Simms, "Classical and Modern Methods of Psychological Scale
Construction," *Social and Personality Psychology Compass* 1 (2007): 1–20.

25 Ibid.

26 Jane Loevinger, "Objective Tests as Instruments of Psychological Theory," *Psychological
Reports* 3 (1957): 635–694.

27 Elizabeth Brondolo et al., "Racism and Social Capital: The Implications for Social and
Physical Well-Being," *Journal of Social Issues* 68(2) (2012): 358–384; Shelly P. Harrell,
"A Multidimensional Conceptualization of Racism-Related Stress: Implications for the
Well-being of People of Color," *American Journal of Orthopsychiatry* 70 (2000): 42–57.

28 Karen Pyke and Tran Dang, "'FOB' and 'Whitewashed': Identity and Internalized
Racism among Second Generation Asian Americans," *Qualitative Sociology* 26 (2003):
147–172.

29 Suzette L. Speight, "Internalized Racism: One More Piece of the Puzzle," *Counseling
Psychologist* 35 (2007): 126–134.

30 Hill, "Skin Color and the Perceptions of Attractiveness."

31 Thompson and Keith, "The Blacker the Berry."

32 Verna Keith, Karen D. Lincoln, Robert Joseph Taylor, and James S. Jackson,
"Discriminatory Experiences and Depressive Symptoms among African American
Women: Do Skin Tone and Mastery Matter?," *Sex Roles* 62 (2010) 48–59.

33 Thompson and Keith, "The Blacker the Berry."

34 Eduardo Bonilla-Silva, *Racism without Racists: Color-blind Racism and the Persistence of
Racial Inequality in the United States* (Lanham, MD: Rowman & Littlefield Publishers,
2003); Victoria C. Plaut, "Diversity Science: Why and How Difference Makes a
Difference," *Psychological Inquiry* 21 (2010): 77–99.

35 Jennifer A. Richeson and Richard J. Nussbaum, "The Impact of Multiculturalism versus Color-blindness on Racial Bias," *Journal of Experimental Social Psychology* 40 (2004): 417–423.

36 Meghan A. Burke and Kira H. Banks, "Sociology by Any Other Name: Teaching the Sociological Perspective in Campus Diversity Programs," *Teaching Sociology* 40(1) (2012): 21–33.

37 Lisa B. Spanierman and Mary J. Heppner, "Psychosocial Costs of Racism to Whites Scale (PCRW): Construction and Initial Validation," *Journal of Counseling Psychology* 51 (2004): 249–262.

38 Thomas G. Cummings and Christopher G. Worley, *Organizational Development and Change*, 9th edition (Mason, OH: South-Western Cengage Learning, 2009).

39 Frances E. Aboud, "A Social-cognitive Developmental Theory of Prejudice," in *Handbook of Race, Racism, and the Developing Child*, eds Stephen M. Quintana and Clark McKown (Hoboken, NJ: John Wiley & Sons, 2008), 55–71; Lawrence A. Hirschfeld, "Children's Developing Conceptions of Race," in *Handbook of Race, Racism, and the Developing Child*, eds Stephen M. Quintana and Clark McKown (Hoboken, NJ: John Wiley & Sons, 2008), 37–54; Phyllis A. Katz, "Racists or Tolerant Multiculturalists? How Do They Begin?," *American Psychologist* 58(11) (2003): 897–909; Meghan M. Patterson and Rebecca S. Bigler, "Preschool Children's Attention to Environmental Messages about Groups: Social Categorization and the Origins of Intergroup Bias," *Child Development* 77 (2006): 847–860; see also generally Debra Van Ausdale and Joe R. Feagin, *The First R: How Children Learn Race and Racism* (Lanham, MD: Rowman & Littlefield, 2001).

40 Evan P. Apfelbaum et al., "In Blind Pursuit of Racial Equality?," *Psychological Science* 21(11) (2010): 1587–1592; Richeson and Nussbaum, "The Impact of Multiculturalism."

41 Apfelbaum et al., "In Blind Pursuit of Racial Equality?"

42 Po Bronson and Ashley Merman, *NurtureShock: New Thinking about Children* (New York: Twelve Books, 2009), 49–52.

43 Louise Derman-Sparks, Pamela G. Ramsey, and Julie Olsen Edwards, *What If All the Kids Are White? Anti-bias Multicultural Education with Young Children and Families*, 2nd edition (New York: Teachers College Press, 2011).

44 Patricia Gurin et al., "Diversity in Higher Education: Theory and Impact on Educational Outcomes," *Harvard Educational Review* 72 (2002): 330–366.

45 Nila R. Branscombe, "Thinking about One's Gender Group's Privileges or Disadvantages: Consequences for Well-being in Women and Men," *British Journal of Social Psychology* 37 (1998): 167–184.

46 Laura A. Liswood, *The Loudest Duck: Moving Beyond Diversity while Embracing Differences to Achieve Success at Work* (Hoboken, NJ: Wiley & Sons, Inc., 2009).

47 Wizdom P. Hammond, Marion Gillen, and Irene H. Yen, "Workplace Discrimination and Depressive Symptoms: A Study of Multi-Ethnic Hospital Employees," *Race and Social Problems* 2(1) (2010): 19–30.

48 Eliza K. Pavalko, Krysia N. Mossakowski, and Vanessa J. Hamilton, "Does Perceived Discrimination Affect Health? Longitudinal Relationships between Work Discrimination and Women's Physical and Emotional Health," *Journal of Health and Social Behavior* 44(1) (2003): 18–33.

49 Wilder and Cain, "Teaching and Learning Color Consciousness."

50 April Harris-Britt, Cecelia R. Valrie, Beth Kurtz-Costes, and Stephanie J. Rowley, "Perceived Racial Discrimination and Self-esteem in African American Youth: Racial Socialization as a Protective Factor," *Journal of Research on Adolescence* 17 (2007): 669–682.

51 Gwendolyn Y. Davis and Howard C. Stevenson, "Racial Socialization Experiences and Symptoms of Depression among Black Youth," *Journal of Child and Family Studies* 15(3) (2006): 293–307.

52 Enrique W. Neblett et al., "Racial Socialization and Racial Identity: African American Parents' Messages about Race as Precursors to Identity," *Journal of Youth Adolescence* 38 (2009): 189–203.

53 "Black or White: Kids on Race," CNN, http://www.cnn.com/SPECIALS/2010/kids.on.race/.

54 Brondolo et al., "Racism and Social Capital."

55 Kira Hudson Banks, Laura P. Kohn-Wood, and Michael S. Spencer, "An Examination of the African American Experience of Everyday Discrimination and Psychological Distress," *Community Mental Health Journal* 42 (2006): 555–570; Hammond et al., "Workplace Discrimination and Depressive Symptoms."

BIBLIOGRAPHY

Aboud, Frances E. "A Social-cognitive Developmental Theory of Prejudice." In *Handbook of Race, Racism, and the Developing Child,* edited by Stephen M. Quintana and Clark McKown, 55–71. Hoboken, NJ: John Wiley & Sons, 2008.

Abrams, Dominic, and Michael Hogg. "Social Identification, Self Categorization and Social Influence." *European Review of Social Psychology* 1(1) (1990): 195–228.

Akbar, Na'im. *Breaking the Chains of Psychological Slavery*. Tallahassee, FL: Mind Productions, 1996.

Albert, Jonathan L. "The Origin of Slavery in the United States—The Maryland Precedent." *American Journal of Legal History* 14 (1970): 195.

Alexander, Michelle. *The New Jim Crow: Mass Incarceration in the Age of Colorblindness*. New York: The New Press, 2010.

Altabe, Madeline. "Ethnicity and Body Image: Quantitative and Qualitative Analysis." *International Journal of Eating Disorders* 23 (1998): 153–159.

Anderson, Margo J., and Stephen E. Fienberg. *Who Counts? The Politics of Census-Taking in Contemporary America*. New York: Russell Sage Foundation, 2001.

Apfelbaum, Evan P., Kristin Pauker, Samuel R. Sommers, and Nalini Ambady. "In Blind Pursuit of Racial Equality?" *Psychological Science* 21(11) (2010): 1587–1592.

Appiah, Kwame Anthony, Amy Gutmann, and David B. Wilkins. *Color Conscious*. Princeton, NJ: Princeton University Press, 1998.

Aptheker, Herbert. *Herbert Aptheker on Race and Democracy: A Reader*. Edited by Eric Foner and Manning Marable. Urbana, IL: University of Illinois Press, 2010.

Arce, Carlos H., Edward Murgia, and W. Parker Frisbie. "Phenotype and Life Chances among Chicanos." *Hispanic Journal of Behavioral Sciences* 9 (1987): 19–32.

Austin, Regina. "Nest Eggs and Stormy Weather: Law, Culture and a Black Woman's Lack of Wealth." *University of Cincinnati Law Review* 65 (1996–97): 771.

Bachman, John. *The Doctrine of the Unity of the Human Race Examined on the Principles of Science*. Charleston, SC: C. Canning, 1850.

Bachman, John. *Selected Writings on Science, Race, and Religion*. Edited by Gene Waddell. Athens, GA: University of Georgia Press, 2011.

Baldwin, James. *The Cross of Redemption: Uncollected Writings*. New York: Pantheon, 2010.

Baldwin, Joseph A. "African (Black) Psychology: Issues and Synthesis." *Journal of Black Studies* 16 (1987): 235–249.

Banks, Kira Hudson, Laura P. Kohn-Wood, and Michael S. Spencer. "An Examination of the African American Experience of Everyday Discrimination and Psychological Distress." *Community Mental Health Journal* 42 (2006): 555–570.

Banks, Ralph Richard. "The Color of Desire: Fulfilling Adoptive Parents' Racial Preferences through Discriminatory State Action." *Yale Law Journal* 107 (1998): 875, 964 n. 20.

Banks, Ralph Richard. *Is Marriage for White People? How the African American Marriage Decline Affects Everyone*. New York: Penguin, 2012.

Banks, Taunya Lovell. "Colorism: A Darker Shade of Pale." *UCLA Law Review* 47 (2000): 1705–1746.

Banks, Taunya Lovell. "Multi-Layered Racism: Courts' Continued Resistance to Colorism Claims." In *Shades of Difference Why Skin Color Matters*, edited by Evelyn Nakano Glenn. Palo Alto, CA: Stanford University Press, 2009.

Banks, Taunya Lovell. "Unreconstructed Mestizaje and the Mexican Mestizo Self: No Hay Sangre Negra, So There is No Blackness." *Southern California Interdisciplinary Law Journal* 15 (2006): 199.

Bardaglio, Peter W. "Shameful Matches: The Regulation of Interracial Sex and Marriage in the South Before 1900." In *Sex, Love, Race: Crossing Boundaries in North American History*, edited by Martha Hodes. New York: NYU Press, 1999.

Bartholet, Elizabeth. *Family Bonds: Adoption, Infertility, and the New World of Child Production*. Boston, MA: Beacon Publishing, 1993.

Baynes, Leonard. "If It's Not Just Black and White Anymore, Why Does Darkness Cast a Longer Discriminatory Shadow than Lightness? An Investigation and Analysis of the Color Hierarchy." *Denver University Law Review* 75(131) (1997–1998): 132–133.

Belafonte, Harry, and Michael Shnayerson. *My Song: A Memoir*. New York: Alfred A. Knopf, 2011.

Bell, Derrick. *Race, Racism, and American Law*. 6th edition. New York: Aspen Publishers, 2008.

Benn, Charles D. *Daily Life in Traditional China: The Tang Dynasty*. Westport, CT: Greenwood Press, 2002.

Berger, Bethany R. "Red: Racism and the American Indian." *UCLA Law Review* 56 (2009) 591.

Berlin, Ira. *Many Thousands Gone: The First Two Centuries of Slavery in North America*. Cambridge, MA: Harvard University Press, 1998.

Berlin, Ira. *Slaves without Masters: The Free Negro in the Antebellum South*. New York: Pantheon Books, 1974.

Berlin, Ira, Marc Favreau, and Steven F. Miller, eds. *Remembering Slavery: African Americans Talk about Their Personal Experiences of Slavery and Emancipation*. New York: New Press, 1996.

Berry, Bonnie. *The Power of Looks: Social Stratification of Physical Appearance*. Burlington, VT: Ashgate Publishing, 2008.

Blackmon, Douglas A. *Slavery by Another Name: The Re-Enslavement of Black Americans from the Civil War to World War II*. New York: Anchor Books, 2009.

Blair, Irene V., Charles M. Judd, and Kristine M. Chapleau. "The Influence of Afrocentric Facial Features in Criminal Sentencing." *Psychological Science* 15 (2004): 674.

Blay, Yaba. "Skin Bleaching and Global White Supremacy: By Way of Introduction." *Journal of Pan African Studies* 4(4) (2011).

Blay, Yaba Amgborale. "Struck by Lightening: The Transdiasporan Phenomenon of Skin Bleaching." *JENdA* 14 (2009).

Bodenhorn, Howard. "Colorism, Complexion Homogamy, and Household Wealth: Some Historical Evidence." *American Economic Review* 96 (2006): 256.

Bodenhorn, Howard. "The Complexion Gap: The Economic Consequences of Color among Free African Americans in the Rural Antebellum South." *Advances in Agricultural Economic History* 2 (2003): 41.

Bodenhorn, Howard. "The Mulatto Advantage: The Biological Consequences of Complexion in Rural Antebellum Virginia." *Journal of Interdisciplinary History* 2 (2002): 23.

Bodenhorn, Howard, and Christopher S. Ruebeck. "Colourism and African-American Wealth: Evidence from the Nineteenth-century South." *Journal of Population Economics* 20 (2007): 601–602.

Bond, Selena, and Thomas F. Cash. "Black Beauty: Skin Color and Body Images among African-American College Women." *Journal of Applied and Social Psychology* 22 (1992): 874–888.

Bondilla, Joanne L., and Paul Spickard. *Is Lighter Better? Skin-Tone Discrimination among Asian Americans.* Lanham, MD: Rowman & Littlefield Publishers, 2007.

Bonilla-Silva, Eduardo. *Racism without Racists: Color-Blind Racism and the Persistence of Racial Inequality in the United States.* 3rd edition. Lanham, MD: Rowman & Littlefield, 2009.

Bowen, William G., and Derek Bok. *The Shape of the River.* Princeton, NJ: Princeton University Press, 1998.

Bracey, Christopher Alan. *Saviors or Sellouts: The Promise and Peril of Black Conservatism, from Booker T. Washington to Condoleezza Rice.* Boston, MA: Beacon Press, 2008.

Bramlett-Solomon, Sharon. *Race, Gender, Class and Media: Studying Multiculturalism and Mass Communication.* Dubuque, IA: Kendall Hunt Publishing, 2012.

Branscombe, Nila R. "Thinking about One's Gender Group's Privileges or Disadvantages: Consequences for Well-being in Women and Men." *British Journal of Social Psychology* 37 (1998): 167–184.

Breen, T. H., and Stephen Innes. *"Myne Owne Ground": Race and Freedom on Virginia's Eastern Shore, 1640–1676.* New York: Oxford University Press, 1980.

Brewer, Marilynn B. "In-Group Favoritism: The Subtle Side of Intergroup Discrimination." In *Codes of Conduct: Behavioral Research into Business Ethics*, edited by David M. Messick and Ann E. Tenbrunsel, 160–171. New York: Russell Sage Foundation, 1996.

Brondolo, Elizabeth, Madeline Libretti, Luis Rivera, and Katrina M. Walsemann. "Racism and Social Capital: The Implications for Social and Physical Well-Being." *Journal of Social Issues* 68(2) (2012): 358–384.

Bronson, Po, and Ashley Merman. *NurtureShock: New Thinking about Children.* New York: Twelve Books, 2009.

Brown, Kevin. *Race, Law and Education in the Post-Desegregation Era: Four Perspectives on Desegregation and Resegregation.* Durham, NC: Carolina Academic Press, 2005.

Brown, Kevin. "Should Black Immigrants Be Favored Over Black Hispanics and Black Multiracials in the Admissions Processes of Selective Higher Education Programs?" *Howard Law Journal* 54 (2011): 255–302.

Brown, Kevin, and Tom I. Romero, II. "The Social Reconstruction of Race & Ethnicity of the Nation's Law Students: A Request to the ABA, AALS, and LSAC for Changes in Reporting Requirements." *Michigan State Law Review* 2011 (2011): 1134–1189.

Brunsma, David L., and Kerry Ann Rockquemore. "The New Color Complex: Appearances and Biracial Identity." *Identity: International Journal of Theory & Research* 1 (2001): 225–246.

Buchanan, Kim S. "Creating Beauty in Blackness." In *Consuming Passions: Feminist Approaches to Weight Preoccupation and Eating Disorders,* edited by Catrina Brown and Karin Jasper, 36–51. Toronto: Second Story Press, 1993.

Burke, Meghan. "Colorism." In *International Encyclopedia of the Social Sciences,* edited by William Darity, Jr, 17. New York: Macmillan Library Reference, 2008.

Burke, Meghan A. and Kira H. Banks. "Sociology by Any Other Name: Teaching the Sociological Perspective in Campus Diversity Programs." *Teaching Sociology* 40(1) (2012): 21–33.

Burrell, Tom. *Brainwashed: Challenging the Myth of Black Inferiority.* New York: Smiley Books, 2010.

Burton, Linda. M., Eduardo Bonilla-Silva, Victor Ray, Rose Buckelew, and Elizabeth H. Freeman. "Critical Race Theories, Colorism, and the Decade's Research on Families of Color." *Journal of Marriage and Family* 72 (2010): 440–459.

Bynum, Victoria E. "'White Negroes' in Segregated Mississippi: Miscegenation, Racial Identity, and the Law." *Journal of Southern History* 64 (1998): 247.

Byrd, Ayana D., and Lori L. Tharp. *Hair Story: Untangling the Roots of Black Hair in America.* New York: St. Martin's Griffin, 2001.

Calhoun, Arthur W. *A Social History of the American Family from Colonial Times to the Present.* New York: Barnes & Noble, Inc., 1945.

Calmore, John O. "Airing Dirty Laundry: Disputes Among Privileged Blacks—From Clarence Thomas to 'The Law School Five.'" *Howard Law Journal* 46 (2003): 175–228.

Carbado, Devon W., and Mitu Gulati, "Acting White? Rethinking Race in Post-Racial America." New York: Oxford University Press, 2013.

Carbado, Devon, and Mitu Gulati. "The Law and Economics of Critical Race Theory." *Yale Law Journal* 112 (2003): 1765.

Carter, Robert T., and Janet E. Helms. "The Relationship Between Racial Identity Attitudes and Social Class." *Journal of Negro Education* 57 (1988): 23.

Charles, Christopher A. D. "Skin Bleaching, Self-Hate, and Black Identity in Jamaica." *Journal of Black Studies* 33(6) (2003): 711–728.

Childs, John Brown. "Toward Trans-Community, the Highest Stage of Multiculturalism: Notes on the Future of African-Americans." *Social Justice* 20 (1993): 35.

Chou, Rosalind. *Asian American Sexual Politics: The Construction of Race, Gender, and Sexuality.* Lanham, MD: Rowman & Littlefield. 2012.

Choy, Catherine. "Asian American History: Reflections on Imperialism, Immigration, and the Body." In *Pinay Power: Peminist Critical Theory: Theorizing the Filipina/American Experience,* edited by Melinda L. Jesus. New York: Routledge.

Clark, Kenneth B., and Mamie Clark. "Racial Identification and Preferences in Negro Children." In *Readings in Social Psychology,* edited by Theodore M. Newcomb and Eleanor L. Hartley. New York: Holt, Rinehart, and Winston, 1947.

Coard, Stephanie I., Alfiee M. Breland, and Patricia Raskin. "Perceptions of and Preferences for Skin Color, Black Racial Identity, and Self-Esteem among African Americans." *Journal of Applied Social Psychology* 31 (2001): 2256–2274.

Collins, Patricia Hill. *Black Feminist Thought: Knowledge, Consciousness, and the Politics of Empowerment.* 2nd edition. New York: Routledge, 2000.

Cook, Anthony E. "Beyond Critical Legal Studies: The Reconstructive Theology of Dr. Martin Luther King, Jr." *Harvard Law Review* 103 (1990): 1016.

Craig-Henderson, Kellina. *Black Men in Interracial Relationships: What's Love Got to Do with It?* Piscataway, NJ: Transaction Publishers, 2006.

Craig-Henderson, Kellina. *Black Women in Interracial Relationships: In Search of Love and Solace?* Piscataway, NJ: Transaction Publishers, 2010.

Cummings, Thomas G., and Christopher G. Worley. *Organizational Development and Change.* 9th edition. Mason, OH: South-Western Cengage Learning, 2009.

Daniel Tatum, Beverly. *Why Are All the Black Kids Sitting Together in the Cafeteria? And Other Conversations about Race.* New York: Basic Books, 1997.

Darder, Antonia, and Rodolfo D. Torres. *After Race: Racism After Multiculturalism.* New York: NYU Press, 2004.

Darity, William A., Jr., Patrick L. Mason, and James B. Stewart. "The Economics of Identity: The Origin and Persistence of Racial Identity Norms." *Journal of Economic Behavior & Organization* 60 (2006): 301.

Davidson, Chandler, and Bernard N. Grofman. *Quiet Revolution in the South: The Impact of the Voting Rights Act, 1965–1990.* Princeton, NJ: Princeton University Press, 1994.

Davila, Arlene. *Latinos, Inc. The Marketing and Making of a People.* Berkeley, CA: University of California Press, 2001.

Davis, Adrienne. *"Don't Let Nobody Bother Yo' Principle": The Sexual Economy of American Slavery, Sister Circle: Black Women and Work* (ed. S. Harley) (2002).

Davis, Adrienne. *Slavery and the Roots of Sexual Harassment, Directions in Sexual Harassment* (eds. C. MacKinnon & R. Siegel) (2003).

Davis, Adrienne. *The Private Law of Race and Sex: An Antebellum Perspective*, Stan LR 51 (1999): 222.

Davis, F. James. *Who Is Black? One Nation's Definition.* University Park, PA: Pennsylvania State University Press, 1991.

Davis, Gwendolyn Y., and Howard C. Stevenson. "Racial Socialization Experiences and Symptoms of Depression among Black Youth." *Journal of Child and Family Studies* 15(3) (2006): 293–307.

Degler, Carl N. *Neither Black Nor White: Slavery and Race Relations in Brazil and the United States.* Madison, WI: University of Wisconsin Press, 1971.

De Gobineau, Count Arthur. *The Moral and Intellectual Diversity of Races, with Particular Reference to Their Respective Influence in the Civil and Political History of Mankind.* Philadelphia, PA: J. B. Lippincott & Co., 1856.

DeMello, Margo. *Faces around the World: A Cultural Encyclopedia of the Human Face.* Santa Barbara, CA: ABC-CLIO, 2012.

D'Emilio, John, and Estelle B. Freedman, *Intimate Matters: A History of Sexuality in America.* Chicago, IL: University of Chicago Press, 1997.

Demo, David H., and Michael Hughes. "Socialization and Racial Identity among Black Americans." *Social Psychology Quarterly* 53 (1990): 364–374.

Derman-Sparks, Louise, Pamela G. Ramsey, and Julie Olsen Edwards. *What If All the Kids Are White? Anti-bias Multicultural Education with Young Children and Families.* 2nd edition. New York: Teachers College Press, 2011.

de Souza, Melanie Miyanji. "The Concept of Skin Bleaching in Africa and Its Devastating Health Implications." *Clinics in Dermatology* 26(1) (2008): 27.

Dovidio, John, Kerry Kawakami, Craig Johnson, Brenda Johnson, and Adaiah Howard. "On the Nature of Prejudice: Automatic and Controlled Processes." *Journal of Experimental Social Psychology* 33(5) (1997): 510–440.

Du Bois, W. E. B. *The Souls of Black Folks, Three Negro Classics.* New York: Avon Books, 1965.

Du Bois, W. E. B. "The Talented Tenth," from *The Negro Problem: A Series of Articles by Representative Negroes of To-day.* New York: James Pott & Co., 1903.

Eberhardt, Jennifer L., Paul G. Davies, Valerie J. Purdie-Vaughns, and Sheri Lynn Johnson. "Looking Deathworthy: Perceived Stereotypicality of Black Defendants Predicts Capital-Sentencing Outcomes." *Psychological Science* 17(5) (2006): 383–386.

Edmonston, Barry, Sharon M. Lee, and Jeffrey Passel. "Recent Trends in Intermarriage and Immigration and Their Effects on the Future Racial Composition of the U.S. Population." In *The New Race Question: How the Census Counts Multiracial Individuals*, edited by Joel Perlmann, Mary C. Waters, and Jerome Levy Economics Institute, 227–255. New York: Russell Sage Foundation, 2002.

Edmonston, Barry, and Jeffrey S. Passel, eds. *Immigration and Ethnicity: The Integration of America's Newest Arrivals.* Washington, DC: Urban Institute Press, 1994.

Ellemers, Naomi, Paulien Kortekaas, and Jaap W. Ouwerkerk. "Self-Categorization, Commitment to the Group and Social Self-Esteem As Related but Distinct Aspects of Social Identity." *European Journal of Social Psychology* 28(2–3) (1999): 371–398.

Ellison, Christopher G. "Are Religious People Nice People? Evidence from the National Survey of Black Americans." *Social Forces* 71 (1992): 411–430.

Emens, Elizabeth F. "Intimate Discrimination: The State's Role in the Accidents of Sex and Love." *Harvard Law Review* 122 (2009): 1307–1402.

Entman, Robert M., and Andrew Rojecki. *The Black Image in the White Mind: Media and Race in America.* Chicago, IL: University of Chicago Press, 2000.

Falconer, Jameca W., and Helen A. Neville. "African American College Women's Body Image: An Examination of Body Mass, African Self-Consciousness, and Skin Color Satisfaction." *Psychology of Women Quarterly* 24 (2000): 236–243.

Fanon, Frantz. *The Wretched of the Earth.* New York: Grove Press, 2005.

Feagin, Joe R. *Racist America: Roots, Current Realities, and Future Reparations.* New York: Routledge, 2000.

Fedders, Barbara. "Race and Market Values in Domestic Infant Adoption." *North Carolina Law Review* 88 (2010): 1687.

Fenton, Zanita E. "In a World Not Their Own: The Adoption of Black Children." *Harvard BlackLetter Law Journal* 10 (1993): 39, 54.

Finkelman, Paul. *Defending Slavery: Proslavery Thought in the Old South.* Boston, MA: Bedford/St. Martin's Press, 2003.

Finkelman, Paul. *The Law of Freedom and Bondage.* New York: Oceana Publications, 1986.

Finkelman, Paul. *Slavery and the Founders: Race and Liberty in the Age of Jefferson.* 2nd edition. Armonk, NY: M. E. Sharpe, 2001.

Firebaugh, Glenn, and Kenneth Davies. "Trends in Anti-Black Prejudice, 1972–1984: Region and Cohort Effects." *American Journal of Sociology* 94(2) (1988): 251–272.

Fischer, Roger A. *The Segregation Struggle in Louisiana, 1862–77.* Urbana, IL: University of Illinois Press, 1974.

Fish, Jefferson M. *The Myth of Race, in Race and Intelligence: Separating Science from Myth.* Edited by Jefferson M. Fish. Mahwah, NJ: Lawrence Erlbaum Associates, 2002.

Foner, Eric. *Reconstruction: America's Unfinished Revolution, 1863–1877.* New York: Harper & Row, 1988.

Force, Pierre. "The House on Bayou Road: Atlantic Creole Networks in the Eighteenth and Nineteenth Centuries." *Journal of American History* 100 (2012): 9.

Franklin, Frazier E. *Black Bourgeoisie.* New York: Simon & Schuster, 1957.

Freeman, Howard E., David Armor, J. Michael Ross, and Thomas F. Pettigrew. "Color Gradation and Attitudes among Middle-Income Negroes." *American Sociological Review* 31 (1966): 365.

Freire, Paulo. *Pedagogy of the Oppressed*. 30th anniversary edition. New York: Bloomsbury Academic, 2006.

Fryer, Roland G., Jr. "Guess Who's Been Coming to Dinner? Trends in Interracial Marriage over the 20th Century." *Journal of Economic Perspectives*, 21 (2007): 77.

Garcia, Alma M. *Contested Images: Women of Color in Popular Culture*. Lanham, MD: AltaMira Press, 2012.

Gary, Lawrence E. "African American Men's Perceptions of Racial Discrimination: A Sociocultural Analysis." *Social Work Research* 19(40) (1995): 207–217.

Gatewood, Willard B. *Aristocrats of Color, 1880–1920*. Bloomington, IN: University of Indiana Press, 1990.

Gatewood, William B. *Aristocrats of Color: The Black Elite, 1880–1920*. Fayetteville, AR: University of Arkansas Press, 2000.

Gellhorn, Ernest. "The Law Schools and the Negro." *Duke Law Journal* 17 (1968): 1077–1085.

Germain, Carel. *Human Behavior in the Social Environment: An Ecological View*. New York: Columbia University Press, 1991.

Gibelman, Margaret, and Philip H. Schervish. "Pay Equity in Social Work: Not!" *Social Work* 40(5) (1995): 622–629.

Gilroy, Paul. *Against Race: Imagining Political Culture beyond the Color Line*. Cambridge, MA: Belknap Press of Harvard, 2000.

Glenn, Evelyn Nakano, ed. *Shades of Difference: Why Skin Color Matters*. Palo Alto, CA: Stanford University Press, 2009.

Golash-Boza, Tanya, and William Darity, Jr. "Latino Racial Choices: The Effects of Skin Colour and Discrimination on Latinos' and Latinas' Racial Self-Identifications." *Ethnic and Racial Studies* 31(5) (2008): 904.

Golden, Marita. *Don't Play in the Sun: One Woman's Journey through the Color Complex*. New York: Anchor Books, 2005.

Goldenberg, David M. *The Curse of Ham: Race and Slavery in Early Judaism, Christianity, and Islam*. Princeton, NJ: Princeton University Press, 2003.

Goldsmith, Arthur H., Darrick Hamilton, and William Darity, Jr. "From Dark to Light: Skin Color and Wages among African-Americans." *Journal of Human Resources* 42(4) (Fall 2007): 701–738.

Goldsmith, Arthur H., Darrick Hamilton, and William Darity, Jr. "Shades of Discrimination: Skin Tone and Wages." *American Economic Review* 96 (2006): 242–245.

Golebiowski, Ewa A. "The Contours and Etiology of Whites' Attitudes Toward Black-White Interracial Marriage." *Journal of Black Studies* 38(2) (2007): 268–287.

Golub, Mark. "*Plessy* as 'Passing': Judicial Responses to Ambiguously Raced Bodies in *Plessy v. Ferguson*." *Law and Society Review* 39 (September 2005): 568.

Gomez, Christina. "The Continual Significance of Skin Colour: An Exploratory Study of Latinos in the Northeast." *Hispanic Journal of Behavioral Science* 22 (2000): 94–103.

Gordon, Lewis R. "Racist Ideology." In *Turbulent Voyage: Readings in African American Studies,* 3rd edition, edited by Floyd Hayes, III, 505–509. San Diego, CA: Collegiate Press, 1997.

Gordon, Milton M. *Assimilation in American Life: The Role of Race, Religion and National Origin*. Oxford: Oxford University Press, 1964.

Gossett, Thomas F. *Race: The History of an Idea in America.* Dallas, TX: Southern Methodist University Press, 1963.

Gotanda, Neil. "A Critique of 'Our Constitution Is Color-Blind.'" *Stanford Law Review* 44(1) (1991): 1–68.

Gould, Benjamin Apthorp. *Investigations in the Military and Anthropological Statistics of American Soldiers.* New York: Hurd and Houghton, 1869.

Gould, Stephen Jay. *The Mismeasure of Man.* New York: W. W. Norton & Company, 1981.

Gould, Virginia M. "The Free Creoles of Color of the Antebellum Gulf Ports of Mobile and Pensacola: A Struggle for the Middle Ground." In *Creoles of Color of the Gulf South,* edited by James H. Dormon. Knoxville, TN: University of Tennessee Press, 1996.

Graham, Lawrence Otis. *Our Kind of People: Inside American's Black Upper Class.* New York: Harper Perennial, 1999.

Greene, Beverly, Judith C. White, and Lisa Whitten. "Hair Texture, Length, and Style as a Metaphor in the African American Mother-Daughter Relationship: Considerations in Psychodynamic Psychotherapy." In *Psychotherapy with African American Women: Innovations in Psychodynamic Perspective and Practice,* edited by L. C. Jackson and Beverly Green, 166–193. New York: Guilford Press, 2000.

Greenfield, Gary A., and Don B. Kates, Jr. "Mexican Americans, Racial Discrimination, and the Civil Rights Act of 1866." *California Law Review* 63 (1975): 692–693.

Greenwald, Anthony G., and Mahzarin R. Banaji. "Implicit Bias Social Cognition: Attitudes, Self Esteem and Stereotypes." *Psychological Review* 102 (1995): 4.

Greenwald, Anthony G., and Linda Hamilton Kreiger. "Implicit Bias: Scientific Foundations." *California Law Review* 94 (2006): 946.

Greenwald, Herbert J., and Don B. Oppenheim. "Reported Magnitude of Self Misidentification among Negro Children: Artifact?" *Journal of Personality and Social Psychology* 8 (1968): 49–52.

Guerra, Lillian. *Popular Expression and National Identity in Puerto Rico: The Struggle for Self, Community, and Nation.* Gainesville, FL: University Press of Florida, 1998.

Gullickson, Aaron. "Black/White Interracial Marriage Trends, 1850–2000." *Journal of Family History* 31(3) (2006): 289–312.

Gurin, Patricia, Eric L. Dey, Sylvia Hurtado, and Gerald Gurin. "Diversity in Higher Education: Theory and Impact on Educational Outcomes." *Harvard Educational Review* 72 (2002): 330–366.

Haizlip, Shirlee Taylor. *The Sweeter the Juice: A Family Memoir in Black and White.* New York: Touchstone, 1994.

Hall, Ronald. "Bias among African Americans Regarding Skin Color: Implication of Skin Color for Human Behavior in the Social Environment." *Journal of Human Behavior in the Social Environment* 13 (2006): 19–31.

Hall, Ronald E. "Bias among African Americans Regarding Skin Color: Implications for Social Work Practice." *Research on Social Work Practice* 2(4) (1992): 479–486.

Hall, Ronald E. "The Bleaching Syndrome: African Americans' Response to Cultural Domination vis-à-vis Skin Color." *Journal of Black Studies* 26(2) (1995): 172–184.

Hall, Ronald E. *An Historical Analysis of Skin Color Discrimination in America: Victimism among Victim Group Populations.* New York: Springer, 2010.

Hall, Ronald E., ed. *Racism in the 21st Century: An Empirical Analysis of Skin Color.* New York: Springer Science & Business Media, LLC, 2008.

Haller, John S., Jr. *Outcasts from Evolution: Scientific Attitudes of Racial Inferiority, 1859–1900.* Carbondale, IL: Southern Illinois University Press, 1971.

Hamilton, Darrick, and William Darity, Jr. "Can 'Baby Bonds' Eliminate the Racial Wealth Gap in Putative Post-racial America?" *Review of Black Political Economy* 37 (2010): 208.

Hamilton Darrick, Arthur Goldsmith, and William Darity, Jr. "Shedding 'Light' on Marriage: The Influence of Skin Shade on Marriage for Black Females." *Journal of Economic Behavior and Organization* 72(1) (2009): 30–50.

Hammond, Wizdom P., Marion Gillen, and Irene H. Yen. "Workplace Discrimination and Depressive Symptoms: A Study of Multi-ethnic Hospital Employees." *Race and Social Problems* 2(1) (2010): 19–30.

Hanger, Kimberly S. "Origins of New Orleans Free Creoles of Color." In *Creoles of Color of the Gulf South*, edited by James H. Dormon. Knoxville, TN: University of Tennessee Press, 1996.

Harrell, Shelly P. "A Multidimensional Conceptualization of Racism-related Stress: Implications for the Well-Being of People of Color." *American Journal of Orthopsychiatry* 70 (2000): 42–57.

Harris, Cheryl. "Whiteness as Property." *Harvard Law Review* 106 (1993): 1707.

Harris-Britt, April, Cecelia R. Valrie, Beth Kurtz-Costes, and Stephanie J. Rowley. "Perceived Racial Discrimination and Self-esteem in African American Youth: Racial Socialization as a Protective Factor." *Journal of Research on Adolescence* 17 (2007): 669–682.

Harrison, Matthew S., and Kecia M. Thomas. "The Hidden Prejudice in Selection: A Research Investigation on Skin Color Bias." *Journal of Applied Social Psychology* 39 (2009): 134–168.

Harvey, Richard D., Nicole LaBeach, Ellie Pridgen, and Tammy M. Gocial. "The Intragroup Stigmatization of Skin Tone among Black Americans." *Journal of Black Psychology* 31 (2005): 237–253.

Hecht, Michael L., Mary Jane Collier, and Sidney A. Ribeau. *African American Communication: Ethnic Identity and Cultural Interpretation*. Newbury Park, CA: Sage, 1993.

Heilemann, John, and Mark Halperin. *Game Change: Obama and the Clintons, McCain and Palin, and the Race of a Lifetime*. New York: Harper Perennial, 2010.

Helms, Janet. *A Race is a Nice Thing to Have*. Topeka, KS: Content Communications, 1992.

Hening, William Waller. *The Statutes at Large; Being a Collection of All the Laws of Virginia, From the First Session of the Legislature in the Year 1619*. vol. 2. New York: R. & W. & G. Bartow, 1823.

Hernandez, Tanya Katerí. *Racial Subordination in Latin America: The Role of the State, Customary Law, and the New Civil Rights Response*. New York: Cambridge University Press, 2012.

Hernandez, Tanya Katerí. "To Be Brown in Brazil: Education & Segregation Latin American Style." *NYU Review of Law & Social Change* 29 (2004–05): 683.

Hernández-Truyol, Berta Esperanza, and Stephen J. Powell. *Just Trade: A New Covenant Linking Trade and Human Rights*. New York: New York University Press, 2009.

Hernstein, Richard J., and Charles Murray. *The Bell Curve*. New York: Free Press Paperback Books, 1994.

Herring, Cedric, Verna Keith, and Hayward Horton, eds. *Skin Deep: How Race and Complexion Matter in the "Color Blind" Era*. Urbana, IL: University of Illinois Press, 2004.

Hersch, Joni. "Profiling the New Immigrant Worker: The Effects of Skin Color and Height." *Journal of Labor Economics* 26 (2008): 345.

Hersch, Joni. "Skin Color, Physical Appearance, and Perceived Discriminatory Treatment." *Journal of Socio-Economics* 40 (2011): 671–678.

Higginbotham, A. Leon, Jr. "An Open Letter to Justice Clarence Thomas from a Federal Judicial Colleague." *University of Pennsylvania Law Review* 140 (1991): 1005.

Hill, Mark E. "Color Differences in the Socioeconomic Status of African American Men: Results of a Longitudinal Study." *Social Forces* 78 (2000): 1437–1460.

Hill, Mark E. "Race of the Interviewer and Perception of Skin Color: Evidence from the Multi-city Study of Urban Inequality." *American Social Review* 67 (2002): 100.

Hill, Mark E. "Skin Color and the Perception of Attractiveness Among African Americans: Does Gender Make a Difference?" *Social Psychology Quarterly* 65 (2002): 77–91.

Hirschfeld, Lawrence A. "Children's Developing Conceptions of Race." In *Handbook of Race, Racism, and the Developing Child,* edited by Stephen M. Quintana and Clark McKown, 37–54. Hoboken, NJ: John Wiley & Sons, 2008.

Hochschild, Jennifer L., and Vesla Weaver. "The Skin Color Paradox and the American Racial Order." *Social Forces* 86 (2007): 643–670.

Hochschild, Jennifer L., Vesla M. Weaver, and Traci R. Burch. *Creating a New Racial Order: How Immigration, Multiracism, Genomics, and the Young Can Remake Race in America.* Princeton, NJ: Princeton University Press, 2012.

Hodes, Martha. *White Women, Black Men: Illicit Sex in the Nineteenth-Century South.* New Haven, CT: Yale University Press, 1997.

Hoerder, Dirk. *Cultures in Contact: World Migrations in the Second Millennium.* Durham, NC: Duke University Press, 2002.

Hoffman, Frederick L. *Race Traits and Tendencies of the American Negro.* New York: Macmillan, 1896.

hooks, bell. *Sisters of the Yam: Black Women and Self-Recovery.* Boston, MA: South End Press, 2005.

Horowitz, Donald. "Color Differentiation in the American Systems of Slavery." *Journal of Interdisciplinary History* 111(3) (1973): 509–526.

Horton, Hayward Derrick. "Racism, Whitespace, and the Rise of the Neo-Mulattoes." In *Mixed Messages: Multiracial Identities in the "Color-Blind" Era,* edited by David L. Brunsma. Boulder, CO: Lynne Rienner, 2005.

Horton, Hayward Derrick. "Rethinking American Diversity: Conceptual and Theoretical Challenges for Racial and Ethnic Demography." In *American Diversity: A Demographic Challenge for the Twenty-First Century,* edited by Nancy A. Denton and Stewart E. Tolnay, 262. Albany, NY: State University of New York Press, 2002.

Hovenkamp, Herbert. "Social Science and Segregation before *Brown.*" *Duke Law Journal* 34 (1985): 655.

Hraba, Joseph, and Geoffrey Grant. "Black is Beautiful: A Re-Examination of Racial Preference and Identification." *Journal of Personality and Social Psychology* 16 (1970): 398–402.

Hudgins, Lara. "Rethinking Affirmative Action in the 1990s: Tailoring the Cure to Remedy the Disease." *Baylor Law Review* 47 (1995): 815.

Hudson, J. Blaine. "Democracy, Diversity, and Multiculturalism in American Higher Education: Issues, Barriers, and Strategies for Change." *Western Journal of Black Studies* 18 (1994): 222–226.

Hughes, Michael, and Bradley R. Hertel. "The Significance of Color Remains: A Study of Life Chances, Mate Selection, and Ethnic Consciousness among Black Americans." *Social Forces* 68 (1990): 1105–1120.

Hunt, Sanford B. "The Negro as a Soldier." *Anthropological Review* 7 (January 1869): 49–50.

Hunter, Margaret L. "If You're Light You're Alright: Light Skin Color as Social Capital for Women of Color." *Gender & Society* 16(2) (2002): 175–193.

Hunter, Margaret. "The Persistent Problem of Colorism: Skin Tone, Status, and Inequality." *Sociology Compass* 1(1) (2007): 237–254.

Hunter, Margaret L. *Race, Gender, and the Politics of Skin Tone.* New York: Routledge, 2005.

Imarogbe, Kamau. "Hair Misorientation: Free Your Mind and Your Hair Will Follow." In *African-Centered Psychology: Culture-Focusing for Multicultural Competence,* edited by Daudi ya Azibo, 201–220. Durham, NC: Carolina Academic Press, 2003.

Jablonski, Nina G. *Living Color: The Biological and Social Meaning of Skin Color.* Berkeley, CA: University of California Press, 2012.

Jacques, Martin. *When China Rules the World: The End of the Western World and the Birth of a New Global Order.* 2nd edition. New York: Penguin Press, 2009.

Johnson, Melissa A., Prabu David, and Dawn Huey-Ohlsson. "Beauty in Brown: Skin Color in Latina Magazines." In *Brown and Black Communication; Latino and African American Conflict and Convergence in Mass Media,* edited by Diana I. Ri_os and A. N. Mohamed, 165. Westport, CT: Praeger, 2003.

Johnson, Michael P., and James Roark. *Black Masters: A Free Family of Color in the Old South.* New York: W. W. Norton, 1984.

Jones, Bernie. *Fathers of Conscience: Mixed Race Inheritance in the Antebellum South.* Athens, GA: University of Georgia Press, 2009.

Jones, James M. *Prejudice and Racism.* New York: McGraw-Hill, 1997.

Jones, Trina. "Intra-Groups Preferences: Problems of Proof in Colorism and Identity Performance Claims." *NYU Review of Law & Social Change* 34 (2010): 657.

Jones, Trina. "Shades of Brown: The Law of Skin Color." *Duke Law Journal* 49 (1999): 1487–1556.

Jordan, Phillip, and Maria Hernandez-Reif. "Reexamination of Young Children's Racial Attitudes and Skin Tone Preferences." *Journal of Black Psychology* 35 (2009): 388–403.

Jordan, Winthrop D. "American Chiaroscuro: The Status and Definition of Mulattoes in the British Colonies." *William and Mary Quarterly* 19 (1962): 184.

Jordan, Winthrop D. *White over Black: American Attitudes toward the Negro, 1550–1812.* Chapel Hill, NC: University of North Carolina Press, 1968.

Jost, John, and Mahzarin Banaji. "The Role of Stereotyping in System-Justification and the Production of False Consciousness." *British Journal of Social Psychology* 33(1) (1994): 1–27.

Jost, John, Mahzarin Banaji, and Brian Nosek. "A Decade of System Justification Theory: Accumulated Evidence of Conscious and Unconscious Bolstering of the Status Quo." *Political Psychology* 25(6) (2004): 881–919.

Judd, Charles M., Bernadette Park, Carey S. Ryan, Markus Brauer, and Susan Kraus. "Stereotypes and Ethnocentrism: Diverging Interethnic Perceptions of African American and White American Youth." *Journal of Personality and Social Psychology* 69(3) (1995): 460–481.

Kalmijn, Matthijs. "Trends in Black/White Intermarriage." *Social Forces* 72(1) (1993): 119–146.

Kam, Cindy D. "Implicit Attitudes, Explicit Choices: When Subliminal Priming Predicts Preference." *Political Behavior* 29 (2007): 345.

Kang, Jerry. "Trojan Horses of Race." *Harvard Law Journal* 118 (2005): 1489.

Kang, Jerry, and Kristin Lane. "Seeing through Colorblindness: Implicit Bias and the Law." *UCLA Law Review* 58 (2010): 476.

Karger, Howard J., and David Stoesz. *American Social Welfare Policy.* New York: Longman, 1990.

Katz, David, and Kenneth Braly. "Racial Stereotypes of One Hundred College Students." *Journal of Abnormal and Social Psychology* 28(3) (1933): 280–290.

Katz, Phyllis A. "Racists or Tolerant Multiculturalists? How Do They Begin?" *American Psychologist* 58(11) (2003): 897–909.

Kaw, Eugenia. "Medicalization of Racial Features: Asian American Women and Cosmetic Surgery." *Medical Anthropology Quarterly* 7 (1993): 74–89.

Keith, Verna M., and Cedric Herring. "Skin Tone and Stratification in the Black Community." *American Journal of Sociology* 97 (1991): 760–778.

Keith, Verna, Karen D. Lincoln, Robert Joseph Taylor, and James S. Jackson. "Discriminatory Experiences and Depressive Symptoms among African American Women: Do Skin Tone and Mastery Matter?" *Sex Roles*, 62 (2010): 48–59.

Kennedy, Randall. *Interracial Intimacies.* New York: Pantheon Books, 2003.

Kennedy, Randall. *Sellout: The Politics of Racial Betrayal.* Reprint edition. New York: Vintage, 2009.

Kerr, Audrey Elisa. *The Paper Bag Principle: Class, Colorism, and Rumor and the Case of Black Washington, DC.* Knoxville, TN: University of Tennessee Press, 2006.

Khanna, Nikki, and Cathryn Johnson. "Passing as Black: Racial Identity Work among Biracial Americans." *Social Psychology Quarterly* 73 (2010): 380.

Kitano, Harry H. L. *Race Relations.* Englewood Cliffs, NJ: Prentice-Hall, 1985.

Klonoff, Elizabeth A., and Hope Landrine. "Is Skin Color a Marker for Racial Discrimination? Explaining the Skin Color Hypertension Relationship." *Journal of Behavioral Medicine*, 23 (2000): 329–338.

Kovel, Joel. *White Racism: A Psychohistory.* New York: Columbia University Press, 1984.

Kozol, Jonathan. *The Shame of the Nation: The Restoration of Apartheid Schooling in America.* New York: Crown Publishers, 2005.

Kramer, Roderick. "Cooperation and Organizational Identification." In *Social Psychology In Organizations: Advances in Theories and Research*, edited by J. Keith Murnighan, 244–268. Englewood Cliffs, NJ: Prentice-Hall, 1993.

Krieger, Nancy. "Shades of Difference: Theoretical Underpinnings of the Medical Controversy on Black/White Differences in the United States, 1830–1870." *International Journal of Health Services* 17 (1987): 265.

Krysan, Maria, and Nakesha Faison. "Racial Attitudes in America: An Update." Institute of Government and Public Affairs: University of Illinois. Accessed August 1, 2012, http://igpa.uillinois.edu/programs/racial-attitudes/detailed5.

Lancaster, Roger N. "Skin Color, Race and Racism in Nicaragua." *Ethnology* 30(4) (1991): 339–353.

Landreth, Catherine, and Barbara Johnson. "Young Children's Responses to a Picture and Inset Test Designed to Reveal Reactions to Different Skin Color." *Child Development* 24 (1953): 63–79.

Landrine, Hope, and Elizabeth A. Klonoff. "The Schedule of Racist Events: A Measure of Racial Discrimination and a Study of its Negative Physical and Mental Health Consequences." *Journal of Black Psychology* 22 (1996): 144–168.

Lane, Kristin A., Jerry Kang, and Mahzarin R. Banaji. "Implicit Social Cognition and Law." *Annual Review of Law and Social Science* 3 (2007): 435–437.

Langbein, John H. "The Twentieth-century Revolution in Family Wealth Transmission." *Michigan Law Review* 86 (1988): 722.

Lawrence, Charles R., III. "The Id, the Ego, and Equal Protection: Reckoning with Unconscious Racism." *Stanford Law Review* 39 (1987): 317, 333.

Leary, Joy. *Post Traumatic Slave Syndrome, America's Legacy of Enduring Injury and Healing.* Oakland, CA: Uptone Press, 2005.

LeConte, Joseph. "The Effect of Mixture of Races on Human Progress." *Berkeley Quarterly* 1 (April 1880): 89–90.

LeConte, Joseph. "The Genesis of Sex." *Popular Science Monthly* 16 (December 1879): 167.

LeConte, Joseph. *The Race Problem in the South.* New York: Appleton, 1892.

Lee, Jennifer, and Frank D. Bean. *The Diversity Paradox: Immigration and the Color Line in Twenty-First Century America.* New York: Russell Sage Foundation, 2010.

Lee, Sharon M., and Barry Edmonston. "New Marriages, New Families: U.S. Racial and Hispanic Intermarriage." *Population Bulletin* 60(2) (2005): 1–40.

Levinson, Justin D., and Danielle Young. "Different Shades of Bias: Skin Tone, Implicit Racial Bias, and Judgment of Ambiguous Evidence." *West Virginia Law Review* 112 (2010): 308.

Lewis, Kelly M., Navit Robkin, Karie Gaska, and Lillian Carol Njoki. "Investigating Motivations for Women's Skin Bleaching in Tanzania." *Psychology of Women Quarterly* 35(1) (2001): 29–37.

Li, Eric P. H., Hyun Jeong Min, Russell W. Belk, Junko Kimura, and Shalini Bahl. "Skin Lightening and Beauty in Four Asian Cultures." *Advances in Consumer Research* 35 (2008): 444.

Lieberson, Stanley. *A Piece of the Pie: Blacks and White Immigrants since 1880.* Berkeley, CA: University of California Press, 1980.

Liswood, Laura A. *The Loudest Duck: Moving Beyond Diversity while Embracing Differences to Achieve Success at Work.* Hoboken, NJ: Wiley & Sons, Inc., 2009.

Lively, Donald E. *The Constitution and Race.* New York: Praeger, 1992.

Loevinger, Jane. "Objective Tests as Instruments of Psychological Theory." *Psychological Reports* 3 (1957): 635–694.

Lopez, Ian F. Haney. "Is the 'Post' in Post-Racial the 'Blind' in Colorblind?" *Cardozo Law Review* 32 (2011): 807.

Lopez, Ian F. Haney. "The Social Construction of Race." *Harvard Civil Rights-Civil Liberties Law Review* 29(1) (1994): 1–62.

Maddox, Keith B. "Perspectives on Racial Phenotypicality Bias." *Personality and Social Psychology Review* 8(4) (2004): 383–401.

Maddox, Keith B., and Stephanie Gray. "Cognitive Representations of Black Americans: Reexploring the Role of Skin Tone." *Personality and Social Psychology Bulletin* 28(2) (2002): 250–259.

Maddox, Keith B., and Stephanie Gray Chase. "Manipulating Subcategory Salience: Exploring the Link between Skin Tone and Social Perception of Blacks." *European Journal of Social Psychology* 34 (2004): 533–546.

Maldonado, Solangel. "Discouraging Racial Preferences in Adoptions." *University of California–Davis Law Review* 39 (2005–2006): 1415.

Maslow, Abraham H. *Toward a Psychology of Being.* New York: Van Nostrand, 1962.

Massey, Douglas S. "The New Immigration and Ethnicity in the United States." *Population and Development Review* 21(3) (1995): 631–652.

McClish, Bruce. *Old World Continents: Europe, Asia, and Africa.* Chicago, IL: Heinemann Library, 2003.

McConnell, Allen, and Jill M. Leibold. "Relations among the Implicit Association Test, Discriminatory Behavior, and Explicit Measures of Racial Attitudes." *Journal of Experimental Social Psychology* 37(5) (2001): 435–442.

McFarlane, Audrey G. "Operatively White? Exploring the Significance of Race and Class through the Paradox of Black Middle-Classness." *Legal & Contemporary Problems* 72 (2009): 183.

McGuire, William J., and Claire V. McGuire. "The Content, Structure, and Operation of Thought Systems." In *The Content, Structure, and Operation of Thought Systems: Advances in Social Cognition*, edited by Robert S. Wyer, Jr. and Thomas K. Srull, vol. 4, 1–78. New York: Psychology Press, 1991.

McIntosh, Peggy. "White Privilege: Unpacking the Invisible Knapsack." *Independent School* 49(2) (1990): 31–35.

McMullen, Ann. "Blood and Culture: Negotiating Race in Twentieth-Centure Native New England." In *Confounding the Color Line: The Indian-Black Experience in North America*, edited by James F. Brooks. 261–291. Lincoln: University of Nebraska Press, 2002.

McWhorter, John. *Authentically Black: Essay for the Black Silent Majority*. New York: Gotham Books, 2003.

Mencke, John G. *Mulattoes and Race Mixture: American Attitudes and Images, 1865–1918*. Ann Arbor, MI: UMI Research Press, 1979.

Merton, Robert. "Intermarriage and the Social Structure: Fact and Theory." *Psychiatry* 4(3) (1941): 361–374.

Mezey, Naomi. "Erasure and Recognition: The Census, Race and the National Imagination." *Northwestern University Law Review* 97 (2003): 1749–1752.

Mills, Charles W. *The Racial Contract*. Ithaca, NY: Cornell University Press, 1999.

Mills, Gary B. "Miscegenation and the Free Negro in Antebellum 'Anglo' Alabama: A Reexamination of Southern Race Relations." *Journal of American History* 68 (June 1981): 26.

Montalvo, Frank F. "Surviving Race: Skin Color and the Socialization and Acculturation of Latinas." *Journal of Ethnic & Cultural Diversity in Social Work* 13 (2004): 25–43.

Moran, Rachel F. *Interracial Intimacy: The Regulation of Race and Romance*. Chicago, IL: University of Chicago Press, 2001.

Morgan, Edmund. *American Slavery, American Freedom: The Ordeal of Colonial Virginia*. New York: W. W. Norton, 1975.

Morrison, Toni. *The Bluest Eye*. New York: Holt, Rinehart, and Winston, 1970.

Morton, Samuel G. *Crania Americana; or, A Comparative View of the Skulls of Various Aboriginal Nations of North and South America: To which is Prefixed an Essay on the Varieties of the Human Species*. Philadelphia: London, Simpkin, Marshall & Co., 1839.

Mullin, Gerald W. *Flight and Rebellion: Slave Resistance in Eighteenth-century Virginia*. New York: Oxford University Press, 1972.

Murguia, Edward, and Edward E. Telles. "Phenotype and Schooling among Mexican Americans." *Sociology of Education* 69 (1996): 276–289.

Myrdal, Gunnar. *An American Dilemma: The Negro Problem and Modern Democracy*. New York: Harper & Bros., 1944.

National Hispanic Media Coalition. "Latino Decisions." *The Impact of Media Stereotypes on Opinions and Attitudes Towards Latinos*. 2012.

Neal, Angela, and Midge L. Wilson. "The Role of Skin Color and Features in the Black Community: Implications for Black Women and Therapy." *Clinical Psychology Review* 9 (1989): 323–333.

Neblett, Enrique W., Ciara P. Smalls, Kahlil R. Ford, Hòa X Nguyên, and Robert M. Sellers. "Racial Socialization and Racial Identity: African American Parents' Messages About Race as Precursors to Identity." *Journal of Youth Adolescence* 38 (2009): 189–203.

Nelson, Camille. "Considering Tortious Racism." *DePaul Journal of Health Care Law* 9 (2005): 905–969.

Nelson, Camille A. "Of Eggshells and Thin-Skulls: A Consideration of Racism-related Mental Illness Impacting Black Women." *International Journal of Law and Psychiatry* 29 (2006): 112–136.

Newby, Idus A. *Jim Crow's Defense: Anti-Negro Thought in America, 1900–1930.* Baton Rouge, LA: Louisiana State University Press, 1965.

Noah, Barbara A. "A Prescription for Racial Equality in Medicine." *Connecticut Law Review* 40 (2008), 698–699.

Nobles, Melissa. *Shades of Citizenship: Race and the Census in Modern Politics.* Stanford, CA: Stanford University Press, 2000.

Nolan, Laurence C. "The Meaning of *Loving*: Marriage, Due Process and Equal Protection (1967–1990) as Equality and Marriage, From *Loving* to *Zablocki*." *Howard Law Journal* 41 (1998): 247–248.

Norwood, Kimberly Jade. "Blackthink's(tm) Acting White Stigma In Education and How It Fosters Academic Paralysis In Black Youth." *Howard Law Journal* 50(117) (2007): 711–754.

Norwood, Kimberly Jade. "The Virulence of BLACKTHINK™ and How Its Threat of Ostracism Shackles Those Deemed Not Black Enough." *Kentucky Law Journal* 93(3) (2004–05): 143.

Nosek, Brian A., Frederick L. Smyth, Feffrey J. Hansen, Thierry Devos, Nicole M. Lindner, Kate A. Ranganath, Colin Tucker Smith, Kristina R. Olson, Dolly Chugh, Anthony G. Greenwald, and Mahzarin R. Banaji. "Pervasiveness and Correlates of Implicit Attitudes and Stereotypes." *European Review of Social Psychology* 18 (2007): 36–88.

Notholt, Stuart. *Fields of Fire: An Atlas of Ethnic Conflict.* London: Stuart Notholt Communications, Ltd., 2008.

Nott, Josiah Clark. "The Mulatto: A Hybrid: Probable Extermination of the Two Races If the Whites and Blacks are Allowed to Intermarry." *Boston Medical and Surgical Journal* 29 (1843): 29.

Nott, Josiah Clark, George Robins Gliddon, Louis Agassiz, William Usher, and Henry Stuart Patterson. *Types of Mankind: Or, Ethnological Researches, Based upon the Ancient Monuments, Paintings, Sculptures, and Crania of Races, and upon Their Natural, Geographical, Philological and Biblical History.* Philadelphia, PA: J. B. Lippincott, Grambo & Co., 1854.

O'Neill, Timothy. *Bakke and the Politics of Equality.* Scranton, PA: Wesleyan University Press, 1985.

Orfield, Gary, and Susan E. Eaton. *Dismantling Desegregation: The Quiet Reversal of Brown v. Board of Education.* New York: New Press, 1996.

Orfield, Gary, and Chungmei Lee. *Why Segregation Matters: Poverty and Educational Inequality.* Cambridge, MA: Harvard Civil Rights Project, 2005.

Orig, Princess. "Kayumanggi Versus Maputi: 100 Years of America's White Aesthetics in Philippine Literature." In *Mixed Blessing: The Impact of the American Colonial Experience on Politics and Society in the Philippines*, edited by Hazel M. McFerson. Westport, CT: Greenwood Press, 2002.

Otto, David. *Insiders' Guide to Shreveport.* Guilford, CT: Globe Pequot Press, 2010.

Painter, Nell Irvin. *The History of White People.* New York: W. W. Norton & Co., 2010.

Papel, Ira D. *Facial Plastic and Reconstructive Surgery.* 3rd edition. New York: Thieme, 2009.

Passell, Jeffrey, Wendy Wang, and Paul Taylor. "Marrying Out: One-in-seven New U.S. Marriages is Interracial or Interethnic." *Pew Social and Demographic Trends.* Washington, DC: Pew Research Center, 2010.

Patterson, Meghan M., and Rebecca S. Bigler. "Preschool Children's Attention to Environmental Messages About Groups: Social Categorization and the Origins of Intergroup Bias." *Child Development* 77 (2006): 847–860.

Pavalko, Eliza. K., Krysia N. Mossakowski, and Vanessa J. Hamilton. "Does Perceived Discrimination Affect Health? Longitudinal Relationships between Work Discrimination and Women's Physical and Emotional Health." *Journal of Health and Social Behavior* 44(1) (2003): 18–33.

Perry, Imani. "Buying White Beauty." *Cardozo Journal of Law & Gender* 12 (2006): 579.

Phillips, Amali. "Gendering Colour: Identity, Femininity and Marriage in Kerala." *Anthropologica* 46(2) (2004): 255.

Pierce, Chester M. "Entitlement Dysfunctions." *Australian and New Zealand Journal of Psychiatry* 12 (1978): 215–219.

Plaut, Victoria C. "Diversity Science: Why and How Difference Makes a Difference." *Psychological Inquiry* 21 (2010): 77–99.

Poran, Maya A. "Denying Diversity: Perceptions of Beauty and Social Comparison Processes among Latina, Black and White Women." *Sex Roles* 47 (2002): 65–72.

Pyke, Karen, and Tran Dang. "'FOB' and 'Whitewashed': Identity and Internalized Racism among Second Generation Asian Americans." *Qualitative Sociology* 26 (2003): 147–172.

Qian, Zhenchao, and Daniel T. Lichter. "Measuring Marital Assimilation: Intermarriage among Natives and Immigrants." *Social Science Research* 30(2) (2001): 289–312.

Rachlinski, Jeffrey J., and Gregory S. Parks. "Implicit Bias, Election '08, and the Myth of a Post-Racial America." *Social Science Research Network,* August 17, 2009, 21.

Randall, Vernellia. *Dying while Black.* Dayton, OH: Seven Principles Press, 2006.

Rankin, David C. "The Impact of the Civil War on the Free Colored Community of New Orleans." *Perspectives in American History* 11 (1977–78): 381–382.

Ravitch, Diane. *The Troubled Crusade: American Education, 1945–1980.* New York: Basic Books, 1983.

Rhode, Deborah L. *The Beauty Bias: The Injustice of Appearance in Life and Law.* New York: Oxford University Press, 2010.

Ribane, Nakedi. *Beauty: A Black Perspective.* Scottsville, South Africa: University of KwaZulu-Natal Press, 2006.

Richeson, Jennifer A., and Richard J. Nussbaum. "The Impact of Multiculturalism Versus Color-Blindness on Racial Bias." *Journal of Experimental Social Psychology* 40 (2004): 417–423.

Richeson, Jennifer A., and Sophie Trawalter. "African Americans' Implicit Racial Attitudes and the Depletion of Executive Function after Interracial Interactions." *Social Cognition* 23(4) (2005): 336–352.

Rivera, Amaad, Jeannette Hueza, Christina Kasica, and Dedrick Muhammad. *State of the Dream 2009: The Silent Depression.* Boston, MA: United for a Fair Economy, 2009. Accessed June 14, 2012, http://www.faireconomy.org/files/pdf/state_of_dream_2009.pdf.

Robertson, David M. *The Buried Story of America's Largest Slave Rebellion and the Man Who Led It.* New York: Alfred A. Knopf, Inc., 2000.

Robertson, Ian. *Sociology.* 3rd edition. New York: Worth Publishers, Inc., 1988.

Robinson, Cedric J. *Forgeries of Memory and Meaning: Blacks and the Regimes of Race in American Theater and Film Before World War II.* Chapel Hill, NC: University of North Carolina Press, 2007.

Robinson, Eugene. *Disintegration: The Splintering of Black America*. New York: Doubleday, 2010.

Robinson, Russell K. "Structural Dimensions of Romantic Preferences." *Fordham Law Review* 76(6) (2008): 2787–2819.

Robinson, Tracy L., and Janie V. Ward. "African American Adolescents and Skin Color." *Journal of Black Psychology* 21 (1995): 256–274.

Rockquemore, Kerry A. "Between Black and White: Exploring the "Biracial Experience." *Race & Society* 1 (1998): 197–212.

Rockquemore, Kerry Ann, and David Brunsma. *Beyond Black: Biracial Identity in America*. Thousand Oaks, CA: Sage Publications, 2002.

Rodkin, Philip C. "The Psychological Reality of Social Constructions." *Ethnic and Racial Studies* 16 (1993): 633–655.

Rodriguez, Junius P. *The Louisiana Purchase: A Historical and Geographical Encyclopedia*. Santa Barbara, CA: ABC-CLIO, Inc., 2002.

Roithmayr, Daira. "Them That Has, Gets." *Mississippi College Law Review* 27 (2007–08): 373.

Romero, Tom I., II. "La Raza Latina?: Multiracial Ambivalence, Color Denial, and the Emergence of a Tri-Ethnic Jurisprudence at the End of the Twentieth Century." *New Mexico Law Review* 37 (2007): 263–270.

Rondilla, Joanne, and Paul Spickard. *Is Lighter Better?* Lanham, MD: Rowman & Littlefield, 2007.

Rosenfeld, Michael J. "A Critique of Exchange Theory in Mate Selection." *American Journal of Sociology* 110(5) (2005): 1284–1325.

Roth, Wendy D. "The End of the One-Drop Rule? Labeling of Multiracial Children in Black Intermarriages." *Sociological Forum* 20 (March 2005): 35.

Rothenberg, Paula. *White Privilege*. New York: Worth, 2011.

Rubin, Lisa R., Mako L. Fitts, and Anne E. Becker. "Whatever Feels Good in My Soul: Body Ethics and Aesthetics among African American and Latina Women." *Culture, Medicine and Psychiatry* 27 (2003): 49–75.

Ruchames, Louis, ed. *Racial Thought in America, From the Puritans to Abraham Lincoln*. Amherst, MA: University of Massachusetts Press, 1969.

Russell, Kathy, Midge Wilson, and Ronald E. Hall. *The Color Complex: The Politics of Skin Color among African Americans*. New York: Anchor Books, 1993.

Sahay, Sarita, and Niva Piran. "Skin-color Preferences and Body Satisfaction among South Asian, Canadian and European-Canadian Female University Students." *Journal of Social Psychology* 137 (1997): 161–171.

Salas, Jesús María Herrera. "Ethnicity and Revolution: The Political Economy of Racism in Venezuela." *Latin American Perspectives* 32(2) (2005): 72.

Salinas, Guadalupe. "Comment: Mexican-Americans and the Desegregation of Schools in the Southwest." *Houston Law Review* 8 (1971): 929.

Sciara, Frank J. "Skin Color and College Student Prejudice." *College Student Journal* 17 (1983): 390–394.

Segall, Marshall H., Pierre R. Dasen, John W. Berry, and Ype H. Poortinga. *Human Behavior in Global Perspective: An Introduction to Cross Cultural Psychology*. 2nd edition. Boston, MA: Allyn and Bacon, 1999.

Sellers, Robert M., Mia A. Smith, J. Nicole Shelton, Stephanie A. J. Rowley, and Tabbye M. Chavous. "Multidimensional Model of Racial Identity: A Re-Conceptualization of African American Racial Identity." *Personality and Social Psychology Review* 2 (1998): 18–39.

Seltzer, Richard, and Robert Smith. "Color Differences in the Afro-American Community and the Differences They Make." *Journal of Black Studies* 21(3) (1991): 279–286.

Shaler, Nathaniel Southgate. *The Neighbor: The Natural History of Human Contacts.* Boston, MA: Houghton, Mifflin and Co., 1904.

Shelton, Nicole. "A Reconceptualization of How We Study Issues of Racial Prejudice." *Personality and Social Psychological Review* 4(4) (2000): 374–390.

Simms, Leonard J. "Classical and Modern Methods of Psychological Scale Construction." *Social and Personality Psychology Compass* 1 (2007): 1–20.

Smith, Elsie M. "Black Racial Identity Development: Issues and Concerns." *Counseling Psychologist* 17 (1989): 277–288.

Smith, Stephen F. "The Truth about Clarence Thomas and the Need for New Black Leadership." *Regents University Law Review* 12 (2000): 513.

Snipp, C. Matthew. "Racial Measurement in the American Census: Past Practices and Implications for the Future." *Annual Review of Sociology* 29 (2003): 566.

Solorzano, Daniel, Miguel Ceja, and Tara Yosso. "Critical Race Theory, Racial Micro-aggressions, and Campus Racial Climate: The Experiences of African American College Students." *Journal of Negro Education* 69(1–2) (2000): 60–73.

Spanierman, Lisa B., and Mary J. Heppner. "Psychosocial Costs of Racism to Whites Scale (PCRW): Construction and Initial Validation." *Journal of Counseling Psychology* 51 (2004): 249–262.

Speight, Suzette L. "Internalized Racism: One More Piece of the Puzzle." *Counseling Psychologist* 35 (2007): 126–134.

Spencer, Rainier. *Spurious Issues: Race and Multiracial Identity Politics in the United States.* Boulder, CO: Westview Press, 1999.

Steele, Claude M., and Joshua Aronson. "Stereotype Threat and the Intellectual Test-Performance of African-Americans." *Journal of Personality and Social Psychology* 69(5) (1995): 797–811.

Stout, Karen D., and William Buffum. "The Commitment of Social Workers to Affirmative Action." *Journal of Sociology and Social Welfare* 20(2) (1993): 123–135.

Strand, Palma Joy. "Inheriting Inequality: Wealth, Race and the Laws of Succession." *Oregon Law Review* 89 (2010): 453.

Stryker, Sheldon. *Symbolic Interactionism: A Social Structural Version.* Menlo Park, CA: Benjamin Cummings, 1980.

Stryker, Sheldon, and Anne Stratham. "Symbolic Interactionism and Role Theory." In *The Handbook of Social Psychology,* edited by Gardner Lindzey and Elliot Aronson, 311–378. New York: Random House, 1985.

Suggs, Robert E. "Poisoning the Well: Law & Economics and Racial Inequality." *Hastings Law Journal* 57(2) (2005): 255.

Sumi Cho, "Post-Racialism." *Iowa Law Review* 94 (2009): 1594.

Sweet, Frank. *Legal History of the Color Line: The Rise and Triumph of the One-Drop Rule.* Palm Coast, FL: Backintyme, 2005.

Tajfel, Henri. "Social Identity and Intergroup Behavior." *Social Science Information* 13(2) (1974): 65–93.

Telles, Edward E., and Edward Murguia. "Phenotypic Discrimination and Income Differences among Mexican Americans." *Social Science Quarterly* 71(1990): 682–696.

Telles, Edward E. *Race in Another America: The Significance of Skin Color in Brazil.* Princeton, NJ: Princeton University Press, 2004.

Tewari, Nita, and Alvin N. Alvarez. *Asian American Psychology Current Perspectives.* Hoboken, NJ: Taylor and Francis, 2012.

Thapar, Romila. "The Theory of Aryan Race and India: History and Politics." *Social Scientist* 24(1–3) (1996): 6.

Thompson, Maxine S., and Verna M. Keith. "The Blacker the Berry: Gender, Skin-Tone, Self-Esteem and Self-Efficacy." *Gender & Society* 15 (2001): 336–357.

Thompson, Vetta L. Sanders. "African American Body Image: Identity and Physical Self-Acceptance." *Humboldt Journal of Social Relations* 30 (2006): 44–67.

Thompson, Vetta L. Sanders. "The Complexity of African American Racial Identification." *Journal of Black Studies,* 32 (2001): 155–165.

Thompson, Vetta L. Sanders. "Factors Affecting African-American Racial Identity Salience and Racial Group Identification." *The Journal of Social Psychology* 139 (1999): 748–761.

Thompson, Vetta L. Sanders. "A Multidimensional Approach to the Assessment of African American Racial Identification." *Western Journal of Black Studies* 15 (1991): 154–158.

Thompson, Vetta L. Sanders. "The Multidimensional Structure of Racial Identification." *Journal of Research in Personality* 29 (1995): 208–222.

Thompson, Vetta L. Sanders, and Maysa Akbar. "The Understanding of Race and the Construction of African American Identity." *Western Journal of Black Studies* 27 (2003): 80–88.

Torre, Elizabeth. "Drama as a Consciousness-raising Strategy for the Self-empowerment of Working Women." *AFFILIA: Journal of Women and Social Work* 5(1) (1990): 49–65.

Touré, ed. *Who's Afraid of Post-Blackness? What It Means to Be Black Now.* New York: Free Press, 2011.

Tucker, Cynthia. "Clarence Thomas Would Kick Away the Ladder He Climbed." *Los Angeles Daily Law Journal*, July 26, 1991.

Turner, John C. "Towards a Cognitive Redefinition of the Social Group." In *Social Identity and Intergroup Relations,* edited by H. Tajfel, 15–40. Cambridge, UK: Cambridge University Press, 1982.

Uhlmann, Eric, Nilanjana Dasgupta, Angelica Elgueta, Anthony G. Greenwald, and Jane Swanson. "Subgroup Prejudice Based on Skin Color among Hispanics in the United States and Latin America." *Social Cognition* 20(3) (2002): 198–226.

Van Ausdale, Debra, and Joe R. Feagin. *The First R: How Children Learn Race and Racism.* Lanham, MD: Rowman & Littlefield, 2001.

Vargas, Lucila. *Latina Teens, Migration, and Popular Culture.* New York: Peter Lang Pub., 2009.

Viglione, Jill, Lance Hannon, and Robert DeFina. "The Impact of Light Skin on Prison Time for Black Female Offenders." *The Social Science Journal* 48 (2011): 250–258.

Villarreal, Andrés. "Stratification by Skin Color in Contemporary Mexico." *American Sociological Review* 75(5) (2010): 653.

Vontress, Clemmont E. "Counseling Blacks." *Personnel and Guidance Journal* 48(9) (1970): 713–719.

Wagatsuma, Hiroshi. "The Social Perception of Skin Color in Japan." *Daedalus* 96(2) (1967): 407–443.

Walker, Alice. "If the Present Looks Like the Past, What Does the Future Look Like?" In *In Search of Our Mothers' Gardens.* New York: Harcourt Brace Jovanovich, 1983.

Wallenstein, Peter. "Race, Marriage, and the Law Of Freedom: Alabama and Virginia, 1860s–1960s." *Chicago-Kent Law Review* 70 (1994): 377–389.

Wallman, Katherine K., Suzann Evinger, and Susan Schechter. "Measuring Our Nation's Diversity: Developing a Common Language for Data on Race/Ethnicity." *American Journal of Public Health* 90 (November 2000): 1704.

Wang, Wendy. "The Rise of Intermarriage: Rates, Characteristics Vary by Race and Gender." *Pew Social and Demographic Trends*. Washington: Pew Research Center, 2012.

Watson, Elwood, and Darcy Martin, eds. *There She Is, Miss America: The Politics of Sex, Beauty, and Race in America's Most Famous Pageant*. New York: Palgrave Macmillan, 2004.

Welsing, Frances Cress. *The Cress Theory of Color-Confrontation and Racism*. Washington, DC: C-R Publishers, 1970.

West, Carolyn W. "Mammy, Sapphire, and Jezebel: Historical Images of Black Women and Their Implications for Psychotherapy." *Psychotherapy* 32 (1995): 458–466.

Wiecek, William M. "The Statutory Law of Slavery and Race in the Thirteen Mainland Colonies of British America." *William and Mary Quarterly* 34 (1977): 258–280.

Wilder, JeffriAnne. "Revisiting "Color Names and Color Notions: A Contemporary Examination of the Language and Attitudes of Skin Color Among Young Black Women." *Journal of Black Studies* 41 (2010): 184–206.

Wilder, JeffriAnne, and Colleen Cain. "Teaching and Learning Color Consciousness in Black Families: Exploring Family Processes and Women's Experiences With Colorism." *Journal of Family Issues* 32 (2011): 577–604.

Willhelm, Sidney M. *Who Needs the Negro?* Cambridge, MA: Schenkman, 1970.

Williams, Kim M. *Mark One or More: Civil Rights in Multiracial America*. Ann Arbor. MI: University of Michigan Press, 2006.

Williamson, Joel. *New People: Miscegenation and Mulattoes in the United States*. Baton Rouge, LA: Louisiana State University Press, 1995.

Wilson, William Julius. *Blacks and Changing American Institutions*. 2nd edition. Chicago, IL: University of Chicago Press, 1978.

Wilson, William Julius. *The Declining Significance of Race: Blacks and Changing American Institutions*. 2nd edition. Chicago: University of Chicago Press, 1978.

Wise, Tim. *White Like Me: Reflections on Race from a Privileged Son*. Brooklyn, NY: Soft Skull Press, 2011.

Wittenbrink, Bernd, Charles M. Judd, and Bernadette Park. "Evidence for Racial Prejudice at the Implicit Level and Its Relationship with Questionnaire Measures." *Journal of Personality and Social Psychology* 72(2) (1997): 262–274.

Woodson, Carter G. "The Beginnings of Miscegenation of the Whites and Blacks." *Journal of Negro History* 3 (October 1918): 335–353.

Yancey, George. "Who Interracially Dates: An Examination of the Characteristics of Those Who Have Interracially Dated." *Journal of Comparative Family Studies* 33(2) (2002): 177–190.

Yoshino, Kenji. "Covering." *Yale Law Journal* 111 (2002): 772.

Zavalloni, Marisa. "Social Identity: Perspectives and Prospects." *Social Science Information* 12 (1973): 65–91.

Zilversmit, Arthur. *The First Emancipation: The Abolition of Slavery in the North*. Chicago, IL: University of Chicago Press, 1967.

Zuberi, Tukufu, and Eduardo Bonilla-Silva, eds. *White Logic, White Methods: Racism and Methodology*. Lanham, MD: Rowman & Littlefield, 2008.

ABOUT THE CONTRIBUTORS

Taunya Lovell Banks is the Jacob A. France Professor of Equality Jurisprudence and the Francis & Harriet Iglehart Research Professor of Law at the University of Maryland School of Law, where she teaches constitutional law, torts, and seminars on law in popular culture (film or literature), citizenship, and critical race theory. Prior to entering legal education in 1976, she worked as a civil rights lawyer in Mississippi, litigating voting rights and housing discrimination cases and providing technical assistance to black elected officials. During the 1979 and 1980 academic years, she worked as a senior trial attorney for the Equal Employment Opportunity Commission in Los Angeles, litigating some of the early sexual harassment cases under the interim guidelines. Professor Banks' most recent publications explore racial reconciliation and reparations, the impact of race, racial formation, and racial hierarchies among and within communities of color, and constructing new legal theories of racial equality.

Kevin D. Brown is the Richard S. Melvin Professor of Law at Indiana University Maurer School of Law and the emeritus director of the Hudson & Holland Scholars Program at Indiana University-Bloomington. Professor Brown has been a member of the faculty of the Law School since 1987. He graduated from Yale Law School in 1982. He has been a visiting professor at the University of Texas School of Law, University of Alabama School of Law, and University of San Diego School of Law, and he is affiliated with universities on four different continents, including the National Law School of India University in Bangalore, India; the Indian Law Institute in New Delhi, India; the law faculty of the University of Capetown in Capetown, South Africa; and the University of Central America in Managua, Nicaragua. Professor Brown has published nearly sixty articles, essays, comments, and encyclopedia entries on issues related to race, law, and education and is considered a leading scholar in the field. In 2005, his book *Race, Law and Education* *in the Post-Desegregation Era* was published by Carolina Academic Press. His current book project is titled *Because of our Success: The Ethnic Cleansing of the African-American Student from the Campuses of Selective Higher Education Programs.*

Kellina M. Craig-Henderson, PhD, is a former professor of social psychology who is currently serving as the deputy division director of the Social and Economic Sciences Division of the Social, Behavioral and Economic Sciences Directorate of the National Science Foundation (NSF). She retains an affiliation with the Department of Psychology at Howard University where she was promoted to full professor shortly before undertaking full-time federal service at the National Science Foundation. Dr. Craig-Henderson graduated from Wesleyan University in Connecticut before attending the University of Chicago where she earned an MA in social sciences. She then attended Tulane University in New Orleans, Louisiana, and earned an MS and a PhD in psychology. She served on the faculty in the Department of Psychology, as well as the Afro-American Studies and Research Program at the University of Illinois in Champaign-Urbana. This was followed by an appointment in the Psychology Department of California State University in Long Beach. She subsequently moved to Howard University in Washington, DC. Dr. Craig-Henderson is passionate about broadening the participation of underrepresented groups, and has been involved in a number of activities that share this focus. She has published reports of empirical research in peer-reviewed journals as well as two books on interracial relationships. Her research program includes studies of groups, cross-cultural, gender, and race issues, as well as aggression and expatriation processes. Her work has been supported by a variety of public and private sources including NSF, the Ford Foundation, and the American Psychological Association, and she has presented findings from her research activities at a variety of regional, national, and international research and pedagogical meetings.

Paul Finkelman is the President William McKinley Distinguished Professor of Law and Public Policy at Albany Law School. A specialist in American legal history, race, and the law, Professor Finkelman is the author of more than one hundred scholarly articles and more than twenty books, and he is the ninth most cited legal historian, according to *Brian Leiter's Law School Rankings*. The study, which measures the scholarly impact of faculty work, was based on citations from 2000 to 2007. Before going to Albany, Professor Finkelman held the Chapman Distinguished Professorship at the University of Tulsa College of Law, the John F. Seiberling Chair in Constitutional Law at the University of Akron, as well as chairs at Cleveland State University Law School and the University of Miami. He received his BA in American studies from Syracuse University (1971), his PhD in U.S. history from the University of Chicago (1976), and was a fellow in law and humanities at Harvard Law School (1982–83). He is an expert in areas such as the law of slavery, constitutional law, and legal issues surrounding baseball. Professor Finkelman was the chief expert witness in the Alabama Ten Commandments monument case and his scholarship on religious monuments in public spaces was cited by the U.S. Supreme Court in *Van Orden* v. *Perry* (2005).

Violeta Solonova Foreman is a J.D. candidate at the Washington University School of Law in Saint Louis. She holds an executive articles editor position on the *Global Studies Law Review*, which published her note "Problems with BitTorrent Litigation in the U.S.; Personal Jurisdiction, Joinder, Evidentiary Issues, and Why the Dutch Have a Better System." Prior to law school, she attended Duke University, graduating magna cum laude. At Duke, she double-majored in English and visual art, receiving both the highest distinction in the English critical thesis and The Benenson Award in the Arts.

Ronald E. Hall graduated with distinction, and his professional career began as a clinical social worker. His professional role encompassed the practice of individual and group psychotherapy with schizophrenic and manic-depressive clients. Subsequent to numerous clinical observations, Dr. Hall incorporated the notion of skin color, among people of color, as a critical dynamic of mental health. Having written his dissertation on skin color, in 1990 Dr. Hall testified as expert witness to America's first skin color discrimination case between African Americans: *Morrow* v. *IRS*. Dr. Hall later devised the Bleaching Syndrome to explain discrimination among people of color and Identity Across the Lifespan as an alternative biracial identity model. Dr. Hall's work includes more than 150 (co)-authored publications, interviews, and presentations on these topics, including pieces on Justice Clarence Thomas and President Barack Obama via *TIME* magazine and Oprah Winfrey via *The Color Complex*, his latest book, which was published in 2013. His previous book is titled *The Melanin Millennium* (2012). Dr. Hall has lectured on skin color both domestically and internationally, including by invitation Bates College (Lewiston, ME), Pennsylvania State University (State College, PA), and Oxford University (Oxford, UK). His most recent speaking events include Paramaribo, Suriname, where he was guest speaker for a medical convention on skin color in November 2010. In October 2012 Dr. Hall lectured on skin color in India at the Jindal Global University in Delhi and the Tata Institute of Social Sciences in Mumbai. In 2003, he won the Mellen Prize for Distinguished Contribution to Scholarship. In 2007, he was invited to Washington by a member of Congress to address issues pertaining to skin color.

Richard D. Harvey received his PhD in psychology from the University of Kansas. He currently holds a double appointment as an associate professor of psychology in both the social psychology and industrial/organizational psychology specialty programs in the Department of Psychology at Saint Louis University. He currently conducts research and/or has published research on a variety of topics including: prejudice/racism, organizational identity, racial identity, and performance management. In addition, Dr. Harvey has more than twenty years of consulting experience in both profit and nonprofit program evaluation. He is a fellow of the Center for the Application of Behavioral Sciences.

Kira Hudson Banks is an assistant professor in the department of psychology at Saint Louis University. Her research examines the experience of discrimination and its affect on mental health and intergroup relations. Professor Hudson Banks has worked in schools, communities, institutions of higher education, and corporations to improve diversity and inclusion efforts and to engage people in productive dialogue and action. Her courses have ranged from abnormal psychology to the psychology of racism. She received her BA from Mount Holyoke College and her PhD from the University of Michigan.

Adrienne Johnson is an Atlanta, GA, native. She graduated from Furman University in 2010 and Washington University School of Law with her J.D. in 2013. Her academic and practice interests include public education law, employment law, and criminal defense, with particular interest in the ways in which race and color affects each. Ms. Johnson is an active participant in several community-based organizations that target minority and/or low-income youth and focus on higher education and social justice. Her recent article, "In Living Color: Examining Color-Based Discrimination Claims Under Title VII," was published in the *Atlanta Bar Association: Labor and Employment Law News* and can be found at http://archive.constantcontact.com/fs120/1101107659171/archive/111271 8034243.html.

Kimberly Jade Norwood is a Professor of Law at Washington University School of Law in Saint Louis, Missouri. She has a BS degree from Fordham University and a J.D. degree from the University of Missouri-Columbia. She clerked for a federal district judge after law school and practiced law as a litigator at a major law firm for several years before joining the faculty of the Washington University School of Law in 1990. Professor Norwood currently teaches torts, products liability, education policy and law, and a seminar on the intersections of race, class, education and the law. She has taught abroad, including in Africa, China, Japan, and The Netherlands. She has published several articles on the black identity/authenticity issues, the toll that the stigma of acting white takes on black students, and on urban education issues. She has also created a high school-to-law school pipeline program at Washington University School of Law, which involves judges, lawyers, and law students working with and mentoring public school students. The program has received both national and local acclaim.

Vetta L. Sanders Thompson is an associate professor at the Institute of Public Health, George Warren Brown School of Social Work, and Urban Studies at Washington University in Saint Louis. Professor Sanders Thompson received her bachelor's degree in psychology and social relations from Harvard University in 1981. She received her master's degree and doctorate in psychology from Duke University in 1984 and 1988, where she also completed the clinical training program. Professor Sanders Thompson is a licensed psychologist and health service provider in the state of Missouri. She teaches courses in human diversity, health disparities, and evidence-based treatments in mental health. Prior to joining the faculty at Washington University, she was an associate professor at the Saint Louis University School of Public Health, Department of Community Health, Behavioral Sciences and Health Education (2004–2008), and a member of the psychology faculty and coordinator of the Black Studies Minor at the University of Missouri–St. Louis from 1989 through 2003. She is a clinical psychologist and a leading researcher in the areas of racial identity, psychosocial implications of race and ethnicity in health communications, access to health services, and determinates of health and mental health disparities.

Rachel E. Tennial received her masters of science (research) from Saint Louis University (SLU). She is currently a doctoral candidate in the area of experimental social psychology at SLU. Ms. Tennial's research interests include racial/ethnic identity, sexual identity, stereotyping, stigma, and prejudice.

INDEX